The Dialect of Modernism

RACE AND AMERICAN CULTURE

General Editors:
Arnold Rampersad and Shelley Fisher Fishkin

Love and Theft
Blackface Minstrelsy and the American Working Class
Eric Lott

The Dialect of Modernism
Race, Language, and Twentieth-Century Literature
Michael North

THE DIALECT
OF MODERNISM

Race, Language, and
Twentieth-Century Literature

MICHAEL NORTH

OXFORD UNIVERSITY PRESS
New York   Oxford

Oxford University Press

Oxford   New York
Athens   Auckland   Bangkok   Bogotá   Bombay
Buenos Aires   Calcutta   Cape Town   Dar es Salaam
Delhi   Florence   Hong Kong   Istanbul   Karachi
Kuala Lumpur   Madras   Madrid   Melbourne
Mexico City   Nairobi   Paris   Singapore
Taipei   Tokyo   Toronto   Warsaw

and associated companies in
Berlin   Ibadan

Copyright © 1994 by Michael North

First published in 1994 by Oxford University Press, Inc.,
198 Madison Avenue, New York, New York 10016

First issued as an Oxford University Press paperback, 1998

Oxford is a registered trademark of Oxford University Press

An earlier version of part of chapter 4 originally appeared in *American Literary History* 4 (Spring 1992).
Reprinted by permission of the publisher. Chapter 3 originally appeared in *Prehistories of the Modern*, ed.
Elazar Barkan (Stanford, CA: Stanford University Press, 1994). Reprinted by permission of the publisher.

Excerpts from "Mélange Adultère de Tout" and "Sweeney Agonistes" in *Collected Poems, 1909–1962* by
T. S. Eliot, copyright 1936 by Harcourt Brace & Company, copyright © 1964, 1963 by T. S. Eliot, reprinted
by permission of Harcourt Brace & Company and Faber and Faber Ltd.
Excerpts from *The Waste Land: A Facsimile and Transcript of the Original Drafts Including the Annotations
of Ezra Pound*, edited by Valerie Eliot, copyright © 1971 by Valerie Eliot; reprinted by permission of
Harcourt Brace & Company and Faber and Faber Ltd.
Selections from *Images of Kin: New and Selected Poems* (Urbana: University of Illinois Press, 1977) by
Michael S. Harper, reprinted by permission of the publisher.
Selections from *Selected Poems of Claude McKay* (Harcourt, Brace, 1979) reprinted by permission of the
Archives of Claude McKay, Carl Cowl, Administrator.
Selections from *The Cantos of Ezra Pound*, copyright 1948 by Ezra Pound, reprinted by permission of New
Directions Publishing Corporation and Faber and Faber Ltd.
"Reapers" and selections from "Her Lips Are Copper Wire" are reprinted from *Cane* by Jean Toomer, by
permission of Liveright Publishing Corporation. Copyright 1923 by Boni & Liveright. Copyright renewed 1951
by Jean Toomer.
Selections from *The Collected Poems of William Carlos Williams, 1901–1939*, vol. 1, copyright 1938 by New
Directions Publishing Corporation, and *Paterson*, copyright 1948, 1962 by Willias Carlos Williams, reprinted
by permission of New Directions Publishing Corporation.
Selections from the correspondence of Langston Hughes, James Weldon Johnson, and Gertrude Stein, and
from the papers of Claude McKay and Jean Toomer are quoted by permission of the Yale Collection of
American Literature, Beinecke Rare Book and Manuscript Library, Yale Library, Yale University.

Library of Congress Cataloging-in-Publication Data
North, Michael, 1951–
The dialect of modernism : race, language, and twentieth-century literature / Michael North.
p. cm.—(Race and American culture)   Includes bibliographical references.
ISBN-13: 9780195122916
ISBN 0-19-508516-7   ISBN 0-19-512291-7 (pbk.)
1. American literature—Afro-American authors—History and criticism.   2. American literature—20th
century—History and criticism.   3. Dialect literature, American—History and criticism.   4. Conrad, Joseph,
1857–1924. Nigger of the Narcissus.   5. Modernism (Literature)—United States.   6. Afro-Americans in
literature.   7. Black English in literature.   8. Language and Culture.   9. Race in literature.
I. Title. II. Series. PS153.N5N67   1994   810.9'896073—dc20   93–36288

9 8 7 6 5

Printed in the United States of America
on acid-free paper

Preface

The white vogue for Harlem has long had an accepted place in histories of the 1920s, and the shallow Negrophilia of this period has often been acknowledged in accounts of the Harlem Renaissance. But it is less often acknowledged just how far this racial cross-identification went or how widespread it was. Writers as far from Harlem as T. S. Eliot and Gertrude Stein reimagined themselves as black, spoke in a black voice, and used that voice to transform the literature of their time. In fact, three of the accepted landmarks of literary modernism in English depend on racial ventriloquism of this kind: Conrad's *Nigger of the "Narcissus,"* Stein's "Melanctha," and Eliot's *Waste Land.* If the racial status of these works is taken at all seriously, it seems that linguistic mimicry and racial masquerade were not just shallow fads but strategies without which modernism could not have arisen.

To see these strategies simply as instances of modern primitivism is to miss a good deal of their importance. That the modern covets the primitive—perhaps even created it—is another frequently acknowledged fact. But to view this attraction merely as a return to nature, a recoil from modernity, is to focus myopically on a rather vapid message while missing its far more intriguing medium. The real attraction of the black voice to writers like Stein and Eliot was its technical distinction, its insurrectionary opposition to the known and familiar in language. For them the artist occupied the role of racial outsider because he or she spoke a language opposed to the standard. Modernism, that is to say, mimicked the strategies of dialect and aspired to become a dialect itself.

This might mean a number of different things, depending on how "dialect" is defined. The dialect of *Uncle Remus,* which was particularly important to Eliot and Pound, certainly offered itself as a natural alternative to more conventional speech, superior precisely to the degree to which it failed to approximate grammatical correctness. Though the dialect mouthed by Stein, Eliot, Pound, and the other white writers to be considered here sounded a good deal more like Uncle Remus than any actual African-American speaker of the 1920s, nonetheless it promised something a good deal more complicated. For the play among rival languages that dialect mimicry made possible led to a breakdown of both the privilege that the standard enjoyed and the myth that there could be a "natural" alternative. In this way, dialect became the prototype for the most radical representational strategies of English-language modernism.

Realizing this makes it easier, I think, to appreciate the true distinction of modern African-American writing, which had to fight its way out of the prison of white-created black dialect. Despite the best efforts of Henry Louis Gates, Jr. and Houston A. Baker, Jr., discussions of African-American writing still tend to focus rather single-mindedly on subject matter. The literary technique of certain writers (Claude McKay being the most glaring example) is dismissed as conventional and uninteresting virtually without a glance. To me there is a certain element of condescension in this bias against technique, an unwillingness to look beyond the obvious in order to see how hard certain African-American writers struggled to be both linguistically and stylistically challenging. The real struggle of writers like McKay, Toomer, and Hurston was often not to preach or inform but rather to free a language from domination. It is this struggle, I think, that allows us to discuss Anglo-American modernism and African-American writing in the same context, and thus to understand how thoroughly each kind of writing was marked, for good or bad, by the other.

I have been keenly aware, while writing on this subject, how easy it is to go wrong where race and language are concerned, and especially when they are connected. From the beginning, I have been guided by a poem by Michael Harper, a poem whose title alone provides a book's worth of introspection on these two subjects. As a memorial for his friend and fellow poet John Berryman, and in final bafflement at the weird racial ventriloquism of *The Dream Songs*, Harper wrote "Tongue-Tied in Black and White." In it Harper interrogates the dead Berryman about "that needful black idiom" that crops up from time to time in *The Dream Songs*, the second poem of which is actually dedicated to the originator of the Jim Crow routine that marked the beginning of American minstrelsy.[1]

The title itself, in all its splendid ambiguity, contains the various answers that Harper conjures up. On one level the title means that actual dialect, of any kind, can never reliably be rendered in the black and white of print. The very sounds of the nonstandard, as Houston Baker and Eric Sundquist have variously reminded us, elude the standard representations. Of course, this means as well that black language can hardly be portrayed by a white poet at all; such a poet can't really "hear" the other language and so cannot render it with any accuracy. Taken a step further, this means that the two races can scarcely communicate: to be tongue-tied in black and white is to be struck deaf and dumb by racial division. The language that Berryman includes in *The Dream Songs* as black dialect is not really black at all but the language of white fear and incomprehension: *"That slave in you was white blood forced to derision. . . ."*[2] Yet the two races, the two languages, the two tongues are nonetheless inextricably joined: "tongue-tied" means that no matter how painfully black and white may speak past one another, they are still linked. In fact, it might be best to say that they are bound by the condition of being tongue-tied, trapped, as it were, in a language that neither can control or dominate. However many other ways there might be to parse this title, its essential ambivalence becomes clear: our language both encodes racial division and traps us all within a common linguistic horizon from which there is no escape. It is this condition that I will analyze in the following pages.

This book is divided into three parts: a general description of the linguistic cross-currents of the period 1880–1920, especially as these concern the triangular relationship of standardization, dialect, and aesthetic modernism; a section devoted to modern expatriates; and a concluding discussion of American writers who faced some of the same linguistic pressures as the expatriates because they were self-consciously American in a time of linguistic Anglophilia. Both of these last two sections contain chapters on African-American writers (or Afro-Caribbean writers; McKay always being very difficult to categorize) not only because they are of great interest in themselves but also because their lives and works offer an illuminating contrast to those of their white counterparts. As I advance chronologically from Conrad at the turn of the century to Hurston in the 1930s, I also consider Anglo-American modernists and African-American writers within the same chapters. I do not mean by this to deemphasize the many differences between these two groups of writers, but only to help demonstrate the central conviction of this book, namely, that where language is concerned the two groups cannot be discussed in isolation.

In addition to my rather distant debt to Michael Harper, I owe a more direct one to my colleague Eric Sundquist, who read and helpfully criticized an early version of part of this book. The John Simon Guggenheim Memorial Foundation and the University of California provided fellowship support that made completion of this project possible.

I would like to thank the librarians and staff of the UCLA Research Library Department of Special Collections and the Beinecke Rare Book and Manuscript Library at Yale University for their assistance.

Los Angeles   M.N.
October 1993

Contents

PART I

Against the Standard

1

Against the Standard:
Linguistic Imitation, Racial Masquerade,
and the Modernist Rebellion

I

In the preface to *Pygmalion* George Bernard Shaw reassures his readers, some of whom might be daunted by the dazzling success of Eliza Doolittle, that she is but an example of the "many thousands of men and women who have sloughed off their native dialects and acquired a new tongue." Sounding a bit like Dale Carnegie, who began his self-help empire at about this time, Shaw promises those who follow Eliza a world of social harmony based on proper phonetics, a world in which words cannot be mispronounced, in which men and women will no longer be divided by differences of speech. "It's filling up the deepest gulf that separates class from class and soul from soul," as Henry Higgins crows in the play itself.[1] The American musical *My Fair Lady* expands on Shaw's expansiveness by staging Eliza's final elocution lesson as a triumphant tango: when "the rine in Spine" finally becomes "the rain in Spain," the three principals drop all decorum and dance.

The same subject is handled rather differently in another famous American musical, one whose slapdash colloquial title, *Singin' in the Rain*, would have made Henry Higgins cringe. In this elocution lesson, Don Lockwood, famous silent movie actor, receives instruction from a prissy professorial type in string tie and thick glasses. Don's lesson also ends in dance, but in this case the student and his sidekick transform the professor's tongue twister into a tap extravaganza, in which the professor himself is merely a dumb prop. They untie his tie, muss his hair, put a lampshade on his head, throw his papers in the air, and end by belting out a perfectly harmonized *a*, the same *a*, incidentally, that Eliza finally masters in *her* triumphant elocution scene. But what a difference! Don and his friend Cosmo dance to demonstrate their utter indifference to verbal exactitude. Taking the tongue twister into tap shows how American verve and creativity triumph over empty formality, American individuality over conformity and authoritarianism. What else would you expect from a movie whose very title drops its *g*'s?[2]

Yet this movie, seemingly so breezy and informal, contains within it a tangle of feelings about speech and language that makes Shaw seem almost as shallow as

Dale Carnegie. The elocution scene is but a part of the larger story of the arrival of the talkies, an arrival that *Singin' in the Rain* portrays, on one level at least, as an unmasking. Lina Lamont, silent movie star and Don Lockwood's longtime screen companion, seems sweet and refined. Her voice, which is carefully kept out of the first few scenes of the movie so as to heighten its impact, reveals the fact that she is not. Her coarse screeching is contrasted throughout to the calm, low voice of the newcomer Kathy Selden, who *is* sweet and also genuine, which is much better than being refined. Thus the whole movie is structured around the contrast between Kathy and Lina: their names, their clothes, their faces, their hairstyles, their personalities. Kathy enters the movie as a critic of the trumped-up, hokey acting of the silent era, and her progress from obscurity to stardom is an allegory of the emergence of movies like *Singin' in the Rain.* Don's screen love scene with Lina involves powdered wigs, heavy brocade, and stilted language on the title cards; for his first love scene with Kathy, he sets up the most ostentatiously simple stage set ever filmed and then croons straight from the heart.

The big difference, of course, is sound, which frees movies from the dodges, exaggerations, and falsehoods of the past and allows them to sing. On the other hand, sound puts film actors to the test, and those, like Lina, whose talent is shallow and unnatural are exposed. But sound brings to the movies not just singing but also another, more equivocal, art: dubbing. The studio's answer to Lina's vocal limitations is not to replace her with Kathy, but just to replace her voice with Kathy's. It is historically true that dubbing was born with the talkies: Warner Oland's "Kol Nidre" was dubbed in *The Jazz Singer;* Alfred Hitchcock's *Blackmail* was completely reshot as a talkie, with Hitchcock's script girl crouching under tables and behind doors to provide a voice for the thickly accented leading lady.[3] But the possibilities of dubbing threaten the whole structure of *Singin' in the Rain,* based as it is on the idea that voice reveals the true measure of one's talent and character.

There is actually a good deal of unacknowledged dubbing in *Singin' in the Rain.* Because Debbie Reynolds, who played Kathy Selden, wasn't a very strong singer or dancer, her high notes and taps were dubbed throughout the movie. Beyond this, two entire songs were dubbed by Betty Noyes, one of them the very song Kathy Selden sings to cover up Lina's vocal limitations. If this seems to smudge the message of the movie somewhat, it's as nothing compared with the scene in which Kathy dubs Lina's spoken voice. Here Reynolds is actually dubbed by Jean Hagen, who played Lina. In other words, Hagen is dubbing Reynolds dubbing Hagen. The reason for this last sleight of hand is that Reynolds had what director Stanley Donen considered a "midwestern" accent, while Hagen, beneath the screech she affected for her role as Lina, actually had just the sort of smooth, cultured voice the scene demanded.[4] One wonders why they didn't just give Reynolds elocution lessons.

Behind its assured surface, therefore, *Singin' in the Rain* reveals the mixed emotions that most Americans have about the national speech. Despite its pose of

4

insouciant nonconformity, the movie is just as prescriptive as Henry Higgins, with the same linguistic hypersensitivity that Americans have always harbored along with their colloquial freedom. And yet hypocrisy is just one element of this complex situation, for while the movie is furtive about its own dubbing, it is quite open about the dubbing of "The Duelling Cavalier," the movie within the movie. When Cosmo Brown comes up with the idea of dubbing, everyone cheers him as a genius, though they promise to use the technique "just this once," as if it were a powerfully seductive drug. The deception is finally revealed to the opening-night audience when Kathy is exposed singing behind the miming Lina, but their reaction is not outrage or confusion but laughter and applause. As Ronald Haver points out in his audio essay on the movie, the audience realizes at once what is happening, though dubbing is so new it should be unrecognizable to them.

Such knowing enjoyment is an actual component of audience reaction to films like *My Fair Lady*, since everyone has known from the very beginning that Audrey Hepburn is not actually singing in the scene that celebrates Eliza's discovery of her new voice. Though Eliza may labor long and hard to sound like a proper lady, Audrey Hepburn can sing like Marni Nixon virtually at the touch of a button. What's really being celebrated in such scenes is not vocal authenticity but rather the technical wizardy that can make anyone sound like anyone else. The real American retort to linguistic authoritarianism is dubbing, carefully manipulated falsehood, and not the naturalism of Don Lockwood's love song to Kathy. If *Singin' in the Rain* is about the entry of the movies into modernity, then that condition is represented as one in which technology sets the whole concept of vocal authenticity aside as irrelevant and is applauded for doing so.

In one of the most peculiar scenes in this movie, the camera follows Don and Cosmo as they cross a vast stage set on which four or five movies are being filmed simultaneously. As they pause near the "African" set, a white extra in blackface and elaborate feathers reads them a notice from *Variety* announcing *The Jazz Singer*. This scene provides the pretext for everything else that happens in the movie, since it is the success of *The Jazz Singer* that motivates the changes in the film studio, and at the same time it reveals an important missing element in this, one of the most lily-white musicals ever made: race.[5]

Except for this one element, *Singin' in the Rain* is a very faithful retelling of *The Jazz Singer*. Rebellion against Old World authority through jazz is also the essence of the earlier movie, as is revealed at the very beginning when old Mr. Yudelson catches Jakie Rabinowitz, the cantor's son, down at the beer garden, singing "Waiting for the Robert E. Lee" and "shufflin'" when he should be practicing the "Kol Nidre" with his father.[6] Later, as an adult, Jakie, become Jack Robin the jazz singer, has an archetypal American argument with his father: "[Y]ou're of the old world! Tradition is all right, but this is another day! I'll live my life as I see fit!"[7] Finally, just as his career is about to take off, Jack is once again summoned to sing the "Kol Nidre," this time as his aged father lies on his deathbed. Like *Singin' in the Rain*, *The Jazz Singer* tells this story partly to reflect and applaud its own technical accomplishments. Jack succeeds as a singer because he sings from the heart; his voice "has that tear in it."[8] The growth to self-realization of such a career could only be told in sound, by a process like the one Vitaphone was introducing with elaborate fanfare in *The Jazz Singer*, so that Jakie's acquisition and defense of his own personal voice recapitulates the advance of movies into the talking era.

On the other hand, *The Jazz Singer* raises the same questions about technical wizardry that *Singin' in the Rain* does: Is a movie with sound more realistic than one without, or is it merely the producer of newer and more powerful illusions? When Jakie becomes Jack and sings his own songs is he unmasked, revealed as himself at last, or is he wearing a new mask instead? These questions, which are posed by the use of dubbing in *Singin' in the Rain*, are presented visually as well as vocally in *The Jazz Singer* by Jolson's blackface makeup. Mr. Yudelson puts it with crude succinctness upon discovering Jack in his dressing room: "It talks like Jakie, but it looks like a nigger."[9] Yet, for the most part, "it" doesn't even sound like Jakie: the music that represents his youthful self-assertion is mostly black music, from the minstrel shuffle he does as a youngster to "Mammy" at the very end. How can Jakie become Jack, become himself, as it were, by donning a disguise? More fundamentally, how can *The Jazz Singer* enter the modern era of talking pictures by recapitulating a minstrel show routine at least a hundred years old?[10] Why should the latest technical accomplishment, one that claimed to provide a new fidelity to nature, rely on such an old-fashioned and painfully obvious masquerade?

Like *Singin' in the Rain*, once again, *The Jazz Singer* keeps these questions out in the open. The later musical makes dubbing not only a major subject but, in fact, the fulcrum of the plot, as if in blissful ignorance of the peril this technique poses to the movie's central message of wholesome naturalness. The earlier movie does the same by pulling its star, Al Jolson, back and forth across the racial boundary. It shows him making up, juxtaposes scenes in the synagogue with those on stage, and, at one point, does a mirror dissolve from his face with black makeup to that of a cantor singing. All this suggests conflict and tension, but it also suggests that the black mask is less important than the process of masking. The alternative to Old World tradition with all its rigidity is not blackface per se but the ability to change identity that blackface implies.

There is a kind of vocal blackface too, a mimicry of "black" speech patterns that serves to cover up what Sampson Raphaelson, author of the story on which *The Jazz Singer* was based, called the "richly filthy East Side *argot*."[11] But visual and vocal blackface don't always coincide in *The Jazz Singer*, and the black makeup is often weirdly incidental to Jolson's performances. He can "sing it jazzy," without his makeup, as he does when singing "Blue Skies" to his mother,[12] and he can sing a sentimental number of his own like "Mother of Mine, I Still Have You" as if he were an Irish tenor, despite wearing blackface. What all

6

of this emphasizes is that blackface is a role, a creation, into which and out of which Jack can slip at will.

It is only partially accurate, therefore, to portray Jakie's transformation into the Jazz Singer as his achievement of a free, authentic personality, an American personality untrammeled by outmoded conventions. For the modern American personality Jakie acquires is free precisely to the extent that it is inauthentic, free to don and change masks at will. The grotesque exaggeration of blackface makeup had always been meant at least in part to emphasize the fact that the wearer was *not* black; in the 1920s Jolson made this old tactic breezy and up-to-date by publicly joking about the inauthenticity of his role. In 1925 *Vanity Fair* published his account of a trip to the South under the title "Maaaaam-my! Maaaaam-my! The Famous Mammy-Singer Explores His Native (?) Sunny Southland." For the purposes of this article, Jolson pretends to believe the clichés he has been purveying about the South, and he reacts with mock horror as the actual South repeatedly fails to conform to the clichés. Finally, he hopes at the very least to find "the southern darky—the banjo strummer whose wit is famous wherever minstrel shows have been played," but when he does find a promising specimen the man tells Jolson one of his own jokes, a joke he had been using on the stage for years.[13]

Jolson does not draw the obvious conclusion from this episode, that he is himself the "southern darky" he is looking for, he and white performers like him the only fleshly reality of this very old stereotype. But neither does he flinch at the contradiction between such knowing self-mockery and the maudlin sentiment of films like *The Jazz Singer*. One does not undermine the other, because the film insists equally on both. On one hand, the black persona carries all the connotations of natural, unspoiled authenticity that Europe has attached to other cultures at least since Montesquieu, and thus Jakie can throw off convention to become himself by becoming "black." On the other hand, blackface declares itself openly as a mask, unfixes identity, and frees the actor in a world of self-creation.[14]

We seem to have come a long way from Eliza Doolittle's masquerade as a lady, and yet all of our masquerades tell the same story, or parts of the same story. *Singin' in the Rain* shows how variously Americans respond to the linguistic and cultural prescriptiveness of experts like Henry Higgins. A single movie can accommodate Stanley Donen's nervous conventionality, Don Lockwood's brash freedom, and Cosmo Brown's technical wizardry, which allows the movie to have both convention and nature by erasing all the boundaries between them. This is what makes *Singin' in the Rain* such a faithfully American movie, its utterly genuine combination of cultural innocence and technological cynicism. But *Singin' in the Rain* is less than faithful to the moment it pretends to portray, the modernist moment of the 1920s, in that it omits any mention of race. The new voice that American culture acquired in the 1920s, the decade of jazz, stage musicals, talking pictures, and aesthetic modernism, was very largely a black one.

In music, on stage, and in film, white artists dubbed in a black voice and often wore, as Jolson did, a black mask. Because this mask, and the voice that issued from it, already embodied white America's quite various feelings about nature and convention, it became an integral part of the cultural and technical innovation of the 1920s. The story that both *Singin' in the Rain* and *The Jazz Singer* tell, the story of modernity's triumphant rebellion against the restrictions of the past, can hardly be told without it.

II

In January 1922, about the time that T. S. Eliot returned from his rest cure in Lausanne with a certain nineteen-page poem in his suitcase, Sampson Raphaelson published "The Day of Atonement" in *Everybody's Magazine*. This is the story of a young Jewish American so taken with "the plaintive blare of 'Alexander's Ragtime Band'" that he becomes a "blackface comedian," a story later made into a play and then the movie *The Jazz Singer*.[15] This protagonist's route to modernity may seem quite different from the one Eliot was about to chart, and yet the story Raphaelson tells of becoming modern by acting black was to be retold over and over in the next decade. It is, in fact, this story that links the transatlantic modernism Eliot and Joyce inaugurated in 1922 with the Harlem Renaissance that began, with Claude McKay's *Harlem Shadows*, at exactly the same time.

At the height of the Harlem Renaissance, in the year of *The Jazz Singer*, Rudolf Fisher reported wryly that all his favorite Harlem haunts had been taken over by whites "playing Negro games. . . . They camel and fish-tail and turkey, they geche and black-bottom and scronch, they skate and buzzard and mess-around—and they do them all better than I!"[16] In the same year Charles S. Johnson published in his anthology *Ebony and Topaz* a story that goes one step further, for the title character of "The Negro of the Jazz Band" is, despite his seemingly black skin and extraordinary sense of rhythm, white.[17] Though the story is meant to be a kind of fantasy, there were at this time many fashionable whites who purposely skirted the racial line, and at least a few who temporarily crossed it. Carl Van Vechten, who was famously caricatured in blackface by Miguel Covarrubias, had first passed for black as an undergraduate. Waldo Frank, author of the racial melodrama *Holiday*, also posed as black when traveling in the South with Jean Toomer.[18]

One might include in this company a number of white writers without Van Vechten's obvious connection to Harlem. Long before the Harlem Renaissance, Wallace Stevens signed himself "Sambo" in a letter to his fiancée, and long after it Ezra Pound was still calling Eliot "de Possum" and using what he imagined was black dialect in his letters.[19] It was in London that Eliot signed himself "Tar Baby," in Paris that Gertrude Stein casually used "dey" and "dem."[20] William

Carlos Williams imagined himself as a black musician in the 1940s, and as late as 1959 John Berryman could go back to the very source by dedicating one of his first *Dream Songs* to Daddy Rice, who "jumped 'Jim Crow' in 1828."[21] In "The Day of Atonement," then, Raphaelson tells a rather common story of white rebellion and escape by means of racial cross-identification, a story Nathan Huggins sums up in three phrases: "They defected, became apostates; they became Negroes."[22]

What ragtime promised Raphaelson's protagonist, what the minstrel show promised Berryman almost two generations later, was a voice. In 1923 Sherwood Anderson wrote to Jean Toomer about listening to some black dockworkers sing, held back from speaking to them by a reluctance he did not quite understand: "Perhaps I did not know how much I wanted a voice from them."[23] The heroine of *HERmione,* H.D.'s autobiographical novel, feels the same sort of vocal magnetism, in her case amounting almost to mesmerism, in talking to her family's black cook: "Her fell into the rhythm of Mandy's speech, the moment she began to speak to Mandy."[24] Though H.D. never let this rhythm pass into her published work, Alice Corbin, one of the early coeditors of *Poetry* magazine, did, in the appropriately named "Mandy's Religion," as did a number of other contributors to the journals of the early modernist avant-garde, including Carl Sandburg, Malcolm Cowley, Mina Loy and, perhaps most famously, Vachel Lindsay.[25] Eliot, Pound, and Stein fell into the same rhythm, in published work and in their letters, where it was often saved for private allusions and in-jokes, as if there were some secrets only a black voice could conceal.

The whole pattern of rebellion through racial ventriloquism is best illustrated by someone who might seem the least likely example: T. S. Eliot. As unlike Jakie as he might seem, as distant as he was from the Hester Street synagogue and from ragtime, Eliot did nonetheless resemble Jakie in defying his father's ancestral expectations to follow a more modern art. Instead of finishing his dissertation and joining the Harvard faculty, as his father had requested, Eliot remained in England to become a poet and free-lance man of letters, and he was very much saddened when his father died apparently thinking his son a failure.[26] Even before he abandoned his dissertation, however, Eliot produced a long-running parody of the kind of scholarship to which he was supposed to devote his life. In 1914 he sent to Conrad Aiken one of the infamous King Bolo poems, an obscene screed about "King Bolo's big black queen," carefully and cruelly annotated: "See Krapp: STREITSCHRIFT GEGEN HASENPFEFFER. 1.xvii §367, also Hasenpfeffer: POLEMISCHES GEGEN KRAPP I.II. 368ff. 490ff." Obscene doggerel is obviously a safety valve for this student sick of scholarly trivia, and eye dialect of a very crude sort becomes an alternative to the cramped language of references and citations: "King Bolo's big black bassturd kween / Her taste was kalm and klassic. . . ."[27] Thus Eliot rejects his family's traditional expectations and becomes a "blackface comedian," a role to which Ezra Pound gave the name "de Possum."

As the comic alternative to the serious scholarship expected by his family, doggerel in dialect becomes the prototype of the audacious poetry Eliot was to write instead of academic philosophy. As early as 1915 he wrote a play with a blackface role, the "REV. HAMMOND AIGS comic negro minister, of the 'come breddern' type."[28] Although the play was little more than an extended joke to entertain his Cambridge friend Eleanor Hinkley, it did suggest close knowledge of the prevailing dramatic stereotypes. So fond was Eliot of these particular clichés that Clive Bell sarcastically suggested in 1921 that Eliot's "agonizing labours seem to have been eased somewhat by the comfortable ministrations of a black and grinning muse."[29] Bell declined to be more specific, but at the time Eliot was laboring to put his knowledge of black music to work in *The Waste Land*, which contained at one time references to a number of rags and minstrel songs. These were finally removed from the final text, so that Eliot's "black and grinning muse" did not emerge in print until the fragments of *Sweeney Agonistes* were published in 1926–27.[30] The climax of this unfinished play is a minstrel show rendition of the Johnson–Cole–Johnson hit "Under the Bamboo Tree," a sensation during the St. Louis World's Fair of 1904, which Eliot attended with his family. Eliot called *Sweeney* a "Comic Minstrelsy" and a "jazz play."[31] It is, in fact, his version of *The Jazz Singer*, which was released that same year, his way of breaking with the very respectability he had so recently achieved.

For Eliot, as for a large number of other writers who were to make transatlantic modernism the dominant movement of the 1920s, the story of *The Jazz Singer* seems paradigmatic.[32] For another modern movement struggling to emerge at the same time, however, the story had a very different import. In 1927 James Weldon Johnson, lyricist of "Under the Bamboo Tree," published *God's Trombones*, which carefully avoided the very voice Eliot, Anderson, H.D., and the others envied to the point of mimicry. Johnson says in his preface that "practically no poetry is being written in dialect by the colored poets of today."[33] Dialect is impossible for a serious black poet of the 1920s because it is "based upon the minstrel traditions of Negro life," on "a happy-go-lucky, singing, shuffling, banjo-picking being," the very being, that is to say, that Jolson became in *The Jazz Singer*.[34]

When Alain Locke, instigator and editor of the landmark anthology *The New Negro*, wanted an example of "the newer motive" in African-American literature, he turned to "The Creation," the first of Johnson's sermons to be published. In this "interesting experiment," says Locke, is to be seen one of the "modernistic styles of expression" coming into being in the 1920s.[35] "The Creation" hardly seems "modernistic" in comparison to its exact contemporary *Sweeney Agonistes*: it has no contemporary references, no stylistic tricks, nothing overtly "experimental." But it could seem modern in the context of *The New Negro* simply by avoiding certain nearly inescapable stereotypes suggested by its subject, stereotypes Eliot had naturally drawn upon for his character the Reverend Hammond Aigs. As Van Vechten put it, "The Creation" was the poem that "broke the chain of dialect which bound Paul Laurence Dunbar and freed the younger generation from this dangerous restraint."[36]

Van Vechten's metaphor tells the whole story of the difference between these two modernisms. Linguistic imitation and racial masquerade are so important to transatlantic modernism because they allow the writer to play at self-fashioning. Jazz means freedom to Jakie Rabinowitz partly because it is fast and rhythmically unrestrained but also because it is not ancestrally his: to sing it is to make a choice of self, to do his own dubbing, as it were. For African-American poets of this generation, however, dialect is a "chain." In the version created by the white minstrel tradition, it is a constant reminder of the literal unfreedom of slavery and of the political and cultural repression that followed emancipation. Both symbol and actuality, it stands for a most intimate invasion whereby the dominant actually attempts to create the thoughts of the subordinate by providing it speech.[37]

Even more ironically, when a younger generation of African-American writers attempted to renew dialect writing by freeing it from the clichés Johnson criticized, fashionable white usage of the same language stood in their way as a disabling example.[38] Locke hoped that the interest of certain white modernists in plain and unvarnished language would help to make a wider audience for writers like Langston Hughes, Jean Toomer, and Claude McKay. At one point, he actually envisioned an alliance between an indigenous American modernism and the younger Harlem writers, to be based on a mutual interest in the language of the folk.[39] But these hopes were to be disappointed, and the younger writers found, as Johnson had, that white interest in African-American language and culture was, if anything, more dangerous than indifference.

Thus two different modernisms, tightly linked by their different stakes in the same language, emerge between 1922 and 1927. Houston Baker, Jr., has argued that Anglo-American modernism is dangerously irrelevant to the movement that was born at about the same time in Harlem.[40] In another sense, Anglo-American modernism is dangerous in its very relevance to the Harlem Renaissance because its strategies of linguistic rebellion depended so heavily on a kind of language that writers like Johnson rejected. For this reason, however, it is impossible to understand either modernism without reference to the other, without reference to the language they so uncomfortably shared, and to the political and cultural forces that were constricting that language at the very moment modern writers of both races were attempting in dramatically different ways to free it.

III

The publication of the *Oxford English Dictionary* (OED), the most important event in the stabilization of the English language, took more than forty years—coincidentally from the 1880s, when most of the transatlantic modernists were born, to the 1920s, when their most important works were published. Hugh Kenner has suggested that this is an important coincidence, that the OED shaped the way modernism looked at language.[41] But the OED, even in all its massiveness, is just one element in a whole complex of tense and tangled relationships within the language, all of which had their effect on the modernisms of the period.

In the beginning, the whole purpose of the OED was to deny the possibility of tense and tangled relationships within the language. To have any hope of success within the lifetime of humankind, the compilers of the dictionary needed to set some limit to the number of words to be defined. The 1858 proposal for the dictionary, therefore, rules out of consideration dialect words more recent than the Reformation, and, in doing so, provides what the OED itself cites as the first recorded use of the phrase "standard language."[42] This phrase was such a useful one that it became more and more common as the century went on. Shaw, for example, claimed that the whole purpose of *Pygmalion* was to dramatize the need for a "standard English."[43] The real danger, of course, is not simply that guttersnipes like Eliza will continue to wallow in linguistic filth, but that perfectly respectable girls like Clara Eynsford Hill will adopt it and make it fashionable. If Henry Higgins does not set the standard, then Eliza and her like will, and the whole country will end up talking a "quaint slavey lingo."[44]

Demands for linguistic standardization had been made from the earliest days of printing, which made variations more obvious by distributing them more widely, and became particularly insistent in the eighteenth century, when decorum of all kinds was highly prized.[45] But there was a distinct increase in volume in the years encompassed by the publication of the OED. It was in the 1880s that criticism of linguistic faults became a "thriving industry." Kenneth Cmiel's tabulation shows forty-one editions of works of verbal criticism or linguistic self-help between 1881 and 1885 and twenty-nine more between 1886 and 1890, almost twice as many as any other decade after 1860.[46] Popular magazines reflected this interest as well, with whole series of articles on standardization and usage in *Harper's, Lippincott's, Scribner's, Appleton's,* and the *Galaxy*.[47] This was also the heyday of spelling reform, Shaw's own hobbyhorse.[48]

There was a change of tone as well as volume. Standardization of the kind advocated after 1880 is different from the process by which one dialect gradually acquires power and prestige and so comes to dominate its rivals, as West Saxon crowded out other dialects to become Old English. What the flood of books and articles published in the 1880s called for was "a process of more or less conscious, planned and centralized regulation of language" in which "new elements threatening to enter the language are limited, and . . . variants within the language are hierarchized, and sometimes eliminated."[49] This program brought with it a moralistic tone and an almost evangelical fervor that made relatively minor infractions seem matters of cultural life or death.

During this period a number of organizations were formed to monitor such infractions. One of these was, of course, the OED itself, although on publication it turned out to be far too inclusive to serve as the mighty bulwark many had hoped for.[50] More stringent was the Society for Pure English (SPE), whose founder, Robert Bridges, was one of Shaw's models for Henry Higgins. The SPE was originally conceived in 1913 to "preserve the richness of differentiation in our vocabulary" and to oppose "whatever is slipshod and careless, and all blurring of hard-won distinctions." It began by objecting to artificial standards, even those promulgated by the new pronouncing dictionaries of the era, and it included among its members writers such as Thomas Hardy and Arnold Bennett, whose novels often included language that was more genuine than correct. Before long, however, the tracts of the SPE became little more than a testing ground for the little articles on *"shall* versus *will"* and the split infinitive that H. W. Fowler was to consolidate in his *Modern English Usage.*[51] Though Robert Graves's accusation that the SPE was "the literary equivalent of political fascism" seems a bit extreme, its tracts did devote a remarkable amount of space to issues, such as the proper use of the hyphen, of greater symbolic social value than linguistic significance.[52]

The SPE allowed Bridges to play Higgins on a larger stage, which grew even larger when he chaired the first BBC Advisory Committee on Spoken English.[53] Some members of the SPE also served on the commission chaired by Sir Henry Newbolt that examined the role of language and literature in the English educational system. The Newbolt Report, or *The Teaching of English in England* as it was properly titled, called unequivocally for "correct pronunciation and clear articulation" of "standard English" as the bedrock of education in all subjects.[54] This report, as well as Bridges's role with the BBC, shows how the pressure for standardization suffused the country by the 1920s.

An American equivalent of these groups was the American Academy of Arts and Letters, which received a grant in 1916 to "determine its duty regarding both the preservation of the English language in its beauty and integrity, and its cautious enrichment by such terms as grow out of modern conditions."[55] By the early 1920s, however, this modest program had become a full-fledged cultural crusade. In a national radio broadcast Nicholas Murray Butler proclaimed, "The preservation of our English speech in its purity is for the Academy a matter of high concern." Thus the academy established a Medal for Good Diction on the Stage and assigned Hamlin Garland to monitor the progress it would encourage.[56]

Garland thus joined the swelling ranks of the linguistic watchdogs, Englishmen like George Sampson, whose *English for the English* warned that the country was "torn with dialects," and Americans like Adams Sherman Hill, who decried in *Our English* the "'local color' and local dialects which jaded minds demand nowadays."[57] So pervasive and so inescapable was the conviction that language was in peril that even in deepest Africa H. Rider Haggard's She complained that the savages among whom she lived had "debased and defiled" the pure Arabic of the past.[58]

The stage was crowded in these years with individuals volunteering to serve as "linguistic conscience" to the nation.[59] In a book that had gone through eighteen editions by 1889, Richard Grant White attempted to enlist his readers in "a sort of linguistic detective police."[60] Noses to the ground, decoder rings at the ready, members of White's club would find and, apparently, punish those variations that so many writers of the time seemed to find disloyal. In fact, what was new and peculiar to the period was not linguistic difference and variation, which had been even more promiscuous in the past, but demands for its elimination. Leonard Forster dramatizes this change by noting that when William Beckford wrote *Vathek* in French in 1784 it excited little comment, but when Oscar Wilde wrote *Salomé* in French in 1894 it caused a scandal. What makes the difference is a concept of "language loyalty" relatively new in history and, John Joseph points out, peculiar to Europe.[61]

The whole idea that language is something to which one must remain loyal, the idea that empowers White's detective police as they search the countryside, is a popularized application of Romantic philology.[62] When Leibniz declared that "tongues differ as profoundly as do nations," he suggested an equation that was to be crucial for Herder, who taught that each language is a spiritual individuality like a nation, and for Humboldt, who took the next and, for our purposes, most crucial step, by maintaining that language is "an accurate index to the grade of intellectual comprehension attained by" a people.[63] Thus language becomes the cornerstone of national identity and an index of cultural health. Over and over, the linguistic conscience tells its captive audience that linguistic unity is not just crucial to national unity but actually synonymous with it. English, according to the Newbolt Report, is not just a medium: "It is itself the English mind." Thus, according to George Sampson, "The one common basis of a common culture is the common tongue." And finally, linguistic nonconformists must be admonished, as American immigrants were in 1916, that "a cleavage in the language now would mean to us a cleavage of the nation in its most vulnerable if not its most essential part."[64]

As powerful, and as powerfully seductive, as these ideas are, they are haunted by a crucial weakness, a self-destructiveness in the very notion of racial, national, or linguistic purity. Etienne Balibar maintains that a "pure race" can never, by definition, coincide with the totality of a national population, so that racism always works in reverse, creating a nation by taking its distance from the rejected.[65] The same is true of languages, which can never be pure despite the best efforts of the SPE. Thus the most shopworn commonplace in all the propaganda for standardization is that the standard language cannot be defined or even adequately described: "We do not expect to hear it, as a matter of course, in any given place where men congregate; when we do hear it, we know it for what it is."[66] This is the infallible, if somewhat mysterious, test: "[W]e all know when we are reading good English and when we are reading bad English. That is the conclusion of common sense. . . ."[67]

Despite these bland assertions, it turns out that, more commonly, we know only when we hear *bad* English. Sampson's second thoughts on the subject are revealing: "There is no need to define Standard English speech. We know what it is, and there's an end on't. Or, to put it another way, we know what is *not* standard English, and that is a sufficiently practical guide."[68] This explains why the campaign for standardization became a chorus of complaint and censure, why, even today, virtually all popular linguistic criticism focuses obsessively on minor errors and why grammar, in the popular mind, consists entirely of prohibitions. Over a hundred years ago, Henry Alford, Dean of Canterbury, condensed the entire tradition into one elegantly self-evident maxim: "Avoid all oddity of expression."[69] Yet this puts the poor speaker in the plight of the person who is ordered not to think of a brown bear. This situation is especially painful because the errors that are most stigmatized are, of course, the most common. The final turn in this paradoxical situation comes when we realize that "a particular usage is not attacked as non-standard until it has become very general and widespread."[70] The standard is not standard, that is to say, but rather the very opposite. Critics willing to play with numbers speculate that perhaps 3 to 4 percent of the population of England speaks standard English,[71] but the truth is that no one speaks standard English because that language is simply whatever shapeless thing is left when all the most common errors are removed.

If standard English is chimerical, however, the social forces that stand behind it are not, and the theoretical weakness of the standard language movement was precisely what gave it such great social strength. The period covered by the publication of the OED was one of great immigration and urban centralization: between 1871 and 1901 the number of towns in England with more than fifty thousand inhabitants doubled, and in the same period there was mass emigration from southern and eastern Europe and Russia at the greatest rate in history. At the same time, European imperialism attained a new pace so feverish it was commonly called a "scramble."[72] If anything, these vast social changes tended to favor linguistic uniformity, and linguists such as Otto Jespersen suggested that dialects were in the process of dying out worldwide.[73] Yet this process was hardly a painless or impersonal one.

Urbanization and mass emigration brought together all sorts of languages, dialects, and idiolects previously separated by space and social difference. The flood of linguistic criticism after 1880 was part of an attempt to sort out these competing languages and arrange them in order of prestige. At the same time, this concentration on linguistic propriety concealed concern for another kind of purity. Defense of the language became an indirect and intellectually respectable way of defending the borders, those outlying borders crossed by foreigners and those closer, less tangible, but even more sensitive borders crossed by a growing urban working class.[74] At the same time, the linguistic thought police struggled against one of the ironies of empire: extending the borders meant including millions of new speakers who might in time exert more influence over English than it could exert over them.

The first consideration given for the creation of the SPE was, therefore, the spread of the English language throughout the world.[75] Originally such anxiety had been directed at the United States. Americanisms had been decried as early as the 1740s, and in the generally unfriendly spirit of the 1860s Alford drew a direct connection between "the process of deterioration which our Queen's English has undergone at the hands of the Americans" and the debasement of the American nation in general.[76] Bridges had chiefly the Americans in mind when he decried "this most obnoxious condition, namely, that wherever our country-men are settled abroad there are alongside of them communities of other-speaking races, who, maintaining among themselves their native speech, learn yet enough of ours to mutilate it, and establishing among themselves all kinds of blundering corruptions, through habitual intercourse infect therewith the neigh-bouring English."[77] The racism inherent in such attacks could be surprisingly indiscriminate. In 1927 an anonymous contributor to the *New Statesman* de-nounced the outrageous idea that "our language belongs to everybody who uses it—including negroes and Middle-Westerners and Americanised Poles and Ital-ians."[78]

If the American experience excited such anxiety about "other-speaking races," the great expansion of empire in the nineteenth century made linguistic critics almost giddy. In 1886 T. L. Kington-Oliphant had serenely decreed that in recompense for all she borrowed, England provided to the empire "her own staple, namely the speech of free political life."[79] Looking back in 1926, however, A. Lloyd James, secretary to the BBC Advisory Committee on Spoken English, took it for granted that the influence had been all in the other direction: "[T]his territorial expansion of our language sowed the seeds of its disintegra-tion. . . ."[80] Between these two dates, "the immense area over which the lan-guage now extends" is routinely cited as one of the most important factors in its decline from purity.[81] The language that was to have symbolized England's cultural preeminence over the world, thus justifying its political and economic domination, became instead a symbol of English vulnerability, and defense of the language became a way of defending England against the cultural consequences of the implosion of the empire.

American concerns of the time about the purity of the language were in part defensive reactions to English prejudice. Richard Grant White batted back Dean Alford's slur on American speech by claiming that the British were even worse. John Hay took another tack by praising the vigor and power of American speech.[82] But Americans also had imperial anxieties quite similar to those of the English. In 1887 William Fowler worried that as "our countrymen are spreading westward across the continent, and are brought into contact with other races, and adopt new modes of thought, there is some danger that, in the use of their liberty, they may break loose from the laws of the English language. . . ."[83] Announc-ing the dedication of the American Academy of Arts and Letters to language issues thirty years later, Paul Elmer More spoke as if this dangerous process were nearly complete, the language "no longer the possession of the people alone who had created it, but . . . spoken and written over a vast territory among many peoples separated from the main stem by political and other traditions."[84] American expansion westward implied the same danger of linguistic contamination for Americans "from the main stem" that the English had feared from America itself.

Worse yet, in this view, was the threat that American English faced even if it stayed put: the threat of immigration. The boom in linguistic criticism in the United States coincided with the increased immigration of the 1880s and was one manifestation of the reaction against it. The "wild motley throng" that crowds in through the "unguarded gates" of Thomas Bailey Aldrich's 1895 poem of the same name bring with them a disturbing cacophony:

> In street and alley what strange tongues are loud,
> Accents of menace alien to our air,
> Voices that once the Tower of Babel knew.[85]

Thus, in a book that had gone through twenty-one editions by 1892, William Mathews declared that since "unity of speech is essential to the unity of a people" even so much as "a daily newspaper with an Irish, German, or French prefix, or in a foreign language, is a perpetual breeder of national animosities."[86] More dangerous yet was the possibility that foreign languages might corrupt English itself, so that Joseph Fitzgerald urged his readers to treat foreign loanwords "as aliens, and to agitate for an exclusion act against them."[87]

This was not merely a jingoistic campaign carried on by xenophobic know-nothings; it was in large part the work of established writers and intellectuals, men like Barrett Wendell, Brooks Adams, and Francis Parkman. For example, when Henry James returned to the United States in 1905, after his own immigration to England, he was appalled to find that he had forgotten to lock the door behind him. In his outrage James felt the presence of newly emigrated speakers of English quite literally as the invasion of a burglar:

> All the while we sleep the vast contingent of aliens whom we make welcome, and whose main contention, as I say, is that, from the moment of their arrival, they have just as much property in our speech as we have . . . all the while we sleep the innumerable aliens are sitting up (*they* don't sleep!) to work their will on their new inheritance and prove to us that they are without any finer feeling or more conservative instinct of consideration for it . . . than they may have on the subject of so many yards of freely figured oilcloth, from the shop. . . .

James's other metaphor for this linguistic violation is even more intimate:

> [T]o the American Dutchman and Dago, as the voice of the people describes them, we have simply handed over our property—not exactly bound hand and foot, I admit, like Andromeda awaiting her Perseus, but at least distracted, dishevelled, despoiled, divested of that beautiful and becoming drapery of native atmosphere and circumstance. . . . [88]

James's choice of allusion may have made the graduating class of Bryn Mawr, to whom he directed this hysterical outburst, uncomfortable in ways that he did not intend, but it struck a sympathetic chord in Paul Shorey, who told the American Academy a few years later:

> [W]e are all hearing every day and many of us are reading and writing not instinctively right and sound English but the English of German American and Swedish American, Italian American, Russian American, Yiddish American speakers, pigeon [*sic*] English, Japanese schoolboy English, Hans Breitmann English, doctors' dissertation English, pedagogical seminary English, babu English.[89]

The verbal excessiveness of these defenses, like a squid shooting ink, suggests that both Shorey and James were so concerned they were willing to destroy the language in order to save it.[90]

It should be clear by now, however, that language is simply a convenient symbol of resistance to social change. The same processes that took the English to the far corners of the world and the Americans to the western shore, that brought emigrants from all over Europe to the United States, tended to erase the most visible means of distinguishing between different classes and nationalities. One of the wry messages of *Pygmalion* is that clothes make the lady, and, as manufacturing made dress more uniform, the leap from flower girl to lady became less extreme. But it is far easier to dress Eliza up in borrowed finery than it is to change her speech. Shaw's play is, therefore, a demonstration of the way that speech came to play the role of chief social discriminator as other means became less effective.[91] Between the 1880s and the 1920s, linguistic criticism became a way of checking social mobility and racial progress without overt illiberalism. Even today, criticism of speech is often, if not always, a way of expressing other social prejudices that polite discourse overtly disavows.[92] Thus the theoretical weakness of Romantic linguistic nationalism, its ghostly, parasitic dependence on that which it would expel, is the source of its social utility. The standard language movement did not need to define the standard language in order to succeed, because its real purpose was to focus attention on the alien, both foreign and domestic, and to provide a means of discriminating where other methods were beginning to fail.

IV

In these years during which dialect words were excluded from the pages of the OED, dialect was, of course, routinely stigmatized. The inconveniences arising "from the existence of local dialects" are, in the opinion of G. P. Marsh, "very serious obstacles to national progress, to the growth of a comprehensive and enlightened patriotism, to the creation of a popular literature, and to the diffusion of general culture."[93] The two great myths of linguistic decline, the Hellenizing of Greece and the fall of Rome, tended to associate the division of a language into varieties with cultural collapse. Thus Paul Elmer More warned the American Academy that English had entered its "Englistic" period, beyond which the future seemed pretty dim.[94]

Yet, in the same set of addresses, Shorey reminded his listeners that it was "the scholarly Lowell who composed poems in a Yankee dialect."[95] And it was the scholarly Bridges who lamented "our perishing dialects" in the tracts of a society devoted by title at least to the preservation of pure English. In fact, the SPE was sometimes seen, from within and without, as a kind of junior branch of the English Dialect Society. In the 1918 *Cambridge History of American Literature* C. Alphonso Smith treated the SPE as if it were a conservator of dialect differences, and Walter Raleigh joined the SPE, by one account, because he thought it would offer opportunities to "coin words, and use dialect, and rap out forcible native idioms."[96] This paradox was hardly limited to the SPE. The Newbolt Report contained an opinion, submitted by the Committee on Adult Education, that dialect literature should be encouraged because "dialect, where it still lives, is the natural speech of emotion, and therefore of poetry and drama."[97]

There seems to be some indecision here, even in this very opinionated propaganda, about which English is really pure. The Newbolt Report was forthright about the need for instruction in standard English, especially if this required the abandonment of dialect, and the tracts of the SPE devoted many pages to monitoring niggling distinctions.[98] And yet there was some suspicion even here that the standard language was a fiction, an artificial convention, and that a mere convention could hardly play the role in the English ethos assigned to the national language. After all, the popular linguist Max Müller had taught since the middle of the century that the standard written languages were mere confections: "The real and natural life of language is in its [spoken] dialects."[99]

In fact, there was a marked increase in English dialect writing at this time, including works by Hardy, Stevenson, Kipling, Barnes, and the writers of the Irish Revival, as well as writers such as Henley and Davidson, who were aggressively vernacular in style.[100] The conflict between dialect, idiolect, and the standard language began to appear as a plot element in literature of the period, but not all writers agreed with Mr. Alfred Yule of Gissing's *New Grub Street*, who was given such exquisite pain by his wife's uneducated speech he never invited guests to his home. Bi-dialectal shifters such as poor Mrs. Yule, who live in two distinct speech communities, begin to appear in a sympathetic light and then in a favorable one, a process that can be traced from *Tess of the d'Urbervilles* to *Lady Chatterley's Lover.*[101]

Dialect writing was pursued even in an atmosphere of linguistic censoriousness because of the hope that it might be "the prince in disguise . . . an original and unique literary medium of expression."[102] Dialect, it was often argued about this time, was "purer" than the standard written language because it was less affected by printing, education, and "elocution masters."[103] If the real culprit in the degeneration of language is education, or the newspapers, or science, or modern slang, as Alford, James, and other watchdogs variously claimed, then perhaps the good old rural dialects of England were the "pure" alternative.[104] This is one way of understanding the enlistment in the SPE of Thomas Hardy, though he was perhaps the leading practitioner of dialect writing at the time.

Times of verbal nicety in England have often coincided with romantic rediscoveries of dialect, a coincidence best exemplified by the careers of Scott and Austen. The sort of recourse to dialect represented by Scott is easy enough to understand, but what of C. M. Doughty's claim that he traveled into Arabia "to redeem English from the slough into which it has fallen."[105] How could a sojourn among the heathen possibly redeem English? Of course, if distance from education, newspapers, science, and modern slang makes for authenticity and pure language, then maybe Arabia is just the place to find it. Or perhaps Africa, as Andrew Lang suggested when he said that "the natural man in me, the survival of some blue-painted Briton" responds best to "a *true* Zulu love story."[106] Or perhaps South America, where Roger Casement found a language so old, so elemental and untouched, no one even knew the meaning of it.[107] The shape of the paradox, at any rate, begins to emerge. On one hand, the standard language movement has as its central purpose the protection of England from other races. Yet, insofar as it recoils from what Henry James called "the high modernism of the condition,"[108] the more it is thrown into the kind of primitivism that contributed to another great trend of the period: the colonial adventure story. Perhaps it is not so odd, then, that when Rider Haggard's heroes Holly and Vincy finally reach the heart of darkest Africa and complete their search for the mysterious She, they find a linguistic critic.

The situation in America is even more complex, since it develops in the shadow of England's authority. American defiance of this authority can take two forms: a claim that Americans are in fact more proper in their speech than the English, or a claim that Americans speak a more vital, natural speech than their decadent co-linguists. Thus American linguistic critics are even more apt than their English colleagues to splay themselves across this paradox. Even Shorey, as pinched an authoritarian as ever addressed the American Academy, praised the "crisp concise verbiage" of popular America because it "unites us in a fellowship of democratic revolt against the pedant" and "differentiates us from the supercilious and slow-witted Englishman who cannot understand it."[109] Both Brander Matthews, another Academician, and Gilbert Tucker wrote to the SPE to alert it to the fact that American English still had all the pith and vividness the SPE was searching for in England.[110]

However true this may have been, it ran against another cherished notion that America had no dialects, at least in the sense of provincial variations. Visitors to the United States in the late eighteenth and early nineteenth centuries reported an amazing uniformity of speech, on which the Americans sometimes plumed themselves when it seemed to contrast favorably with the divisiveness of English provincialisms.[111] There was, of course, one significant exception to this general uniformity: "Dialect in general is there less prevalent than in Britain, except among the poor slaves."[112] In fact, there grew up a theory that was to enjoy an extremely long life, that the English dialect variations were preserved in America only in the untutored speech of the slaves. Joel Chandler Harris, for example, claimed that the language he used in the Uncle Remus stories was simply white English three hundred years out-of-date. In the 1920s, George Philip Krapp made this claim into a full-fledged scientific theory, one which enjoyed a certain popularity in the black press of the time perhaps because it seemed to rescue black speech from the worst prejudices against it.[113]

If the slaves had preserved the "good old Elizabethan pronunciation," as R. Emmett Kennedy put it, then did it not follow that theirs was the purest English? Kennedy followed the SPE line of reasoning perfectly: the true index of a race or nation is found in its "native melodies and folk literature," preserved as much as possible from "the artificialities of civilization." Yet this authentic national voice belonged only to the unlettered folk "who have not lost the gracious charm of being natural." Ambrose Gonzales, like Kennedy a white dialect writer of the 1920s, said much the same thing: "The peasantry, the lower classes generally, are the conservators of speech."[114] As an anonymous critic observed in an 1889 review of Harris, such ideas fit perfectly within the confines of Romantic philology, except that "Putnam County . . . becomes like the Central Plateau of the Hindu-Kush Mountains—'east of the moon and west of the sun'—so dear to the myth-mongers and philologists of the Müller school."[115]

And yet, on the other hand, black English had long been considered not just corrupt in itself but also the cause of corruption in others. As early as 1740, dire notice was taken of the way that a colonial speaker who regularly consorts with slaves "acquires their broken way of talking."[116] In the next century, Dickens noticed with disapproval that "women who have been bred in the slave States speak more or less like negroes, from having been constantly in their childhood with black nurses."[117] Writers like Kennedy and Gonzales do not disavow such notions: the black speakers in their works are abundantly provided with the sort of malapropisms that have always characterized literary representations of "broken English." Somehow the language included in works like Kennedy's *Black Cameos* and Gonzales's *Black Border* is both broken and pure, twisted and authentic. And yet perhaps it is this very inconsistency that explains why the 1880s, the decade in which the standard language movement became a "thriving industry," also marked the beginning of another, seemingly quite different, industry: dialect literature.

From the hint given by Irwin Russell's "Christmas Night in the Quarters" in 1878, Joel Chandler Harris and Thomas Nelson Page developed a style of writing that was soon to dominate American magazines to such an extent it provoked pleas for relief.[118] In 1897 T. C. De Leon called it "a sort of craze." Even Page himself admitted that the result of Harris's success with Uncle Remus was "a deluge of what are called 'dialect-stories,' until the public, surfeited by them has begun almost to shudder at the very name." Prominent magazines such as *Harper's,* the *Atlantic, Scribner's,* the *North American Review,* and *Century* ran hundreds of stories and vignettes in dialect in this period.[119] At first this may seem to be a realization of the standardizer's worst fear, that popular language would be determined from below and not from above. On the other hand, however, it may be that these stories in dialect are simply another way of managing the social pressures behind the standard language movement.

C. Alphonso Smith did not consider it especially peculiar that his survey of "Negro Dialect" in the 1918 *Cambridge History of American Literature* was almost totally devoted to white writers. Smith dismisses Booker T. Washington and W. E. B. Du Bois not because they did not write in dialect but because they were not of "unmixed negro blood," and he ignores Charles W. Chesnutt altogether.[120] Here Smith simply reflects the fact that the dialect movement was almost exclusively a matter of white mimicry and role-playing. Harris may have been the most successful such writer because he had the greatest psychological investment in the role. Painfully shy and a stutterer, Harris preferred to appear before his public, and sometimes even before personal friends, as Uncle Remus. Like Jakie Rabinowitz forty years later, it seems that Harris could not find a voice until he found a black one.[121]

On the other hand, Harris was an accomplished editorialist for the Atlanta *Constitution,* where he helped Henry W. Grady define the New South that was to follow the demise of Reconstruction.[122] Harris's dual role is more than a psychological curiosity: it expresses the duplicity of the whole dialect movement. It is no accident that this movement coincides with the dismantling of Reconstruction and the birth of Jim Crow, with a legal retrenchment that began in 1883 with the overthrow of the Civil Rights Act and culminated in *Plessy v. Ferguson* in 1896, and with an increase in racist propaganda and hate crimes.[123] For the comic stories of the dialect movement firmly establish in the minds of the white readership a picture of the freed slaves as hapless, childlike, and eager for paternalistic protection.

The essential conceit on which these works are based is that their subject is fast disappearing. Over and over, it is said that Harris caught Uncle Remus at the moment he and his kind had ceased to exist.[124] Oddly enough, such figures continued to disappear for at least the next thirty years, at which time E. K. Means congratulated himself for preserving in print a new generation of vanishing Negroes.[125] The central trope of the movement, the "disappearing Negro," was serviceable on several levels. It functioned as wish fulfillment, revealing the barely submerged hope that the freed slaves would simply die off. It served as a metaphor of the temporal reversal of the post-Reconstruction period, taking readers imaginatively back in time as the South was being taken politically back in time. And it fed nostalgia for a time when racial relationships had been simple and happy, as least for whites, suggesting that they might be simple and happy again if southern whites were simply left alone to resolve things themselves.[126]

What was really vanishing, in other words, was a racial relationship that Jim Crow laws were meant to recreate. The black of the dialect stories was little more than a metaphor for the antebellum way of life. As Page put it, "It has been very often suggested that I was writing up the darkey; but my real intention has been to write up the South and its social life, using the darkey as a medium. . . ."[127] Yet Page seems unaware of the full implications of this metaphorical identification, as Julia Peterkin certainly was when she ingenuously rephrased it: "I shall never write of white people; to me their lives are not so colorful. If the South is going to write, what is it they are going to write about—the Negro, of course."[128] If the South has no subject but the Negro, as Harris had no voice but that of Uncle Remus, then the region has come to be defined entirely in terms of that which it hates and fears. The freed slaves are submerged, expelled, and expanded until they become coterminous with the region itself.

In the same way, black speech is mocked as deviant and at the same time announced as the only true voice of the South. This has the effect of affirming the standard about which the standardizers were so concerned while simultaneously creating an escape from it. Smith claims that "the American passion for a standardized average of correctness" has checked the use of dialect among whites, but he does not suspect that the "Negro dialect" to which he devotes his article *is* white dialect in that it stands in for that which has apparently been abandoned.[129] Bad grammar has long been the privilege of the upper classes, who demonstrate their superiority to social constraints by slipshod speech. The dialect tradition extended this privilege to the entire white race, which could pay homage to and in the same breath demonstrate its independence from the standard language.

The difficulties this created for African-American writers of the time are indicated by the absence of Charles W. Chesnutt from Smith's encyclopedic article. Chesnutt himself included a sort of allegory of this situation in his novel *The Marrow of Tradition*, in which Tom Delamere, "a type of the degenerate aristocrat," excels in "cakewalk or 'coon' impersonations, for which he was in large social demand." Delamere's talent turns to crime when he robs and kills his own aunt while disguised as the faithful black houseservant Sandy, who is nearly lynched for the crime.[130] The way that Delamere goes free while Sandy is confined and almost executed represents the unequal effects of the racial mimicry of the dialect tradition, which represented imaginative license for its white practitioners but quite literal imprisonment for blacks. These effects impinged in the same way on the most noted African-American poet of the period, Paul Laurence Dunbar, who complained that praise of his dialect verse had become a trap because readers would pay attention to nothing else.[131] This is the very "chain of dialect" that Johnson had to break in the 1920s, while another young aristocrat named Tom practiced his "coon impersonations."

In the generation between *The Marrow of Tradition* and *God's Trombones* the chain became, if anything, even tighter. According to Thomas Gossett, the widespread race riots of 1919 marked an intensification of American racism that lasted throughout the 1920s: "[B]ooks and articles expounding the transcendent importance of race as a key to civilization poured from the presses in the 1920's." There was an increase in racial violence, in overt discrimination, and in prejudices about language: in 1919 fifteen states passed laws requiring that all instruction, public and private, be in English.[132] At the same time, there was a second boom in dialect writing, even larger, if anything, than the first. So strong was the "vogue" that Edgar Billups feared that the field would be given over to mere "faddists." Julia Peterkin complained that her Gullah stories were ignored because so many of the potential reviewers wrote dialect stories of their own.[133] These might have included Irvin Cobb, Hugh Wiley, T. S. Stribling, Robert McBlair, Gertrude Sanborn, Ada Jack Carver, John Trotwood Moore, Marceilus Whaley, E. C. L. Adams, Roark Bradford, John B. Sales, and many others. In addition to the magazines and journals that had been publishing dialect since the 1880s, *The Saturday Evening Post* began to make it a particular speciality.[134]

By the 1920s, then, dialect was solidly established in a quite equivocal role: it reflected increasingly shrill demands for adherence to a chimerical standard and at the same time defied those demands. As "broken English," dialect was the opposite without which "pure English" could not exist. In fact, "pure English" could never adequately be represented except by implication, so that dialect, slang, and other forms of linguistic slovenliness had to be kept in currency to keep "pure English" alive. At the same time, however, dialect served as the "natural" form of "pure English," its unmarked counterpart, to which even the strictest schoolmaster had to pay lip service at times. Finally, dialect preserved an escape from all the social pressures implied by the standard language movement: "black" dialect was white dialect in hiding. This is not to say that there was no actual black speech with its own order and rules, only that the acted, sung, and published versions of this language were almost always white products, no matter how much they may have resembled their black prototypes. Black dialect was a resort freely open only to whites, and thus its popularity matched and in fact reflected the influence of the standard language movement so inimical to non-European cultures and languages.

V

Born in the 1870s and 1880s, modernists such as Eliot, Pound, Stein, H.D., Williams, and Stevens grew up at a time when the English language was being pulled apart by competing political and social forces. Schoolchildren, both white and black, "were taught that the speech of their fathers was not proper English speech. They were encouraged to leave behind their dialects and regional and ethnic idioms."[135] This, for many, was a rather more difficult process than Shaw supposes when he speaks of the "many thousands of men and women who have sloughed off their native dialects and acquired a new tongue." At the same time, however, youngsters like Ra Pound were presented with a romanticized alternative in the stories of Uncle Remus and the dialect tradition of the popular magazines.[136]

When their movement climaxed with *The Waste Land* in 1922, the modernists' linguistic horizon also enclosed "The Day of Atonement," the Newbolt Report, *The Book of American Negro Poetry, Harlem Shadows,* Clement Wood's *Nigger,* and Wittgenstein's *Tractatus,* all of which were published in the same year. And though it may seem that these various linguistic productions have little to do with one another, they are in fact joined by a rather dense network. Brander Matthews, a member of the American Academy and a contributor to the tracts of the SPE, introduced James Weldon Johnson's dialect poetry to the nation.[137] C. K. Ogden, inventor of Basic English and translator of the *Tractatus,* published two dozen poems by Claude McKay in the same issue of the *Cambridge Magazine* that included "The Linguistic Conscience."[138] Eliot stole from Johnson; Johnson advised Van Vechten; Van Vechten introduced Gertrude Stein to Harlem by quoting her in *Nigger Heaven.*[139]

The position of literary modernism in this network of linguistic relationships is almost necessarily equivocal. In a 1926 comment in the *Dial,* Marianne Moore welcomed the SPE because she found its tracts "persuasively fastidious." Though she admitted that "perfect diction" is less to be found in America than mastery of slang, she did find enough of it to mention James, Poe, Whistler, Stevens, Pound, and Cummings as examples. Moore was clearly entranced by the possibilities for fine distinction presented by the articles of the SPE, which she saw as the ally of poets interested in the infinite variousness of words.[140] On her own side of the Atlantic, however, the forces of linguistic criticism had chosen Moore herself for attack. One of the papers published by the American Academy in 1925, Robert Underwood Johnson's "Glory of Words," is in fact an extended attack on literary modernism: on free verse, on contemporary subject matter, on colloquial diction, on Eliot, Conrad Aiken, Carl Sandburg, Amy Lowell, and on Marianne Moore. Quoting a stanza from "Those Various Scalpels," Johnson asks, "what is the remedy for this disease?" The answer is "to dwell upon the glory of words in our inexhaustible and imperishable treasures of great poetry," which is probably about what Moore thought she was doing.[141]

The irony reveals how variously modernism might be defined as bringing greater precision to language or as destroying just those rules and usages that made precision possible. But there is another, more specific, twist in this relationship as well. Moore declares a "fascinated interest" in the variability of American pronunciation, "when in New York seabirds are *seaboids,* when as in the Negro vernacular, the tenth becomes the *tent,* certainly is *certainy,* and Paris is *Parus.* "[142] Moore's examples are fairly weak, and one is apparently a piece of eye dialect, but the message is clear: vernacular and dialect distortions of the language are a resource to be mined. Eliot praised Moore in the pages of the *Dial* precisely for her ability to exploit this resource, "the jargon of the laboratory and the slang of the comic strip."[143] But in Johnson's ears this same mixture of sounds causes exquisite pain. "The free verse of to-day," he says, "disdains the lute, the harp, the oboe, and the 'cello and is content with the tom-tom, the triangle, and the banjo."[144] The racial implications of Johnson's musical examples are fairly clear: modernism disdains great literature for black minstrelsy. Its rebellion against pure English and the great literature written in it is figured as racial treason.

Johnson may have had in mind Vachel Lindsay's poem "The Congo" or Carl Sandburg's "Jazz Fantasia." He might well have trained his sights on two plays not published until two years after his talk, *Sweeney Agonistes* and E. E. Cummings's *Him*, both of which use minstrel instrumentation. Cummings's play, which Moore admired so much she arranged to have parts of it published in the *Dial*, aims to give offense in exactly the quarter defended by Johnson.[145] Perhaps this is what endeared it to Moore, because the play is an unruly compendium of variant Englishes from drunken slurs to soap box oratory to advertisement slogans to vaudeville to medicine show barking.

Cummings tends to arrange these languages in competing pairs. A drunken Englishman who asks to have his "topper" replaced on his "nut" is met by an American policeman who says things like "Lissun. Wutchuhgut dare." An Ethiopian who claims "Ah ain goin nowhere" meets some suspicious centurions. A "gentleman" whose hypercorrectness of speech leads him to misuse the word *infer* meets a shapeless mob. The climax, in a way, of this fairly shapeless bit of modernist vaudeville is the confrontation between six "coalblack figures" in full minstrel regalia, singing to an invisible jazz band, and John Rutter, "President pro tem. of the Society for the Contraception of Vice." Rutter spins out an enormously bloated indictment of "harmful titillation provocation or excitation complete or incomplete of the human or inhuman mind or body" whether it "be oral graphic neither or both and including with the written and spoken words the unwritten and unspoken word or any inscription sign or mark." Rutter is, in brief, one of the "linguistic thought police" let loose by Richard Grant White and egged on by Robert Underwood Johnson. Meanwhile the minstrel singers say things like "Gway yoh poor whytrash."[146]

The confrontation between linguistic authoritarianism and American dialects is but one version of a more general conflict between repression and freedom, which Cummings dramatizes by having the minstrels confront Rutter with "something which suggests a banana in size and shape and which is carefully wrapped in a bloody napkin."[147] This object symbolizes what Rutter, despite his name, does not have, what he fears, and what his language in all its convoluted Latinate obscurity attempts to hide. The ultimate affront to Rutter and his ilk would obviously be actual obscenity, and yet Cummings shrinks from this final outrage, letting black speech and jazz innuendo suggest what he is too squeamish to say.

Johnson is perfectly right, then, to associate the modernist affront with minstrel instruments. Minstrel dialect is for Cummings one of the languages of rebellion, and the rebellion against stifling linguistic authoritarianism that it makes possible is the type of a much broader rebellion against repression and standardization of all kinds. In the year of *The Jazz Singer* and *Sweeney Agonistes*, Cummings also breaks away from the fathers, from the Robert Underwood Johnsons, by donning a minstrel disguise. Thus the terms of *The Jazz Singer* are recapitulated, with Robert Underwood Johnson in the role of the outraged father who shouts, "Singing nigger songs in a beer garden! You bummer! You no good lowlife!"[148] and E. E. Cummings as the cheeky lad who demands the right to express himself by putting shoeblack on his face.

Thus the generational conflict between the older critics clustered behind the American Academy's walls and the younger writers outside was fought over the body of a third figure, a black one. When Sherwood Anderson wanted to express his fear about creeping standardization and linguistic intolerance, he drew on the old metaphor of the vanishing Negro: "Will the love of words be lost? Success, standardization, big editions, money rolling in. . . . Words goin the way of the black, of song and dance." It is no accident that Anderson actually begins to speak in dialect here, because he implicitly aligns the free language of the modern artist with the despised dialect of African America. In this analysis only the standard language is actually "white." Artistic language is, by virtue of its deviation from that standard, black: "In the end they will make factory hands of us writers too. The whites will get us. They win."[149]

Because the American Academy had long associated immigration with linguistic decline, it also viewed the conflict over language as a racial one. Modernism became another form of mongrelization, another impurity stirred into the terrifying mixture that America was becoming. Like Johnson, Stuart Sherman attacked the younger generation as if its literary experiments had introduced some sort of alien bacillus into the bloodstream of the republic. Such young people, he charged, were in league "against virtue and decorum and even against the grammar and idiom of English speech." This league might never have gathered, Sherman suggests darkly, if not for a group of leaders "whose blood and breeding are as hostile to the English strain as a cat to water." Sherman's metaphor for these "alien-minded" writers is peculiarly inappropriate: he calls them "Mohawks," as if American Indians were somehow more alien to America than the English immigrants of the 1660s. But his point is clear nonetheless: writers who tamper with the English language are, ipso facto, racial aliens.[150]

The figure in the midst of all this, the racial alien, is, of course, a cipher, and yet it actually represents the one point of agreement in the battle of literary generations. Both sides tend to see this figure as natural, primitive, life-affirming, and impatient of restraint. This unspoken agreement shows how little threat was actually posed to the reigning order by plays like *Him*. Despite the outrage of Robert Underwood Johnson, such plays merely offered the sort of escape that confirmed authority by confirming its categories, no matter how thoroughly they may have reversed the value judgments attached to those categories. When Cummings or Anderson romanticize dialect as a natural and spontaneous alternative to a restrictive standard, they merely repeat what Johnson has already said, albeit in a different tonality. And yet *Him* shares something else with *The Jazz Singer:* a tendency to undermine its own oppositions. The jumble of competing languages in Cummings's play makes it very difficult to nominate one as the most "natural." Cummings's vaudevillian ventriloquism is so indiscriminate it undermines the status of dialect itself, leveling all language. This is the real threat it poses to the forces of standardization.

VI

The third member of the linguistic ménage à trois at the center of *Pygmalion* is Colonel Pickering, author of *Spoken Sanscrit,* who comes home to England especially to meet Henry Higgins. One of Higgins's real-life prototypes, Henry Sweet, had predicted Pickering, in a way, when he argued that the widening of the Empire would provide linguists with innumerable useful and exotic examples, of which Sanskrit was only the first. Studying Sanskrit in India, Sir William Jones had proposed the notion of a common ancestor behind it and most of the European languages, an ancestor that came to be called Indo-European. Jones's suggestion gave rise to a kind of "unified field theory" of language, with a new etymological principle of human universality to replace that once provided in a narrower sphere by Latin grammar.[151]

Eliza's education is in part an experiment to test this theory, which she corroborates by ably learning a whole panoply of languages besides standard English, including African dialects and "Hottentot clicks."[152] Higgins's ability to teach and Eliza's to learn these quite different languages suggests a common substratum and therefore a brotherhood among them. Given enough time and study, perhaps all languages could be arranged around a single standard, a possibility that would assuage all the anxieties of the Society for Pure English by transforming it into the Society for Pure Language. But this is just what troubled the opponents of the Indo-European theory. If there is a common substratum linking English and Sanskrit, then there is a fundamental cultural commonality linking the English and what Müller called "the black inhabitants of India," and if there is such a commonality then it seems impossible to maintain the superiority on which the empire depended.[153]

The ironic result of the "unified field theory," as Linda Dowling points out, is that, instead of affording linguists a standard by which they could construct some vast pecking order of world languages, it reduced all languages to the same plane.[154] In this way the ethnographic appetite of imperialist Europe led in the end to the very opposite of the vast order once envisioned; it led to contemporary cultural and linguistic relativism. The very gesture that extended European intellectual sway over all the globe undermined the pretensions of European thought and language. Thus professional linguists have been utterly at odds with the standard language movement since its beginnings, because they tend to look at language as purely conventional and relative.[155]

In part this relativism grew naturally out of the linguistic difficulties faced by the earliest ethnographers. Franz Boas, attempting to deal with the basic ethnographic problem of linguistic transcription, realized that it was impossible to treat a European language, no matter how "scientific," as a neutral container for other languages. Trapped inside his own linguistic system, the European observer could only approximate what he heard. Thus there was no way to rank or hierarchize languages; they were simply different sound systems, mutually incompatible.[156] The same was true for Bronislaw Malinowski, who claimed that ethnographic research had "driven" him away from the idea of language as a stable repository of meaning toward a new theory he called "the principle of Symbolic Relativity." This theory, which held that each language is governed by a "pragmatic world vision," frees us, Malinowski says, "from logical shackles and grammatical barrenness."[157] It also made the whole notion of a standard language a philosophical incoherence.[158]

This dual development, this link between ethnographic interests and linguistic relativism, was recapitulated within the international modernism that grew up at the same time. In some cases the connection between ethnography and artistic experiment was remarkably direct. The American painter Max Weber, for example, sat down in the American Museum of Natural History one day in 1911 and began to write free verse. Weber began with a piece called "To Xochipilli, Lord of Flowers," inspired by a pre-Columbian sculpture in the museum's collection, and finished fifteen years later with a book called *Primitives: Poems and Woodcuts*, which included poems like "Congo Form" and "Bampense Kasai," which was written about an African mask.[159] For the most part, however, the influence of ethnographic collections was mediated through scholars like Wilhelm Worringer and Lucien Lévy-Bruhl. In both cases ethnography fed the desire George Steiner identifies particularly with the avant-garde of the period 1870–1900, the desire to investigate—through destructive experimentation if necessary—the very bases of language.[160]

The writers who felt this necessity most keenly all seem to have been polyglot cosmopolitans: Pound, Kandinsky, Cendrars, Tzara, Apollinaire. Richard Huelsenbeck's 1917 dada manifesto "The New Man" describes this miscellaneous group as "saturated, stuffed full to the point of disgust with the experience of all outcasts, the dehumanized beings of Europe, the Africans, the Polynesians, all kinds. . . ."[161] Peculiarly, Africans and Polynesians come to stand for all outcasts, and their languages, or imaginary versions of their languages, for the new speech of the new man. Pound declared that "the artist recognises his life in the terms of the Tahitian savage," and he sat for a portrait bust that made him look like an Easter Island idol.[162] And when Huelsenbeck appeared at the first of many evenings at the Cabaret Voltaire, he recited "some Negro poems that I had made up myself."[163]

These poems were the first of many "chants nègres" to grace a dada evening at the Cabaret Voltaire, where the entertainment also often included Huelsenbeck's drumming and "African" masks by Marcel Janco.[164] Dada poetry of the period depended heavily on "pseudo-African" languages made up of nonsense syllables like the "umba umba" that graced Huelsenbeck's first essay in the genre. At its extreme, such poetry went beyond nonsense syllables to the very letter itself, as in Huelsenbeck's "Chorus Sanctus":

> aao a ei iii oii
> ou ou o ou ou e ou ie a ai
> ha dzk drrr br obu br bouss boum
> ha haha hi hi hi l i l i l i leïomen[165]

Using an ersatz African language as a wedge, Huelsenbeck pries language loose, letter by letter, from sense and meaning.

In this the dadaists came closer than they realized to one of the oldest and most traditional of all American entertainments. The original minstrel shows themselves were somewhat dadaistic. Dan Emmett, composer of "Dixie," also became famous for something called "Machine Poetry," "a babble on a single tone, fizzling out into prose."[166] And this history shows how deeply conventional the association between black speech and nonsense was. Yet dada pushed the disintegrating power of nonsense so far as to upset the easy dichotomy that kept the alinguistic safely in Africa or in the slave quarters of the plantation.

In 1926, for example, Hannah Höch produced the visual counterpart of a dada poem with her series of photocollages entitled *From an Ethnographical Museum*.[167] These mix African images with bits and pieces of conventional European beauty: lips, eyes, seductive female legs. The mixture disrupts conventional European notions of beauty by putting cover girl lips on an African mask and high-heeled legs beneath a sculptured African torso. It also disrupts the dichotomy that places only African images in ethnographic museums. Here the ethnographic gaze is all-encompassing, and it has the dadaistic effect of reducing every cultural icon to the same level, making nonsense of all. The collages are an exact visual equivalent of the effect that ethnography had on European linguistics, relativizing the European by including it in the same frame of analysis as the foreign, and they also reflect the reversal of values that lurked in the heart of the avant-garde poetry of this period that used African models.

Blaise Cendrars, to take an even more significant example, was an amateur ethnographer of some popular importance, since the *Anthologie nègre* that he published in 1920 became widely known in Europe and the United States.[168] Though Cendrars was not himself a dadaist, selections from the anthology were in fact used at a 1919 "Fête nègre" in Paris that very much resembled the goings-on at the Cabaret Voltaire.[169] Cendrars, who was born Frédéric Louis Sauser in Switzerland and was a relentless traveler, agreed with Huelsenbeck that there was some essential correspondence between this condition of modern statelessness and the life of "le sauvage": "Quand le poète a voulu exprimer le monde moderne, 'il a souvent employé le langage du sauvage. C'était une nécessité.'" The poet faces the modern world "pauvre et démuni comme un sauvage armé de pierres devant les bêtes de la brousse."[170] Thus it was that one of the great themes of Cendrars's life was "le renouvellement du langage poétique par l'imitation de certaines caractéristiques des langues archaïques."[171]

This process produces certain poems, such as "Mee Too Buggi," that reproduce in poetry the relativizing effect of Höch's collages. "Mee Too Buggi" is, in fact, a collage, a tissue of quotations from a nineteenth-century English ethnographic work. Since this work depends on quotation itself, the words of Cendrars's poem sometimes have three or four competing resonances. "Mee Too Buggi" is, it turns out, the name of a Tongan dance, apparently rendered from the indigenous language into pidgin English and then imported by way of French translation into the text of Cendrars's poem. Though one American translator twisted the line into "Me too boogie," the circle cannot be closed that easily. The competing interests of Tongan, English, and French cancel one another out, producing a nonsense term that has no secure home in any language.[172]

As Jean-Pierre Goldenstein points out, this use of a language unintelligible to virtually all readers of the poem "crée un effet d'étrangeté et d'illisibilité."[173] "Mee too buggi," "fango fango," "Mee low folla" become mere signs torn loose from any signification. Thus Cendrars uses the ethnographic material in collage to reproduce the effect achieved by artists like Höch and, on a grander scale, Picasso, who used the clash between European and African materials to create an effect of cultural disorientation that would finally expose the pretensions of the sign to natural signification. "Mee Too Buggi" also juxtaposes "Bolotoo" and "Papalangi," as if these were two remote and unknown places, but "Papalangi," it turns out, was a Tongan word for Europe.[174] The European reader, in almost certain ignorance, looks back at himself or herself as at a foreigner from a distant country with a funny, nonsensical name. This effect is, for the most part, a private joke, but the poem makes the same point frequently on the surface. At the beginning of the poem, the poet takes up his sacred lyre and touches it to his nose. The whole production of literature, of history, of poetry ("Rimes et mesures dépourvues"), is reduced to slapstick ("L'homme qui se coupa lui-meme la jambe ruississait dans le genre simple et gai") and low pidgin ("Mee low folla").[175] The mockery reduces the privilege of poetry, of language itself, to nothing.

Unlike Cummings, who resorts to racial models so as to find an authentic language, a natural one to counterpose to the artificial languages of authority, Cendrars mixes pidgin in with French to emphasize the artificiality of both. His nearest counterpart in English is perhaps Joyce, especially the Joyce of *Finnegans Wake,* but also the Joyce of "Oxen of the Sun," which ends its history of English prose styles with a "frightful jumble" of "Pidgin English, nigger English, Cockney, Irish, Bowery slang and broken doggerel. . . ."[176] This mélange may represent drunkenness or moral chaos, but it may also represent the present as an era without a dominant linguistic standard, one in which pidgin can replace Macaulay at the center of power. It is as if Joyce offers this as the language of modernism, of the modern condition in which dialect and idiolect take the place of standard English as the rightful language of literature.

Cendrars may find other counterparts among the transatlantic modernists, other expatriates such as Conrad or Stein, or writers who lived in the United States all their lives in a condition of linguistic disaffinity, like Williams. Such writers see their own language, once taken for granted, as a distinct and arbitrary set of conventions. According to Seamus Heaney, this is a condition that afflicts more and more poets in this century: "Many contemporaries writing in English have been displaced from an old at-homeness in their mother tongue and its hitherto world-defining heritage."[177] This is like the condition Marianna Torgovnick has discussed under Lukács's term "transcendental homelessness," but it is rather more specifically linguistic and political than transcendental. And it is a global condition that affects millions beyond the literate elite.[178] The forces behind the linguistic conflicts of the last hundred years are so vast as "to convert what had been an experience of small minorities to what, at certain levels, and especially in its most active sites and most notably in the United States, could be offered as a definition of modernity itself."[179]

As Torgovnick shows, primitivism seems necessarily to accompany a condition of exile, as the exile searches man's primeval past for another home.[180] But racial primitivism provides a home only for some exiles; for others, like Cendrars, it calls into question the whole notion of "at-homeness," especially if that condition goes along with a heritage once thought to be "world-defining." What "The Negro of the Jazz Band" finally learns by passing for black is that "everyone disguises his own personality. . . . The world is a marketplace of falsefaces."[181] This is the revelation that waits at the heart of *The Jazz Singer,* that there is no true voice at all, only a shuttling back and forth made possible by makeup.

Of course, this sort of restless relativism contains its own possibilities of romantic primitivism. Stephen Greenblatt maintains that the elemental cultural sin of the European colonizers was their refusal to grant "opacity" to the other peoples they encountered. Nowadays, as Sara Suleri has complained, such opacity is virtually enforced, as the "unreadability" of the colonial other becomes fetishized.[182] Thus the romantic nomadism of Deleuze and Guattari depends quite unself-consciously on the racial other as the type of the asignifying sign, and on dialect as the prototype of a nomadic language: "To be a foreigner, but in one's own tongue, not only when speaking a language other than one's own. To be bilingual, multilingual, but in one and the same language, without even a dialect or a patois. To be a bastard, a half breed, but through a purification of race. That is when style becomes a language." This is what might be called postmodern primitivism, and it differs from the older modernist variety only in romanticizing the relativity and opacity of language instead of its concreteness.[183]

Thus the new aesthetic may look a great deal like the old, as Pasolini's African romanticism looks like Eliot's:

> I have been rational and I have been
> irrational: right to the end.
> And now . . . ah, the desert deafened
> by the wind, the wonderful and filthy
> sun of africa that illuminates the world.
>
> Africa! My only
> alternative . . .[184]

That such lines could be written by a postmodern hero as late as 1960 suggests that some things will never change, no matter how much the categories may be shuffled. On the other hand, the notion of linguistic and cultural relativism brought about by the dislocations of the late nineteenth and twentieth centuries does make possible a reversal of terms, of points of view, very useful to writers who have never before been able to feel "at home" in English.

Something like this is suggested, at any rate, in Salman Rushdie's *Satanic Verses* by the character of Saladin Chamcha, the Man of a Thousand Voices and a Voice. Chamcha makes his money doing voice-overs: "On the radio he could convince an audience that he was Russian, Chinese, Sicilian, the President of the United States."[185] Chamcha's placelessness is thus played for laughs, but the humor is mostly at the expense of his listeners, who have no idea they are docilely listening to a man they might refuse to sit next to in the subway. What Rushdie is dramatizing here is a global reversal of the situation of *The Jazz Singer*, a fundamental contravention of the old law that mimicry meant freedom only for the European.

Like *The Jazz Singer*, *The Satanic Verses* is also self-reflexive, for Chamcha's voice-overs dramatize a situation of which Rushdie himself is one of the best examples:

> What seems to me to be happening is that those peoples who were once colonized by the language are now rapidly remaking it, domesticating it, becoming more and more relaxed about the way they use it—assisted by the English language's enormous flexibility and size, they are carving out large territories for themselves within its frontiers.[186]

Rushdie's final metaphor precisely reverses the standard imperialist language, as his whole statement represents his own hopeful reversal of the standardizers' worst fear. *The Satanic Verses* "rejoices in mongrelization and fears the absolutism of the Pure."[187] Across the century, Henry James and Rushdie agree that this is "the high modernism of the condition," that the movement and mixture of peoples and their languages, dialects, and vernaculars is the defining condition of the literature of our time. How we get from James's shudder of rejection to Rushdie's celebration, and from the racial mimicry of T. S. Eliot to that of Saladin Chamcha, is one of the most important stories that modern literature has to tell.

PART II

The Dialect of the Expatriate

2

The Nigger of the "Narcissus" as a Preface to Modernism

I

According to at least one suggested genealogy, modernism begins with the preface Joseph Conrad wrote after finishing *The Nigger of the "Narcissus."*[1] Written at the turn of the century, as Conrad himself turned decisively from the sea to literature, the preface has received the kind of rapt attention given to short, epoch-making statements like the preface to *Lyrical Ballads*.[2] It even seems easier, somehow, to consider this brief essay as prefatory to a whole new century than to the novel of which it was an afterthought. Though most critics would agree with Michael Levenson's levelheaded judgment, "If we are to consider the preface, we must consider that to which it is prefatory," very few actually attempt to connect the preface to the subject of the novel, as announced in its title. Levenson himself hardly mentions James Wait and does not discuss his race. For all the rivers of ink that have flowed over the tortuous racial politics of *Heart of Darkness*, it is hard to find a critique of *The Nigger of the "Narcissus"* that takes seriously the race of its title character.[3]

For John Frederick Matheus, one of the contributors to *The New Negro* and Nancy Cunard's *Negro* anthology, Conrad's novel has an important role in a very different genealogy of modernism. Writing in 1934, Matheus looks back on the proliferation of black figures in literature by white writers, mentioning Van Vechten, Anderson, Du Bose Heyward, Marc Connelly, and Eugene O'Neill, among others. Summing up this popular trend, Matheus says, "So it is in spite of the insistence of the enemy, intentional or unwitting, the Negro looms a larger and larger figure in the white literary world, as did that weird West Indian Negro in Joseph Conrad's *Nigger of the "Narcissus,"* whose strange insinuations dominated finally hate, repugnance, intolerance, all that ship and crew from fore to aft, body and soul."[4] Matheus's metaphor makes *The Nigger of the "Narcissus"* prophetic of a modernism increasingly obsessed with and finally taken over by its black subjects. How can we reconcile this sense of the powerful domination of race as the subject of *The Nigger of the "Narcissus"* with the general critical indifference to it? And how can we square this genealogy derived from the subject of the novel with the far more prominent one derived from the aesthetic program of the preface?

A short version of that aesthetic program is usually found in Conrad's defiant response to those who would hold the novel to any purpose outside itself: "My task which I am trying to achieve is, by the power of the written word, to make you hear, to make you feel—it is, before all, to make you *see*! That—and no more: and it is everything!" (*NN*, p. 147). It might seem almost embarrassing, after all that has been said about this statement, to ignore its implicit defense of the aesthetic motive and simply take it literally, and yet Conrad's works often confront us with the laboriously physical process by which dry print becomes a visual and auditory experience. If this task to which Conrad dedicates himself can be understood as one that transforms what is read into something overheard and then, finally, into something actually seen, then it is a task to which he frequently confessed himself unequal. *Lord Jim*, to take just one example, degenerates from an omniscient and all-seeing account into Marlow's version, told "audibly," and then into the packet of written documents left for the "privileged man" in chapter 36, declining from the seen to the heard to the written as the story compounds its mysteries (*LJ*, pp. 21, 205). The aesthetic attempt to conjure out of some sensually unrewarding marks on paper a full sensory experience is constantly qualified in this way by Conrad's sense of its structural impossibility.

To succeed even provisionally, the writer depends on the connivance of his audience. As Ian Watt points out, Conrad did not and could not believe in a simple process of transference by which sense impressions are encoded in words and then decoded by readers. Rather, the writer appeals to certain "latent" feelings in his audience that already crucially resemble those he wants to convey, to "the subtle but invincible conviction of solidarity that knits together the loneliness of innumerable hearts: to that solidarity in dreams, in joy, in sorrow, in aspirations, in illusions, in hope, in fear, which binds men to each other, which binds together all humanity—the dead to the living, and the living to the unborn" (*NN*, pp. 145–46). In Watt's rather fine phrase, this solidarity is "orectic and conative in nature" because it is what Conrad wishes for and longs to achieve rather than what he actually believes in.[5] In the words of the preface, the writer makes an "appeal," a plea, as it were, to a potential sense of kinship in the audience by which it can recreate and reexperience his experiences.

Conrad is not so naive as to believe that there are latent feelings that bind together *all* humanity, but he does feel that insofar as differences within humanity exist, they complicate the writer's attempt to awake sensations by means of mere words. As a Pole writing in English, Conrad was only too aware of such complications, but even apart from this inescapable rift, his work presented real obstacles to perfect solidarity. He wrote almost exclusively of places far from England in a literary tradition strongly marked by French masters such as Flaubert. As D. C. R. A. Goonetilleke says, "[T]he presence of cultural and racial difference in his fictional worlds made it hard for Conrad to subscribe to some of the codes by which the English novel confidently inscribes its own reality. . . ."[6] But Goonetilleke is too conservative, for it is clear that cultural and racial differences make it hard for Conrad to subscribe to his own code, which relies on common experience and feeling to overcome the opacity of words.

The relationship that seems to exist between the aesthetic program of Conrad's preface and the subject of his novel is, therefore, one of blank contradiction. In fact, the opening scene of the novel seems to be an allegorical enactment of the defeat of reading, and therefore of writing, by difference. First, James Wait's name appears on the ship's log as an unreadable blot: "Can't make out that last name. It's all a smudge" (*NN*, p. 10). When, as if in answer to this confusion, the newly arrived Wait sings out his last name, it is misheard as an imperative: "What's this? Who said 'Wait'? What. . . ." Of course, writing down the sound is already to resolve at least part of the aural confusion it causes, so that Conrad wavered between "Who said 'Wait'?" and "Who said wait?"[7] Somehow, it seems particularly ironic that writing cannot even represent confusion without making a mess of things. When Wait clears this up—"Naturally I called out my name. I thought you had it on your list, and would understand. You misapprehended" (*NN*, p. 11)—his understatement is crushingly grand. How could anything disrupt the easy and natural conversion of written symbols into aural sensations and finally into things themselves?

Yet the error in reading ascribed so comically to the white mate is almost immediately reassigned to Wait himself, as if failure to signify were some innate racial characteristic: "He held his head up in the glare of the lamp—a head powerful and misshapen, with a tormented and flattened face—a face pathetic and brutal; the tragic, the mysterious, the repulsive mask of a nigger's soul" (*NN*, p. 11). Unlike the verbal misapprehension, the first confused visual impression, that his head is "indistinguishable" and his hands "gloved" (*NN*, p. 10), is not dispelled but confirmed under better light. There is no way around confusion when the face itself is a mask, when mystery resides right at the surface in the color of the skin. It is no wonder that Conrad was haunted by Stephen Crane's story "The Monster," in which a black burn victim hides his destroyed face under a veil.[8] When the skin itself is a mask, there can be no unmasking; underneath the veil is another surface even more opaque.

Conrad seems fully aware that what appears as the obliquity of black skin is in fact white ignorance mesmerized by itself, and yet such is the threat of difference to his notion of solidarity that this knowledge counts for nothing.[9] At this stage, Wait is nothing more than a physical embodiment of the threat posed to discursive meaning by racial and cultural difference. The mate's challenge to him, "What do you mean, coming shouting here" (*NN*, p. 10), has at least three possible paraphrases, all potentially translatable into one another: "What is your intention in thrusting yourself in where you don't belong?"; "How dare you speak out of turn?"; and "If you don't assume your assigned place, how can I tell what you mean?" Not to belong is the same as not to mean, and vice versa. In the drama of the story, according to Albert Guerard, Wait is *"something the ship and the men must be rid of before they can complete their voyage.*"[10] On the level of aesthetics, Wait seems to be something the ship and crew must be rid of so as to achieve any meaning.

Wait rarely speaks what Conrad once called "the debased jargon of niggers."[11] But when he finally dies, his once clear and precise speech becomes a kind of venomous nonsense, like the gibbering of a devil forced out by exorcism. Behind his "fantastic and grimacing mask of despair and fury" there are only "hollow, moaning, whistling sounds," a "mutter," a "murmur," a "gibberish of emotions, a frantic dumb show of speech pleading for impossible things, promising a shadowy vengeance" (*NN*, p. 93). This burst of asignifying noise stands in marked contrast to the deep "Ah—h—h!" that comes from the crew "like one man" when Wait's body is dropped overboard (*NN*, p. 99). Levenson, among many others, has noticed Conrad's distrust of noise and his characteristically nineteenth-century association of it with social discord.[12] Here, at the end of *The Nigger of the "Narcissus,"* the contrast between dissonance and solidarity becomes almost audible.

The title character of *The Nigger of the "Narcissus"* thus seems to have entered the story only to be expelled, as if to illustrate the threat that racial and cultural difference pose to the solidarity on which successful reading and writing depend. His dying gibberish is, we might think, the final descent into nonsense of words that can never make us hear or see, whose plea to our solidarity falls, as it were, on deaf ears. What does it mean, then, that about a month after the publication of *The Nigger of the "Narcissus"* Conrad referred to his own speech as gibberish? Writing to Cunninghame Graham about an overture to Frank Harris, Conrad warned, "But You know I am shy of my bad English. At any rate prepare him for a 'b——y furriner' who will talk gibberish to him at the rate of 10 knots an hour. If not forewarned the phenomenon might discourage him to the point of kicking me downstairs."[13] It almost seems as if Conrad fears a literal enactment of the opening of his novel, with Harris in the role of the impatient mate and himself as "the nigger." This transference of the word *gibberish* from Wait's dying tirade to his own speech has more than a biographical significance, however. Goonetilleke maintains that it is Conrad's inability to make his language and his foreign subject matter fit into prescribed novelistic forms that "motivates partly his technical innovations and intricacies." Significantly, especially considering the association he draws between civil unrest and dissonance, Levenson refers to these innovations and intricacies as Conrad's "modernist clangour."[14] If this is an apt characterization, then it seems that Conrad's personal position as the outsider who must be expelled from his own novel simply reflects the powerfully ambiguous role difference plays in the modernism inaugurated by *The Nigger of the "Narcissus."* Racial and cultural difference is both constitutive and radically disruptive of the work announced in Conrad's preface. This is why that preface remains a valid introduction to the rest of modern literature.

I I

The Nigger of the "Narcissus" is a liminal work for many reasons peculiar to Conrad's career. It is set en route to England, and ends by arriving there, after two other novels set on the extreme outskirts of the empire. Perhaps this success with a subject that is at least in transit to England emboldened Conrad to directly address his English reading public in the preface; heretofore he had not appealed to their solidarity but to their taste for the outlandish and exotic. In his preface to *The Rescue,* Conrad says that finishing *The Nigger of the "Narcissus"* "brought to my troubled mind the comforting sense of an accomplished task, and the first consciousness of a certain sort of mastery. . . ." (*R,* p. xi). Perhaps it was this sense of accomplishment and mastery that emboldened him to step out from behind the Malayan backdrop which, according to Zdzislaw Najder, had conveniently hidden "the lack of a common cultural background with his readers."[15]

Yet the South Seas from which the *Narcissus* departed, and especially the East Indies, remained an important background to all of Conrad's work, keeping alive in it the question raised by his "lack of a common cultural background with his readers," the question of linguistic difference. The East Indies, to which Conrad returned again and again until he had finally finished *The Rescue,* was peculiarly well suited to keeping this question in mind. An area that combined extreme physical isolation, as in the interior of Borneo, with the incessant emigration and trade fostered by its waters, the Indies brought dozens of languages in contact with one another. Alfred Russel Wallace's *Malay Archipelago* (1869), a favorite of Conrad's, ends with an appendix entitled "Nine Words in Fifty-Nine Languages of the Malay Archipelago." Faced with such extreme linguistic diversity, English travelers naturally fell back on a familiar biblical prototype: for Sherard Osborn in 1838, Singapore harbor was "a perfect commercial Babel."[16]

If this exotic locale shielded to some extent Conrad's own linguistic and cultural difference, it nonetheless raised a troubling technical question, the very first Conrad had to answer as a novelist: how to represent to a monolingual English public the many different languages of the East Indies. In Goonetilleke's opinion, Conrad solves this problem by fashioning "an English equivalent for the Malayan vernacular of his characters . . . an alien English which is alive and sounds natural."[17] Conrad's dialogue does seem less artificial than that concocted by Hugh Clifford, to whose superior knowledge of Malaya Conrad obsequiously bowed, and yet it still contains such twisted idioms as "You get him away as you can best" (*AF,* p. 130).[18] The responsibility for such mistakes floats intriguingly between Conrad and his characters. Another, more clearly purposeful, technique is to smatter the text with a few Malay words, like the shouted "Makan" that begins *Almayer's Folly.* Yet there is no way for the first-time reader to know that the line "Kaspar! Makan!" (*AF,* p. 3) is the main character's first name and a call to dinner, since the latter is not translated or even referred to for another seventy pages. It almost seems as if Conrad confronts his readers with these unexplained foreign sounds at the very threshold of his first work to emphasize the radical difference of what is to follow.

Far less challenging is a Malay word that had become English so that it could signify the weirdness of the foreign: *amok*. No travelogue of Malaya was complete without a little essay on the quaint native custom of "running amok," a tradition toward which Conrad gestures once in *Almayer's Folly* and twice in "Karain," where it is spelled both *amok* and *amuck* (*AF*, p. 133; *TU*, pp. 37, 45).[19] The uncertain spelling is perhaps revealing of the way languages assimilate the foreign to the familiar and of Conrad's uncertainty as to whether to emphasize or diminish the un-English nature of his subject matter.

In general, however, Conrad avoids the whole problem of difference in language by depriving his characters of words altogether, describing their voices instead of transcribing their statements. Rather than translate the sweet Malay nothings Dain Maroola whispers to Nina Almayer, Conrad simply calls them "the rude eloquence of a savage nature" (*AF*, p. 69). Oxymoronic tags like "rude eloquence" are one way of avoiding the real issues posed by a foreign language; onomatopoeia is another. *Murmur* is perhaps the most significant nonword in Conrad's vocabulary, covering a multitude of cases from Dain's rude eloquence to the hubbub of Malay voices just out of earshot to the sound of the river or sea itself (*AF*, pp. 14, 154). At times Conrad needs both onomatopoeia and oxymoron, as in *Heart of Darkness*, when there is a low drone "with an effect of audible and soothing silence" (*HD*, p. 63), or in "Karain," when a crowd erupts in "silent tumult" (*TU*, p. 8), a perfect description of this speech so confusing it fails not just as language but also as sound.

Representing speech in the Indies as murmur, rumor, mutter, or tumult is one way of representing European incomprehension, but taken literally such words simply deny that a foreign language is a language at all. From the time of Herodotus, of course, non-European speech has been represented as noise, as "the squeaking of bats," or the barking of dogs.[20] Conrad's descriptions of non-European languages frequently fall into this tradition. The Africans in "An Outpost of Progress" make an "uncouth babbling noise" (*TU*, p. 92), and those in *Heart of Darkness* emit a "steady droning sound" like "the humming of bees" (*HD*, p. 63). In *An Outcast of the Islands*, Conrad speaks eloquently of "the talk of barbarians, persistent, steady, repeating itself in the soft syllables, in musical tones of the never-ending discourses of those men of the forests and the sea," but he never transcribes any of it so that it remains simply a confused murmur of repeated soft musical syllables, without meaning (*OI*, p. 95).

In some cases, however, Conrad gives his characters voices rather than words to represent not his incomprehension of them but their incomprehension of one another. Mrs. Almayer, for example, is for many pages little more than a shrill voice behind a curtain. In this case, the gag is clearly more than a mere convenience. The curtain that muffles her words, leaving only a vague but characteristic intonation, stands for the barrier of incomprehension that divides her from Almayer, and it ultimately comes to stand for all similar barriers in this novel so dominated by secrets, special knowledge, and misunderstanding. In this atmosphere, even empty space sometimes seems too dense for meaning to penetrate: "[I]n the space between him and the obstinate phantom floated the murmur of words that fell on his ears in a jumble of torturing sentences, the meaning of which escaped the utmost efforts of his brain" (*AF*, pp. 159–60). When, in *An Outcast of the Islands*, Willems ceases to understand Aissa, "Her words seemed to fall round him with the distracting clatter of stunning hail" (*OI*, p. 346).

Conrad's Malay works are full of such scenes in which words lose their meaning and become incomprehensible sound and finally inert physical objects. A voice murmuring behind a curtain, many voices murmuring across the empty distance, these are images that sum up the early work in which cultural rivalries and differences proliferate lies, secrets, confusion, and finally tragedy. These are also images that defy the ambition of the celebrated preface, since they show how easy it is for words to recede behind a muffling veil when there is no common experience by which to interpret them. James Wait with his masklike skin is simply the final physical embodiment of the muffling veil of racial and cultural difference that Conrad seemed to find in the East Indies.

Such was the effect of the extreme linguistic diversity of the area, however, that there was no way for Conrad, not himself a native English speaker, of course, to keep even English from disappearing behind the veil. Approaching Bangkok at the end of the harrowing voyage described in "Youth," Marlow hears "a murmur of voices" on the deck of a strange ship: "And then, before I could open my lips, the East spoke to me, but it was in a Western voice" (*Y*, p. 39). The confused gobbledygook he hears seems to be, and finally resolves itself into, English, the ranting curses of an angry English skipper. The young Marlow's romanticism is such that it remains undaunted by this surprise, but the mature Conrad clearly intends the irony produced by this reversal of the standard colonial scene, when the mysterious and incomprehensible voice of the East turns out to be speaking English. The reversal suggests that, under the right conditions, even English might be reducible to murmur, tumult, mere babble. It makes it harder to see incomprehensibility as a fixed characteristic of particular languages, or a racial trait like skin color. In short, it opens up a kind of linguistic and cultural relativism the East Indies seemed peculiarly suited to teach.

III

There is a scene of linguistic role reversal in *The Malay Archipelago* that intrigued Conrad so much he referred to it in *The Secret Agent*, many years after he had first read Wallace's book (*SA*, p. 118). In the scene a group of Aru Islanders asks Wallace to tell them the name of his country. Unable to pronounce the name he offers, they simply refuse to believe him: "One funny old man, who bore a ludicrous resemblance to a friend of mine at home, was almost indignant. 'Ung-lung!' said he, 'who ever heard of such a name?—Ang-lang—Anger-lang—that can't be the name of your country. . . . My country is Wanumbai—anybody can say Wanumbai. I'm an orang-Wanumbai; but N-glung! who ever heard of such a name?'" Wallace sometimes handles this sort of reverse ethnography with pre-dictable racist stereotypes. When another old man doubles up in laughter as Wallace takes great pains to catch and preserve an insect, he serenely observes, "Every one will recognize this as a true negro trait." But he can also admit, in a self-deprecating way, that if an Aru Islander can resemble an old friend of his in England, then he might resemble an Aru Islander: "A few years before I had been one of the gazers at the Zulus and the Aztecs in London. Now the tables were turned upon me, for I was to these people a new and strange variety of man, and had the honour of affording to them, in my own person, an attractive exhibition, gratis."[21]

With whom did Conrad most identify, one wonders, the Englishman travel-ing through the wilds of the Malay Archipelago or the old man unable to pro-nounce even so much as the name of England? As Wallace realizes, the conditions of colonial exploration can just as easily erase as solidify the difference. To Sherard Osborn, floating in the babel of a Malay anchorage, "The Saxon cry of 'All's well!' and the Malay sentry's 'Jagga jagga!' struck strangely on the ear." In England at about the same time, Southey was complaining bitterly against the idea of doing up the Bible in "mingle-mangle speech," but Osborn had been wearing Malay garb and exchanging devout greetings of "God is great," so that it did not seem at all odd that Saxon might seem just as odd as "Jagga jagga."[22]

The perspective granted to Wallace and Osborn when their own language becomes an incomprehensible object of scrutiny was about to make its mark on ethnography even as Conrad sailed the South Seas. Conrad took the *Otago* through the Torres Straits in August of 1888;[23] there at the same time was A. C. Haddon, who was so struck by the possibilities of the area that he returned ten years later with the Cambridge Anthropological Expedition, the first extended fieldwork of what was to be called the Cambridge School of anthropology. The expedition produced a massive multivolume ethnographic study of the area and a new approach to anthropological fieldwork; indeed, Haddon was apparently the first to give this form of inquiry its name.[24] That new anthropological practice was given its full modern form, however, by a scientist who followed the Cambridge expedition to New Guinea and who had even closer connections with Conrad: Bronislaw Malinowski.

When Malinowski traveled in Australia and New Guinea during the First World War, he took a number of Conrad's novels along. Though he once de-clared that he would become "the Conrad" of anthropology, it seems that the novels were less a model than an escape from the fieldwork he frequently found boring and exasperating.[25] The two Poles with careers in England and in English became correspondents and even acquaintances, though there is no solid evidence that Conrad actually read *The Family Among the Australian Aborigines*, which Malinowski sent him in 1913.[26] There can have been few other Poles who came to the East Indies with English as a kind of linguistic screen, and this shared background shows in the macaronic style that both Malinowski and Conrad allowed themselves when not writing for print. Malinowski kept his now notorious New Guinea diary in Polish with frequent interpolations in English and then, as he acquired the languages of the people he studied, in Motu, Mailu, Kiriwinian, and Pidgin. Conrad's letters were similarly "macaronic" and "polyglot," to use his own words, sometimes containing English, French, German, Spanish, and Italian within a few lines, while also containing at least scraps of Arabic, Malay, and Pidgin.[27]

The macaronic style is a linguistic version of the geographical and cultural dislocation that Malinowski and Conrad peculiarly shared. In fact, the ironies of that situation might be summed up in a single word, a word that was to become the most notorious of all the unguarded words Malinowski dropped into his diary, the word by which Conrad always metonymically designated the novel that concerns us here: *nigger.* Other, earlier, anthropologists had referred to their fieldwork as "niggering," and British sailors in the East Indies, we know from Conrad's novels, used this word indiscriminately to designate virtually anyone not English.[28] Yet it was considered improper in polite anthropological discourse even of Malinowski's time, and Conrad was forced to remove it from the American edition of his novel for fear of giving offense.[29] Why did these two Poles, whose background and upbringing could hardly have conduced to the casual use of this word, both resort to it? Perhaps it was the very vulgarity of the word, which gives such discomfort now, that was its appeal. By using it, these two outsiders could become, as it were, linguistic insiders, a shared colloquialism being one of the best ways to make common company. And what better colloquialism, from the point of view of a European alien, than one that draws lines not in terms of culture or language but in terms of race? Thus it seems revealing and significant that the word *nigger* is one of the most common to appear in English amid the Polish of Malinowski's diary.

Or does it? George Stocking points out that close scrutiny of the photographed page of the diary that appears as frontispiece to its English edition reveals that the word actually written in Malinowski's handwriting is *nigrami*, apparently a coinage made from the English stem and the Polish case ending *ami*.[30] The intent is obviously the same, but the linguistic material reveals something equivocal in Malinowski's own position. It represents quite succinctly his own hybridity, his own cultural dislocation. It reveals that he could not confidently demean the Mailu or the Kiriwinians from the standpoint of a British colonizer because he was just as much an outsider in British culture as they were, more so, in fact, because as a Pole he was subject to interment as an enemy alien. Thus the term actually reveals in its Polish user just the linguistic and cultural difference it was apparently meant to obscure.

In so doing, this single word becomes an epitome of Malinowski's work in the East Indies. So aggravated did he become at times with his unwilling informants that he emulated Conrad's most dangerous character: "On the whole my feelings toward the natives are decidedly tending to *'Exterminate the brutes'"*; "I under-stand all the *German and Belgian colonial atrocities.'*"[31] On the other hand, he also experienced the same sort of reverse ethnography that amused and disturbed Wallace on his visit to the same part of the world: the entry for January 27, 1918, includes the succinct confession, "Posed before the *niggers.'*"[32] The increasing oppression he feels from the mere presence of the people he has come so far to study may be due to this reversal of roles; more and more the anthropological point of view is trained not on New Guinea and its inhabitants but on Malinowski and his many "homes": "At moments I feel like writing the story of my life. Entire periods already seem so remote, so alien." The entry into an alien society re-quired by the fieldwork method causes an uncanny loss of self: "I saw and felt the utter drabness of the Kiriwinian villages; I saw them through their eyes (it's fine to have this ability), but I forgot to look at them with my own." Then, having entertained the alien point of view, and lost his secure foothold as the observer, the anthropologist finds himself becoming the subject of his own scrutiny: "At this point we are confronted with our own problems: What is essential in our-selves?"[33] Thus Malinowski's verbal savagery against the *"niggers"* is the obverse of his own insecurity: the more they confront him with the alien content of his own life, the more he tries to reposition them, and with them the alien itself, on the other side of some solid line.

Malinowski's real value for anthropology, and for a study of Conrad, lies in the way he managed to accept what at first had so unsettled him. Bringing anthropology home so that it would scrutinize England with the same methods once used only on remote societies became something of a motto of his later life.[34] Implicit in this reversal of ethnographic roles is a cultural relativism that led Malinowski to accept the implications of his macaronic diary, even though he never allowed it to be published. What he called the "ethnographic view of language" is utterly relativistic: each language has its own context, outside of which it is quite meaningless. In fact, Malinowski went well beyond this, to say that the primary function of language, all language, is not to convey meaning at all but to facilitate the social communion without which it has no existence. Lan-guage, he says, "is a mode of action and not an instrument of reflection." But it is a peculiar kind of action, "an act serving the direct aim of binding hearer to speaker by a tie of some social sentiment or other."[35]

Thus language has its primary existence as what Malinowski called "phatic communion," examples of which might be found in "savage life" or in more "civilized" examples, "the binding tissue of words which unites the crew of a ship," for example.[36] At this point, one begins to see the use to which Malinowski put those Conrad novels he brought with him to New Guinea. Conrad liked to say that "a good book is a good action," and he liked to claim that writing is "action in its essence . . . [which] may be compared to rescue work carried out in darkness against cross gusts of wind. . . ."[37] This is exactly the example used by Malinowski when he cites "the preparedness of a lifeboat crew and the corresponding preparedness of an ordinary crew of sailors. . . ."[38] Perhaps the most famous instance of language used in this way occurs in *The Nigger of the "Narcissus"* when the crew is galvanized into action by the single command of their skipper. And it was in the preface to that work that Conrad placed all his faith in "the binding tissue of words," which he called "solidarity." What Malinowski discovered, either in the East Indies or in Conrad's novels or in both, is an entirely new way of looking at the relationship between meaning and that solidarity, and even of the way that racial difference seems to intervene between them.

According to Malinowski's theory, the asignifying murmur so common in Conrad's early work is not simply the failure of savage language to mean but a vital component of all language.[39] Thus it characterizes not just language faintly heard across a barrier but also, and perhaps most especially, that exchanged within the most intimate groupings. The lovers in *Almayer's Folly*, it has already been noted, converse by "murmuring disjointed words of gratitude and love" (*AF*, p. 172), but so do the lovers in *Victory*, and these are not by any stretch of the imagination rude, sublinguistic savages. In fact, the conviction Heyst proclaims to Lena in what seems a moment of idiotic transport—"Your voice is enough. I am in love with it, whatever it says" (*V*, p. 88)—expresses a Conradian credo: "The power of sound has always been greater than the power of sense." Over and over, Conrad's characters are swayed by what he quite revealingly calls "the right accent."[40] Heyst is so moved by Lena's words—"the sound of them more than the sense"—that he exclaims to her, "What power there must be in words, only imperfectly heard" (*V*, pp. 214, 221). Thus the most crucial conversations in Conrad's works tend to be carried on "by shrugs, in interrupted phrases, in hints ending in deep sighs" (*HD*, p. 56), in every mode of communication, that is, other than words.

If this sort of communication seems to be necessitated at times by the linguistic differences between Conrad's characters, it is constantly frustrated by the fact that nothing is more particular, less easily translatable, than intonation. "There is nothing for us," Conrad observes in *An Outcast of the Islands*, "outside the babble of praise and blame on familiar lips, and beyond our last acquaintance there lies only a vast chaos; a chaos of laughter and tears which concerns us not; laughter and tears unpleasant, wicked, morbid, contemptible—because heard imperfectly by ears rebellious to strange sounds" (*OI*, p. 198). What distinguishes our language from another is not that the first is meaningful—it is just as much a babble as the foreign—but merely that it is familiar, and yet this counts for everything because the ear simply rejects the unaccustomed. Thus Conrad's characters experience the utter dependence of language on solidarity long before he describes it in the formula of his famous preface. At the climax of *Almayer's Folly* Nina cries out to her father, "You wanted me to dream your dreams, to see your own visions," thus casting this hapless failure as a prototype of the Conradian artist. He fails, Nina exclaims, because his visions are "visions of life amongst the white faces of those who cast me out from their midst in angry contempt." When speaking with Dain Maroola, on the other hand, Nina says, "I found that we could see through each other's eyes" (*AF*, p. 179). This final scene, in which Nina must choose between her father and her lover, is a struggle not of arguments or even of languages—though the shifts from English to Malay to Dutch are significant—but of voices. Dain Maroola wins because his voice chimes with Nina's for reasons that can hardly be enunciated, since they lie so far from the discursive.

Nina's position, suspended between a European and a Malay voice, reveals the great paradox at the heart of the linguistic theory Conrad shared with Malinowski. Language depends so heavily on the kind of solidarity Conrad describes in his preface because it is primarily asignifying, phatic, and practical, a mode of action and not a system of meaning.[41] But this truth is apparent only to someone like Nina who is outside that solidarity or pulled by competing loyalties. When language produces a perfect "phatic communion," its workings are, almost by definition, indiscernible; only when it fails can it be apprehended. Conrad and Malinowski were particularly apt to find this aspect of language in the East Indies because their own conflicted linguistic situation had already alerted them to it: what another European observer might have dismissed as mere babble appeared to them as a necessary constituent of all language.[42] For the same reason, they remained ethnographers when they returned to England. Edward Garnett once observed, "It is good for us English to have Mr. Conrad in our midst visualizing for us aspects of life we are constitutionally unable to perceive."[43] What Conrad was able to perceive, more by hearing than by sight despite Garnett's metaphor, was that solidarity is not just the basis of all communication but also its goal, yet this solidarity was apparent to him only because he was unable fully to enjoy its protection. It is still true, then, to say that the racial and cultural difference represented by James Wait stands in the way of full seeing and hearing as described in Conrad's preface, but it is also true that only someone in James Wait's position can know this.

IV

Conrad's career as a writer in English (1886–1924) neatly parallels the period already identified as the heyday of standardization. In fact, Robert Graves, an unregenerate rebel against standardization as against so much else, identified Conrad as "the most striking example of a writer bent on reforming English." Graves had in mind Conrad's complaint, transcribed by Ford Madox Ford, against the word *oaken,* which Conrad apparently found far more blurred by connotation than its French counterpart.[44] In making his charge, Graves was apparently unaware of how many times Conrad had been corrected on minor matters of English usage: after *The Nigger of the "Narcissus"* was published, for example, W. H. Chesson instructed Conrad on the difference between *like* and *as, shall* and *will, who* and *that, that* and *which,* and *lay* and *lie.* Conrad tended to accept as his inescapable lot in life such incursions into his style, but he also broke out from time to time in testy hostility against the language whose spelling and grammar were so difficult to master.[45] Rather than favoring the trend toward standardization, Conrad was, along with other foreign speakers of the time, one of its prime targets.[46]

Conrad's English and the English in Conrad's works raise larger issues as well. The geographical sweep of his fiction, and, indeed, his very presence in England, seem exemplary of the close relationship between the English language and imperialism. The early propaganda for the OED spoke confidently of "the race of English words which is to form the dominant speech of the world."[47] Conrad panders to such feelings, explicitly with statements like "deliberations conducted in London have a far-reaching importance" (*AF,* p. 34), and implicitly in the very language he uses, which is the language of use even for a far-flung subject of the Dutch such as Almayer (*AF,* p. 5). But, as we have already seen in chapter 1, the very expansion of English influence carried with it a threat. Gunnar Landtman, who had first gone to the Torres Straits with the Cambridge expedition, observed on a later visit to Papua New Guinea that Pidgin was taught to newcome Europeans by the Papuans: "Thus the native use of pidgin-English lays down the rules by which the Europeans let themselves be guided in using it."[48] This is precisely the situation that terrified a true standardizer like Bridges, that some odd race in some remote corner of the globe would exert influence on the language of Shakespeare and Milton. Malinowski's calm statement that "English changes east of the Suez; it becomes a different language in India, Malaya and South Africa"[49] summarizes the ironic reality that by spreading English, England did not extend its cultural sway but lost control over its own language.

Yet this situation is ironic only if language is thought of as developing within national boundaries and almost as a confirmation of them. The real threat of Conrad's example to the standard language movement lay in the way his experience and his works confounded this most basic way of conceiving language. It may seem a trivial matter that Conrad learned to speak English on board ship, but it is one on which he always lay great emphasis.[50] It is also true, though Conrad was always less emphatic about this, that the crews he served with were polyglot in the extreme. For example, the crew of the *Vidar,* on the decks of which Conrad learned virtually everything factual that went into his early Malay novels, consisted of "two European and one Chinese engineer, a second mate Mahamat, eleven Malayans, and eighty-two Chinamen." The ship was, incidentally, owned by an Arab.[51] The language actually spoken in such a situation must have been either what the Dutch called "gibberish Malay" or some variation on the international maritime pidgin that had been current in the East Indies since the time of the Portuguese. Though remote, this lingua franca was not isolated from English itself, to which it contributed a number of words, including, interestingly, both *linguist* and *nigger*.[52]

In the view of the standardizer, of course, these two terms would have more in common that the mere accident of their origin. It seems safe to say that maritime English was the first variety to suffer the stigma later attached to the transplanted colonial Englishes, of which it was the forerunner.[53] Even Black English, according to J. L. Dillard, can be traced back in part to maritime English, through the West Coast African lingua franca that was formed from the pidgin used by traders, including those in slaves.[54] The English Conrad learned on board ship was, therefore, the very antithesis of the standard. This is not to say that it was a formless language without rules. In fact, Conrad's few literary representations of it tend to mock inept speakers like Jukes in "Typhoon," who, "having no talent for foreign languages mangled the very pidgin-English cruelly" (*T*, p. 13).[55] But it remains threatening to the standard language because it is formed entirely outside national boundaries and by borrowings and transplantations, not by purification.

It should be no surprise, then, that the first linguists (from the Portuguese *linguoa*) were sailors who had learned to work with languages by living with a polyglot crew and traveling the globe. As Richard Bailey says, such interpreters, known by 1649 as "linguisters," were crucial to British exploration and colonization, though they were, ironically, marginal or bicultural themselves. They are the "go-betweens," to use Stephen Greenblatt's term, who appear in nearly every account of exploration and conquest, like the Spanish castaways who interpret for Cortés.[56] These figures, with their insight into the infinite fungibility of language, are the embodied antithesis of a standard language. They are also, almost by definition, racial outsiders, suspended between the races, languages, and cultures they translate.

Conrad's early work is full of both seagoing and landlocked versions of these outsiders: Almayer, who plots with the Malay Dain Maroola against the Dutch; Willems, who plots with the Malay Lakamba against Almayer and Tom Lingard; even Lingard himself, torn between the British Mrs. Travers and his Malay allies. The early work is also full of scenes in which the bilingual protagonist is the human prize in a contest between languages: Nina Almayer, who shifts to Malay to signify rejection of her Dutch father and her new allegiance to Dain Maroola (*AF*, p. 181); Lingard, who stands between Immada, imploring him in Malay, and Mrs. Travers, who says, "It is intolerable to think that their words which have no meaning for me may go straight to your heart . . ." (*R*, p. 218). The situation recurs in part because Conrad felt it as his own. When he offered his first book to the Unwin Pseudonym Library, Conrad suggested that it be published under the name Kamudi, Malay for rudder.[57] Thus Conrad comes before his British public as a foreigner, a racial alien, a linguistic translator, and a sailor all at once. The history of maritime English shows that these different roles were necessarily related. Approaching English, as Conrad did, from the sea, was to approach it in the role of racial outcast.

Of course, "Joseph Conrad" was only slightly more appropriate as a pseudonym than Kamudi.[58] And yet it is quite surprising to realize how frequently Conrad's Polish nationality appeared to his English friends and associates as a racial difference. The heavy Polish accent that he never managed to erase is represented quite inconsistently in contemporary accounts; the strangest but by no means the least common association is with the Orient: "he expressed himself as an Oriental and not as a Nordic." Wells once warned Ford against tampering with Conrad's "wonderful Oriental style." Perhaps this very strange impression represents a transference of the subject matter of Conrad's early novels to the novelist himself. Before meeting Conrad, Edward Garnett had imagined he "might have Eastern blood in his veins," so that he might just as well have used the name Kamudi. In fact, Conrad's friends sometimes treated his language as he so frequently treated that of his Malay subjects, demoting it from the human level altogether: "He was only thrilling when he lost his temper and chattered and screamed like a monkey."[59]

Conrad's appearance, his hunched shoulders and hooded eyes, excited the same peculiar set of reactions. Though nearly every English visitor found him "foreign looking," a few went beyond this vague designation: Perriton Maxwell found his mannerisms "identical with that of the stage Hebrew," and at least one reviewer hinted that Conrad might actually be Jewish.[60] Both Wells and Ford found his appearance and mannerisms "very Oriental indeed," Ford characteristically elaborating this impression so that in his account Conrad resembles "a Caliph entering a slave market." Sir Henry Newbolt, a nautical writer himself and chief architect of the Newbolt Report, also thought that Conrad had "an Oriental face."[61] This pattern of fanciful estrangement reaches bottom with Edwin Pugh's impression of a "savage pungency" so strong Conrad seemed positively "simian." Conrad suffered such impressions frequently enough that they even marked his own view of himself: a 1907 photograph taken with Richard Le Gallienne seemed to him "a gorilla with an angel."[62]

How is it that a foreign accent, a few grammatical mistakes, and heavily lidded eyes can plunge an erudite and cosmopolitan gentleman right out of the human race? We might recall that when Conrad says, in the preface to *A Personal Record*, that sound is more important than sense, he cautions, "Of course the accent must be attended to. The right accent. That's very important."[63] By "accent," he apparently means something like intonation, but the word is revealing nonetheless. For what Conrad learned in the East Indies, what he experienced as a Pole in the British Merchant Service, what he realized both personally and professionally in England, was that the seemingly asignifying aspects of language, the tone, the rhythm, the accent, are by far the most important, because they are the components of what Malinowski called "phatic communion" and Conrad himself called "solidarity." Every solidarity is fostered and enforced by its own particular accent, but, of course, no one can ever hear his or her own accent. Conrad could hear the English accent only because of what he once fearfully deprecated as "my barbarian ear."[64] It was in fact the very barbarism of that ear, schooled, as it were, in the East Indies and at sea, that made Conrad so thoroughly aware of how language structures civilization. But to have this awareness, to live and write in constant remembrance of linguistic difference, is, as Conrad's friends and associates always reminded him, to be a racial outcast.

V

Conrad always managed to keep any hint of Polish out of his writing in English. The one significant exception occurs in *The Nigger of the "Narcissus"* when James Wait sneers at Donkin, "Don't be familiar. We haven't kept pigs together" (*NN*, p. 14). This, according to Zygmunt Frajzyngier, is a close approximation of a Polish idiom, delivered "when a person who is not entitled to do so uses the second person singular pronoun in addressing someone."[65] Of course, such a grammatical slight cannot occur in English, and the imputation of keeping pigs does not carry quite the social sting in English-speaking countries that it apparently does in Poland. The strangest thing about Conrad's use of this idiom is not, however, the cultural inappropriateness or the lame literal translation but the attribution of it to a black West Indian. Though it seems wildly off base, this attribution does have a certain element of self-justification: its very ineptness reveals that Conrad is just as out of place in English as Wait is on board the *Narcissus*.

There is a possibility, albeit an extremely remote one, that Conrad calculated this equation of Pole and West Indian. Twice he called Poland an "outpost" of European civilization, oddly recalling his first African story, "An Outpost of Progress," and he complained, moreover, that the Germans were wont to assume toward the indigenes of this outpost "the attitude of Europeans amongst effete Asiatics or barbarous niggers."[66] While the comparison seems farfetched, Conrad could have called upon his friend Cunninghame Graham, who declared in his satiric screed "Bloody Niggers" that "all those of almost any race whose skins are darker than our own, and whose ideas of faith, of matrimony, banking, and therapeutics differ from those held by the dwellers of the meridian of Primrose Hill, cannot escape" being called by that epithet.[67]

One aspect of Conrad's Polish background does seem to have entered Wait's story: the treatment of his name. Norman Sherry reports that he could not find a single instance in which Korzeniowski was spelled correctly in the Singapore, Bangkok, and Australian newspapers that reported Conrad's voyages in the East Indies.[68] No wonder, then, that Conrad used his two Christian names "so that foreign mouths should not distort my real surname—a distortion which I cannot stand." Of course, Conrad's dynastic name, Nałęcz, cannot even be printed properly in many cases, much less pronounced.[69] Thus Conrad must often have experienced the humiliation Wait brushes off at the beginning of *The Nigger of the "Narcissus"* when his name is deemed an unreadable blot and then misheard even when pronounced very clearly.

What kind of kinship, if any, is suggested by these details? In the American preface to *The Nigger of the "Narcissus"* Conrad says of the real-life prototype of Wait, "I had much to do with him. He was in my watch. A negro in a British forecastle is a lonely being. He has no chums" (*NN*, pp. 167–68). These statements suggest, at the very least, a knowledge of the lonely plight of a black sailor on board an English vessel. This plight, at any rate, Conrad seems to have shared. In "Geography and Some Explorers" Conrad roundly declares that he felt lonely in Africa but "never so at sea. There I never felt lonely, because there I never lacked company." Yet his company is not that of other sailors but that of the "great navigators, the first grown-up friends of my boyhood."[70] This suggests that even when he was an adult, Conrad's closest friends were his books. All the biographical evidence confirms this. In *A Personal Record*, Conrad admits that he had never met another Pole in British service (*PR*, p. 119). Not only did this situation mean total estrangement from the language of his own country, but it also ensured that his fellow seamen would see him as a curiosity, "the Russian count," according to one story.[71] Yet this might have been the mildest reaction he encountered; according to Najder, because of a diminishing number of berths in the merchant service, "a dislike of the 'invasion' of foreigners permeates all contemporary sea writing."[72]

Conrad may have referred to himself as a "b——y furriner" and called his own speech "gibberish" so soon after publishing the story of James Wait because he had written out some of his own experience in that story. In Wait's situation Conrad suggests, as Frederick Karl says, "a marginality that was one part of his own mental baggage."[73] Figuring that marginality in the person of a black alter ego would not have been at all uncommon even for a more securely English writer of the time. Sir Richard Burton delighted in exotic masquerade, so much so he was called "the White Nigger" by his colleagues in Sind. H. Rider Haggard was convinced that in a previous incarnation he had been black.[74] Conrad's friend Cunninghame Graham had played a similar game a number of times, masquerading as Sheik Mohammed el Fasi in order to reach "the forbidden city of Tarudant."[75] This is perhaps the genre into which we should enter Conrad's brief masquerade as Kamudi. But the differences between Conrad and these Englishmen are perhaps more significant than the apparent similarities.

What was for Burton, Haggard, and Cunninghame Graham an exotic escape could not be so for Conrad, because it expressed a condition he could not escape. At the writing of *The Nigger of the "Narcissus,"* Conrad was no longer a European voyaging in remote climes but a foreigner trying to make a career in England, and the novel expresses this change, since it is not about a marooned European as its predecessors had been but about an alien presence on an English ship. The transitional nature of this book in Conrad's career, its odd status as the dog wagged by the great tail of the preface, its celebrated structural difficulties, which Levenson refers to as its "modernist clangour," all can be shown to derive from Conrad's simultaneous identification with and desire to escape from all that James Wait represents.

VI

Conrad displayed a certain indecision about the title of his third novel even before his American publishers objected to *The Nigger of the "Narcissus."* He titled it successively *The Nigger of the "Narcissus," The Forecastle: A Tale of Ship and Men, The Nigger: A Tale of Ship and Men, The Nigger of the "Narcissus"—A Tale of the Forecastle,* and *The Nigger of the "Narcissus"—A Tale of the Sea,* before retitling the American edition *The Children of the Sea: A Tale of the Forecastle.*[76] These vacillations may reveal a certain indecision about the central focus of the novel, which does seem almost painfully splayed between Wait and the crew. This indecision may be related to another, more notorious inconsistency, that of point of view, which wavers queasily from third person to first to second.[77] All of these inconsistencies may be related to an indecision about point of view in more than a technical sense. For it seems that all the vacillations come from the fact that it is impossible to look at the crew both from its own point of view and simultaneously from that of an outsider. And yet this is precisely the position Conrad was in, writing the novel that was to convince him he could succeed as a writer and leave the sea, a novel, moreover, that brought him back to England after several works set in the remote East.

Perhaps the oddest violation of point of view is the one that allows Conrad to report the private musings of Wait, lying sick in his bunk. It is odd and yet crucial, for what Wait discovers in this scene is the voice of the ship, if not of life itself:

> He could hear on the quiet deck soft footfalls, the breathing of some man lounging on the doorstep; the low creak of swaying masts; or the calm voice of the watch-officer reverberating aloft, hard and loud, amongst the unstirring sails. He listened with avidity, taking a rest in the attentive perception of the slightest sound from the fatiguing wanderings of his sleeplessness. He was cheered by the rattling of blocks, reassured by the stir and murmur of the watch, soothed by the slow yawn of some sleepy and weary seaman settling himself deliberately for a snooze on the planks. Life seemed an indestructible thing. It went on in darkness, in sunshine, in sleep; tireless, it hovered affectionately round the imposture of his ready death. (*NN*, p. 64)[78]

Wait hears in these creaks, murmurs, rattles, and stirs the habitual life of the ship, a life that goes on repetitively and surely even in the presence of darkness and death. What the passage seems to say, in spite of the preface, is that it is not necessary to see as long as one can hear, but in hearing it is not really necessary to understand in a discursive way, because simply sensing the voice at the most basic level, the level of rhythm, of pure, asignifying sound, is enough. Wait hears, in other words, the sound of solidarity itself, the phatic communion that links breath to breath in a single murmur.

In *The Nigger of the "Narcissus"* the sea itself speaks such an onomatopoeic language of murmurs, sighs, and hisses, to which the ship responds in kind when the men work it in perfect solidarity: "The sails filled, the ship gathered way, and the waking sea began to murmur sleepily of home to the ears of men" (*NN*, p. 99). So close is Conrad's identification of the crew with the language of the ship that at one point he transferred a murmur from one to the other. In chapter 4 of the Heinemann edition, after the ship is righted, Conrad changed the "deep rumour" of the forecastle to "deep murmurs" and the "awestruck murmurs" of the men to "awestruck exclamations" (*NN*, pp. 59, 117). In a language of murmurs it matters very little, apparently, who or what is actually doing the talking. When in the last line of the novel Conrad calls his crew the best that ever "gave back yell for yell to a westerly gale" (*NN*, p. 107), he means it quite literally, for the crew and the sea have been trading exclamations and murmurs throughout the book.

In the usual romanticization of this language, one Conrad does a lot to advance in *The Mirror of the Sea,* it is considered concrete, motivated, and strictly denotative.[79] But the fiction makes it clear that this is far from true. It is not a communicative language at all but one of action. Mr. Baker, the mate, leads by grunting, Singleton by pointing, and when the captain rouses his sodden crew to wear ship it is "the commanding sharp tones" as much as the content of the command that saves them: "His voice seemed to break through a deadly spell" (*NN*, p. 52). This voice succeeds because it is instantly echoed by "hardly audible murmurs." At their finest moment, fired by "the cries of that silent man," the crew "sighed, shouted, hissed meaningless words, groaned" (*NN*, p. 53). This is the audible expression of the "unexpressed faith, of the unspoken loyalty that knits together a ship's company" (*NN*, p. 6). It is, as Malinowski would have it, a solidarity made by sound and not sense.

The catch is that this language works only for those who are unconscious of its workings. Singleton actually speaks directly to the ship itself, answering a "loud tap" from the anchor cable with a rough "You . . . hold!" (*NN*, p. 16). He can carry out these gnomic colloquies because he has become little more than a sounding board for the sea itself: "The wisdom of half a century spent in listening to the thunder of the waves had spoken unconsciously through his old lips" (*NN*, p. 14). In a well-known letter to Cunninghame Graham, Conrad scoffs at the idea of "Singleton with an education": "Would you seriously, of malice prepense cultivate in that unconscious man the power to think. Then he would become conscious—and much smaller—and very unhappy."[80] What now sleeps in Singleton is the knowledge that his seemingly natural language is in fact a language of habit and convention and therefore utterly arbitrary.

Conrad dearly wanted to pretend that he was such a man himself. He rages, for example, against the idea that his writing in English is the result of conscious choice, that he might just as easily have written in French. He wants, instead, to pretend that English somehow chose him, so that he can avoid the implications of self-consciousness that would necessarily distance him from the language: "I always had but one literary language as if I were born English."[81] For the same reason, Conrad strategically reduces the international nature of the crew of the *Narcissus*. Najder exposes the reality behind Conrad's claim that the crew depicted in "Youth" possessed "a discourse of something secret—of that hidden something, that gift of good or evil that makes racial difference": the crew was in fact almost half foreign.[82] But Conrad wants his crews to manifest that phatic communion that exists far below the level of discourse, that comes from national and racial commonality, and so he makes them all, including that of the *Narcissus*, more English than they were. As Gerald Morgan reports, the crew that sailed on board the *Narcissus* when it left Bombay included "an Argyll captain, a Yorkshire mate, a Polish second mate; Norwegian carpenter, Canadian boatswain, Australian sailmaker; two English cooks, and sixteen foremast hands from seven countries" (*NN*, p. 205). In the novel, the foreign contingent is reduced to a Scot, a Finn, "two Scandinavians," and one West Indian.

This crew comes together, out of the "distracting noise" of Bombay harbor, into a noisy hubbub of its own (*NN*, p. 1). It is the job of the mate, the job of Conrad himself on the actual voyage, to settle this "clash of voices and cries" (*NN*, p. 3) and to make it one, but just as this is about to be accomplished, a "sonorous voice" breaks into the silence and returns it to "hum" and "mutter" (*NN*, p. 10). When Wait shouts out his own name, the crew naturally interprets it as an order, so used are they to hearing short, monosyllabic directions of that kind. They respond not to his word but to the commanding tone that carries it, the tone that tells a listener he has heard an imperative and not a question or a statement. Of course, the only thing that really differentiates the name from the imperative is intonation, and it is just because the crew cannot properly interpret Wait's tone, because he introduces ambiguity into language at the most basic level possible, that he causes such distress on the ship.

The threat of that voice comes not from any meaning it contains but from the mere sound of it.[83] From the beginning Conrad places the emphasis on the "tones," the "intonation" of Wait's words (*NN*, pp. 10–11). These set up a countermurmur that breaks into and disrupts the voice of the ship. The first moment of real commonality on the voyage is "a ripple of laughter" that "ran along, rose like a wave," and then "burst with a startling roar" (*NN*, p. 20). This is interrupted by "a weak rattle," a "murmur," a "sighing groan," the result of which is almost immediate: "The circle broke up" (*NN*, p. 21). From that moment on, Wait's voice resounds "like a solo after a chorus" (*NN*, p. 41), dissolving the crew's solidarity and making it mutinous. The problem created by his original irruption into shipboard routine remains: the sound of his voice can never be made to jibe with the sight of his body. When at first he seems healthy and vigorous, he disturbs the crew with racking coughs; later when he is clearly dying he confounds them with his strong, steady baritone voice.[84] Such is the distress and confusion of the crew that they lose their own voices and become a cacophonous rabble: "shadows that growled, hissed, laughed excitedly" (*NN*, p. 74).

Wait dissolves the crew merely by making it aware that the circuit connecting sound and sense is not automatic. To reverse the terms of the preface, he destroys solidarity by making it impossible for the crew to see clearly what they think they hear. To do this, he merely needs to insert racial difference into the otherwise unconscious workings of phatic communion. The narrator's statement of this principle is both confident and insecure at the same time: "You couldn't see that there was anything wrong with him: a nigger does not show" (*NN*, p. 27). The narrator's own cultural ignorance appears as the unreadability of the black face, but this transference cannot dispel the "discursive fear" caused by the unfamiliar.[85]

Yet all that Wait has really done is to extend to the crew a knowledge of language he has gained as an outsider on other ships, a knowledge that was Conrad's own because he had been in the same position. This, then, is the central conflict of *The Nigger of the "Narcissus."* Conrad celebrates a communal use of language the awareness of which he gained by being excluded from it. Thus he is simultaneously an outside observer, rendering his account in the third person, and an anonymous member of the crew; he is both "the nigger" and the crew that can hardly understand him. And the ship is simultaneously the site of entry for any and all foreigners who may come, Polish or West Indian, a polyglot linguistic community in which communication is carried out in a language that belongs to no one, and a metaphorical version of dear England itself, safe only when it has finally dropped its racial outsiders overboard.

VII

In his preface Conrad dedicates himself to "never-discouraged care for the shape and ring of sentences" (*NN*, p. 146). Actually, that care was discouraged before he had completed another book. In *Lord Jim* Marlow wearily admits, "I have given up expecting those last words, whose ring, if they could only be pronounced, would shake both heaven and earth" (*LJ*, p. 137).[86] In both cases, in self-dedication and in the discouragement of his narrator, Conrad revives the literal, aural meaning of the old idiom "the ring of truth." What matters is the convincing sound of words, the tone or accent by which we recognize and respond to them. But why is Marlow so discouraged when Conrad himself had been hopeful?

Perhaps the answer lies in an even greater literalization of "the ring of truth," the silver ring that Jim sends as token to Dain Waris. As Tamb 'Itam says before he receives it, "the message is important, and these are thy very words I carry" (*LJ*, p. 241). Yet the ring comes back with Dain Waris's body, seemingly as a symbol of Jim's faithlessness, and thus seals his own death. Does this fatal circuit represent some radical failure of translation, some cultural gap that even Jim's sincere words cannot leap? Perhaps the "ring of truth" cannot be handed over as freely as Jim gives his ring to Tamb 'Itam. Perhaps the "ring" that gives words all the truthfulness they have is so particular it cannot be conveyed to another people. If so, then Marlow might well be discouraged, because then there would be no "last words" so final their ring would sound everywhere on earth, and the dedication of his Polish creator to "the shape and ring" of English sentences would lead not just to failure but to cultural suicide.

Yet this is where Conrad situated all his work, at the border between languages, the boundary across which the ring can never quite pass unaltered. He took up residence there as a racial alien, a speaker of gibberish, and he helped to situate transatlantic modernism there as well, at least insofar as it was created by other much-traveled "linguisters" like himself. Because these modernists so often followed Conrad in feeling their linguistic difference as a racial distance, the arrival of James Wait on board the *Narcissus*, wearing what seems to be a mask and speaking what seems gibberish, is, as Matheus suggests, the prelude to much of the literature they would create.

3

Modernism's African Mask:
The Stein–Picasso Collaboration

I

Not long after the publication of *The Nigger of the "Narcissus,"* European artists were attracted en masse to an African art they knew virtually nothing about and were mesmerized by the way that African masks and statues dislocated all conventional artistic strategies.[1] A 1924 *Opportunity* editorial described this new influence as a "forcible entry" and an invasion, promising or warning, it is hard to tell, "Soon primitive Negro art will invade this country as it has invaded Europe. It is inevitable." For aesthetes like Alain Locke and Albert Barnes, the African vogue that influenced Picasso, Apollinaire, Cendrars, Stravinsky, Satie, and many others augured a new prominence for African-American creativity as well, a rise in attention, if not estimation, that Matheus later compared to Wait's arrival and domination.[2]

The questions raised by Conrad's preface and novel are also relevant to this wider African influence on modern art. What is the role of race, of racial prejudice, stereotyping, and romantic identification, in the crisis of representation that Picasso purposely provoked in paintings like *Les Demoiselles d'Avignon?* Was this new interest primarily ethnographic, fixated on the culture that could be rather luridly imagined behind a single African artifact, or was it aesthetic, with the artifact seen as a new arrangement of shapes in space? Was it part of an escapist daydream or a radical disruption of European representational conventions?

One way of answering these questions is to examine the role of Africa in one of the most celebrated relationships in European modernism, namely, that of Pablo Picasso and Gertrude Stein. Their meeting took place at a crucial moment both for them and for the arts they practiced, with Stein just beginning to write under the influence of postimpressionism and Picasso on the verge of disrupting his canvases with actual words. This crossing of old boundaries had a lot to do with the beginnings of modernism, but it was accompanied by another, rather different, crossing, as Stein and Picasso simultaneously discovered African art. Though the first of these "transgressions" seems aesthetic and the second ethnographic, it may be that their relationship is more than coincidental.

Both Stein and Picasso came to resent the myth that modernism began on the day Matisse showed them an African figurine he had found in a secondhand shop.[3] Late in his life, Picasso strenuously denied that he had been crucially influenced by African art, and Stein said of herself in *The Autobiography of Alice B. Toklas:* "She was not at any time interested in African sculpture."[4] And yet the original frontispiece of this very work shows Stein ensconced behind her writing desk, awaiting Alice, with a piece of African sculpture prominently displayed

Man Ray: Gertrude Stein and Alice B. Toklas (ca. 1922). Frontispiece, *The Auto-biography of Alice B. Toklas* (New York: Random House, 1933). © 1993 ARS, New York/ADAGP/Man Ray Trust, Paris.

before her. This is perhaps one of a group of objects Stein purchased for Picasso at Nîmes in 1918.[5] Her acting as Picasso's agent in this case is emblematic, despite the disclaimers, of their collaborative use of African models in inventing modernism.

One of the most important episodes in the birth of that movement occurred shortly before Matisse brought his find to Stein's studio. In the winter of 1906 Picasso ended a long struggle with his portrait of Stein by repainting a likeness he had labored over for as many as ninety-two sittings. On this generally realistic portrait he superimposed a flat, expressionless mask with two eye slits cut against the angle of the rest of the face and body, a mask derived from ancient Iberian reliefs he had seen at the Louvre. This portrait was the first in a series of paintings, all featuring rock-solid figures with impassive faces, that culminated in the women of *Les Demoiselles d'Avignon*, some of whom have faces much like the mask Picasso had fashioned for Stein, some of whom wear masks inspired by his visit to the Musée d'Ethnographie at the Palais du Trocadéro. In its finished state, therefore, *Les Demoiselles* is a virtual map of Picasso's progress from 1905 to 1907, from the Stein portrait, through Africa, to the first intimations of "what two years later would become Cubism."[6]

Even while sitting for Picasso, Stein was composing the work she herself would call, with a disarming lack of modesty, "the first definite step away from the nineteenth century and into the twentieth century in literature."[7] Stein took this step in a way remarkably like that of Picasso, for she composed this crucial work by covering a failed self-portrait with an ethnic mask. Having struggled unsuccessfully to account for an unhappy love affair in *Q.E.D.*, a book that remained unpublished until after her death, Stein rewrote the story, sometimes leaving whole lines of dialogue nearly intact, as "Melanctha," the story of a young black woman's emotional trials.[8]

Thus, Stein and Picasso take the first steps into cubism and literary modernism by performing uncannily similar transformations on the figure of Gertrude Stein herself. Placing a painted mask over his naturalistic portrait, Picasso duplicates the linguistic mask Stein was just devising for herself. By rewriting her own story for black characters, Stein anticipates, and perhaps even motivates, Picasso's use of African masks in *Les Demoiselles d'Avignon*. In each case, in painting and in literature, the step away from conventional verisimilitude into abstraction is accomplished by a figurative change of race.

Of course, Picasso's immediate models are not the same as Stein's, but the fact that Stein drew her inspiration from black Baltimoreans she encountered as a medical student and not from African art would not have mattered much at the time.[9] "Melanctha" was composed in a time of growing pan-Africanism, from the international pan-African conference in London in 1900 to the collapse of Marcus Garvey's movement in the early 1920s.[10] Stylized African masks drawn by the American Aaron Douglas figure prominently in the decorative artwork of *The New Negro*, and similar masks were at one time commissioned for Carl Van

Pablo Picasso: Portrait of Gertrude Stein (1906). All rights reserved, The Metropolitan Museum of Art, Bequest of Gertrude Stein, 1946. © 1993 ARS, New York/ SPADEM, Paris.

Vechten's *Nigger Heaven*.[11] In that work itself the main character, who fitted Van Vechten's image of an up-to-date young black woman, collects African sculpture and quotes a long stretch of "Melanctha" from memory.[12]

For Van Vechten, apparently, the difference between sculpture and literature was no more important than that between Africa and America. In fact, it was common in the early years of the century for critics as different as I. A. Richards and Zora Neale Hurston to draw a line of comparison from African art to African-

American language and literature without bothering overmuch about differences between the arts.[13] Thus the other difference between Picasso and Stein, that his masks were visual while hers were verbal, might not have mattered much either. But, in fact, it is just this crossing of ordinary aesthetic boundaries, this jump from the visual to the verbal and back again, that the African mask makes possible, not, of course, by eliding the actual processes of representation but by highlighting them. This is one reason why the African mask can stand as a sign of the aesthetic collaboration of Picasso and Stein.

From the very beginning, however, this mask has inspired quite different, even contradictory, reactions among Europeans and Euro-Americans. One sort of response to Picasso's version of Africa is felt by William Rubin, who finds in *Les Demoiselles d'Avignon* "something ominous and monstrous such as Conrad's Kurtz discovered in the heart of darkness."[14] To sum up his own very similar reaction, Leo Steinberg applies to the painting Nietzsche's phrase "wild naked nature with the bold face of truth."[15] So insistent are these metaphors of exposure and discovery, of nakedness and wildness, that it is almost impossible to recall that the figures so described are wearing masks. What Steinberg calls "the bold face of truth" is in fact an African mask, clapped violently over the face of Picasso's prostitute. Yet there is no real contradiction here because in Steinberg's account the mask *is* the bold face of truth, revealing inner depths that flesh ordinarily conceals. The mask is not really a cultural artifact, worn for purposes of concealment or adornment, but a psychological revelation exposing what usually lies *behind* the face.[16]

On the other hand, André Salmon saw *Les Demoiselles* as "almost entirely freed from humanity . . . white signs on a blackboard."[17] The same metaphor is used by D. H. Kahnweiler, Picasso's early dealer, who insisted that African art had revealed the true nature of all art, "which is that of handwriting."[18] Quite independently, it seems, Stein decided that African art had made Picasso's painting "calligraphic."[19] In this interpretation, the African mask is convention embodied, the sign of signs. As such, it inaugurates Western abstraction by exposing the conventional nature of all art. Instead of revealing what lies behind the face, the mask grinningly exposes a void where the face should be. Yet it is at least strange that a continent widely perceived in Europe as analphabetic and illiterate should have helped transform European art into calligraphy. At a time when colonized Africans were systematically denied instruction in the European languages, how could African art teach European art how to write?[20]

These are just a few of the contradictions in the feelings of Europeans about the African art they began to incorporate into their own in 1907. African art is portrayed as both abstract and naturalistic, highly conventional and thrillingly crude, opaque and yet more naked than any merely unadorned face. Such contradictions have survived even the most recent developments in cultural criticism. After placing Picasso's primitivism in the context of colonialist controversies of 1905–6, Patricia Leighten concludes that Picasso was a kind of "shaman," one whose painting expressed the "anxiety that civilization had done its work too well, made us too tame, and thus cut us off from sources of magic, fear, and dread. . . ."[21] In Leighten's account, Picasso's paintings seem to have no formal properties at all, just resonance within a context, but for Yve-Alain Bois the same paintings are formalist exercises par excellence, made so by their exposure to an African art that is morphologically provocative because it is so arbitrary.[22] It is no accident that Bois's article is entitled "Kahnweiler's Lesson," because it repeats the analysis in which the African mask is a collection of arbitrary signs, a semiotic exercise curiously unconnected to the people who must have made it, just as Leighten repeats that part of Steinberg and Rubin that breathes heavily over revelations of "the heart of darkness."

Similar inconsistencies occur in interpretations of Stein's story of African-American life in a fictionalized Baltimore. Stein herself said in a 1909 notebook, "I believe in reality as Cezanne [*sic*] or Caliban believe in it."[23] Is she claiming in such a statement that Cézanne introduces us to a reality as basic as that lived by Caliban, or that Caliban has as unsettling an effect on our notions of reality as Cézanne? "Melanctha" seems the first representation of this paradoxical reality, presided over as it was by Cézanne, Stein's first aesthetic model, and by Caliban, the freakishly distorted stereotype who mixes "strong black curses" with "the wide abandoned laughter that gives the broad glow to negro sunshine."[24] But how are critics to understand this mixture of aesthetic experimentation and racist crudity? Very rarely have they been up to the implications of Stein's statement that Cézanne and Caliban see the *same* reality. It is far easier to concentrate on aesthetics, as critics of *Three Lives* have for so long, or to demolish the racism of "Melanctha," as is now becoming more common.[25] Thus the gap between Conrad's preface and the subject of his novel recurs, and it becomes impossible to account for the radical effect of racial difference on the representational schemes of modern art.

These are the difficulties critics face when they attempt to understand the role of Caliban in the art that follows Cézanne. How could the works of a people supposedly so close to primal realities, so "authentic," in a word, awaken a jaded European intelligentsia to the arbitrariness of its own semiotic system? On the other hand, how could an art so morphologically arbitrary, so semiotically vertiginous, beat jungle drums in the hearts of European art critics? And what sort of movement was it that, if the critics are to be believed, appropriated African models to make its own art more immediate *and* more consciously artificial? Like many masks, the African mask that Stein and Picasso drew across the face of European art reveals a good deal about what it is supposed to conceal. It reveals, of course, the deeply contradictory response of Europe to the cultures it was colonizing as the first modernists were born. It also reveals the mixed motives behind the rebellion of early modernism against that dominating European culture. Like the culture they challenged, Stein and Picasso found African art to be both elemental and intriguingly artificial: modernism is, at least in part, what they made of this contradiction.

II

From the very first, contradictions existed in the reactions of Europeans to the cultures they discovered in Africa and America. Columbus first found the people he called Indians to be remarkably generous and peaceable, "the best people in the world"; only later did he decide that these same people were wicked and deceitful.[26] Three hundred years later, European invaders of the deepest Amazon remarked that the people they found there were "unreliable, betraying under different circumstances, and often apparently under the same, . . . all the opposite traits of character."[27] What these explorers discover in the Amazon is, of course, their own preconceptions oscillating mysteriously before their very eyes. Europeans like Columbus were charmed at first by how easy it was to fit the aboriginal inhabitants of the strange continent into European molds; as this fit became less and less satisfactory, charm gave way to disquiet and unease, the people who had seemed comfortingly familiar becoming odd and unaccountable. Hundreds of years later, European notions of the other continents still waver between these linked opposites of identity and difference, since the first impulse of assimilation seems to have no more moderate an alternative than utter, blank incomprehension.

For Sara Suleri one important version of this dichotomy is "the great contradiction of the excessive literalism or the excessive metaphoricity of the racial body." The colonial subject is either a part of nature, utterly literal and therefore soothingly simple, or menacingly unreadable, mysterious, and suggestive of some vast unknown. In the latter case, the signs of the colonized culture appear for the moment *as* signs—hieroglyphs, handwriting, calligraphy, whatever—because they cannot be read except as signifying the European's own fascination with the unreadable.[28] European reactions to other cultures tend to oscillate between these two poles, and thus the same culture can seem simple, authentic, concrete, or, on the other hand, odd, uncanny, and arbitrary.[29]

These incompatible but strongly linked alternatives persist even in the reaction of the avant-garde against Eurocentrism. Long before Cummings wrote *Him,* the European avant-garde used Africa to make its rebellion seem a return to nature. Often this involved pretending to *be* African, as Richard Huelsenbeck and Marcel Janco did with their "African" masks at the Cabaret Voltaire. Picasso went them one better. After his interest in African art became well known, Picasso enjoyed spreading the rumor that he actually was of African descent.[30]

Like her friend Van Vechten, who began passing for black as an undergraduate, Stein had toyed with such notions from the time of her days at Radcliffe.[31]

The "dark-skinned" alter ego named Hortense Sänger who appears in one of the themes she wrote there lives a life that is strangely mirrored in the racial genre pieces written the day before and the day after: on one hand, Hortense's frustrated sensuality is echoed in the "sensuous sunshine" filled with "the voices of negroes singing," on the other, her melancholy is shared by a "melancholy looking porter" who is abused because he is black.[32] This odd, adolescent combination of elemental happiness and deep melancholy certainly reflects the dialect literature of the time, which offered these two stereotypes precisely as models for the kind of daydreaming Stein indulges in. The original publisher of "Melanctha" attempted to feed the same sort of daydreams, boasting that its realism is such "the reader himself, for the time, is a coloured person too."[33] This promise would have resonated strongly in a culture that was very soon to make "Alexander's Ragtime Band" a runaway hit for promising that everyone could play ragtime, a promise Jakie Rabinowitz took so seriously he decided to become a "blackface comedian." This kind of racial role-playing appealed as much to the white reading audience as it did to Stein and Picasso.

Nonetheless, the racial mask also functioned for Stein and Picasso as a sign of expatriation. Rubin speculates that Picasso's adoption of African motifs completed a necessary estrangement from Barcelona. Though "Picasso's father was not around to be shocked when the young painter's primitivism culminated in *Les Demoiselles d'Avignon,*" the painting violated all the bourgeois artistic conventions inherited from the father, a professor at the Fine Arts Academy, breaking a hold that was for Picasso both aesthetic and familial.[34] Stein's father was also safely dead by the time *Les Demoiselles* was painted, but the picture freed her from a far more thorough domination by disgusting her brother Leo. The "Negroid things" were a dead end, he felt, and thus began the split that would leave his sister with all the Picassos they had jointly collected.[35] *Les Demoiselles* became the occasion for a break that would have had to come sooner or later if Stein were to continue with the avant-garde writing that exasperated her brother as much as did Picasso's painting.

In this way Stein and Picasso act out twenty years in advance the other side of *The Jazz Singer,* the generational drama, donning the African mask to make a break with their own cultural past.[36] The affectation of racial difference represents the radical difference Stein and Picasso felt between themselves and those to whom they had been born. Thus Picasso told Malraux that the African sculptures he saw at the Trocadéro were "against everything" and that they supported him in his feeling that "I too am against everything . . . everything is an enemy! Everything!" Yet these fearsome and violent figures also became protective, totemic for those bound together by their opposition to everyone else. Just because they stood with him against a hostile world, the African pieces were "intercesseurs," or mediators, for Picasso.[37] Thus they also protected those whom they isolated. In this way, African figures become the totem of the avant-garde, that tiny tribe unified by its shared opposition to the rest of European society. It is no accident, then, that the earliest propaganda for aesthetic modernism often repre-sented its practitioners as racially alien to Europe, as "The Wild Men of Paris" or "the heirs of the witch doctor and the voodoo."[38]

The role of racial alien is, therefore, a very flexible one for this branch of the international avant-garde. Insofar as its expatriation is willed in revolt against the social constraints and falsehoods of Europe and America, this role completes the process of exile. As Nathan Huggins says of these aesthetic rebels, "they became Negroes" to complete their defection from bourgeois society.[39] Insofar as exile is simply an extreme version of the "transcendental homelessness" of all modern citizens, an unwelcome and even tragic condition, the black role promises another home, very much like the one intellectuals have searched for since the German Romantics.[40] The avant-garde rejects European society, and thus enjoys the freedom of living outside the law, while simultaneously savoring connection to something more authentic found in Africa.

And yet, on the other hand, a mask of authenticity seems a contradiction in terms. The very transformation by which a deracinated European bourgeois becomes a vital African tribalist must appear in its own right as a duality, a tension between what is and what might be. Modernism sometimes seems to base itself on such tensions. In the year of *Les Demoiselles*, Ezra Pound wrote a poem called "Masks," as W. B. Yeats did a year or two later.[41] These poems are versions of what would become one of the recurrent motifs of modernism, a movement obsessed with personae, metamorphoses, doubles, and mythic parallels. This obsession with what Robert Langbaum once called the "mysteries of identity" is especially strong, for obvious reasons, among the expatriates who form such a large proportion of the early generation of modernists. To feel oneself in two places at once, at home and abroad, is almost to feel as two persons and thus to acquire a skepticism about the possibility of ever having an identity, if that means being just one thing. Seen in this light, a mask is the embodiment of the variability and indeterminacy of human identity.[42]

This might be considered a quality of all masks, which are, as A. David Napier maintains, "devices for analyzing the relationship between illusion on one hand and the recognition and integrity of a human face on the other."[43] As Conrad's example shows, however, the African mask is a particular case of rare power for Europeans, because it is so difficult for them to distinguish it from the African face. For a writer like Conrad, an African face *is* a mask because there is some-thing essentially mysterious about it, something paradoxical and ambiguous. It is at once brutally repulsive, far *too* real, and mysteriously elusive, abstract, and distant. It is no accident that James Wait's name appears in the ship's log and thus in the novel as an indecipherable blot, an unreadable sign, because the character himself is an unreadable sign.[44]

The African mask that appears in Picasso's works is, therefore, much more than a metaphor for some primitive authenticity. The figure at the far left of *Les Demoiselles*, for example, wears a mask that has been variously identified as

Pablo Picasso: *Les Demoiselles d'Avignon* (June–July 1907). Oil on canvas, 8' x 7'8".
Collection, The Museum of Modern Art, New York. Acquired through the
Lillie P. Bliss Bequest. © 1993 ARS, New York/SPADEM, Paris.

Iberian, African, and Oceanic. If, however, one were to lift this mask, an act made
possible by the survival of Picasso's studies for the painting, one would see under
it another mask much like the one Picasso used to finish the Stein portrait. The
evidence suggests that Picasso painted over this first mask at about the same time
he repainted the two figures on the far right, sometime after his famous trip to the
ethnographic collections at the Trocadéro.[45] Even beneath this layer, however,
one could find yet another, this time male. For the figure began its life in Picasso's
studies for the painting as a male medical student, apparently hesitating on the
edge of dissipation. In fact, the figure apparently represented Picasso himself
until he changed its sex and gave it a mask.[46] Steinberg says of this mask that it
"protects a secret history," by which he means that the "sex change" the figure
has undergone is obscured. And yet it may be that the mask expresses Picasso's

secret as succinctly as possible, that a mask is in itself expressive of the way that "conventional sexual character traits seem reversed."[47]

The mask worn by Stein in her portrait apparently expressed certain complex feelings raised in Picasso by her unconventional sexuality. As John Richardson puts it, Stein appeared to Picasso as an "hommesse," at once "more feminine and more masculine than the adolescent waifs of 1905."[48] The mask she wears is a sign of this sexual ambiguity, the impersonal immobility of it associated in Picasso's work of the time with a physical bulk and power not at all conventionally feminine. Between the Stein portrait and *Les Demoiselles*, there stands a whole line of solid, sometimes openly phallic, women, often in intimate pairs, their masklike faces expressive only of this sexual indeterminacy. Picasso shares in this indeterminacy himself by using the same mask to change the sex of his alter ego, creating an ambiguity that remains in visible form in *Les Demoiselles* in the hesitation of the masked figure on the threshold of the brothel. This figure, raising a curtain on the edge of *Les Demoiselles*, is both inside and outside the brothel, both male and female, customer and commodity.

Though the "secret history" behind the mask is no longer fully apparent to the audience, much of the power of *Les Demoiselles* resides, nonetheless, in the

Pablo Picasso: Study for *Les Demoiselles d'Avignon* (1907). © 1993 ARS, New York/SPADEM, Paris.

way it challenges, physically and figuratively, conventional notions of female passivity. A good deal of this challenge comes from the primal savagery of the masks, which seem weirdly alive, contorted as if in the act of moving. Something even more radical happens as the masks communicate their geometry to the unclothed bodies of the prostitutes, which can seem no less composed, no less artificial, than the masks themselves. The difference between mask and nakedness is removed by the geometric angularity of the composition, so the body comes to seem as arbitrary, as constructed, as the painted mask. And once the bodies become twisted geometric forms, even their nakedness is not enough to reveal their gender. As Brigitte Leal says in her edition of Picasso's sketchbook for *Les Demoiselles*, once the figures "undergo this primitive stylization," there is nothing but hairstyle to distinguish the women from their male customers: "Like them, they have that aura of sorrowful dignity—with their impassive faces and absent gaze—which Gertrude Stein so admired."[49] Perhaps Stein admired this masklike stillness precisely because of the sexual ambiguity it brought to the painting, making gender a matter of convention, of art, rather than a biological necessity. The tension in the painting between mask and nakedness seems to break down the difference between surface and depth and to make gender a matter of role-playing rather than essence. Thus the body is no longer a natural and inescapable datum, and gender is no longer a given, but something much more like clothes or—a mask.

Stein created a version of this mask for herself in "Melanctha." Just as Picasso had performed a sex change on one of his own alter egos to produce *Les Demoiselles*, Stein, in rewriting *Q.E.D.*, transformed Adele, her mouthpiece, into Dr. Jeff Campbell. On one hand, this change provides a convenient mask for the sexual feelings that disorder *Q.E.D.*, since it changes the lesbian relationships of that book into heterosexual ones. On the other hand, the revisionary masquerade sets up an uncanny oscillation, especially in that all of Adele's most conventional fears and prejudices have been transferred to Dr. Jeff, as if Stein chose to represent the more retrograde parts of her own psyche as male. Certainly, much of the shock value of "Melanctha" comes from the blithe reversal by which the woman "wanders" while the man fidgets at home.

One of the most objectionable aspects of "Melanctha" is certainly its fixation on the sexual lives of its subjects, as if African-American characters are to be understood primarily in sensual terms. Yet the shift of race seemed to make it easier for Stein to see the senses, even the body itself, as ruled by convention. Perhaps Stein, like her publishers, invites her predominantly white readership to identify with the characters and thus play a black role, and yet presenting race *as* a role seems an open invitation to consider it as culturally constituted and perhaps to consider gender a role as well. The residual ambiguity created by the racial masquerade makes gender and then finally the body itself seem a mask. Once again, then, the mask is not a cover for an unconventional sexuality but a revelation of it, even a means of achieving it. Like other forms of masquerade, particularly cross-dressing, the racial mask highlights what Kaja Silverman calls "the dislocation between subjectivity and the role."[50] The ambiguous relationship between mask and face, costume and body, makes it impossible to see biology as destiny.

Like the Arab robes of T. E. Lawrence or the Indian regalia of E. M. Forster, the racial masks that Stein and Picasso give to their own sexual ambiguity have a complex motivation and effect. There is, no doubt in each case, a longing for a certain kind of sensual freedom, found in Africa or Arabia or India because such freedom is always found "elsewhere," just as the natural is always found "elsewhere."[51] On the other hand, the mask maintains a tension between nature and convention, essence and accident, that expresses, even if it does not explain, the very process of displacement that simultaneously links and separates the two halves of each pair. The virtue of works like *Les Demoiselles* and "Melanctha" is that they bring out into the open the dialectical relationship between the mask as raw nature and the mask as cultural convention, and thus approximate the power of the African mask in its own context.

According to Henry Louis Gates, Jr., the African mask is a dialectical synthesis of all sorts of discordant qualities: "Mask is the essence of immobility fused with the essence of mobility, fixity with transience, order with chaos, permanence with the transitory, the substantial with the evanescent."[52] Picasso seems to have sensed in the African art he found in Paris similar possibilities, since he spoke of that art as both "raisonnable," that is to say, formally ordered, and "magicaux," uncanny, mysterious, occult.[53] Stein also spoke of African art as "natural, direct and civilised" as if to defy the usual contrast between the natural and the civilized.[54] These modernists were attracted to African art because it seemed to promise direct access to nature but also because it broke down the whole dichotomy between nature and culture.

Thus the mask that Picasso gives first to Stein is both ancient and impersonal while somehow also being a perfectly individual likeness, "the only reproduction of me which is always I, for me," as Stein put it.[55] A representation that is so obviously a "reproduction" can hardly be a perfect likeness as well, but Stein's insistence that the portrait *is* her is more than merely playful. What the portrait most faithfully represents is the tension, the slippage, between mask and face, between impersonality and individuality, conventional representation and likeness, which it was Stein's program in life and art to explore. Picasso's mask presents this program by only indirectly representing Stein's face.

In other words, the duality of the mask forces a confrontation between representation by likeness and representation by convention or habit. Kahnweiler once said that "in certain Ivory Coast masks, the Cubist painters discovered marks which, without recourse to imitation, compelled the spectator to imagine the face whose 'real' shape these masks did not imitate."[56] This is how the mask erases the distinction between writing and painting so as to make the latter "calligraphic," by confronting the viewer with marks that imitate because they seem real and marks that imitate because they allow us to imagine the real. By questioning the presumed difference between these two kinds of marks, which is the difference between conventional and natural signification, the mask becomes what Walter Benjamin called a "dialectical image."[57] It is in this sense that the African mask is the most characteristic sign of the collaboration of Stein and Picasso, because it was the means by which their different arts could unsettle one another and, by eliding their own differences, make a modernism that would transform both.

IV

According to Adam Gopnick, the mask that Picasso painted over the Stein portrait became, in its mixture of styles and forms, "a kind of creole." The beginnings of modernism are thus compared to what happens when two different dialect groups exchange vocabularies.[58] The same comparison between mask and dialect is frequently made from the other direction. For example, Gates has used the African mask as a metaphor for certain American linguistic and literary tactics. According to Gates, the literary version of the mask is dialect, which he calls "a verbal mask."[59]

Yet the "self-conscious switch of linguistic codes" that Gates identifies as one of the primary strategies of dialect speakers is a mask that does more than just cover or obscure. Under this definition dialect is not a particular kind of language, not a mere deviation or deformation, but a particular *use* of language. It puts the standard language in conflict with itself, "constructing a continuum of variation," to quote Deleuze and Guattari, "negotiating all of the variables both to constrict the constants and to expand the variables. . . ."[60] Social linguists such as Shirley Brice Heath have discovered a similar conflict in the course of empirical studies: different social and ethnic groups use language for different purposes, call on it for different reasons, and only a very few of these have to do with correctness of expression.[61] Dialect is most like "a verbal mask" when it plays against such correctness because then it approximates the mask's uncanny power to focus the natural and the arbitrary in a single spot. Instead of merely setting up a screen behind which nonstandard speakers might plot or smirk, dialect actively contrasts what poses as natural to its own conventions. It is this play *between* dialect and the standard language that resembles the tension the mask creates between the face and its facsimile.

It is in this sense that Stein creates a mask of dialect in "Melanctha." The language in this work has been called "photographically exact."[62] Though this may seem a bit extreme, the first publishers of the story did send a representative to Stein's studio to determine if she were in fact an educated native speaker, the language apparently coming a bit too close to crude reality for perfect comfort.[63] But when Stein wanted to write in dialect, as she did rather frequently in her letters, she used the same phonological and syntactical conventions that white

American writers had been using for decades: "The cakes did arrive and dey was damn good," or "We is doin business too."[64] There is very little of this sort of dialect in "Melanctha" itself.[65] What Stein does instead is to create a dialect in which conventions of verbal verisimilitude are played against themselves so that the speech seems simultaneously concrete and highly artificial.

The first readers of "Melanctha" were promised photographic realism because it was inconceivable in the atmosphere created by the dialect literature of the time that writing about black people could have any other purpose than photographic realism. Dialect was concrete language made and used by down-to-earth literalists, which is precisely why it appealed to—indeed, why it was most often created by—people who felt a surfeit of connotation. Thus R. Emmett Kennedy presented to his audience "crude, semi-barbarous poetry, if you will, but savoring of the real, original essence."[66]

Stein seems to feed the same appetite for the real and concrete by trapping her characters within a round of numbing repetition. In his study of colloquial language in American literature, Richard Bridgman observes, "In the dialogue of uninstructed characters, iteration is understood to result from their inability or superstitious unwillingness to substitute synonyms, pronouns or verbal auxiliaries for the concrete terms of their discussion. This steady, relentless hewing to a line of particulars suggests then that material reality is all that is trusted, all that can be depended upon to convey meaning."[67] Stein seems to make the same point by choosing a particular class of words for repeated repetition, words like *real, regular,* and *certainly.* Particularly in the speech of Jeff Campbell, reliance on these words suggests a desire to stabilize reality by fastening language to it ineluctably.

Yet this technique has the curious power to complicate even as it reiterates. As Kenneth Burke observes, "The most clear-sounding of words can be used for the vaguest of reference, quite as we speak of 'a certain thing' when we have no particular thing in mind." Burke points out that when we say that something is "essentially" true we often mean that it is not true at all.[68] In the same way, when we protest that something is "really" true, our emphasis suggests that there is some reason for doubt. Stein wedges an entire argument into the minute space between the adjective and its adverbial qualification. What does it mean, for example, that Rose Johnson is "married really" to her husband? (p. 88). Why is it necessary for her to assure her friends that she is not married "falsely"? There are even more possibilities in the negative case, as, for example, when the narrator assures us that for all her wandering Melanctha never did anything "really wrong" (p. 96).

In such cases, it seems that the very effort to nail language to a single unequivocal reality defeats itself, as if the very act of invoking the real over and over actually multiplied it. "It was all so nearly alike it must be different and it is different," as Stein says elsewhere.[69] Repetition of simple, basic words often has this effect in Stein, as, for example, when Melanctha accuses Jeff Campbell:

"[Y]ou want to have a good time just like all us others, and then you just keep on saying that it's right to be good . . ." (p. 118). To have "a good time" is obviously the very opposite of being "good," as becomes clear at the end of the story when Rose Johnson observes that Melanctha "never come to no good" because she insisted on her right "to have a good time" (p. 235). If "good" can mean both bad and good, then it seems that very little is stable in the system of language or in the morality it supports.

By taking the real and the good and transforming them into terms of qualification, Stein raises a general suspicion about the way that language attaches attributes to things. Several times in the course of this story, Stein calls Jane Harden "a roughened woman" (pp. 104, 107). Thus, it would seem that her name is an appropriate one, designating some essential hardness in her nature. Yet she is called "roughened," not "rough," and, if what Stein says elsewhere is true and "people can be made by their names"[70] then perhaps Jane was roughed up by her own name. Perhaps her "roughness" is merely an impression that others have about her. Or perhaps it designates her ability to "harden" others. But when Jeff Campbell accuses Melanctha of having "hard" ways like Jane, he exclaims, "I can't believe you mean them hardly" (p. 138) so that "hardly" means both hardly and hardly at all.

Thus the paradox on which Stein constructs the peculiar dialect of "Melanctha." A patois with a very restricted vocabulary and a repetitious, looping sentence structure, it seems on the surface to correspond to Bridgman's description of a kind of speech that sticks almost superstitiously to the known and familiar. And yet the more Stein's speakers reiterate the few simple words allotted to them, the more unstable those words become. Even in the act of assuring their hearers that they can speak the truth, speakers like Jeff Campbell convict themselves of lying: "It's easy enough for me always to be honest, Miss Melanctha. All I got to do is always just to say right out what I am thinking. I certainly never have got any real reason for not saying it right out like that to anybody" (p. 128). The more he uses *certainly, real,* and *right* as magical intensifiers, the more one begins to doubt what he is saying. In fact, Jeff has just admitted, in the very same paragraph, "I just can't say that right out that way to you" (p. 128).

So much of the drama of "Melanctha" is about what characters say, instead of what they do, that this conflict between the sayable and the unsayable comes to dominate the story. It is Jeff's destructive habit of using words to pull intimate emotions to the surface that threatens and destroys his relationship with Melanctha. "You always wanting to have it all clear out in words always, what everybody is always feeling," Melanctha complains. "I certainly don't see a reason, why I should always be explaining to you what I mean by what I am just saying" (p. 171). The phraseology here clarifies the conflict between the characters. Jeff demands words that justly represent habitual feelings, words that commit the speaker. For Melanctha, however, words are something that she is "just saying." If Jeff maintains that it is easy "just to say" what he is thinking, Melanctha counters that whatever she is "just saying" need not represent her innermost thoughts.

This sexual conflict might also be seen as an interracial difference of the kind Heath documents in her study of language acquisition. The white families Heath describes emphasize saying "the right thing." One way that parents school their children in this discipline is by rejecting "children's descriptions of things by their attributes before they have learned to respond with the *name* of the item."[71] This clears away the inessential, the attribute, and emphasizes the single essential designation, the name. But, as Stein says, "the reason that slang exists is to change the nouns which have been names for so long."[72] The dialect Stein puts in the mouths of her black speakers does correspond to the black speech Heath describes in her study in that it multiplies attributes and uses them, moreover, to undermine the solidity of the name.[73]

Long before Stein came to it, the conflict between dialect and the rigidity of the standard language was fought across lines of race and gender. Dialect that could trace itself back to Anglo-Saxon was always referred to as "manly."[74] Its concrete reliability corresponded to a sacred myth of sturdy yeomanry. On the other hand, the dialects of foreigners and, most especially, of blacks, were seen as effeminate. The Italian language itself, according to G. P. Marsh, was "inconsistent with being bold and manly and generous and truthful."[75] And it was no accident that the influence of slave speech was so often perceived as coming through the domestic household, through the idle women who prattled thoughtlessly with their servants.[76]

In "Melanctha," however, the male and the female use the same words: only tiny differences of arrangement separate what Jeff wants so badly "just to say" from what Melanctha is "just saying." How can the difference between truth and falsehood, concrete reality and fantasy, male and female, hinge on such minute differences? By making her dialect both direct and indirect, distinct and very slippery, Stein also undermines the associated differences of race and gender. The masks worn by her characters, which transform Stein herself into Dr. Jeff, correspond to these verbal masks. Like the dislocations of Picasso's finished canvas, which preserve in altered form the secret history of race and sex change, Stein's verbal dislocations represent in the final text the indeterminacy that made her hover between male and female, white and black.

V

Zora Neale Hurston, among many others, lists as one of the "characteristics of negro expression" a "will to adorn," to embellish, to bring an angularity and asymmetry to language that she traces to African sculpture. But Hurston also tells her readers that the terms of "negro expression" are all "close fitting.[77] How can there be a close fit between word and thing and at the same time room for angularity and asymmetry? Gates says more explicitly what Hurston seems to be suggesting, that what truly distinguishes "negro expression" is the ability to play back and forth between the close fitting and the loosely approximate. According to Gates, the "masking function of dialect" is its "self-conscious switch of linguistic codes from white to black or, more properly, from standard English to the black vernacular."[78] At the most general level, such switching moves back and forth between signs that seem to be motivated and signs that advertise and even revel in their conventional nature. Though Stein includes in "Melanctha" very little that could be recognized as actual black dialect, her whole linguistic strategy is to produce this tension between two quite different kinds of language.[79]

Perhaps it was something like this that Richard Wright meant when he said of "Melanctha" that "Miss Stein's struggling words made the speech of the people around me vivid."[80] Critics have always had a hard time accepting this testimony because the speech in "Melanctha" is so clearly inauthentic and because Wright's work seems so little like Stein's, despite the extravagance of his praise for her. But perhaps Wright valued the way Stein's "struggling words" struggled against one another, producing the tension that Gates identifies as the "masking function of dialect." If so, then the step that Stein had taken in 1905 by assuming an African mask had opened the way to a far more radical twentieth century than even she had imagined.

In Picasso's case it becomes clear that the African mask is an aesthetic element like the stenciled numerals or the squares of real newsprint that Rosalind Krauss credits with bringing into modern art its most fundamental representational tension.[81] But this is not because of the purely formal properties of the mask, and surely not because the arrangements of African masks are, as Bois suggests, somehow more "arbitrary" than European forms. The mask can become a radically disturbing image because of the ethnographic generalizations attached to it, because these contain contradictions so acute, and because these contradictions match so closely other contradictions of gender, nationality, and genre that modernism made it its business to explore. Modernism could not escape the contradictions of European colonialism; indeed it was only because it pushed these to extremes that it could exist as a movement at all.

4

Old Possum and Brer Rabbit:
Pound and Eliot's Racial Masquerade

I

When Ezra Pound first tagged T. S. Eliot with the nickname Possum, he no doubt meant to mock his friend's caution and reserve, but he also used the name, which he had found in Joel Chandler Harris's *Uncle Remus*, to turn Eliot's timidity into a subversive mask. In acting out his nickname, Eliot was to mimic what Alain Locke once called the "'possum play' of the Negro peasant,"[1] to use the traditional strategy of the powerless, assuming a bland conformity that conceals an explosive charge, and in so doing become a milder, subtler version of the trickster from whom Pound had taken his own nickname, Brer Rabbit.[2] Thus Pound used a strategy from the popular literature of his youth to create a mask for transatlantic modernism, behind which he and Eliot might mock the literary capital they hoped to conquer.[3] Eliot accepted his nickname and, at least for a time, the insurrectionary role it implied, and he even introduced his own variations, offering at one point to play Uncle Tom to Pound's Little Eva, at another point sending a postcard to Pound signed Tar Baby.[4]

With these nicknames and the roles they implied came a language, a private, distorted version of the dialect that Harris had first popularized. When, in the course of a quarrel with Lady Rothermere about the *Criterion*, Pound advised his ruffled friend to play possum, he did so, appropriately, in dialect: "Dear ole SON. You jus set and hev a quiet draw at youh cawn-kob" (*EL*, p. 590). Later, when Eliot needed to calm Pound, he responded in kind: "So chaw yore old corn cob & think of God & Maise Huffer" (*EL*, pp. 612–13). This dialect became in their correspondence an intimate code, a language of in-jokes and secrets like the one to which Pound alluded in 1922: "Dere z also de stoorey ob de poker game, if you hab forgotten it" (*EL*, p. 505). In the late 1930s Pound dubbed this private dialect "epistolary," and he distinguished it from the Queen's English, the language of public propriety.[5] As a violation of standard English, dialect became the sign of Pound and Eliot's collaboration against the London literary establishment and the literature it produced. Dialect became, in other words, the private double of the modernist poetry they were jointly creating and publishing in these years.

The few bits and pieces of dialect embedded in the Pound–Eliot correspondence thus reveal more than might be expected about the relationship between their poetry and the literature it challenged. Pound suggested as much, in form and in substance, when he told a correspondent in the mid-1930s: "I wuz riz among nigguhs / the uneven forms of the camp meetin . . . dos jes get right down into my blood / regular strophes BORE ME."[6] In this crude and offensive way, Pound ties defiance of the standard language, presented here as an essentially black habit, to his own literary experimentation. Black dialect is a prototype of the literature that would break the hold of the iambic pentameter, an example of visceral freedom triumphing over dead convention. The dialect *in* modernism is a model for the dialect *of* modernism, since black speech seems to Pound the most prominent prior challenge to the dominance of received linguistic forms.

Eliot also confessed the hold of black speech over his imagination, but in an entirely different way. Just two years after signing himself Tar Baby on a postcard to Pound, Eliot wrote to Herbert Read: "Some day, I want to write an essay about the point of view of an American who wasn't an American, because he was born in the South and went to school in New England as a small boy with a nigger drawl, but who wasn't a Southerner because his people were northerners in a border state and looked down on all southerners and Virginians, and who so was never anything anywhere. . . ."[7] What Pound parades with such bluster, the influence of black speech on his own language, Eliot confesses as a dirty secret. For Eliot, black dialect is a flaw, a kind of speech impediment, a remnant of the inarticulate that clogs his language and stands in the way as he attempts to link his own individual talent with tradition.

The two poets seem almost to be speaking two different dialects, one earthy and natural, at one with sensation, the other inarticulate and inauthentic. Indeed, Pound finally turned the private language the two once shared against Eliot, who had become so much more successful—"Waaal Possum, my fine ole Marse Supial"—punning on the old nickname to suggest that his friend had gone over to the masters (*PL*, p. 306). But this contrast may be more apparent than real, for Pound was hardly free of the sort of racial anxiety Eliot confessed to Read. In a country "flooded with 'inferior races,' with the 'off-scourings of Europe,'" it was the pure Anglo-Saxon like Pound, or so he thought, who was "racially alien to the mass of the population," and therefore landless and even homeless.[8] Thus Pound could say, apparently without a trace of irony, "The decline of human liberty in the States may quite possibly date from the year of the emancipation proclamation," dramatizing the drastic contrast between his own political calendar and that of the race he liked to imitate.[9] Pound's version of the racial masquerade may be so full of insurrectionary bluster precisely because it concealed an anxiety even deeper than Eliot's. In any case, the language and the roles the two poets adopted from *Uncle Remus* are obviously shot through with ambivalence and contradiction. The proximity of black speech to their own seems to Pound and Eliot both an opportunity to be seized and an affliction to be regretted.[10]

It may be no mere coincidence, then, that the assumption of Uncle Remus's language by these white American poets is synchronized with its repudiation by black American writers. In 1921, just as Pound and Eliot were choosing nicknames from *Uncle Remus,* James Weldon Johnson remarked "a tendency to discard dialect" and the traditional subject matter of dialect poetry, including "'possums, watermelons, etc." Johnson saw this as a positive trend because "Negro dialect is at present a medium that is not capable of giving expression to the varied conditions of Negro life in America. . . ." Dialect poetry of the time suffered from rigid and shallow conventions such as "mere mutilation of English spelling and pronunciation," conventions that he very tactfully suggests were imposed on African-American writers "from without."[11] By this time white-written black dialect had been in vogue for forty years, and the most popular contemporary practitioners of it were those like Octavus Roy Cohen and E. K. Means who drew the broadest caricatures.[12] In other words, the language Pound and Eliot assume as part of their attack on convention is itself a convention; the linguistic tool they use to mock the literary establishment is in fact part of that establishment. On close examination the dialect adopted by these early modernists proves to be of that peculiar kind that confirms the standard even in deviating from it. Indeed, this may be one of the advantages of this dialect for writers like Eliot and Pound, that it can contain and at least in part conceal their deeply mixed feelings about race, language, and the social authority that links them.

I I

According to Malcolm Cowley, the creators of the first modernist works were members of a generation "divested of their local peculiarities, taught to speak a standard American English and introduced to the world of international learning."[13] They were, in other words, some of the "many thousands of men and women" whom Shaw praised for having "sloughed off their native dialects and acquired a new tongue."[14] But, as Eliot's letter to Read confesses, this process of linguistic retooling was neither so successful nor so painless as Shaw supposed. When the two poets first met, Eliot still had what Wyndham Lewis called a "ponderous, exactly articulated drawl," and Pound was routinely mocked by the English literati for his "nasal twang."[15] These divergent accents were just the most obvious manifestations of deeper and more troubling variations. Pound's tenuous linguistic position, even in the years of his greatest success, is exemplified by his abject groveling before Thomas Hardy over *Homage to Sextus Propertius.* Pound apologized for using "homage," which was "not an English word at all," and he explained himself by revealing that "I come from an American suburb—where I was not born—where both parents are really foreigners, i.e. one from New York and one from Wisconsin. The suburb has no roots, no centre of life."[16] In this, his version of Eliot's letter to Read, Pound rushes to confirm what the English suggested by mocking his twang, that as an American he had only secondary rights to the English language.

If Eliot had felt linguistically anomalous at Harvard, how much more so in London itself, where the arrival of transatlantic modernism coincided with a surge in the movement to defend and advance the standardization of English. The founding of the Society for Pure English in 1919, the filing of the Newbolt Report in 1921, and the publication of books like George Sampson's *English for the English* in the same year exemplify the concentration of standardizing activity in the years during which Pound and Eliot were formulating their revolt. The title of Sampson's book is especially revealing. As far back as 1863, Henry Alford's anti-American attacks on the nonstandard had inspired newspaper articles entitled "English for the English."[17] In 1922, the year of *The Waste Land,* H. W. and F. C. Fowler complained that "there is a real danger of our literature being Americanized. . . ."[18] And though the SPE had opened communications with some American academics by that time, Bridges reportedly scuttled the cooperation and by 1925 was pointing to the United States as one of the areas of gravest danger for English.[19]

One of the chief sources of this danger was the proximity of what Bridges called "other-speaking races."[20] When Henry Newbolt announced "the imminent demise of English" in 1926, his list of causes included Chinese pidgin, the English spoken by Japanese businessmen, Babuisms from India, and "the Negro influence on the language of the United States," which he illustrated with a "genuine sentence" that might have come from Pound and Eliot's correspondence: "No, suh, he ain't come back sence I sawn him went out."[21] In this atmosphere of linguistic xenophobia, even solidly Anglo-Saxon Americans such as Pound and Eliot could be denounced as denationalized "riff-raff" imperiling the linguistic health and harmony of England.[22] Yet such attacks really expressed no more than what the two poets felt themselves, that their language branded them as cultural interlopers. Even late in his life, when he might have seemed quite comfortably English, Eliot referred to himself as a "metic," a foreigner, but in his early years in London this feeling was so strong he confessed the fear that "I may simply prove to be a savage."[23]

Despite his impeccably Anglo-Saxon background and his command of standard English, Eliot still felt as if he were "a nomad and an immigrant and a gypsy in relation to his own language."[24] He wrote, that is to say, what Deleuze and Guattari have called a "minor literature," a literature located "within the heart of what is called great (or established literature)," and yet separated from it by differences of region, ethnicity, or class. Like the writers Deleuze and Guattari discuss, Eliot makes use of this very alienation "to oppose the oppressed quality of this language to its oppressive quality, to find points of nonculture or underdevelopment, linguistic Third World zones by which a language can escape. . . ."[25] That is to say, he converts his linguistic estrangement into an insurrectionary strategy. Thus at the very time Eliot was disclosing his fear of savagery he was also claiming in print that the artist "is more *primitive,* as well as more civilized, than his contemporaries."[26] At the very time he confessed his uneasiness about his "nigger drawl," he was playing Tar Baby with Pound. The same factors combined even more explosively in the case of Pound, who was able to transform his embarrassment at having grown up in a suburb into the crude boast that modern artists are "the heirs of the witch-doctor and the voodoo."[27]

For Eliot and Pound, the world of *Uncle Remus* is a sort of linguistic "Third World zone," as Malaya is for Conrad and black Baltimore for Stein, and the dialect they find there is less a kind of language than a particular use of language, a deployment of variety against consistency. At the same time, of course, this language and its associated roles feed the very prejudices from which Pound and Eliot had originally suffered. In fact, preemptive mimicry of blacks is a traditional American device allowing whites to rebel against English culture and simultaneously use it to solidify their domination at home. Robert C. Toll suggests that minstrel shows gained in popularity during the antebellum period because they both fed and fed upon American cultural defensiveness. On one hand, minstrel shows in all their crudity offered an outlet for egalitarian sentiments outraged by the conventional English stage. On the other hand, minstrel shows offered the white American common man an example even he could feel superior to, the black American common man, who was used to exemplify just those qualities white Americans were most nervous about.[28] Minstrel shows allowed white audiences to have it both ways, to mock tradition, aristocracy, European culture by comparing them to something earthier, more natural, more "American," while simultaneously distancing all these qualities in a figure to which even the commonest white audience could condescend.

Dialect had played a similar role ever since Harris gave it its first popularity among white readers. Uncle Remus's animal tales preserved a good deal of the original violence and trickery of the African and African-American originals, enough at any rate to appeal to a young upstart like Ezra Pound. But Harris also enclosed these stories within a framing device, placed them behind another mask, as it were, that neutralized their unpleasant implications.[29] Dialect writers of the 1920s such as E. C. L. Adams were doing the same even as Pound and Eliot adopted their roles from Harris. Adams called his second book of dialect stories *Nigger to Nigger* so as to place a black mask over his very real criticisms of southern society, yet the epithet itself layers another, safer, white mask over the whole.[30] Thus white masquerade behind black dialect became a well-established strategy that allowed for both rebellion and a reinforced conformity.

This strategy was, of course, about to break out onto an entirely new stage even as Pound and Eliot began to play with it. Blackface was exceedingly common onstage and in film during this period: one Tom Wilson performed in nineteen different blackface roles between 1917 and 1927.[31] In the latter year, however, Al Jolson gave the convention an entirely new prominence by making it a figure for jazz age rebelliousness. Like Harris before him, Jolson went behind a black mask to mime for his audience a certain kind of break with cultural authority. Yet the very mask that makes this rebellion possible also guarantees that it will not go beyond mime. The blackface masquerader can give himself up to the insurrectionary rhythms of jazz and at the same time identify these with another race, which he resembles so little in his clumsy makeup as almost to emphasize his distance from it.

According to the account given by Conrad Aiken, dialect played such a role for Eliot long before he met Pound and became the Possum. As Aiken tells it in *Ushant*, his pseudonymous autobiography, the main question that he and Eliot debated as students at Harvard was "whether one could, or should, lay siege to one or another of the European countries, or cultures, and with what prospects of success. . . ." The two were obviously haunted by "the shadow of the Old Country," a shadow that cast such gloom over the new country as to make it seem impossible for art. But the two students resisted the dismal conclusion of Henry James, insisting in protest that "a new language, the language of a new biological and social continent, a new biological and social climate, was this minute in its most fascinating stage. . . ." Evidence of this new emerging language was to be found in movies, comic strips, and smutty stories: "The very language of the street had genius in it."[32]

Aiken and Eliot thus assume the traditional American pose, that of vital, new, raw, egalitarian, common men as against the gray cultural authorities established in Europe, and they also remodel it so that it can become a component of literary modernism with its generational revolt against old literary conventions. All the conviction for this pose is drawn from American dialect of social classes and situations far removed from Harvard. Like Eliot and Pound a few years later, the two position themselves as class outlaws, defying the standard language as a way of breaking the grip of the standard literature. And yet the one specific example of this new language that Aiken gives is a racial epithet: "Hadn't the Tsetse [T. S. Eliot] and D. [Aiken], just the moment before, been revelling in the latest slang word for Negro, 'dinge'—? Could one find in England any comparable fecundity?"[33] Suddenly Aiken's account of the new language splits open to reveal an irony as old and shopworn as the minstrel show. This language appears natural and unaffected by affronting English propriety, but it achieves this effect only by mocking blacks. These white Harvardians can approach the lower depths by slumming in slang while simultaneously solidifying their position as white by using racial slurs.

Yet even as they enjoyed such language, Aiken and Eliot were also reimagining themselves as racial aliens. "Was it for nothing," Aiken continues, "that William Blackstone had left the banks of the Cam for those of the Charles, to be alone with his books, and the Indians, and his own concepts of goodness and truth, and above all for his own invention of freedom and innocence—freedom from the enslaving bonds of society, and hierarchy in society?"[34] Cultural rebellion of this kind seems almost synonymous with a shift in racial allegiance, but this shift is attended by certain ironies. In Aiken's account, Blackstone repudiates English culture in two ways, by living alone and by joining the Indians, but Aiken perceives no contradiction here because he is quite capable of imagining life among the Indians as life alone. He considers the Indians as mere context or landscape, like the trees of the forest in which Blackstone hides. Aiken is similarly unaware of any irony in his speaking against slavery and hierarchy just after having enjoyed the word *dinge*. Identification with another race is Aiken's way of freeing himself from the authority of Europe, but his individual freedom requires not just the suppression but also the nullification of the other race. Though his fantasies take him out of the orbit of conventional white culture, they simultaneously show how deeply implicated in it he remains.

Years later, in a celebratory volume on Eliot, Aiken would repeat this account almost verbatim, recalling, "How delighted we were with the word 'dinge' for negro." He then continued, "This rich native creativeness was to be reflected, of course, in [Eliot's] poetry, notably in Prufrock. . . ."[35] The unintended irony speaks volumes about the dialect of modernism. By "rich native creativeness" Aiken means the language that refused to abide by English standards, the language that was to make the early works of modernism an affront to conventional linguistic propriety. Yet it is also true that Aiken's unfortunate taste in epithets is reflected in Eliot's work and in that of Ezra Pound. One might almost say that in this way Aiken has captured in a single word one of the most basic ironies of the modernism of Eliot and Pound, which used the language of race to strike down restrictive linguistic boundaries and social conventions and simultaneously to solidify boundaries whose loss both Eliot and Pound deeply feared. Dialect, which was to signify the subversive freedom of the modernist, also marks the language of modernism with this fear.

III

A good example of these ironies is one of the poems Eliot wrote in French in 1916, a poem so close to Deleuze and Guattari it might have been written to illustrate both the range and the limits of their theory. "Mélange Adultère de Tout" takes its title and its tone from Tristan Corbière and its conclusion from Rimbaud, perhaps from "Mauvais sang," a text quoted twice in *Anti-Oedipus*.[36] The basic theme is deracination, which the poem defines in three different but related ways. The speaker wanders fitfully from place to place, and the recurrent conceit on which the poem is built is that this movement through space means alteration of personality as well: "En Amérique, professeur; / En Angleterre, journaliste."[37] Finally, the poem expresses instability of place and identity by variations in language. Written in French about an American much like Eliot himself, the poem includes German terminology, American place-names, French slang, and sheer nonsense like "tra la la," to which Eliot gives the emphasis of rhyme. The poem rubs familiar names like "Omaha" up against the exotic: "De Damas jusqu'à Omaha." It holds "Emporheben" and "Tra la la" at an equal if opposite distance, defining its own idiom by the vast difference between them. The very idea of linguistic decorum, of a single standard of diction or tone, is mocked by the easy movement between these extremes. In short, the language of the poem is what Deleuze and Guattari call "a schizophrenic mélange, a Harlequin costume in which very different functions of language and distinct centers of power are played out, blurring what can be said and what can't be said. . . ."[38]

As such, Eliot's "Mélange" represents perfectly the process Deleuze and Guattari call *deterritorialization,* for the protagonist's movements from country to country unsettle identity and language at once, so that Omaha can seem as distant as Damascus and sound as foreign as *Emporheben*. The natural goal of this deterritorializing progress about the globe is, of course, Africa, and the final version of the harlequin costume is a savage skin robe: "Je célébrai mon jour de fête / Dans une oasis d'Afrique / Vetu d'une peau de giraffe" (*CPP*, p. 29). Thus Eliot's speaker becomes William Blackstone, albeit in Africa rather than the wilds of America. His restless linguistic peregrination comes to rest in the savage desert, where racial cross-dressing represents his independence and solitude.

Precisely because he is wayward and free, the speaker gravitates toward Africa, which is in this sense the place of placelessness. In the same way, the African role is the vacant center around which the other roles play, the empty epitome of the speaker's lack of consistent identity. Tending toward Africa frees the speaker from restrictive linguistic and psychological standards, liberating him into a state very much like the schizophrenia Deleuze and Guattari celebrate, but this tendency also leads toward the grave. The poem ends: "On montrera mon cénotaphe / Aux côtes brulantes de Mozambique" (*CPP*, p. 29).The cenotaph implies that even after death the body continues to perambulate the globe. The African oasis is itself this cenotaph, marking the speaker's habit of always being elsewhere, a quality this poem makes typically modern and necessarily African. An adulterate mixture, an international polyglot, the modernist as African is symbolized by his empty grave, which is the opposite of everything definite. The empty, silent grave is both the conclusion and a negative inversion of the rest of the poem. Its dazzling linguistic variety drains away to nothing down this hole in the sand, and mute absence alone remains where the speaker had once displayed his many colors.

The peculiar tone of the poem comes from the jaunty way its speaker accepts, even courts, this self-extinction. A number of modernist theories about impersonality, including Eliot's, could be illustrated by this poem, with its magic sleight of hand, its removal of veil after veil to reveal at last an empty tomb where the protagonist should be. But the African cenotaph also reveals a deep and very personal fear, the exact fear Eliot confessed to Read, that of a "small boy with a nigger drawl," who was not a southerner or a northerner or a midwesterner "and who so was never anything anywhere. . . ." Eliot felt himself to be just such an adulterate mixture, and his fear of that placelessness, that lack of identity, is expressed, in the letter to Read and in the poem, by the fantasy of being black.[39]

As suave as the poem is, the choice is really rather stark, for being black means to Eliot either to be everything or to be nothing, to have the freedom and the power of the cosmopolitan modernist or to be locked alone in utter darkness. Three years after writing "Mélange," Eliot sketched out the "impersonal theory of poetry" in a letter to Mary Hutchinson. It was a theory he seemed apt to illustrate himself until he confessed a nagging fear: "But I may simply prove to be a savage" (*EL*, p. 318).

Given the many obvious similarities between "Mélange" and *The Waste Land*, which is also a restless peregrination and a mélange, one might expect to find a tendency toward Africa in the later poem as well. Such a tendency did exist, most notoriously in the original epigraph from Conrad's *Heart of Darkness*, but all examples of it ended up, like that epigraph, on the cutting-room floor. The original opening scene, scribbled over in the preserved manuscripts, took a group of partygoers reeling around Boston to the combined tunes of a host of popular songs. For this scene Eliot toyed with lines from a number of songs suggesting minstrel shows. One example, "Meet me in the shadow of the watermelon vine / Eva Iva Uva Emmaline," combines, as Valerie Eliot's notes say, lines from "By the Watermelon Vine" and "My Evaline." The first of these was, as the title suggests, a "Negro song," and the second was part of a vaudeville extravaganza that included the traditional minstrel olio and at least one dialect number: "Rag-time Will Be Mah Finish." The other song line inserted into the draft at this point is from "The Cubanola Glide," a minor dance craze descended from the cake-walk.[40]

These lines are the first examples in the draft of the famous techniques of quotation and juxtaposition, and their provenance suggests an unexpected proto-type for Eliot's experiments: the minstrel show.[41] From the beginning, the min-strel show was an art of mélange, of star turns, mock oratory, sentimental songs, melodrama, ragtime, and slapstick comedy. Besides the obvious motive of con-trolling blacks through preemptive parody, there was also an element of what might be considered deterritorialization, as bits and pieces of conventional white culture were shifted into blackface. Famous American speeches, parts of operas, or scenes from Shakespeare might appear in or with a minstrel performance. *The Waste Land*'s famous "Shakespeherian Rag" is a vestige of this practice, to which, it seems, Eliot turned for inspiration at the very beginning of his poem.[42]

"Meet me in the shadow of the watermelon vine" is also, however, a blackface version of a line that had haunted Eliot for years with its primal complex of temptation and threat: "Come under the shadow of this grey rock." For *The Waste Land*, it seems, Eliot intended to take this line, the first line of "The Death of Saint Narcissus," dating from 1915, and merge it with the minstrel song "By the Watermelon Vine."[43] "Meet me in the shadow of the watermelon vine" combines sexual temptation, the allure of the sensual black stereotype with its promise of release from guilt and convention, and the dread of spiritual annihila-tion that appears in the final draft, where all that is found in the shadow under the rock is "fear in a handful of dust." Both possibilities, release and annihilation, seem associated in Eliot's mind with another race and what he fancies is the language of that race. When Clive Bell suggested that Eliot had assuaged his anxieties with "a black and grinning muse," he had little idea how inextricably Eliot had entwined the two.[44]

Though neither watermelon vine nor Saint Narcissus appears in the final draft of *The Waste Land*, the trembling ambivalence they reveal seems to lie at the very heart of the poem. Eliot was obsessed, as Christopher Ricks has said, with the quality of "between-ness," which appears everywhere in his work—from Tiresias, who throbs "between two lives," to the compound ghost of "Little Gidding," wandering "between two worlds."[45] One of the earliest versions of this key phrase appears in "Song. For the Opherion," a poem once destined for a place in *The Waste Land*. In this poem the speaker is torn "bleeding between two lives." The suspension is clearly psychological, but it is also geographical and quite possibly racial, as the speaker is paralyzed before a river that seems to incarnate "between-ness": "I saw across [an alien] river / the campfire[s] shake the spears."[46] The image seems to express a mingled attraction to and horror of that beyond the border, the alien and savage. The passage also serves as a complex bridge between several seemingly different parts of Eliot's work.

When Eliot published the poem by itself as "Song to the Opherian," he used the pseudonym Gus Krutzsch. This obscure figure turns out to be one of the revelers of the excised original opening of *The Waste Land*, a reference that seems to draw an explicit, if ironic, parallel between the devotees of the music hall and this explorer of the alien river.[47] "Krutzsch" also inescapably evokes "Kurtz" and thus the original epigraph to *The Waste Land:* "The horror, the horror." In the preserved typescript this torn confession from *Heart of Darkness* leads directly into the vaudeville opening, as if there were some connection between that night on the town and Kurtz's fall. In fact, Eliot preserved "Song to the Opherian" for a time by working it into the drafts of "The Hollow Men," a poem that begins with one of his most notorious pieces of dialect: "Mistah Kurtz—he dead."[48] Thus the alien river of "Song" is inextricably identified with the Congo, the shaken spears with those of the Africans who menace Marlow, and the torn confession of "between-ness" with Kurtz's confession of crossing into savagery.

"Song to the Opherian" reveals a fearsome aspect of the sort of racial crossing Eliot toys with in "Meet me in the shadow of the watermelon vine." To feel the pull of the spears, to be on both sides of the river, is, as the title of "The Hollow Men" suggests, to be null. Like Kurtz himself, who is described in *Heart of Darkness* as a pasteboard mask, a hollow figurine, Eliot's speaker suffers the utter loss of identity that comes from crossing the line that delimits the races. *The Waste Land* was informed from the beginning by the drastically different possibilities opened up by such a transgression: the modernist freedom afforded by the drastic mix of styles; the paralyzed horror, the loss of an identity once underwritten by secure racial boundaries. Even as he worked on *The Waste Land,* however, Eliot turned to something even more revealing.

IV

In 1922, while working on the drafts of *The Waste Land,* Pound responded to Eliot's scathing review of Gilbert Murray's Euripides by trying to find a livelier language into which to translate the classics: "I twisted, turned, tried every elipsis [*sic*] and illumination. I made the watchman talk nigger. . . ."[49] Though the attempt failed, it did produce one odd dividend, for in the same letter in which he confesses his own failure with Euripides, Pound responds to Eliot's news that he is now reading Aristophanes by saying, "Aristophanes probably depressing, and the native negro phoque melodies of Dixie more calculated to lift the ball-encumbered phallus of man. . . ."[50] This suggestion evidently helped Eliot to produce his "Fragments of an Aristophanic Melodrama," otherwise known as *Sweeney Agonistes,* which Eliot also titled in a late typescript "Fragment of a Comic Minstrelsy."[51] In this work Eliot accomplishes the combination of the Greek classics and black dialect that Pound had tried but failed to achieve.[52]

The result is an especially extreme example of deterritorialization, one that Barbara Everett suggests Eliot is able to manage because of his own "dislocation between two available traditions."[53] She argues, against the prevailing view that the protagonists are clearly English, that their speech is at least partially American. The title given to the first published version of "Fragment of an Agon" was "Wanna Go Home, Baby?"—which is, as Everett insists, self-consciously American.[54] And yet there is a good deal in the speech of Dusty and Doris that is equally self-conscious of being English. Dusty uses the phrase "ring up" (*CPP,* p. 76), which is, as Eliot observed rather pedantically in correcting James Joyce, not American but English.[55]

At one or two points in the play, the difference between American and English is thrown into relief by the characters themselves. Dusty says to Pereira over the phone, "Yes, this is Miss Dorrance's *flat*—" (*CPP,* p. 75). The italics apparently signify sarcastic emphasis on the English term for what Americans call an apartment. If Dusty is herself English, this would perhaps mean that Pereira is a foreigner trying unsuccessfully to appear English. If she is American, she may be mocking the English idiom. In either case, the italics focus suspicion on the most innocuous words, exposing cultural distinctions within them. The result is that the characters cannot be securely placed. They are deterritorialized as much as their speech and thus stand in living mockery of the idea of cultural homogeneity. In this way Eliot breaks down the distinction between what George Sampson was calling at this very moment "English for the English" and the English spoken by the rest of the world. It is perhaps effects like these that prompted Henry Louis

Gates, Jr., to hold up *Sweeney* as a positive model for black writers of the exploitation of slang.[56]

Yet this ability to cross back and forth over linguistic boundaries also appears thematically in the text as a debilitating alienation. When Doris reads the cards they predict "A quarrel. An estrangement. Separation of friends" (*CPP*, p. 76). Though the women look forward to a party and dream of weddings, the cards predict the very opposite: separation and finally death. This message of absence and alienation read in the cards governs the drama of the first of Eliot's two surviving fragments, "Fragment of a Prologue," which is almost completely concerned with arguments about home and homelessness. "Are you at home in London?" is the implicit question that underlies the conversation with Klipstein and Krumpacker, the Americans. "Sam of course is at *home* in London," says Krumpacker, emphasizing the word to underscore his own status as a mere visitor. But Sam is a former lieutenant of the Canadian Expeditionary Force and is referred to as "the Loot," a term that was famously associated with the North American Expeditionary Forces by the British, who pronounce the word *lefte*-nant.[57] Thus he is no more "at home" than anyone in this ominous fragment. It may be, then, that no one is truly at home, that everyone suffers from the estrangement and separation predicted by the cards, the awful end of which is foretold when Doris turns up the card that stands for the coffin.

The tension between Eliot's deliberate deterritorialization of language and the threat of estrangement is even greater in the second fragment, "Fragment of an Agon." The centerpiece of "Fragment of an Agon" is a distorted version of "Under the Bamboo Tree," written in 1902 by the team of Bob Cole, Rosamond Johnson, and James Weldon Johnson, with the last responsible for the lyrics.[58] There is a certain irony in Gates's feeling that *Sweeney* might serve as a model for black writers, since the tone of that work depends at least to some extent on Johnson, who was advising African-American writers to abandon dialect just as Eliot borrowed it from him.

Eliot's use of the song makes it clear why Johnson was wary. Though the song was received by the white press as "a pretty coon ballad," Johnson was proud of the way it departed from the conventions of the standard "coon song" of the time.[59] The dialect contained only minimal distortion and the situation actually suggested that a Zulu man and woman might feel for one another an emotion recognizable as human love and not the mere randiness of minstrel cliché. In *Sweeney*, however, Eliot imprisons the song once again in the minstrel tradition, arranging to have it sung by "SWARTS AS TAMBO. SNOW AS BONES" (*CPP*, p. 81). Tambo and Bones are the two players, one on tambourine, the other on bones, who take seats opposite one another during the main part of the minstrel show. These "end men" were usually more heavily made up than the other performers, used a more exaggerated dialect, and were called upon to perform more ludicrous and demeaning gyrations.[60] Eliot gives his end men names, Swarts and Snow, that suggest this sort of blackface comedy, and he stoops to the obnoxious device of predicting their arrival with the Knave of Spades (*CPP*, p. 77).

Eliot adapts Johnson's lyrics to put the whole play into a complex, ambivalent blackface:

> Under the bamboo
> Bamboo bamboo
> Under the bamboo tree
> Two live as one
> One live as two
> Two live as three
> Under the bam
> Under the boo
> Under the bamboo tree.
> (*CPP*, p. 81)

This lyric is the central example of the repetitive and disintegrative language of the whole fragment, the language spoken, for example, by Sweeney when he becomes a mock cannibal: "I'll convert *you*! / Into a stew. / A nice little, white little, missionary stew" (*CPP*, p. 80). Such language does fit the definition Gates gives of the African-American idiom, "paradigmatic (y-axis) substitutions determined by phonetic rather than semantic similarity."[61] In fact, Eliot pushes this exploitation of phonetic similarity so far as to eliminate the syntagmatic axis altogether, reducing the poem to a few chanted nonsense syllables. "Bam" and "Boo" finally become "Ha" and "hoo" to form the conclusion of the drama: "Hoo ha ha / Hoo ha ha / Hoo / Hoo / Hoo" (*CPP*, p. 85).

If this seems like mere fooling, it should be remembered how crucial a role is played in *The Waste Land* by the syllable "Da." The reduction of language to its barest elements, especially when these are associated with cultures outside of Europe, represents a radical challenge to the primacy of conventional European culture. As Deleuze and Guattari note, this is one of the common strategies of a minor literature, to produce a "language torn from sense, conquering sense, bringing about an active neutralization of sense," a language that puts the purely phatic, material sound in the way of the usual linguistic order.[62] These final lines also seem a perfect example of what Houston Baker, Jr., calls the "deformation of mastery," the purposeful exaggeration and display of what seem to the outsider inarticulate hoots.[63]

Like Conrad in his Malay novels, Eliot reduces the imperial language to babble, starting with nonstandard speakers but gradually extending their hoots to level the entire language. Thematically, however, "Fragment of an Agon" resembles other, more lurid aspects of Conrad's tropical works, with which Eliot was obsessed at this time. Beginning with Sweeney's offer to carry Doris off to a cannibal isle and ending with his odd exposition of the psychological state of a man who has killed a girl, the fragment illustrates a dual transgression. In "Eeldrop and Appleplex," Eliot says that the man who murders his mistress has "crossed the frontier."[64] *Sweeney* is the story of that crossing, which is both psychological and geographical. To commit murder is to cut oneself off in utter savagery, to cross the river to the cannibal isle. Crossing this boundary also dislocates language:

> I gotta use words when I talk to you
> But if you understand or if you don't
> That's nothing to me and nothing to you
> (*CPP*, p. 84)

Language becomes null, as if each word were a mere "hoo" or "ha." This nullity is the dead end of one kind of deterritorialization, as the reduction of language to its bare elements goes too far and results in dumb stupidity. Life on the cannibal isle is the epitome of this state since it is nothing but the universal negation of everything outside it:

> There's no telephones
> There's no gramophones
> There's no motor car . . .
> (*CPP*, p. 80)

Sweeney's chant piles up *nothing*s line after line until he reaches the climax: "Nothing at all but three things . . . Birth, and copulation, and death" (*CPP*, p. 80). As in "Mélange," the savage life is an utter absence, a death marked only by a cenotaph.

Thus *Sweeney* does, as Gates suggests, present a powerful model of the deployment of slang against the standard language. Eliot is able to use his anomalous position, the position that seems to have caused him such anguish, as a vantage point from which to lever one kind of language against another and in so doing move all language a few inches off its pedestal. Eliot's fear that he may sound black appears in this poem as the assumption of a black voice to remake the English language. Yet that fear also appears in itself when Eliot remakes Johnson's song to force it back into minstrel stereotypes. This seems the reaction of a writer for whom conventional racial boundaries were necessary to avoid moral chaos and disintegration. In *Sweeney*, as in so much of the work of this period, blackness is both freedom and servitude, opportunity and obstruction, variety and a blank absence.

Eliot published the two fragments of his Aristophanic melodrama in 1926–27, about a year before sending the letter to Read about his estranging childhood. Of course, Eliot was about to resolve these doubts about his proper place in the world by becoming English and Anglican. The uneasiness of his letter stands in marked contrast to the bluff confidence with which he delivered, only a year later, his famous tripartite self-definition: "classicist in literature, royalist in politics, and anglo-catholic in religion." This seems to leave no room for ambiguity, and, in fact, Eliot says in the preface that contains this formula that he gives it "to refute any accusation of playing 'possum."[65] Does this signify Eliot's withdrawal from the modernist project, from subversive teamwork with Pound? Does it mean that Eliot is attempting to put aside with his modernism the black role so closely identified with it? If so, it is also significant that even in defining himself as English, Eliot has recourse to an American idiom, and there certainly seems to be a private joke here, since Eliot *was* Possum and continued to be Possum even as he became a classicist, a royalist, and an Anglo-Catholic.

Even the famously hollow voice retained some evidence of the original Possum.[66] Despite Eliot's conviction that he had lost his St. Louis drawl in Boston, Edward Brathwaite claimed that "in that dry deadpan delivery, the riddims of St. Louis (though we didn't know the source then) were stark and clear for those of us who at the same time were listening to the dislocations of Bird, Dizzy and Klook." According to Brathwaite, Eliot's voice "subverted the Establishment" and "made the breakthrough" for Caribbean Anglophone poets like himself who were moving from "standard English to nation language."[67] Is there some cunning in history after all that the voice that so embarrassed Eliot at Harvard should return, despite all his efforts, to inspire a new generation of poets to use their own idiom against standardization? Brathwaite's testimony suggests that even after Eliot thought he had put dialect aside the racial irony of modernism had another turn left in it, as if, having once let dialect in, Eliot could not control its effects or the extent of its influence.

V

Oblivious to what remained of Eliot's slyness, Pound continued to use the old nicknames to goad his friend, as if to shame him into renewed insurgency. In Pound's view, the Eliot of the *Criterion* had ceased to be the Possum he knew and had become a "Marse Supial" whose deadness was no longer feigned:

> Sez the Maltese dawg to the Siam cat
> "Whaaar'z ole Parson Possum at?"
> Sez the Siam cat to the Maltese dawg
> "Dahr he sets lak a bump-onna-log."
> (*PL*, p. 307)

The dialect signifies that, despite what has happened to Eliot, Pound remains the Rabbit, and thus it becomes thicker and more impenetrable as his ire against Eliot's celebrity and respectability rises. The pain behind the Rabbit role exploded more than once, for example when Eliot asked Pound to contribute to the *Criterion* something on Robert Bridges: "Rabbit Britches indeed!!! Whaaar he git the plagiarization of Babbitt [sic] aza name anyhow? . . . All the pseudo-rabbits: Rabbit Brooke, Rabbit Britches. Wotter hell. Your own hare or a wig, sir???" (*PL*, p. 280). The pseudorabbits are at least in part stand-ins for the pseudopossum T. S. Eliot, so emasculated by popular success that he would divert Pound from the real business of making a literary revolution to praise dead laureates. The real Rabbit remains outside convention, exiled from success, raw, crude, and therefore authentic.

There is more to this opposition between Brer Rabbit and Robert Bridges, however, than Pound's juvenile desire to show the hair on his chest. As the real Brer Rabbit, Pound takes his challenge into the heart of Eliot's domain, into the *Criterion*, into Faber, and into the culture Eliot was defining through these publishing outlets. "An how you gwine ter keep deh Possum in his feedbox," he taunted F. V. Morley of Faber, "when I brings in deh Chinas and blackmen?? He won't laaak fer to see no Chinas and blackmen in a bukk about Kulchur. Dat being jess his lowdown Unitarian iggurunce" (*PL*, p. 288). For all its crudeness, both as masquerade and as anthropology, this challenge does represent a significant alternative to the exclusive notion of culture that Eliot was promulgating at this time. In Pound's view the culture Eliot was trying to define in purely English terms had long since ceased to be either the creation or the property of the English. His "bringing in" of China and Africa was simply the last in a long series of what he called "exotic injections": "Rossetti brought in the Italian primitives; Fitzgerald made the only good poem of the time that has gone to the people; it is called, and is to a great extent, a translation or mistranslation. . . . Morris translated sagas. . . ." The transatlantic modernism that Pound himself had done so much to advance was merely the last of these infusions:

> [T]he Irish took over the business for a few years; Henry James led, or rather preceded, the novelists, and then the Britons resigned *en bloc;* the language is now in the keeping of the Irish (Yeats and Joyce); apart from Yeats, since the death of Hardy, poetry is being written by Americans. All the developments in English verse since 1910 are due almost wholly to Americans. In fact, there is no longer any reason to call it English verse, and there is no present reason to think of England at all.[68]

So much for the laureate.

There is obviously a significant gulf here between the conception of English that Bridges had been pushing through the SPE and Pound's idea that the language was "in the keeping of the Irish" and the Americans, a gulf that Pound purposely widens by writing in the most extreme dialect he knows. Where Bridges was trying to purify English, especially of those influences it might pick up from Americans or other far-flung speakers, Pound maintained that it was the "bringing in" that kept the language alive: "It has taken in lashin's of Greek, swallowed mediaeval French, while keeping its Anglo-Saxon basis. It then petrified in the tight little island. . . . Throughout all history and despite all academies, living language has been inclusive and not exclusive" (*PL*, p. 347). Pound's letters, with their lashings of black dialect, cockney slang, Greek, Latin, Chinese, and demotic Ezraese, are a model of this inclusivity, as was his poetry, which was scooping up and spilling out the same collection of languages.

Thus Brer Rabbit becomes a representative, not just of transatlantic modernism but also of a whole countertradition of "exotic injections" from Swinburne's Greek to the "Japerican" that Pound foresees arising from commerce between Japan and America (*PL*, p. 347). The dialect spoken by that Rabbit is the macaronic result of all these infusions, and its miscellaneous nature seems almost calculated to affront the other Rabbit, the academic imposter, Rabbit Britches. By the time he appears in the *Pisan Cantos*, Bridges has become a quick index of arthritic diction—"'forloyn' said Mr Bridges (Robert) / 'we'll get 'em all back' / meaning archaic words" (80/507)—as his colleague Henry Newbolt had become a model of syntax lamed by rhyme: "'He stood' wrote Mr Newbolt, later Sir Henry / 'the door behind' and now they complain of cummings" (80/507).[69]

However, the telegraphese of the *Cantos* obscures the rather significant fact that the archaic words welcomed by Bridges were in Pound's own poetry. Reading *Personae* and *Exultations*, Bridges had been thrilled by the reappearance in a young man's verse of what Pound called "archaic dialect" (*PL*, p. 179). In fact, it was part of SPE dogma that archaic terms like "teen," "dole," "meed," etcetera, were heartier and pithier than contemporary verbiage and therefore deserved preservation.[70] Thus Bridges's exultant "we'll get 'em all back" must have sprung from the hope that younger poets like Pound would refresh contemporary speech with this "archaic dialect." This hope was not entirely delusory. Not only did Pound abundantly use this old dialect, but he also followed other SPE directives. Early in the 1920s he formulated a short list of significant moments in his literary development, one he repeated virtually without change for the next forty years. On this list appeared Robert Bridges's "caution against homopnones [*sic*]" (*PL*, p. 178).[71] The crusade against homophones was one of Bridges's earliest and most durable hobbyhorses, one that Robert Graves singled out for special ridicule, but it apparently struck a chord with Pound, whose opinions about diction did fall into the SPE ideology that there should be as many distinct, specific words as possible.[72] At this early stage in his career, Pound looked like anything but an insurrectionary opponent of the SPE. Thus Bridges might be forgiven for having expected that *this* young poet, at least, would help bring the ideals of the SPE to fruition in verse.

In fact, the person Pound later referred to as his first literary friend in London, Frederic Manning, was an early member of the SPE, along with Henry Newbolt, whom Pound may have met at the Poet's Club as early as 1909.[73] In 1914, when the original SPE committee was begun, Pound reported breathlessly to his fiancée that he was to read at the Poetry Bookshop with Newbolt and later meet with Bridges.[74] Though Pound later complained about "the stilted language that then passed for 'good English' in the arthritic milieu that held control of the respected British critical circles, Newbolt, the backwash of Lionel Johnson, Fred Manning, the Quarterlies and the rest of 'em," he still included Newbolt among the blessed, and not among the blasted, in *Blast*.[75] Newbolt repaid the compliment by including Pound in his anthology *New Paths on Helicon*, which was forward-looking enough to include Eliot, Sitwell, and Lawrence as well.[76]

Like Bridges, Newbolt might have thought of Pound as the most promising of the lot, since his most popular early effort, "The Ballad of the Goodly Fere," reads at times like a virtual mimicry of Newbolt's first great success, "Drake's Drum." Newbolt's rough-hewn narrator proclaims his faith in the return of Sir Francis Drake in language that suggests he has never left: "Slung atween the round shot, listenin' for the drum, / An' dreamin' arl the time o' Plymouth Hoe." Pound's equally salty narrator accomplishes the same feat where Christ himself is concerned: "I ha' seen him drive a hundred men / Wi' a bundle o' cords swung free."[77] The resemblance suggests that dialect might not mark the dividing line between transatlantic modernism and the standardizing movement of men like Bridges and Newbolt at all but might rather constitute a link between them. Archaic diction and dialect usages appealed to standardizers like Bridges and Newbolt because they seemed to inject vigor into the language, which is what Pound thought he was doing in "The Ballad of the Goodly Fere." The crucial difference, of course, is that Pound did not stop at English dialects but welcomed American varieties and then global versions of English as well. But the convergence of his career and interests with those of Bridges and Newbolt exposes a conservative substrate within the insurrectionary shell of the Brer Rabbit pose, a substrate that was to rise to the surface as Pound grew older.

VI

In 1934 Pound lashed out against "the Afro-American intelligentzia" for its supposed ignorance of Leo Frobenius, "who has shown their race its true charter of nobility and who has dug out of Africa tradition overlaid on tradition to set against the traditions of Europe and Asia."[78] Actually, Claude McKay had mentioned Frobenius in print as early as 1922, and Léopold Sédar Senghor and Aimé Césaire were about to discover Frobenius for themselves, without any help from Pound.[79] Pound himself became more and more entoiled in Frobenius's African researches, which appealed precisely because they offered a definition of tradition and of culture quite different from the one that prevailed in the *Criterion*. In Frobenius's version, Africa possessed the power of tradition, since its culture seemed both cohesive and very old, and the charm of insurrection, since that tradition seemed incompatible with the one in place in Europe. Thus Pound's references to Frobenius could be solemnly quasi-religious or insultingly rude, as in the letters threatening to sneak "deh Chinas and blackmen" into the *Criterion*.

It is no wonder, then, that Pound came to rely heavily on this version of Africa as he languished in the Disciplinary Training Center at Pisa. On the one hand, it promised a tradition "indestructible" to replace that destroyed with the fall of Fascist Italy; on the other hand, it functioned as a symbol of resistance to the authorities, military and cultural, then holding Pound in jail. It is no accident that

Pound's black guards and fellow prisoners become associated with Frobenius's Africa when they are committing acts of insubordination:

> niggers scaling the obstacle fence
> > in the middle distance
> and Mr Edwards superb green and brown
> > in Ward No 4 a jacent benignity,
> of the Baluba mask: "doan you tell no one
> > I made you that table"
> . . . the greatest is charity
> to be found among those who have not observed
> > regulations
> > > (74/434)

Mr. Edwards, whose face supposedly resembles one of the African masks collected by Frobenius, becomes the living symbol of this wonderful tradition that does not observe regulations, a tradition inimical to European culture but apparently native to Africa for centuries:

> What counts is the cultural level,
> > thank Benin for this table ex packing box
> > "doan yu tell no one I made it"
> > > from a mask as fine as any in Frankfurt
> "It'll get you offn th' groun"
> > > (80/518–519)

Thus, despite the ignorance of the African-American intelligentsia about Frobenius, the American blacks of the DTC are living representatives of the African tradition Pound hoped to set against the traditions of Europe. Their speech is a constant affront to and correction of European cultural presumption:

> Criminals have no intellectual interests?
> "Hey, Snag, wot are the books ov th' bibl'"
> "name 'em, etc.
> "Latin? I studied latin."
> > said the nigger murderer to his cage-mate
> (cdn't be sure which of the two was speaking)
> "c'mon, small fry," sd/ the smaller black lad
> > to the larger.
> "Just playin'"
> > > (75/454–55)

Set this, as we are clearly meant to do, against the official guardians of Latin:

> But on the other hand the President of Magdalen
> (rhyming dawdlin') said there were
> too many words in "The Hound of Heaven"
> > a moddddun opohem he had read . . .
> > > (74/445)

Given a choice between the drawling intellectual laziness of the don and the peppery give-and-take of the black prisoners, it would not be hard for any reader to decide in favor of the latter.

All of these nonstandard voices that stream through the *Pisan Cantos*—American, Irish, Catalan, Romagnese, "Japanerican"—might be summed up in the African chant that celebrates Frobenius's indestructible city:

> 4 times was the city rebuilded, Hooo Fasa
> Gassir, Hooo Fasa dell' Italia tradita
> now in the mind indestructible, Gassir, Hoooo Fasa . . .
> (74/430)

Some of the mystery of these lines can be dispelled by a reading of Frobenius's *African Genesis*, but surely much of their impact is thereby lost. The repeated "Hoooo" is meant to be mystifying, challenging, alien. It is Pound's hoot against the demands of linguistic and cultural conformity, his version of the "Hoo ha ha" at the climax of *Sweeney Agonistes*. It pushes linguistic nonconformity so far as to exceed sense altogether, and it functions rather as a mask functions, as display and not as communication. As one of the most extreme of the "exotic injections" Pound administered to the language, it can stand for all the rest, even the non-standard noises Pound himself made as a crude American knocking on the door of English literary society.

At the same time, however, black speech can represent the most reactionary impulses in these very reactionary cantos. When Pound invokes Frobenius in Canto 80, it is to introduce a nostalgic scene from his childhood:

> Hier wohnt the tradition, as per Whitman in Camden
> and an engraving 596 Lexington Ave.,
> 24 E. 47th,
> with Jim at the checquer board by the banana cage
>
> "Funny looking wood, James," said Aunt F.
> "it looks as if it had already been burnt"
> [Windsor fire]
> "Part o deh roof ma'am."
> (80/508)

The memory of "playing checquers with black Jim" (74/447) at his Uncle Ezra Weston's in New York somehow becomes wrapped up with a whole definition of "refinement, pride of tradition" (74/447), which is weirdly double, extending back on one side through Jim to the culture Frobenius discovered in Africa and on the other side to Pound's own Weston forebears.

Pound had been meditating on this scene for some years until it had become a little cinematic vignette of powerful significance:

> Lookin' back and rememberin' my far distant childhood on the corner of 47th
> and Madison Avenue . . . right where my Great Uncle used to keep his

> bunch of bananas, and I used to play checquers with him; my old Great Aunt's black man of general all work, or rather any work, some work, that he used to dodge to play checquers on top of the apple barrel . . . An' yaller Martha. She used to take snuff. That's a long time before the great night life of Harlem.

The significance of this scene of racial cooperation, which Pound drops into one of his anti-Semitic radio speeches, is that it occurs "before the invasion,"[80] before some mythical moment in Pound's warped understanding of history at which time the Jews arrive to disrupt the smooth functioning of American life.

In other words, these black characters and voices function exactly as they did in the most reactionary examples of the dialect tradition to represent a mythical, "lost" stability in American culture. Pound himself calls the servants "the remains of the old South" (74/447), which was in one sense literally true because they had been acquired during his uncle's travels behind enemy lines during the Civil War. But it is true in a more extended sense as well, since the servants represent a way of life founded on secure racial and cultural boundaries. Blacks who had lived in plantation society were, J. J. Wilhelm reports, far more acceptable to the Westons than the European immigrants of the 1880s and 1890s "because they were menials, trained to keep their place."[81] In fact, such black menials are evoked so as to provide proper models for relationships between races, cultures, and creeds, which is why Pound harks back to his experiences with them when he laments the supposed influence of the Jews. What he does here is in a sense to reverse the process on which *The Jazz Singer* is based, using a carefully chosen black model to block Jewish entry into and influence in American life. The "tradition" evoked by these black voices is the polar opposite of the modern world of jazz with its improvisation and mobility: it is rural, repressive, stratified, and static.

The dialect Pound assumes in order to evoke this tradition is of the sort dear to the heart of the SPE, only with black servants playing the role assigned to rough but servile sailors in Newbolt's poetry. Thus Newbolt himself, who appears trailing clouds of mockery in Canto 80, actually winds up the catalogue of "Lordly men . . . to earth o'ergiven" in Canto 74: "and Newbolt who looked twice bathed / . . . to earth o'ergiven" (74/433). Like Bridges, Newbolt is alternately mocked and installed in one of Pound's minipantheons, along with Ford, Yeats, and Joyce. The inconsistency is telling, since it represents a deeper vacillation in Pound's attitude toward the language, which overlapped the efforts of Bridges and Newbolt even as it posed an exaggerated and blustery challenge to them.

There is an equally telling vacillation in the way race works in this relationship. In Canto 80 Pound's mockery of Newbolt and Bridges follows hard on his vignette about black Jim, as if Jim's dialect had brought to mind the tangled, academic jargon of the standardizers. In Canto 74, however, Newbolt is swept up in Pound's retrospective embrace of the lordly men, who are called "the companions," and at the same time Mr. Edwards of the Baluba mask becomes one of the *"comes miseriae"* (74/436). The two groups of *comites* are never explicitly connected, and yet both seem to crowd round in comfort, as if having much in common with Pound they also had something in common with one another. Yet there still seems a world of difference between the "twice washed" Newbolt and his friend "Maurie [Hewlett] who wrote historical novels" and the black soldiers and prisoners whose company Pound values because they say things like "fer a bag o' Dukes" and "c'mon small fry" (74/436).

Finally, however, in the extremity of the death camp, such differences disappear, subsumed within the one grand opposition that gave Pound's mind whatever structure it had at this time: "authenticities disputed by parasites" (74/448). At this late stage in his life, Pound believes that the difference between the authentic and the parasitic can actually be heard, so that Bridges's avid "we'll get 'em all back" will chime somehow with "c'mon small fry" and strike dissonant sparks off "Napoleon wath a goodth man, it took uth / 20 yearth to crwuth him" (78/477). The *Pisan Cantos* are profoundly schizoid, echoing with voices as they do, and it would be easy to find in Deleuze and Guattari the means of glorifying their disorder. They certainly let onto the page, as into the psyche of their author, more different dialects and idiolects than any other poem ever printed, approaching at times the invented languages of Cendrars and dadaists like Huelsenbeck, the *Klanggedichtung* of Hugo Ball, or the secret speech of Stefan George.[82] Unlike the dadaists, however, Pound folds all his languages back into an "authenticity" all-encompassing enough to include even Bridges and Newbolt. The program of Cendrars, like that of Stein, was to unseat language, to destroy its privileges, but Pound, for all his attacks, could not shake an essentially conservative desire to make language real again.

Thus Brer Rabbit makes his final appearance in the work Pound turned to immediately after the *Pisan Cantos*, the Confucian Odes. In what is either an act of great cultural daring or a clumsy and insensitive mistake, Pound uses black dialect for a few of the folksier odes:

> Yalla' bird, you stay outa dem oaks,
> Yalla' bird, let them crawps alone,
> I just can't live with these here folks,
>   I gotta go home and I want to git goin'
>   To whaar my dad's folks still is a-growin'.[83]

Donald Davie is so much taken with the "risks, and perhaps the liberties" that Pound takes in such translations that he begins *The Poet as Sculptor* with an extended discussion of the odes, and L. S. Dembo begins his defense of the poems by citing the first in which Pound uses black dialect.[84] At their best, as these critics insist, the odes deftly balance word against word, cadence against cadence, and manage their jumble of historical and racial dialects in such a way as to force the reader to contemplate a language usually taken for granted.

And yet there must be some connection between the dialect Pound chooses for ode number 16 and its message of eternal servility:

> Don't chop that pear tree,
> Don't spoil that shade;
>
> Thaar's where old Marse Shao used to sit,
> Lord, how I wish he was judgin' yet. [85]

Here the oldest cliché of the dialect tradition, the black freedman's nostalgia for the plantation, is deployed in a setting that suggests it is a universal and eternal human impulse. And what Dembo calls "living dialect" is in fact the chosen language for a condition that is the very opposite of life, since it foreswears change. Brer Rabbit still stands for something so frisky it can never be captured:

> Ole Brer Rabbit watchin' his feet
> Rabbit net's got the pheasant beat . . .[86]

But this mood is rare, and it sorts poorly with the other black voice that wants only preservation and protection.

Together, the two voices define the limits of the Brer Rabbit persona that Pound had adopted nearly thirty years before. Far more overtly than Conrad or Stein, Pound deploys dialect against the standard language to make way for an entirely new literature. At times it seems that an entire cultural program might follow from the unlikely example of *Uncle Remus*, a program that would demolish the authority of the European languages and even of the Roman alphabet. In this way Pound would carry the social and cultural dislocations of the modern period, dislocations of which he felt himself to be the deracinated product, to their logical conclusion in a new language. But dialect was also a way for Pound, as for Eliot, to guard himself against the implications of those vast cultural changes, an involved defense against the very dislocations of language that give rise to his most challenging work. These two writers therefore carried the radical challenge to the standard language and literature farther than Conrad and Stein, or at the very least they made it much more explicit, but at the same time they showed how easily any challenge using a racial masquerade might turn back and neutralize itself.

5

Quashie to Buccra:
The Linguistic Expatriation of Claude McKay

I

When Claude McKay visited England in 1919, he was pleased to find on the London stage four plays by George Bernard Shaw, a writer he had admired since his school days in Jamaica. McKay attended all four and even met Shaw himself, who rather stunned his young disciple by suggesting he might be better off as a boxer than as a poet (*ALWH*, pp. 60, 62). This obtuseness might have cast an ironic light on one of the plays McKay had just seen, namely, *Pygmalion*, which Shaw was even then proclaiming as a manifesto of equal access to the King's English and which, for that reason, had special relevance to McKay. As a well-spoken young Jamaican, McKay might have seemed to Shaw a signal example of those "many thousands of men and women who have sloughed off their native dialects and acquired a new tongue." McKay even had his own Henry Higgins in the person of Walter Jekyll, a wealthy Englishman long resident in Jamaica. Yet he was a Higgins with a significant difference, for McKay came to him already speaking and writing perfect standard English, which Jekyll urged him to drop, at least on paper, in favor of the Jamaican dialect. In these hands, Eliza Doolittle might have ended up writing something like "Song of the Shirt," and yet it is doubtful whether she would have been any happier than she was under Higgins's tutelage. For it is one of the central ironies of McKay's career that Jekyll's patronage of dialect, and other patronage like it, did not lessen the pressure of standardization but doubled it.

Growing up in Jamaica, McKay was schooled in what he once called "my native adopted language"[1] according to a system strongly influenced by the standardization movement. What he mainly remembered of it as an adult was a list of "expressions which we were told not to use," a list heavy on Americanisms (*GHJ*, pp. 16–17). To be a good "black Briton" one had to avoid a long list of seemingly trivial mistakes and to be particularly careful about words like *schedule* because American pronunciation was associated with young upstarts who had gone off to work on the Panama Canal and had "come back ruder" (*BB*, p. 35). McKay once claimed, "I was brought up to use the same language to a white person as a colored,"[2] but that language could only have been standard English because "the common Negro dialect . . . was regarded as the mark of an inferior person" (*GHJ*, p. 113).[3]

In this atmosphere Walter Jekyll must have seemed eccentric indeed. A lapsed clergyman with more than sufficient financial independence, Jekyll had come to Jamaica to escape the processes of modernization that, in his view, were rapidly ruining the rest of the world.[4] Even in England, the language and lore of the peasantry had seemed to him a bulwark against such change, and he developed a taste for choice bits of country dialect,[5] a taste his sister Gertrude was later to share with Logan Pearsall Smith of the Society for Pure English.[6] "The peasants were his hobby," as the narrator of *Banana Bottom* puts it, speaking of Squire Gensir, whose character was based on Jekyll. "Any new turn of speech, any original manner of turning English to fit peasant ways of thinking and speaking, could make him as happy as a child" (*BB*, p. 71).

Wayne Cooper draws a telling comparison between this proclivity and the interest that "southern country gentlemen of the United States in the same period" sometimes took in "their black agricultural laborers."[7] Jekyll's interest, in fact, exactly parallels that of aristocratic southerners like Irwin Russell and Thomas Nelson Page, who gathered dialect as an imaginative defense against the demise of plantation life. When Jekyll published his collection of stories about Anancy, the African trickster figure whose personality overlaps that of Brer Rabbit, the resemblance was so obvious that he was credited with "doing for Jamaica what Mr. Chandler Harris, *e.g.* has done for Georgia."[8] In both cases, however, the conservative bias of the very act of preservation, which was underscored by the antimodern romanticism they brought to collecting, ran against the rebellious content of the Anancy/Brer Rabbit stories to produce a very equivocal combination. It was this equivocation, more than anything, that Jekyll bequeathed to Claude McKay.

When they met, Jekyll had just published *Jamaican Song and Story* but was still collecting, and he clearly looked on McKay as a worthy specimen. He laughed at the poems McKay had written in standard English but praised his single offering in dialect, saying "[T]his is the real thing. The Jamaican dialect has never been put into literary form except in my Annancy stories. Now is your chance as a native boy [to] put the Jamaica dialect into literary language" (*GHJ*, pp. 66–67). McKay was understandably bewildered, "because to us who were getting an education in the English schools the Jamaican dialect was considered a vulgar tongue. . . . All cultivated people spoke English, straight English" (*GHJ*, p. 67). But Jekyll prevailed, not just from sheer authority but also because McKay enjoyed writing in dialect and found a ready audience for it among his friends. In 1912 McKay published two volumes, *Songs of Jamaica* and *Constab Ballads*, that gained him widespread praise as the first educated black West Indian to bring the dialect into English verse.[9]

At the age of twenty-two McKay was a great success, but the irony of this achievement stayed with him a good deal longer than any of its rewards. The irony emerges in *Banana Bottom,* McKay's last significant literary work and one he conceived as a tribute to Jekyll. This novel doubles *Pygmalion,* as it were, pitting Mrs. Craig, who wants to cultivate young Bita Plant until "she would be English trained and appearing in everything but the colour of her skin" (*BB,* p. 31), against Squire Gensir, who is Jekyll in a very light disguise.[10] Gensir chastizes Bita for turning against Jamaican culture: "Obeah is a part of your folklore, like your Anancy tales and your digging jammas. And your folklore is the spiritual link between you and your ancestral origin. You ought to learn to appreciate it as I do mine" (*BB,* p. 125). This argument forms the basis of the novel, as Bita wavers between dialect, tea meetings, obeah, and sex, on the one hand, and standard English, hymn singing, Scotch Presbyterianism, and loveless marriage on the other.

This may seem a wildly unequal match, and yet there is some reason to wonder if there are really two sides at all. It is only because the Squire is willing to accompany her, and thus to shield her with his aristocratic probity, that Bita has the courage to attend a tea meeting, a sort of Jamaican cakewalk much disdained by the Craigs, and the Squire remains at her side as she steps deeper and deeper into the forbidden waters of Jamaican folk life. But Bita's trust in the Squire, which is what gives her both the courage and the social sanction to keep stepping, is founded on solidly English values. She is willing to listen to him going on about obeah because he is the friend of the son of her favorite English poet, a distant connection but strong enough nonetheless to collect "a romantic cloud" around him (*BB,* p. 127). McKay can never have been quite this starry-eyed himself, and yet he too needed to transfer the glory of England to the dialect of Jamaica before he could appreciate it: "A short while before I never thought that any beauty could be found in the Jamaica dialect. Now this Englishman had discovered beauty and I too could see where my poems were beautiful" (*GHJ,* p. 69). Dialect, tea meetings, perhaps even obeah and sex, become beautiful only when touched by the wand of English approval. Thus the essential contest of *Banana Bottom* is not really between Bita and the Craigs, Jamaica and England, but between the Craigs and Squire Gensir, England and England's Jamaica.

It was a contest that Jekyll had outlined for McKay back in 1912—the aristocracy and the peasantry in league against the pinched and pinching middle class.[11] There were certain obvious attractions for McKay in an alliance with an aristocrat, and yet it dropped him into a trap from which he was never quite to emerge, a trap formed of the false dichotomy between rigid, life-denying Scotch Presbyterianism and free, life-affirming Jamaican paganism. This dichotomy was a trap because both sides were actually defined by the English, and it was false because it posed England as culture against Jamaica as nature. Jekyll needed such a contrast as protection against the ills of an overly developed civilization, but for a Jamaican poet anxious to redeem a culture from colonialism the primitive stereotype proved crippling.

Several commentators have noticed how McKay tended to replicate his relationship with Jekyll, first with Frank Harris and then with Max Eastman and Joel Spingarn in America, and with C. K. Ogden in England.[12] Such patrons were certainly necessary to the practical process of publication: Spingarn arranged for McKay's first magazine publication in America and for the publication of *Harlem Shadows* in 1922; Eastman gave McKay an outlet at the *Liberator;* and Ogden published verses in the *Cambridge Magazine* and arranged for the publication of *Spring in New Hampshire* in 1920.[13] All this took place before white interest in Harlem created widespread opportunities for black writers. But the price tag was often displayed quite openly in the form of the patron's introduction, which typically validated the author in terms that were at best condescending and stereotypical. Jekyll's preface to *Songs of Jamaica*, for example, ended by informing his readers that "they have here the thoughts and feelings of a Jamaican peasant of pure black blood" (*SJ*, p. 9). Eastman repeated this unnecessary and inaccurate validation in the introduction to *Harlem Shadows* (*HS*, p. ix) and, many years later, in the introduction to *Selected Poems*.[14] I. A. Richards did the same in the preface that Ogden asked him to write for *Spring in New Hampshire*, beginning with the declaration that "Claude McKay is a pure-blooded Negro."[15]

In Jamaica such a statement might have signified McKay's own pride at *not* belonging to the mulatto elite, but in the United States and England it simply registered astonishment that poetry could be produced where white ancestry did not exist. Thus the other stereotypical piece of misinformation that appears and reappears in these introductions is that McKay's poems are "the first significant expression of [his] race in poetry" (*HS*, p. ix).[16] McKay was disgusted at what he called the "flippant note" of astonishment "at the idea of a Negro writing poetry" (*ALWH*, p. 88), but he could not prevent even his closest admirers from striking that note again and again. He was introduced over and over as a phenomenon, a human oxymoron, bringing raw nature into the cultured realm of poetry. It put him in an impossible bind, for the more conventional his poetry was the more astonishment it raised, thus confirming the notion that, under it all, he was still some sort of savage.

If McKay tried to wriggle out of this trap, his credentials were simply withdrawn. You are "not a real Negro," Robert Minor informed him when he confessed to liking E. E. Cummings. "He thought of a Negro," McKay mused later, "as of a rugged tree in the forest" (*ALWH*, p. 103). In its crudity Minor's outburst reveals the perverse illogic of the trap that McKay was confined in. It was vitally necessary to his white patrons and readers that he be "real"—recall Jekyll's commendation of his one dialect poem as "the real thing"—so that he could symbolize a nature that had escaped from the culture they found stifling. And yet that nature could only be defined and validated by white authority itself, which rigidly enforced its own standards of the natural as if sublimely unaware of the contradiction.

Is it any wonder, then, that each of McKay's major changes in literary direction coincided with a change of place and thus of patron? He wrote no dialect poetry after leaving Jamaica and Jekyll, no significant poetry at all after leaving the United States and Eastman. He did not return to the United States from Europe and Africa until his career as a writer of fiction was thoroughly played out. There were certainly practical reasons for some of these changes, but the last, at least, was impractical and even inexplicable. The fact that McKay is now so hard to place—novelist or poet? Jamaican or American? Harlem Renaissance or Lost Generation?—may be due to the fact that he was so firmly placed every time he settled. Perhaps the very role that signified escape for Walter Jekyll and, in another place and time, for T. S. Eliot and Ezra Pound was one that McKay could never quite escape *from*.

In this sense McKay's situation exemplifies a difficulty facing all colonial writers in the European languages. Ever since Sartre's 1948 preface to the negritude poets, European theory has tended to focus on the threat of standardization: "[S]ince words are ideas, when the Negro declares in French that he rejects French culture, he accepts with one hand what he rejects with the other. . . ." The answer to this intimate colonization is what Sartre calls the "auto-destruction of language," a "holocaust of words" caused by linguistic frustration. This holocaust razes the language to the ground, reduces its signifying powers to nothing, and in so doing passes "judgment on the foolish" and repressive "business of naming things."[17] Sartre's formulation is an obvious forebear of Deleuze and Guattari's notion of a minor literature that devours the significations of a major language. It stands behind more recent theories as well, particularly those that place great hope in creolization as resistance to the domination of a centralizing standard.[18]

McKay's situation, however, exposes the fact that very often the creole has been defined by the same forces that define the standard. As McKay himself put it in 1921, it is the blackface "impersonators" and "imitators" who set "the current standards" for "Negro art" (*PCM*, p. 63). Thus the nonstandard is maintained as a carefully limited escape from the standard, a "natural" alternative to the rigid conventions of culture. Sartre remains blind to this stereotype because he is himself one of its chief perpetrators: "Negritude is the far-away tam-tam in the streets of Dakar at night; voo-doo shouts from some Haitian cellar window, sliding along level with the roadway; the Congolese mask. . . ."[19] Deleuze and Guattari cannot truly examine the limitations of their theory of a minor literature because their defining examples—Rimbaud, Artaud, Nijinsky—are among the impersonators McKay accused. For Deleuze and Guattari, Nijinsky's boast—"I am a red Indian. I am a Negro. I am a Chinaman. I am a Japanese. I am a foreigner, a stranger"—is a complex act of disaffiliation, and Rimbaud's metaphor—"I am a beast, a Negro"—a key to his deterritorialization.[20] For McKay the creole itself, the minor literature as a necessary shadow of the major language, posed the greatest threat, from which he spent his entire life trying to escape.

Perhaps McKay's life story does not differ so much from *Pygmalion* after all.

Though he felt somewhat snubbed by Shaw, he did strike up a valuable friendship with C. K. Ogden, who duplicated Shaw's interest in radical politics and language reform. Like Shaw, Ogden set himself up as "linguistic conscience" to the nation, with his own scheme for lowering the barriers raised by language, a scheme that became Basic English.[21] But Ogden's linguistics were far more radical than Shaw's because he came to believe that European thought was mesmerized by "word magic," the mistaken belief that there was an essential connection between sign and referent.[22] About the time he met McKay, Ogden also met Malinowski and was intrigued by the way Malinowski's researches in the East Indies supported the notion that most language was mere phatic convention. It is tempting to think that some of Ogden's interest in McKay may have stemmed from the hope of finding more proof in the West Indies.

Ogden and Malinowski represent an early version of Sartre's view that the colonized languages will expose "the foolish business of naming things." In fact, the notion presented in Malinowski's supplement to Ogden and Richards's *Meaning of Meaning* that language does not reflect the rules of logic was to become vitally significant for British philosophy up through Austin.[23] And yet it did not prevent Ogden from introducing McKay's perfectly standard poems as displaying "some of those peculiar qualities which rendered the visit of the Southern Syncopated Orchestra so memorable last Autumn, and for which we are becoming accustomed to look as the distinctive contribution of African Art in general."[24] Capable of finding convention everywhere else, Ogden finds here, in McKay's utterly conventional sonnets, unmediated nature. Despite the passage of ten years and a complete change of literary direction, McKay still found himself up against a Henry Higgins determined to teach dialect.

II

When James Weldon Johnson noted with satisfaction the general abandonment of dialect in African-American poetry, he made one exception. McKay's Jamaican poems, he said, are "quite distinct in sentiment and treatment from the conventional Negro dialect poetry, . . . free from both the minstrel and plantation traditions, free from exaggerated sweetness and wholesomeness. . . ." One reason for this, Johnson supposes, is "that McKay had the advantage of not having to deal with stereotypes."[25] Perhaps McKay did enjoy a greater geographical distance from the crippling stereotypes left behind by Dunbar, but he suffered nonetheless from the same kind of preemptive patronage that Dunbar felt he had received from Howells. This, in fact, is what at least a few of the more significant dialect poems are about.

Songs of Jamaica begins with "Quashie to Buccra," a poem whose defiant tone might have pleased Johnson but one that is at the same time utterly entangled in the problematic of the dialect stereotype. The poem delivers its entire message, or so it seems, in one rush at the outset: "You tas'e petater an' you say it sweet, / But you no know how hard we wuk fe it. . . ." (*SJ*, p. 13). For seven stanzas, each made up of two rhymed couplets, the poem elaborates on this message of practical demystification, directed by Quashie to Buccra. The notes, with which *Songs of Jamaica* is liberally supplied, enclose the lesson in a dramatic context: "The buccra (white man) looking over the hedge at the black man's field, is addressed by the latter as follows" (*SJ*, p. 13). This is, in fact, the very first note and, as such, it conjures up a dramatic scene before the first-time reader thinks to ask why there *are* notes. Surely a Jamaican reader will not need to be told, for example, that *calalu* is spinach, "but not the English kind" (*SJ*, p. 81). To be sure, the notes may simply make the poems available to the English reader as well as to Jamaicans conversant with the dialect, who could ignore them, but even so they expose, by their very existence, a metatextual situation that their content tries to obscure. The Buccra to whom Quashie addresses his warning is also the white reader unfamiliar with black Jamaican life. As the first poem in the collection, "Quashie to Buccra" assumes the traditional role of addressing itself to the reader, in this case warning the white reader in particular against a superficial reading of what is to follow.

But there may be an even more specific warning enclosed in Quashie's address to Buccra. Intrinsic evidence suggests that the notes are not McKay's creation: indeed there are a few "Author's notes," which are distinguished from the others (*SJ*, pp. 26, 129). Since Jekyll supplies a good many general linguistic notes in his preface, it seems likely that the notes to specific poems are his as well, especially since they strongly resemble the notes attached to *Jamaican Song and Story*. This would certainly bear out the impression given by the preface that Jekyll is serving as a virtual translator, as well as introducer, to interpret these poems for an audience unfamiliar with dialect or Jamaica. Perhaps, then, "Quashie to Buccra" is McKay's own introduction, his own interpretation of what will follow, meant to counter and correct the preemptive introduction of his patron. Perhaps the dialogue it dramatically portrays is precisely this dialogue between introductions, between rival interpretations of Jamaican experience.

Jekyll certainly seems a worthy object of Quashie's instruction. In his preface he says that dialect is "an expression of the languorous sweetness of the South" especially appropriate to "charmingly naive love songs" (*SJ*, p. 5). To this, it seems, Quashie retorts, almost before Jekyll has closed his mouth, "you say it sweet / But you no know how hard we wuk fe it." This retort may be directed at an earlier preface as well. In *Jamaican Song and Story*, the contents of which were "taken down from the mouths of men and boys in my employ," Jekyll speaks of "the joyous labour of this sunny, happy land." No wonder the workers in this land "never stop chattering and laughing."[26] But in "Quashie to Buccra" it is the buccra who laughs and so cruelly he must be corrected: "You laughin', sir, you must be t'ink a fun" (*SJ*, p. 14). In other words, the defiance of "Quashie to Buccra" seems aimed at fairly close range, at a patron who would associate dialect with happy-go-lucky peasants, at an introducer who would counsel the wide white reading world not to take too seriously anything that follows.

Actually, the struggle takes place in even tighter quarters than this, since the Quashie role is but a variation on the trickster figure most commonly exemplified by Anancy, the hero of the largest part of *Jamaican Song and Story* itself. According to Patrick Taylor, "Anancy is Quashee, the master of 'congo-saw,' or double-talk. His aim is to protect himself by cringing before the white master, lying, avoiding the issue, and misleading him."[27] Quashie is, in Lloyd Brown's words, "a smiling mask," one of many proliferating throughout African and diaspora literature from Brer Rabbit to the signifying monkey.[28] But how can this mask work if it has been collected, annotated, interpreted, and introduced by a white editor? What if the black trickster becomes, as Ralph Ellison once charged, a white fashion?[29] Perhaps the most serious struggle in this, the first poem in McKay's first book, is the fight to get Anancy back.

What seems at first to be a fairly limited retort against a white tourist, gazing over a hedge and admiring the neat field beyond, is in fact a defensive gesture against the sort of interest a white reader might take in a book like *Songs of Jamaica*, and against the white editor who encourages stereotypical misconceptions. The reaction against tourism is also overt in "Fetchin' Water":

> Watch how dem touris' like fe look
> Out 'pon me little daughter,
> Wheneber fe her tu'n to cook
> Or fetch a pan of water:
> De sight look gay,
> Dat is one way,
> But I can tell you say,
> 'Nuff rock'tone in de sea, yet none
> But those 'pon lan' know 'bouten sun.
>   (*SJ*, p. 42)

On one level this simply claims that only those who work outside can know how hot the sun is. But there is a larger warning against the aestheticization of hard work in this and other similar lines: "De fiel' pretty? It couldn't less 'an dat, / We wuk de bes', an' den de lan' is fat" (*SJ*, p. 14). In "Quashie to Buccra" the expansion of this warning into a metatextual comment can only be accomplished outside the poem by taking into account its title, placement, and relationship to other works. In this way the hedge between Quashie and Buccra becomes the line between poem and commentary, between poem and introduction, between creator and commentator, Jamaican and Englishman, black and white.[30]

However, no matter how strictly this line is drawn, no matter how prickly the hedge, Jekyll still manages to get on both sides of it. Even Quashie's deviousness has already been included in his list of the black Jamaican's peculiar charms. "The Black man is such an accomplished actor," Jekyll tells the readers of *Jamaican Song and Story*, "that he can assume any character." Anancy in particular delights in "enigmatic language," so much so, in fact, that he illustrates better than anyone else the old saw that speech "is the art of disguising thought."[31] Jekyll senses no particular threat to himself here, even though he realizes full well that certain aspects of black Jamaican life will remain forever hidden to him, because he can easily reduce the obfuscation and indirection of the Anancy role to the level of childish playacting. How could Quashie's devious critique disturb an Olympian calm so secure it is charmed even by devious critiques? How can it break through an interpretive screen that has aestheticized in advance all possible strategies of rupture?

In the end, "Quashie to Buccra" seems to capitulate to the greater interpretive powers of the white introducer:

> You tas'e petater an' you say it sweet,
> But you no know how hard we wuk fe it;
> Yet still de hardship always melt away
> Wheneber it come roun' to reapin' day.

The last couplet is either a massive non sequitur or a sly joke, an ironic assumption of the very happy-go-lucky role the poem rejects in every other line. In this indeterminacy the last couplet serves as the most accurate introduction of all to the rest of McKay's dialect poetry, which rather frequently uses the very language that "Quashie to Buccra" rejects:

> I hear above the murmur of the dale
> The tropic music dear to great and small,
> The joyous outburst of the nightingale.
> . . . .
> I feel the sweetness of those days again . . .
>   (*SJ*, p. 97)

The problem posed by McKay's dialect poetry, and, for that matter, by all of his poetry, is how to reconcile this nostalgic romanticism with the militant rejection of the romantic found in other poems. As "Quashie to Buccra" shows, this discontinuity exists not just between poems but often within them. Within the space of two pages, McKay can reject the aesthetic strategy that sweetens hard work— "High people fabour t'ink it sweet / Fe batter in de boilin' heat" (*SJ*, p. 42)—and embrace it himself: "Dis water-fetchin' sweet dem though . . ." (*SJ*, p. 43).

Perhaps this ability to turn on a dime, to play it hot and then play it sweet, is a characteristic of the Quashie role, a role that enables the powerless peasant to jab and then hide. But is this really the key we need to unlock poems like "Old England," in which McKay himself becomes the tourist:

> Just to view de homeland England, in de streets of
>   London walk,
> An' to see de famous sights dem 'bouten which dere's
>   so much talk,

> An' to watch de fact'ry chimneys pourin' smoke up to
> de sky,
> An' to see de matches-children, dat I hear 'bout,
> passin' by.
>
> (*SJ*, p. 63)

A bold interpretation might read this as reverse colonization, the Jamaican worker now reducing England's own downtrodden masses to charming match girls and its factory smoke to "atmosphere."[32] But is the ironic mode established by "Quashie to Buccra" strong enough to transform this act of literary and political abasement, in which the empress of half the world becomes "our Missis Queen, Victoria de Good," into satire? Elsewhere, McKay seemed quite genuine in his touristic awe of the sights of England.[33] And yet he also rejected the idea that black Jamaicans needed any other home than Jamaica. It would be tempting to read these shifts of point of view as ironically manipulated shifts in allegiance, the aesthetic resistance of a writer who is formally but not actually English. But in the end it hardly seems to matter whether "Old England" is as truly submissive as it seems or covertly and ironically resistant, because Jekyll has already included both alternatives within his definition of the charm of the black Jamaican.

Perhaps it is wrong to look for resistance at the discursive level at all. Edward Brathwaite's complaint against McKay's dialect poetry has to do with its rhythms, which never break away from the conventional English iambic pentameter. This is significant because for Brathwaite, as for many Caribbean theorists, true creolization takes place at the level of sound itself. According to Edouard Glissant, "Creole organizes speech as a blast of sound. . . . Since speech was forbidden, slaves camouflaged the word under the provocative intensity of the scream. No one could translate the meaning of what seemed to be nothing but a shout."[34] To really break free of the hold of English or French, then, it is necessary to disorder it at the most fundamental level, in the underdrone of phatic communion where, as Conrad discovered, a language does its most effective social work.

McKay's best opportunities to create a counterdrone come in *Constab Ballads*, where he rather frequently slips an illicit beat into the rhythm of military orders:

> Quick march!—halt!—a sharp right tu'n,
> Wid de right han' smart salute,
> All attention poker-stiff,
> An' a-standin' grave an' mute . . .
>
> (*CB*, p. 54)

"A-standin'" is obviously not the same thing as "standing." It is far more "at ease," both dramatically and rhythmically, where it slips a bit of anapestic looseness into the poker-stiff rhythms of the military orders. This rhythmic opposition rises closer to the discursive surface in the next stanza of the same poem:

> 'Ter all de formalities,
>   Dis an' dat an' warra not,
> Salute,—'tion,—right about turn,—
>   Den de precious pay is got . . .
>   (*CB*, p. 55)

The tendency of the military to reduce its own formalities to mere grunts ("tn*shun!*") is parodied by the constab's dismissive "dis an' dat." The ritual of discipline is one to be rushed through to get to the real business, payday, which gives this poem its title, and so the drill is squeezed until it becomes little more than the chanting of meaningless syllables. These are so highly stressed as to seem comically stiff against the devil-may-care rhythm of "dis an' dat an' warra not." The effect rhythmically duplicates the generally two-faced nature of the whole poem: "Constable wid a solemn face / Constab only full o' fun" (*CB*, p. 54). Underneath the constable mask there is a dialect figure, the constab, who makes his mocking existence in between words by adding a syllable here and clipping one there.

Unfortunately, McKay makes sure that the fault in this mismatch of mask and face will be found in himself and in his race. "We blacks are all somewhat impatient of discipline," he says in his preface to *Constab Ballads* (p. 7). And Jekyll helps to make sure that linguistic indiscipline will also be read as a charming fault and not a serious protest. Jamaican rejection of the "harder sounds" of English and its regular rhythms is characterized in terms traditionally appropriate to women and children: "a pretty lisp" (*SJ*, p. 5); "the prettiest little twirks and turns of intonation, sometimes on the words, sometimes mere vocal ejaculations between them."[35] What he calls the "sweetness" of the black Jamaican dialect is, in fact, to be found here, at the level of sound, where the masculine rigors of standard English are softened and feminized. What Brathwaite would like to hear resounding like a scream is preemptively characterized as a lisp.

How could any writer break out of a circle of expectations as solidly drawn as this one? Beginning *Songs of Jamaica* in the role of Quashie might seem a bold enough move if Jekyll had not already used all of Jamaican dialect literature to pose himself as Quashie against the stern, utilitarian England he had fled. Because Jekyll persists in seeing black Jamaicans as natural, childlike, and full of tomfoolery, against an overly cultured England, dialect can never confront English directly, culture to culture. The language a writer like McKay might use against the standard English he was taught in school has already been turned into a harmless curiosity before he can get to it. This double dispossession provides both the condition and the subject of the rest of McKay's writing, even after he abandons dialect itself.

III

When *Harlem Shadows* was published in 1922, it was received as "a clean break with the dialect tradition of Dunbar" (*PCM*, p. 17). Of course Dunbar himself had tried to make a break from dialect poetry but without success, and though McKay seemed to succeed by continuing to write in standard English, it can hardly be said that the break was a clean one. Indeed, the gap between his standard English poetry and the dialect was full of all sorts of entanglements, from which McKay was never to be free.

The linguistic dilemma of the standard English poetry McKay wrote in America is fittingly revealed by a break, the first stanza break in "The Tropics in New York," which expresses more effectively than anything else in the poem the break between the tropics and New York. The whole poem is structured around this break as a kind of double take, both for the author and for the reader. The first stanza chews over a catalogue of tropical names as if they were real enough to taste:

> Bananas ripe and green, and ginger-root,
>   Cocoa in pods and alligator pears,
> And tangerines and mangoes and grape fruit,
>   Fit for the highest prize at parish fairs . . .
>   (*HS*, p. 8)

There is an implicit synesthesia here in the way certain repeated consonants, particularly the *g*'s and *r*'s and the *g*'s and *n*'s, give the lines a concrete, almost crunchy sound. Some of the names, such as cocoa and grape fruit, also force compromises on the generally iambic pattern, further clogging lines already very high in consonance. The result is an extraordinary effect of sensory presence, which is instantly and utterly dispelled by the stanza break.

Stanza breaks of any kind are relatively rare in McKay's American poetry, where the most characteristic form is the sonnet. Stanza breaks that do not coincide with a full stop are even rarer. This stanza break jumps over a mere comma to a phrase that sets the preceding scene in an entirely new context: "Set in the window, bringing memories . . ." What seemed present, close enough to smell and taste, is suddenly flung behind glass, and the tropical scene is revealed as a mere memory, evoked by a grocer's display. The effect, with its displacement and consequent disorientation, is almost modernistic, particularly in a book of poetry that plays very little with point of view.

The shift in point of view coincides with a decided change in tone and diction. Where there was "cocoa in pods" there are now "low-singing rills," and alligator pears give way to "dewy dawns" and "mystical blue skies / In benediction over nun-like hills." The language is the language of memory, softened by distance. "Poetry," announcing itself as such—the word *rill* does not get much use outside of poetry—replaces what was insistently the language of sensory experience. In this way, "The Tropics in New York" resembles a rather more famous modern poem of memory, "The Lake Isle of Innisfree," which also began with a young colonial's vision in a metropolitan shop window.[36] There, too, the "clay and wattles" of a primary rural existence give way to the "glimmer" and "glow" of memorial longing. The resemblance suggests that, though alligator pears and wattles are particular, the language of memory is universal, for both poets rely on a certain dewy dimness to describe their longing for home.

Of course, what really happens in both poems is that the particular language of the colony loses out to the generalized language of empire. In McKay's case the conflict between these two competing vocabularies is concentrated on a single word: *hungry.* When McKay says in the third stanza that he is "hungry for the old, familiar ways," he is certainly speaking metaphorically, and yet it may be that this trope, which governs the entire stanza, retains a shadow of the literal reality described so vividly at the beginning of the poem. There is a special irony in the situation of the transplanted Jamaican staring at the fruit imported from his homeland and carefully displayed behind glass. What was common at home, and commonly available, becomes a rare delicacy, not the recipient of prizes but a prize itself. But the Jamaican, offspring of the families who grow such valuable fruit, seems mysteriously to have fallen in value during his transplantation to New York: he can only gaze at the fruit with unsatisfied longing. What strange process is it that can bring both product and person so far from home and then erect a wall of glass between them? As it happens, McKay first came to America on a United Fruit Company passenger–cargo ship (Cooper, p. 60). "The Tropics in New York" is, at this level, about the radically different fates of passenger and cargo in the global economy, the cargo assimilated as an exotic treat, the passenger cut off from both tropics and New York.[37]

As literal hunger, McKay's longing might mark the beginning of a visceral awareness of the costs of uneven development, not at all inappropriate for a writer who at this time was becoming deeply involved in radical politics. As metaphor, the same longing seems nothing more than standard romantic dispossession: "I turned aside and bowed my head and wept." The original readers of the poem were apt to place it in an even more specific context. Since the eighteenth century, pathetic songs about slavery such as "The Desponding Negro" had been a staple of the British music hall stage. Sometimes these were abolitionist tracts about the ravages of slavery, but as time went on the same emotional clichés were adapted to another genre especially popular in America: the freedman lamenting the old plantation.[38] In either case the cliché depended on and reinforced the notion that Africans are out of place in a modern urban civilization: in the South they may long for Africa, in New York for the South.

When "The Tropics in New York" was originally published in England, it was recognized as a sophisticated reworking of this minstrel-show cliché. The *Westminster Review* said of *Spring in New Hampshire:*

> The greater part of its contents are inspired by memories, made dearer by exile, of a childhood spent in a warm, semi-tropical country, and the intense fidelity of the negro to places and scenes familiar in early youth, the longing to return and revisit them expressed (and vulgarised) in the hundreds of crude music hall songs which have captured the public ear both in London and New York. . . .[39]

The longing of an African for his home was, in other words, a popular commodity with a well-established market. Whatever McKay's own intentions may have been, and despite the superior technical achievement of the verse, his poems fed this market. In England I. A. Richards, who wrote the preface to *Spring in New Hampshire,* compared his poems to "the Spirituals," and in the United States Max Eastman, who wrote the introduction to *Harlem Shadows,* modified Jekyll's charcterization of "the Negro" so that he was not merely quick of laughter but also quick "of tears" (*HS,* p. ix).

Thus the fate of the passenger on the United Fruit cargo ship is not so different from that of the cargo: the company sells its fruit and he sells his longing for the fruit. But this means that McKay is further separated from his homeland by the very language he uses to express his separation from his homeland: even his sense of dispossession is already part of a vicarious experience to be enjoyed by a white readership. Thus the ultimate level of dispossession in this poem, beyond literal hunger and metaphorical nostalgia, is linguistic.[40] There is no language for McKay to use about his experiences that cannot be worked into the synthetic racial tradition created by white performers and writers. Leaving dialect behind and leaving the dialect tradition behind turn out to be two entirely different things.

In fact, leaving dialect behind while also leaving Jamaica behind led McKay into a linguistic no-man's-land from which he never quite emerged. That these two departures were actually related is suggested by *My Green Hills of Jamaica,* an unfinished autobiography, at the end of which McKay steps off into the future like Adam leaving Eden: "At last I had left the beautiful green hills of Jamaica for another world. What did this new world hold for me?" It did hold at least one hope: "Someday I would write poetry in straight English and amaze and confound them [his Jamaican readers] because they thought I was not serious, simply because I wrote poems in the dialect which they did not consider profound" (*GHJ,* p. 87). Adolesence, universal bourgeois conformity, and a colonial inferiority complex merge in this plan to leave behind an audience that can only be pleased by those who leave them behind. To write in standard English just to show this audience that he can do it is to invite his white editors to make him into the sort of stuffed exhibit he became in all their prefaces.

Unfortunately, the alternative to standard English that McKay discovered in America was just as limiting. He received his first real welcome from rebellious, forward-looking journals like *Seven Arts* and the *Masses,* both of which acknowledged that racial prejudice was one real impediment to American renovation.[41] But McKay was aesthetically at odds with *Seven Arts*, at least, whose editors did not care for sonnets. James Oppenheim, who edited *Seven Arts*, was rather more interested in things like Lindsay's poem "The Congo," but he agreed nonetheless to publish two of McKay's sonnets, "Harlem Dancer" and "Invocation," "which though traditional sonnets in form were clearly racial in theme."[42] The terms of this compromise are fairly clear: dealing with racial themes could make even a relentlessly traditional poet a kind of honorary modernist. The compromise remains in force today, and, in fact, still governs most critical commentary on McKay: "If his style was in most respects anachronistic and sometimes clumsy, his essential message of alienation, anger, and rebellion was thoroughly modern."[43]

Though McKay certainly wanted to be published, the terms of the compromise meant that no matter how carefully he polished his sonnets, he was still read in an atmosphere determined by works like "The Congo." Ogden introduced the two dozen poems he published in the *Cambridge Magazine*, all of them in traditional forms and standard English, by recalling to his readers "the Southern Syncopated Orchestra." The indiscriminate association of race and modernism appears quite clearly in the next issue, in which Ogden published his own review of *Spring in New Hampshire*, some photographs of Benin bronzes with a note on African art, a Pierrot by Picasso, and a Matisse lithograph.[44] In his introduction to *Harlem Shadows*, Eastman also invoked African art. Though he assured his readers that there was nothing exotic about McKay's poems, he compared them nonetheless to "the sculptures and wood and ivory carvings of the vast forgotten African Empires of Ifé and Benin" (*HS*, pp. ix–x), which must have seemed at least a little exotic to most American readers.

McKay disliked Lindsay and resented the notion that he was beating the same kind of drum.[45] As early as 1922, he published a general denunciation of modernist primitivism: "The slogan of the aesthetic art world is 'Return to the Primitive.' The Futurists and Impressionists are agreed in turning everything upside down in an attempt to achieve the wisdom of the primitive Negro. . . . Homage is rendered to dead Negro artists, while the living must struggle for recognition. . . ."[46] McKay particularly objected to the idea that everything needed to be turned "upside down" in order to render the experience of "the Negro," and he resisted the notion that he should write in a disorderly way simply because he was black. Thus, in his own foreword to *Harlem Shadows*, he feels obliged to note that though he is "very conscious of the new criticisms and trends in poetry, to which I am keenly responsive and receptive," he has "not used patterns, images and words that would stamp me a classicist nor a modernist." Rather, he says, he has taken inspiration from "our purely native songs the jammas (field and road), shay-shays (yard and booth), wakes (post-mortem), Anancy tales (transplanted African folk lore), and revivals (religious)," which are "all singularly punctuated by meter and rhyme" (*HS*, p. xx). It is, in his view, such "regular forms" that most faithfully express his own particular version of the black experience.

What an irony, though, that the sonnet form should somehow seem closer to jammas and shay-shays than modernist experimental free verse. The irony dramatically demonstrates how little free space there was for McKay between traditionalism and modernism. If he departed from the standard language and its conventional poetic forms, he became a modernist cliché, beating Lindsay's drum, but if he resisted modernism, it seems there was no other alternative but the most traditional standards.[47] McKay sympathized with those modernists he considered true crusaders "against the dead weight of formal respectability" (*PCM*, p. 151), but he bristled when he was told, "If you mean to be a modern Negro writer, you should go meet Gertrude Stein" (*ALWH*, p. 248). In Paris, where such advice was apparently common, McKay conceived a strong dislike for Stein, whom he considered one of the "eternal faddists who exist like vampires on new phenomena" (*ALWH*, p. 348). The source of this animosity is certainly the idea that a "faddist" like Stein held the key to becoming "a modern Negro writer," that if he should wish to be accepted he would have to write like "Melanctha." Instead, he clung defiantly to words that he knew were "in some circles considered poetically overworked and dead," and he pointedly refused "to stint my senses of the pleasure of using the decorative metaphor where it is more truly and vividly beautiful than the exact phrase" (*HS*, p. xxi). Ezra Pound be damned.

Perhaps, then, there is no real conflict between the defiant subject matter and the conventional form of McKay's American poems, as is so often supposed. Perhaps the conventional form is also defiant of a modernism that had steadily identified Africans and African Americans with primitive spontaneity. McKay suggests as much in "Black Belt Slummers," an unpublished poem of the 1920s, in which he denounces the dilettantes who come to Harlem for its "background modern and bizarre."[48] But, if so, then this resolve simply demonstrates the rigid closure of the two choices facing McKay, which are really the same two choices that faced him back in Jamaica, where he could write in standard English or the dialect already packaged by Jekyll. By the time he left the United States he had tried both possibilities without permanently satisfactory results.

McKay admits as much in "Outcast," a sonnet that gropes for a way to describe a language he cannot even name: "Words felt, but never heard, my lips would frame; / My soul would sing forgotten jungle songs" (*HS*, p. 45). If the aspiration to sing jungle songs seems strangely contained in a sonnet, the strategy may be justified by the fact that the whole poem is simply a negative image of another poem that cannot manage to take its place:

> Something in me is lost, forever lost,
> Some vital thing has gone out of my heart,

> And I must walk the way of life a ghost
> Among the sons of earth, a thing apart. . . .
> *(HS*, p. 45)

The vagueness of the language here is itself the point, for the "thing" he longs for is a language that would save him from periphrastic place holders like "thing." That language would enable him to write an entirely different poem, free of these evasions. Lacking it, he is himself a "thing" without positive characteristics, definable only in negative terms: "born, far from my native clime, / Under the white man's menace, out of time." The space "out of time" is, among other things, the limbo of one who tries to use the language of "the great western world" to describe an unknown language that would be its very opposite.[49]

That language would obviously be an African one, and yet one of the great failings of McKay's poetry of this period is still, as Cooper says of the dialect poetry, that it lacks "any effective image of Africa to counter the one" presented by whites.[50] For the most part Africa remains, like Jamaica, an object of romantic longing, and one of the difficulties for readers of his poetry is, as Johnson said long ago, to read the poems of protest and rebellion and then "imagine him dreaming of his native Jamaica. . . ."[51] The non-European parts of his heritage, defined as romantic escape, cannot be mobilized to challenge the overweening culture of Europe. This is precisely what McKay says, with perfectly appropriate diction, in "O Word I Love to Sing":

> O tender word! O melody so slender!
> O tears of passion saturate with brine,
> O words, unwilling words, ye can not render
> My hatred for the foe of me and mine.
> *(HS*, p. 63)

This is stilted language complaining against itself without effect. McKay began his career in America with "Invocation," which tried to conjure "an ancient music" out of the past so as to give words to "my modern heart" *(PCM*, p. 117). In at least one poem, "Heritage," he claims to have read and heard this language. But the line "I can feel and I can write the word" *(HS*, p. 30) is no less periphrastic than "Some vital thing has gone out of my heart." Whether in this one brief moment of false confidence or in the more durable mood of despondency, McKay reveals that, without a language different from the two he had tried, poetry itself had become for him a dead end.

IV

McKay once contended, through the fictional mouthpiece who speaks for him in *Home to Harlem* and *Banjo*, that it is natural "that a youth should pass from the colorful magic of poetry to the architectural rhythm of prose" *(B*, p. 264). Since both Jekyll and Eastman had advised him to stick to poetry, it was perhaps natural for him to think of growing into prose, and natural as well for him to go to Europe to do it.[52] But this departure to a new genre and a new continent may also have been part of an attempt to solve the linguistic problem that had dogged his poetry, whether it was in dialect or standard English. In a defense of his novels written in 1932, McKay claimed that "what I did in prose for Harlem was very similar to what I had done for Jamaica in verse" (*PCM*, p. 135). McKay's desire, at least, seems the same, to bring into English literature a new language, but his success was, as it turned out, still limited by the same forces he had first encountered in Jamaica.

Alone among his white sponsors, Frank Harris had suggested a switch to prose because it seemed to him less burdened by convention, freer to be modern: "Language is loosening and breaking up under the pressure of new ideas and words" (*ALWH*, p. 20). Ten years later, in *Home to Harlem*, McKay put the same opportunity before his alter ego, Ray, who seems bewildered by it: "Dreams of patterns of words achieving form. What would he ever do with the words he had acquired? Were they adequate to tell the thoughts he felt, describe the impressions that reached him vividly? What were men making of words now?" (*HH*, p. 227). Here Ray confronts the problematic freedom of modernism, both generally and quite specifically as he considers Joyce, Anderson, and Lawrence as possible models to replace the old "spiritual masters [who] had not crossed with him into the new" (*HH*, p. 226). Though McKay confesses for Ray a strong generational association with the modernists—he is happy to leave behind the old masters like Ibsen, Wells, and, significantly, Shaw—he cannot resolve this episode of aesthetic and spiritual groping by sending Ray off to write a modernist novel. For if Ray is pulled toward Joyce and Lawrence on one hand, he is pulled even more strongly toward the African-American language and culture exemplified by his friend Jake, who seems rather difficult to place in a modernist work: "Could he create out of the fertile reality around him? Of Jake nosing through life, a handsome hound . . ." (*HH*, p. 228).

This moment of self-reflection in the middle of *Home to Harlem* sheds light over the whole of McKay's fiction. As Harris had suggested, there was an opportunity for McKay in the modernist explosion of the novel form, and a possible model in Joyce, who had transformed Irish linguistic dispossession into a comprehensive refashioning of English fiction, or in Lawrence, who had also started with dialect verse, moved to poetry in standard English, and then to novels that contained, in McKay's own description, a "reservoir of words too terrible and too terrifying for nice printing" (*HH*, p. 227). But what about Jake? The problem is not that there is no place for Jake in modernist fiction, but that there was already a place far too well prepared. How could McKay make the sort of defense of black folk culture he wanted when it constantly appeared in the literature of the time in the form of the comic primitive? Joyce may have demolished every other convention dear to Western civilization, but he still introduced a line of darky minstrels into "Circe" when he wanted to raise the wild comedy another notch.

Ray's paralysis comes from the fact that all his desire to put the "warm accent" of the Harlem voice into literature is blocked by his fearful respectability, which is in fact little more than fear of a phrase: "Harlem nigger strutting his stuff . . . Harlem niggers! How often he had listened to those phrases . . ." (*HH*, p. 264). Like Prufrock, Ray is afraid of words because he dreads the loss of self-control and dignity that comes when one is "formulated" by a phrase. His path to a new language is blocked by such phrases, which drain away all the possibility he senses in the modern moment. If, however, he were somehow to escape his scruples and become just like Jake, who seems so instinctive and free, he might find himself hedged in on the other side, for Jake confesses a shame-faced admiration for precisely those qualities Ray would most like to escape: "Ef I was edjucated, I could understand things better and be proper-speaking like you is . . ." (*HH*, p. 273). Thus the false dichotomy between the reflective Ray and the instinctive Jake becomes a complex square, with Jake shamed because he cannot speak standard English like Ray and Ray shamed because he does not have the courage to put Jake's speech in a book. Despite Ray's sense that the language is changing, the old opposition between standard English and dialect has the characters in a vise.

Of course, to put this dichotomy into a novel is to subject it to scrutiny, if not to transcend it, and those critics who complain that McKay fails to achieve a dramatic resolution in *Home to Harlem* may be asking for a lesser novel than McKay wanted to write. The introduction of Ray, McKay told his agent, was to "give just enough of the modern touch of sophistication to the writing and achieve a kind of subjective-objective fusion—a mosaic that puzzles and yet intrigues and holds the reader."[53] In other words, the fusion was to occur as the reader fit various pieces of the mosaic together in different patterns, a plan that has a good deal of the "modern touch" about it. The end of *Home to Harlem*, in which Ray simply wanders off to resolve his problem elsewhere, is, after all, no more irresolute than the end of *Ulysses*. It may have been McKay's intention to achieve his "subjective-objective fusion" where Joyce does, somewhere in the minds of the readers, by forcing them to examine the tension between the two characters and in this way to understand the linguistic and social forces that keep them apart.

The controversy that followed the publication of *Home to Harlem* thus became a living part of the novel itself because the audience turned out to be incapable of either mosaic or fusion, locked as it was in the same problematic that held McKay's characters.[54] White appreciation of the novel relied on the very stereotype that paralyzed Ray, a stereotype that constantly compared black English to jazz and jungle drums. Herschel Brickell, writing in *Opportunity*, found the novel "rich in Harlem slang" and "refreshingly primitive . . . a modern symphony scored for saxophones and snare-drums which were once tom-toms."[55] T. S. Matthews praised the novel as "a simple picture of the crude and violent life of the jungle nigger in the jungle city" in a review revealingly titled "What Gods! What Gongs!" In fact, Matthews's review captures with brilliant crudity the linguistic dilemma facing McKay. Using a distinction offered by white dialect writer Roark Bradford, who admitted he was more interested in "the nigger" than in "the Negro," Matthews praises *Home to Harlem* over Nella Larsen's *Quicksand*, and Jake over Ray because "Jake is a 'good nigger.' He is a Negro unaware of our world." Ray and Larsen's characters "make us uncomfortable" by reminding "us" of "the Problem," but Jake reminds us only of Uncle Remus and the unself-conscious "niggers" of Roark Bradford.[56]

Thus the line is drawn between Ray and Jake, the very line Ray himself feared to cross lest he be seen as "a Harlem nigger strutting his stuff." It is no wonder, then, that irate black reaction formed up on the opposite side of the same line. Allison Davis, writing in the *Crisis* in 1928, accused virtually the entire younger generation of African-American writers of pandering to stereotypes first promulgated by white faddists like Lindsay and Van Vechten. From the publication of McKay's "Harlem Dancer" back in 1919, he charges, "The jazz band became the model which the Negro poet sought to imitate." Because jazz had become for many whites a point of delicious connection between the modern and the primitive, Davis criticizes jazz-influenced literature both for reckless innovation and for animalistic atavism. Davis does not mention *The Jazz Singer* or Eliot's "jazz play," both of this year, but he does attack both Lawrence and Joyce, perhaps because they are mentioned approvingly in *Home to Harlem*, and modernism in general.[57]

The controversy raised to the level of publicity the superficial dichotomy between the educated Ray and the instinctive Jake. Though the two sides seem utterly at odds, they actually agree on the one false premise that keeps the whole machinelike argument going: that there is something threatening to good order in the primitivist stereotype. To the charge that he was pandering to a white fashion, McKay answered that his critics were the ones tied to white apron strings: "These nice Negroes think that the white public, reading about the doings of the common Negroes, will judge them by the same standards" (*PCM*, p. 136).[58] Yet it was not really one side or the other that was dominated by whites but the very terms of the argument itself. The identification of African and African-American culture with nature meant that it could not actually challenge European and Euro-American culture but could only serve as a complementary escape. McKay reveals an ironic awareness of this fact in *Home to Harlem* when a group of white nightclubbers who claim to be "wearied of the pleasures of the big white world" and in search of "the primitive joy of Harlem" turn out to be undercover agents from the vice squad (*HH*, p. 109). Thus McKay slyly closes the illusory gap between the freedom seemingly offered by the primitivist stereotype and the repression of conventional authority.[59]

At the same time, slight satirical touches like this one reveal McKay's growing awareness of a literary strategy that might avoid the closure of the *Home to Harlem* debate, which was, after all, the same closure that had dominated his career from the beginning. McKay was hardly unaware of the fact so often educed by his critics that the primitivist stereotype is used by whites to demean blacks.[60] As he commented in *Banjo,* it was as if an African or African-American "could not be seen in any other light but that of a funny actor on the stage" (*B,* p. 192). Yet he was more and more amused that no one noticed the obvious contradiction that occurred whenever anyone, white or black, *acted* primitive. McKay elaborately stages this contradiction in *Banjo* when Ray poses for an art class of "fierce moderns." At first they are interested in him purely as an object, a model that will allow them to produce their own version of the African-inspired art sweeping Paris, but then they begin talking to their model about "primitive simplicity and color and 'significant form' from Cezanne [*sic*] to Picasso." They are astounded at Ray's ability to discourse on such subjects: "Their naked savage was quickly getting on to civilized things" (*B,* p. 130). The joke is an obvious one as European eagerness to learn from African savagery is exposed as itself an intellectual preoccupation. Thus Ray exposes the thinness of the line between civilization and savagery not by exposing Conradian gulfs beneath the social surface but by showing how often "savagery" is itself a civilized creation. He enacts this paradox in his own person, better able to pose as a thoughtless physical specimen because he is conversant with the artistic fashion the students are trying to mimic.

Yet the joke is really on the reading audience, if it does not realize the self-reflexive nature of this episode. Ray's posing as a savage before the moderns is an allegory of McKay's own career from the moment he arrived in America and, more specifically, an allegory of the appearance of *Banjo* before its white audience. Like "Quashie to Buccra," it is a veiled warning to the reading audience not to take the happy primitive at face value. It suggests that black performers and writers could not possibly satisfy white demand for the primitive without being exquisitely cultured. Even Banjo himself, who seems the very type of the thoughtless jiver, precisely calculates the commercial possibilities of his role: "The American darky is the performing fool of the world today. He's demanded everywhere. . . . That's the stuff for a live nigger like me to put ovah . . ." (*B,* p. 14). Thus McKay stakes a good deal on the supposition that the one who acts primitive must have a much more finely tuned consciousness than the audience that takes his act at face value.

As if to illustrate this supposition, McKay's fiction became more self-reflexive as it became more outrageously provoking. *Home to Harlem* and *Banjo* both contain in miniature McKay's own satirical versions of the debates that had been occasioned by his work. In *Home to Harlem* the grotesque and openly stereotypical Strawberry Lips taunts his friend Susy, a high-living Brooklynite who becomes primly anti-Harlem when she discovers her boyfriend with another woman in a Harlem cabaret (*HH,* p. 99). *Banjo* is full of debates about banjo music (pp. 90–91), "common darky language" (p. 85), race pride and racial jokes (pp. 181–83). Though these give McKay a chance to at least try to settle scores with the real-life

Susies who had received *Home to Harlem* with such horror, they also demonstrate an intriguing contradiction: there is a lot of talk in this novel about singing, banjo playing, drinking, sex, and other apparently unreflective activities. There is so much discussion of earthy primitivism in the novel, in fact, that it is easy to miss how much of it remains pure discussion and how the unreflective activities of the international cast of *Banjo* are raised time and again to consciousness. As McKay defended what seemed to some critics primitivist stereotypes, he actually defined a peculiarly reflective spontaneity, avidly dissected and evaluated even as it was enjoyed.

By means of a similar process, McKay slowly consumed his own earlier career until he arrived back at Jamaica and Jekyll, who in the guise of Squire Gensir finally unties the knot that had held him tight for over thirty years. *Banana Bottom* seems to be McKay's simplest and sunniest novel, a pleasant return to his native Jamaica, but it is in fact a return to nature by way of a very complex cultural experience.[61] *Banana Bottom* is a useful introduction to McKay's entire career in part because it is faithfully autobiographical and in part because it is autobiography reexperienced and reexamined, as if McKay had realized that all the controversies of his life had roots in Jamaica.

McKay claims in his author's note to *Banana Bottom* that "all the characters, as in my previous novels, are imaginary, excepting perhaps Squire Gensir." The qualifying "as in my previous novels" seems almost calculated to raise doubts, since all of McKay's fiction was strongly autobiographical, but it could not have been calculated to raise doubts about Squire Gensir, who has always been taken as a fairly straightforward portrait of Jekyll. And yet the Jekyll who emerges from this portrait delivers an important message not at all congruent with what the real Jekyll had to say in *Jamaican Song and Story*. Praised by a visitor for the primitive simplicity of his life, the Squire replies "that primitive living was more complex than his visitor imagined" (*BB*, p. 119). As if to illustrate this principle, the Squire plays for Bita a native tune he had collected, a *minto*: "But what had excited the squire was his discovery that with a little variation of measure the melody was original Mozart" (*BB*, pp. 123–24). When Bita wonders if other native tunes might have been borrowed, the Squire replies "I don't think it matters. Everyone borrows or steals and recreates in art. . . . I think some of our famous European fables have their origin in Africa" (*BB*, p. 124).

Here the whole dichotomy between the primitive and the complex, nature and culture, the Afro-Caribbean and Europe, is demolished without so much as a blink of the eye. Perhaps Jekyll once said something just like this to McKay; perhaps he had it in mind even when he urged McKay to write in dialect, but what McKay records about that advice is Jekyll's opinion that only the dialect poem was "the real thing," while the standard language poems were for him a false affectation. Now, at what proved to be the end of his career, McKay returns to put Jekyll himself into a novel, a genre of which he disapproved, and a standard English novel at that. In so doing, is he not illustrating the very theory of cultural cross-fertilization that the fictional Squire enunciates? To make a true Jamaican novel would be to make a *minto* out of a minuet, or rather to make the difference between the two seem illusory. To make a Jamaican novel with Walter Jekyll as a character is to reverse the process by which Jekyll introduced McKay to the world back in 1912.

Squire Gensir himself is a mixture of the Jekyll of 1912 and the McKay of 1932, with Jekyll's collecting interests and a relativism that McKay himself had picked up through much traveling. McKay once refused an invitation to follow in Jekyll's footsteps: "One of my most considerate critics suggested that I might make a trip to Africa and there write about Negro life in its pure state. But I don't believe that any such place exists anywhere upon the earth today, since modern civilization has touched and stirred the remotest corners" (*PCM*, p. 137). When he imaginatively returns to Jamaica, then, he returns to a place irremediably marked by European culture, not to a refuge from modern civilization, which was apparently what Jekyll had been seeking. And he returns with an insight that undid the opposition that had structured his entire career: "Getting down to our native roots and building up from our own people . . . is not savagery. It is culture" (*B*, p. 200). This is an insight with a negative thrust, which exposes the necessarily self-conscious basis of any hankering after the primitive, and with a positive thrust, since it shows that the primitive is never there, only another culture. Delivering a version of this message in the person of Squire Gensir is McKay's way of going back to his own native roots, finally aware of how strongly he had been marked by a culture that had imagined him and his as mere primitives.

V

Reviewing McKay's own summation of his life, Alain Locke searingly accused him of "spiritual truancy."[62] McKay himself once wrote an autobiographical story entitled "The Enigmatic Expatriate."[63] Like Pound, Eliot, Conrad, and Stein, McKay was at odds with his own community; he was spiritually, geographically, and linguistically restless. The arc of his career suggests, at first glance, that the expatriate writers of all modern communities share a single experience: like Pound and Eliot he was schooled in a standardized English from which he broke away; like them he rebelled by linking his language to jazz; and his jazziest novel, *Home to Harlem,* appeared at about the same time as *Sweeney Agonistes.* Yet the differences are even more apparent. For one thing, the career arcs are hardly the same at all: for the white modernists, early struggle finally issued in stability, success, and honor, even for Ezra Pound. McKay's early success dissolved with the notoriety of Harlem, and he ended life a forgotten pauper. The long sonnet cycle he prepared in the 1940s is almost entirely consumed with resentment and hatred for those he considered false friends of his race, most especially the white liberals who had made the race itself into a fad.[64]

A more fundamental difference has to do with the figure of rebellion. Brer Rabbit represented Pound's chosen strategy of escape and resistance; for McKay Quashie was a role he was never entirely free either to occupy or to resist. Pound and Eliot felt pressure to avoid dialect, and thus it became for them a language of rebellion. And yet in this way dialect was transformed into a barrier as rigid as the standard itself for writers like McKay, who had somehow to negotiate their way past two sets of white expectations, diametrically opposed in spirit and yet in fundamental agreement about the character of black language and art. McKay's situation brings to the surface the subterranean connections between dialect and the standard, which need each other for definition, and perhaps the similar collusion between European culture and blackface rebellions against it.

Despite these crucial differences, however, all the enigmatic expatriates considered here did come, perhaps by way of expatriation, to the same realization about language. There is in all these writers a realization that language exists and grows by inclusion, that it is most accurately placed not within land boundaries but somewhere on the high seas, in the keeping of travelers and linguisters. Language itself is in a condition of spiritual truancy, a condition that has been most apparent, in this century at least, to those who have been truants themselves. This realization of the malleability of language in general, and of the arbitrariness and relativity of particular languages, is the common property of all the expatriates considered here, and it is this realization that makes them all users of the dialect of modernism.

PART III

Plain American

6

Race, the American Language, and the Americanist Avant-Garde

I

The coincidence that *The Waste Land* and *Harlem Shadows* were published in the same year may seem merely to dramatize the differences between the literary movements these works have come to represent. After all, when Eliot and McKay both returned to the United States in the mid-1930s after long absences, transatlantic modernism was an accepted literary fact and Eliot was given a respectful and even distinguished reception, while McKay found the Harlem Renaissance virtually moribund and so few opportunities for himself he soon ended up in a state work camp.[1] The distance between Eliot, delivering his most notoriously narrow-minded opinions on race and culture before an audience at the University of Virginia, and McKay, doing manual labor with a crew of partially detoxified alcoholics, could not be greater. Such differences are so hard to ignore that modernism and the Harlem Renaissance have come to seem not just mutually exclusive but even inimical terms. Yet there was a time when it seemed natural to couple the two, when at least some Harlem writers sought an alliance with their white compatriots in the modernist avant-garde, albeit a modernist avant-garde rather different from the one that Eliot had come to represent.

The month *The Waste Land* was first published, the little magazine *Broom* carried an announcement proclaiming "The Oldest and the Newest Art of America. . . . The *January* number of *Broom* is a challenge to Americans to recognize a national art as profoundly American as BASEBALL / THE CINEMA / THE JAZZ BAND / AND THE DIZZY SKYSCRAPER / while fundamentally in harmony with the Art of the ancient Mayas." Listed as practitioners of this new/old art were Marianne Moore, William Carlos Williams, Malcolm Cowley, Gertrude Stein, and Jean Toomer, among others.[2] When the promised issue arrived, it duly contained works by Williams, Toomer, Cowley, and Hart Crane, all decorated with Mayan masks, statues, and architecture, though there was nothing having to do with baseball. The issue also included Matthew Josephson's dismissive review of *The Waste Land*, the spirit of which seemed to extend to the back cover, which carried a quote from Moore's "England": "America where . . . letters are written / not in Spanish, not in Greek, not in Latin, not in shorthand / but in plain American which cats and dogs can read."[3]

Despite Eliot's youthful enthusiasm for American slang, his work in England seemed to many American writers of the time a linguistic affront, one that Williams was still answering twenty-five years later when he composed *Paterson* as "a reply to Greek and Latin with the bare hands."[4] By this time Eliot's opinions had also solidified, so that he accused H. L. Mencken of "issuing a kind of linguistic Declaration of Independence, an act of emancipation of American from English."[5] This is, in fact, exactly what the editors of *Broom* were doing at the very moment of *The Waste Land*, for they felt that the success of the literary avant-garde and the linguistic independence of the United States were necessary to one another. Special issues like the one they promised for January 1923 represented the hopes of a wing of the modernist avant-garde also represented, in varying degrees, in little magazines such as *Others, Poetry, Seven Arts, Secession*, the *Little Review*, and *Contact*. This homegrown avant-garde devoted itself to American popular culture, to the multiracial heritage of the Americas, and above all to modern writing in "plain American."[6]

This effort toward an indigenous American cultural renewal coincided with a similar movement in Harlem. As Alain Locke observed in 1928, "It is a curious thing—it is also a fortunate thing—that the movement of Negro art toward racialism has been so similar to that of American art at large in search of its national soul." The fight of the avant-garde "against conventionality, against Puritanism," has found a natural ally in the black movement that has come to accept "the folk music and poetry as an artistic heritage." Because of this convergence of interests, Locke says, "there is every reason for the Negro artist to be more of a modernist than, on the average, he yet is, but with each younger artistic generation the alignment with modernism becomes closer." By modernism Locke apparently meant something like the theater of Eugene O'Neill or the novels of Carl Van Vechten, but he might almost have been quoting Williams when he cited "the equally important movement for re-rooting art in the soil of everyday life and emotion."[7]

Locke realized that this movement toward "plain American" would inevitably bring white modernists like Williams to African-American language and literature for inspiration:

> Indeed, contemporary American poets, engaged in spite of all their diversities of outlook and technique in a fundamentally common effort to discover and release the national spirit in poetry, have sensed a kindred aim and motive in Negro poetry, and have turned with deep and unbiassed interest to Negro materials as themes and Negro idioms of speech and emotion as artistic inspiration.[8]

Thus Locke hoped that white modernists and the Harlem movement would meet in a common effort to make a new national art that would free all writers from inhibiting standards and traditions. And, in fact, there was a rumor current in the early 1920s that *Broom* was going to follow its "All-American number" with a "Negro number." Though this did not come to pass, the mere fact of the rumor suggests how natural was the connection between a commitment to American linguistic independence and an interest in African-American language and literature.[9]

Locke was not by any means the only critic of the time to refer to the younger Harlem writers as modernists or to suggest, as Herbert Gorman did in the *New York Times Book Review*, that American writers both white and black differed from their English contemporaries in being aesthetically modern.[10] And yet by the early 1950s when Frederick Hoffman published what is still considered a standard overview of the new writing of this period, he found it so easy to disentangle the Harlem Renaissance from the other movements of the time that he did not so much as mention a single African-American writer.[11] It is little wonder, then, that Houston Baker, Jr., has found it necessary, in his turn, to disentangle the Harlem Renaissance from critical generalizations about modern literature formed in virtual ignorance of black writing.[12]

The promise that *Broom* made in 1922 was, in short, never fulfilled. Instead of growing from these shallow beginnings, this facile enthusiasm for skyscrapers and the Mayas, into a truly multicultural modernism, the Americanist avant-garde demonstrated instead a persistent inability to understand how race fit into its conception of modern America, or how the language of African America fit into its conception of "plain American." It was in many ways the American language and its fight with everything English that made this branch of the avant-garde what it was, and that powerful and yet curiously undefinable dialect hovered throughout the 1920s as the possible point of contact for all kinds of adventurous American writing. That this contact was not finally made, that Locke's hopes were disappointed, remains one of the most significant facts about American literature of the twentieth century.

I I

In a 1920 essay in the *Dial*, James Oppenheim nominated poetry as "Our First National Art," as long as it used "only our American speech, the resultant of a new environment, mixture of races and new experience." What Oppenheim added could almost have gone without saying, namely, that this new speech "is decidedly different in flavour and construction from English speech."[13] Eliot had advised Matthew Josephson to move to London to "maintain contact with the pure English language," but he and most of his colleagues chose to stay home and remain impure.[14] Even those who went to London did not take instruction quite as mildly as earlier generations of expatriates. Skipwith Cannell's poem "On a London Tennis Court" begins with the following:

> The land is new to me,
> And the people, too; and the speech
> Is strange to me
> As words
> Spoken from another star.[15]

Most of the new American poets felt this way, according to Richard Aldington, who noted in 1920 how far removed the Americans were from the "discussion [that] has occurred recently in London on the subject of 'pure English.'"[16]

Actually, the American poets were not just removed from but actively antagonistic to that discussion. As Malcolm Cowley later said, they felt the standardization movement as a positive impediment to the new American literature: "A definite effort was being made to destroy all trace of local idiom or pronunciation and have us speak 'correctly'—that is, in a standardized Amerenglish as colorless as Esperanto."[17] Magazines that favored the new American writing necessarily ran up against the same difficulty, as Baker Brownell said of *Others* in 1918: "Words are fluid and beautiful things which the increasing rationalization of grammar surely is freezing. The 'others' evidently are trying to break through the encrustation and immobility that has gradually grown about the cooling language, and with some success."[18] Thus the motto of *Others*, "The old expressions are with us always, and there are always others," purposely situated the magazine and its contributors outside accepted linguistic territory, associating the new poetry by definition with the violation of old linguistic standards. For other little magazines such as *Broom*, which deployed the *Others* motto in a specifically nationalistic way, those standards were inevitably English.[19]

This might seem a rather late date in America's history as a free country to wave the banner of linguistic independence. But there is evidence to suggest that the long linguistic tug-of-war between England and the United States intensified at this time for the simple reason that the United States was becoming markedly less English. It was at this time, at any rate, that Kipling darkly warned his friend Brander Matthews "that non-Anglo writers were degrading American literature."[20] The trouble, from Matthews's point of view, was that the term "non-Anglo" was distressingly elastic. He had been complaining for years against the English tendency to treat all Americans as "outer barbarians, mere strangers, wickedly tampering with something which belongs to the British exclusively."[21] Now it seemed that even so thoroughly Anglicized an American as Henry James might be deemed a "foreigner," forever incapable of using the English language fully and correctly, as Virginia Woolf claimed quite without conscious malice, in the *New Republic* in 1929.[22]

Perhaps the Anglophilia of the American academic establishment of the time was meant to ward off such withering condescension, to avoid any guilt by association with the hordes of "non-Anglos" pouring into the United States. At any rate, men like Stuart Sherman, Bliss Perry, Robert Underwood Johnson, and Barrett Wendell carried on the old New England tradition of opposing immigration on one hand and preaching literary solidarity with England on the other. American literature, according to this line of reasoning, "can only come from pure English racial stock uncontaminated by alien European races—from those 'thoroughbred' Americans who are indistinguishable in taste, manners, and speech from cultivated Englishmen."[23] It is little wonder, then, that the next generation should have made its war with the old a war against England as well, a war that frequently assumed a starkly racial character. As Malcolm Cowley put it, the "revolt against gentility" was also a "conflict of racial strains," with the genteel writers representing "the older immigration" from England and the younger generation representing, sometimes by choice rather than ancestry, the "non-Anglos."[24]

Thus the culture wars of the 1920s were fought in terms that were simultaneously linguistic and racial. In 1922 Harold Stearns dedicated his iconoclastic collection *Civilization in the United States* to the proposition that "whatever else American civilization is, it is not Anglo-Saxon. . . ."[25] A year later H. L. Mencken devoted most of his preface to the third edition of *The American Language* to an attack on the "Anglomaniacs." Both men attacked those Stearns simply called "the standardizers," literary and academic authorities who had robbed America of its true character by holding its language and culture to an English measure.[26] Of course, the standardizers were not about to take this lying down. In 1923 the American Academy of Arts and Letters, armed with a twenty-five-thousand-dollar grant, dedicated itself to the "preservation of our English speech in its purity." "Minor errors in speech," the American Academy was told by no less an authority than Hamlin Garland, "are multiplied by radio into major offenses against society." These the American Academy was determined to eliminate, all the more so in that the newer critics and writers seemed bewilderingly aligned with the very aliens who were undermining America's English speech and heritage.[27]

In short, the debate between the academic establishment and the young writers of the 1920s linked language, literature, and race so closely together that aesthetic experimentation seemed racially alien to certain authorities even if it had nothing overtly to do with race. Thus, at the same time that the American Academy was mounting its campaign against alien influences in the language, the art critic Royal Cortissoz attacked what he called "Ellis Island Art": "The United States is invaded by aliens, thousands of whom constitute so many acute perils to the health of the body politic. Modernism is of precisely the same heterogeneous alien origin and is imperilling the republic of art in the same way." Cortissoz was not so crude as to name names, but the issue of the exact racial or ethnic origin of particular artists was beside the point anyway, because what made the new art perilously alien was its purposeful flouting of the accepted principles of aesthetic order. When Cortissoz says that modernism has been promoted by "types not yet fitted for their first papers in aesthetic naturalization," he commits an elaborate pun, for he simply means that modernism defies what is natural, "what is normal

131

and sane."[28] In this analysis, art and the body politic reproduce one another so closely that an invasion of one is an invasion of the other, and both depend for their health on order, unity, and homogeneity, so that difference is indistinguishable from disease.

This is precisely the metaphor used by the American Academy against literary modernism, as when Robert Underwood Johnson, reading a stanza from Marianne Moore, exclaimed, "[W]hat is the remedy for this disease?"[29] Sometimes the hysteria assumed a more aggressive and more specifically racist tone. Dreiser's English was, according to Paul Elmer More, "of the mongrel sort to be expected from a miscegenation of the gutter."[30] But the American Academy chose as spearhead of its attack on all novelty in language and literature a youngish academic who could be relied on to take a smoother tone. The purpose of Stuart Sherman's *Americans* of 1922 was simply to deny that name to a rather large group of readers and writers, to a new public that "shows little trace of the once dominant Puritan stock and nothing of the Puritan temper. It is richly and curiously composed of the children of parents who dedicated themselves to accumulation, and toiling inarticulately in shop and field, in forest and mine, never fully mastered the English definite article or the personal pronoun." These immigrant children speak the new slang and, instead of reading the good old New England writers, look into the works of moody European misanthropes or, worse yet, lured by "primitive instinct" and "barbaric impulses," succumb to Sandburg, Masters, Anderson, or Dreiser.[31]

Sherman's attack on the ethnicity of these writers and their critical champions is utterly frank. In the course of his exposé of the "alien-minded" among the new writers, he names Huneker, Spingarn, Mencken, Hackett, Brooks, Bourne, Frank, and Stearns, and then suavely concludes, "It is not a group, taken as a whole, however it may be connected with the house of Jesse, which should be expected to hear any profound murmuring of ancestral voices or to experience any mysterious inflowing of national experience in meditating on the names of Mark Twain, Whitman, Thoreau, Lincoln, Emerson, Franklin, and Bradford."[32] Jaded perhaps by the old-fashioned anti-Semitism of such attacks, Sherman finds something a little jazzier in the concept of "literary Mohawks," as he calls "the fighting organization of the younger generation," whose "chieftains have advanced whooping to the portals" of the American Academy.[33] Thus he attempts to combine his favorite metaphors of barbarism and ethnic invasion, forgetting perhaps both the historical priority of the Mohawks in North America and the circumstances of the Boston Tea Party.[34]

Against Sherman's *Americans* the avant-garde could offer Waldo Frank's *Our America*, a book considered by much of the American avant-garde as the first shot in their campaign of cultural independence. Frank spoke for a younger generation eager to leave behind a time "when our land in all but the political surface of its life was yet a colony of Britain." He spoke as well for a multiethnic populace whose "tongues were stilled before the clear articulation of New England."

These tongues, he said, were being given voice in the literary renaissances of Chicago and New York, in the hubbub created when immigrants from the East met rebellious malcontents from the Middle West to create artistic circles like that around Alfred Stieglitz. Above all, Frank preached the positive value of the "ethnic chaos from which a new world must be gathered" and which would give Americans the strength to throw off "English culture [which] has been a growing incubus upon us."[35]

Frank was one of the major intellectual forces behind *Seven Arts*, which had begun publication in 1916 with this charge from Romain Rolland: "You must make of your culture a symphony that shall in a true way express your brotherhood of individuals, of races, of cultures banded together. You must make real the dream of an integrated and entire humanity." The journal apparently tried to meet this charge immediately: the first story it published was "Simply Sugar-Pie," a dialect tale about a pregnant black woman in Louisiana.[36] The editors seemed to have more difficulty finding material by black writers, though the very last poems it published before ceasing publication in 1917 were two sonnets by Claude McKay.[37] Members of the *Seven Arts* group also tried to discharge their responsibility in more substantial ways. Randolph Bourne carried on a long campaign for what he called "Trans-National America," a part of which Paul Rosenfeld illustrated in *Port of New York*, a collective portrait of the avant-garde, which concluded with an appendix giving the varying ethnic extractions of the writers and artists discussed.[38]

Bourne believed that racial and cultural differences were vitally important and should be preserved in the new transnational nation of America: "What we emphatically do not want is that these distinctive qualities should be washed out into a tasteless, colorless fluid of uniformity." On the other hand, Bourne did most emphatically want cultural unity, and he felt very keenly that "[i]n our loose, free country, no constraining national purpose, no tenacious folk-tradition and folk-style hold the people to a line."[39] In fact, he felt that it was the loss of cultural differences that had rendered the United States such a chaos, but he was quite incapable of suggesting how to unchop this tree, putting difference back in so as to achieve a new unity. As Gorham Munson said years later, "He strove to make his concept of transnational America clear but only made it picturesque."[40]

Achieving unity within a polity that also preserved ethnic and racial differences was a difficult task that no one at *Seven Arts* managed to accomplish, even in theory. When forced to choose, Frank for one preferred unity. In fact, before the 1920s were out, he had started to sound uncannily like Stuart Sherman. In "Seriousness and Dada," Frank calls for control and high seriousness in a way that the American Academy itself might have applauded, and as he does so a distressing note of racial fear and prejudice begins to creep into his version of the American language: "Our brew of Nigger-strut, of wailing Jew, of cantankerous Celt, of nostalgic Anglo-Saxon, is a brew of Dada."[41] The heterogeneous mixture of this brew is no longer cause for celebration; "ethnic chaos" becomes instead a force that has to be controlled lest it result in the wildness and indiscipline of dada. When a slightly younger group of writers began a new journal, *Secession,* Frank contributed a surprisingly mild "Declaration of War," in which there was very little about war or chaos but much about the need for cultural unity, which he accused the dadaists of undermining.[42]

On the surface, nothing seems less threatening to good order than the dadaism of *Broom* and *Secession,* belated, transplanted, and diluted to half strength as it was. Yet it worried Frank because it violated his own most cherished precepts simply by carrying them out to their natural extreme. When Josephson, Munson, and Cowley spoke of a new American culture, they enthusiastically included billboards, machines, and vaudeville, about which Frank was notoriously queasy. When they spoke of the "knockabout vitality, vigor, raciness, authenticity, humor, poetry, and vividness of the American language," they included examples that did not look or sound much like language at all: "alldressdupinher *sun* daycloes / and there she goes."[43] Though Frank shifted ground slightly where some movies and some vaudeville were concerned, he realized that a full-scale embrace of skyscrapers and machine culture was inconsistent with his organic definition of culture. He also realized that attacks on language per se would sweep away American along with English.

Obviously, Frank had been counting on "ethnic chaos" to resolve itself into a new order, and he was deeply shocked when the new literature included only the chaos. Others recoiled in the same way, and when they did, the reaction brought with it the same distressing note of racial and ethnic discrimination that had crept into Frank's voice. Edmund Wilson, for example, took vaudeville as a metaphor for the contemporary literature of 1926: "polyglot, parvenu, hysterical and often only semi-literate."[44] It seems that for Wilson the equation between the polyglot and the parvenu and semiliterate was as unarguable as it was for, say, Stuart Sherman. This equation reached its natural conclusion in no less a venue than *Broom* itself, in an essay by Emmy Veronica Sanders about a New York crowd: "And all around, from thousands of lips, bastard sounds reach the ear. Hybrid mixtures of a score of tongues. —And these dishonored crippled tongues, this verbal patchwork, this absence of pure speech, offends the ear. It longs for a clean language as the soul and body long for a clean breeze. Melting pot sounds and melting-pot crowds. . . ."[45] Thus the demand for "pure speech" returns in the very journal that had declared itself for the variety and vigor of a hybrid American tongue. Royal Cortissoz himself would hardly have put it any differently.

It is quite remarkable how the American Academy language of chaos, hybridity, mongrelization, and cacophony reduplicates itself in what is supposed to be the very heart of Mohawk territory. The return of this language and the racial fears it represents marks the emergence of a contradiction, a conflict of motives, in the program of the avant-garde itself. Like Frank, the avant-garde in general counted on the American language to preserve difference and to open up new freedoms, while also building a new unity. How any language, no matter how flexible, might do this without becoming another standard just as limiting as the old academic one was a question they never managed to answer. How they might attack the privilege of the English language without also undermining the privilege of all language, as the dadaists were doing, was a question they seemed afraid even to ask. The Americanist avant-garde advanced racial and linguistic diversity as a wedge in its campaign against English and New Englandish domination, and it was only too glad to play the role of racial outsider in this campaign, but it failed to anticipate how its efforts against the twin authorities of race and language would also thwart its own plans for a new cultural unity.

III

The cover of Williams's *Kora in Hell,* published in 1920, was a visual expression of the multicultural ideal which had animated *Seven Arts:* it showed "a design using sperms of various breeds, various races let's say," surrounding a single ovum.[46] The fact that only one sperm could actually penetrate the egg suggested competition rather than cooperation, but this only makes the cover a more revealing picture. For in this case even a picture could not succeed where a thousand words had failed, and Williams was no more capable than Frank or Bourne of actually describing how diversity would coexist with unity in the new American literature.

The abstract problem of describing the role of difference within a unity emerged quite concretely whenever these writers tried to describe the exact function of other races within the culture that had been Anglo-Saxon. One of the reasons discussions of American language and culture always ended up as discussions about race is that the truly original American art forms—jazz, vaudeville, the movies—were created by blacks or dominated by black impersonators like Jolson. As V. F. Calverton put it in 1929, the contribution of African Americans "to American art and literature is far more free of white influence than American culture is of English. In fact, they constitute America's chief claim to originality in its cultural history." Logically, then, the new American writers would be black, for, as Calverton says, "In respect of originality . . . the Negro is more important in the growth of an American culture than the white man."[47]

This is not exactly what the white avant-garde had in mind. Though they were often quite happy to predict great things for black writers in the future, for the present these folk materials and cultural creations would remain raw material for white writers to use. A candid description of this relationship in the *New York Times* reveals its vampirish qualities: "[T]hrough negro culture our novelists and playwrights hope to find colorful folklore that our starved literature needs most of all."[48] This metaphor of spiritual, if not bodily, transfusion was rife in the 1920s. According to John Rodker, European discovery of the "natural man" means that "[n]ew vitality flows in. The artist has tapped a natural spring which we feed ourselves continually."[49]

Alice Corbin Henderson attempted to describe this process as reciprocal but ended by revealing more than she knew: "As the Negro has absorbed us, so we have absorbed him. His songs, of which he borrowed the inspiration from us, now belong to us quite as much as to him; perhaps more, since the Negro is losing his native strain of song as rapidly as the white man is taking it up."[50] Henderson herself was a good example of this rather tricky transfer. As Alice Corbin she had contributed to an early issue of *Seven Arts* a poem entitled "Echoes of a Child-hood: A Folk-Medley," which included two dialect poems and this refrain:

> Underneath the southern moon
> I was cradled to the tune
> Of the banjo and the fiddle
> And the plaintive negro croon.
> (p. 599)

In the same year, however, she reviewed Fenton Johnson's *Songs of the Soil* for *Poetry* and recommended that black poets not write in dialect but rather in some "new and individual idiom."[51] The fact that she was herself writing in dialect while recommending that black poets give it up illustrates only too well why "the Negro is losing his native strain of song as rapidly as the white man is taking it up."

The transfusion metaphor suggests that the role of African Americans is simply to make European Americans whole again, drained as they have been by the effort of creating Western civilization. Or, to vary the metaphor somewhat, they provide what Gorham Munson called "anti-bodies" against the machine.[52] The literature of the period is full of such antibodies, which seem to enter the white body not by injection or transfusion but by sexual transmission. In "Sloth," published in *Others* in 1917, Mark Turbyfill brings this trope down to its irreducible minimum:

> In the sun
> A date-palm sways,
> And one brown girl
> Struts copiously.
>
> O days
> Pass thus over me.[53]

Other writers gave the theme fuller, less languid exposition. In Stephen Hudson's "Southern Woman," published in the *Little Review* in 1920, the narrator, frustrated by the enticing but rather frigid white woman he has met on a trip to Nashville, follows a black woman back to her shack and pays to watch her undress, while a black chorus sings "Carry me back to ole' Tennessee" under a full moon.[54]

Frank criticized such works because in them "the negro is not a negro at all; he is the healing and resolving norm within the white man's soul," but his own attempts were hardly any better.[55] The hero of his short story "John the Baptist" burbles to his black cleaning lady, "Nigger woman . . you are all *one!*" "Hope," another story in the same collection, reproduces the same elemental scene as "Southern Woman." A lonely and confused white man wanders until he meets a black woman, whom he follows home in order to watch her undress. Bolder than Hudson's narrator, Frank's also undresses, and soon "she undulous easeful, black like a buried sea" and he, "separate white," join, and the "black dead body," receiving his "impress of life," becomes "song."[56] He has finally lost the beingless and thoughtless state in which he began the story, and she, having received impress of life, kisses his feet. Years later, Frank said that the southern whites he met on his travels with Jean Toomer resented their black neighbors because they had escaped the machine.[57] This story shows how that resentment might be so mingled with envy as almost to disappear.

Of course, it never quite disappears but curdles in secret, as other contributions from the same journals can illustrate. Exactly a year before the *Little Review* published "Southern Woman," it published Aldous Huxley's "Happy Families" in an issue that also included prose by William Carlos Williams, an installment of *Ulysses*, and the first part of Pound and Fenollosa's *Chinese Written Character as a Medium for Poetry*. Huxley's story explores the boundary between passion and the pretensions of polite society by giving its male and female protagonists two alter egos each. Aston J. Tyrell is flanked by his two brothers, Sir Jasper, a Wildean aesthete, and Cain, "a Mendelian throw-back to the pure Jamaican type." Miss Topsy Garrick, who really seems quite anxious to get on with Aston, is accompanied by her sisters Henrika, in white muslin, and Belle, who is bosomy, forward, and coarse. The possibilities of the ensuing crowd scene are numerous, but Huxley seems most interested in the shock produced when Cain, with his "black greasy face, . . . pink thick lips, [and] goggling eyeballs of white enamel," steals a kiss from Henrika, who responds with fainting and tears. Cain, who struts up and down clacking a set of bones and saying "nyum nyum," is the traditional minstrel-show version of black sensuality, which becomes negative when the sensuality becomes active and male instead of being passive and female. Huxley tries to deploy this stereotype as if it were a piece of smart comedy, but the hatred and fear at the heart of it keep leering out whenever Cain licks his lips or "runs a thick black finger along Topsy's arm."[58]

The basic assumption, that black and white somehow form one whole human being, a being that feels a sexual longing to repossess its own unity, runs from Hudson's romanticism to Huxley's nasty humor, and it reaches one of its natural conclusions in a story that immediately preceded Huxley's in the *Little Review*. In Ben Hecht's "Rouge," the black alter ego is "a dwarfed and paralytic nigger boy" named Goliath, who lives with and serves a white, middle-aged sculptor. In Goliath the physical distortions that mark Cain reach horrific proportions: he shuffles along, dragging huge apelike hands across the floor, lolling a gigantic head with rolling eyes and gaping mouth. The aesthete with whom Goliath is paired is a similarly distorted version of Sir Jasper, alone in an unhealthy dream-world populated by his own deformed sculptures. This story also ends with a sexual attack, only this time Goliath kills the sculptor and violates the clay statue of a virgin. Thus the aesthete pays for his own violation of nature, which he teases and provokes with his distorted statues and with his perverse and isolated life.[59]

What possible connection can there be between Sugar-Pie and all her sisters, who bring health and wholeness to a white society exhausted by its own civiliza-tion, and the racial nightmare of "Rouge"? In one way this contrast merely marks the emergence of the negative racial stereotype from its romanticized opposite. What seems at one point like fullness and unity emerges more and more as lack: instinct becomes mindlessness, physical presence becomes brutish size, natural submission becomes sullen surrender, deceit, and then death. Goliath may also represent bad conscience revenging itself on the ideal. The scene of white sexual domination that appears in these works was always a travesty of Rolland's "dream of an integrated and entire humanity"; the murder at the end of "Rouge" is its utter inversion.[60]

The murder also exposes an insidious slippage in the very metaphor of an "integrated and entire humanity." If at first African Americans are idealized as whole in themselves, it soon appears that they are so only by virtue of certain qualities that white civilization craves to make itself whole. Since these qualities—physical assurance, instinctive ease, artistic creativity—are but mirror images of other qualities highly prized in most modern societies, they are always just a hair's breadth away from becoming vices—the sloth, animal violence, and brute strength of Goliath. Yet even at their most positive these qualities are nothing more than necessary *parts*, antibodies, antiselves, antidotes to civilization, and thus inevitably and eternally subordinate to the European mind that craves them.

Thus the image of racial and cultural unity cherished by Frank and the others in the Americanist avant-garde is always shadowed by its twin opposite, racial oppression and murder. And the literary propaganda of the period always carries an undertone of fear and mistrust, exemplifed by Cain and Goliath, a fear of the very "ethnic chaos" that Frank promoted in *Our America*. Because the avant-garde could not imagine an integrated and yet independent place for African Americans in its new America, oppression and chaos remained the only two alternatives.

IV

It had been the promise of the avant-garde from the beginning that its revolution would take place first in language, that it would be the new American idiom that would form the basis for a better culture. But it was just here, in its conception of language, that the contradictions in the avant-garde's approach to race appeared most acutely. The American dialect, which was supposed to contain the speech of all ethnicities and all races, turned out to be a good deal less capacious and flexible than the avant-garde had hoped.

Even before the First World War, Max Weber had tried to extract this new speech from the silent lips of Chac Mool:

> Oh my brother in eternity, Chac-Mool of Chichen Itza,
> Would that I could but hear thine unuttered speech
> In silence and heavenly mood . . .
> Thy stern lips of thy firm mouth have spoken, do speak,
>   and will for ever speak.

A bit like Frank's narrator gushing to his black cleaning lady, Weber exclaims to Chac Mool: "Thou knowest more, thou feelest more, thou seest more, thou rememberest more, thou art more."[61] Properly propitiated, Chac Mool is supposed to extend this wholeness and fullness to Weber's art, to give it some of the eternal repose that Weber apparently finds so heavenly. The repetitive phrasing of the free verse and the selectively archaic diction are perhaps the first indications that Chac Mool's "unuttered speech" is appearing by ventriloquism in Weber's own poetry.

Both phrasing and diction seem wildly inappropriate, however, in a volume that Weber entitled *Cubist Poems*. It is hard to see why any of these poems would have been considered "cubist," except insofar as they appeal to African and Meso-American art for inspiration. Yet the effect of that inspiration is curiously inconsistent. The most "cubist" of the poems, "Bampense Kasai," which is a hymn of praise to an African mask, does include a few blocky clumps of adjectives that may have been meant to mimic the abrupt angularity of the mask: "Crudely shaped and moulded, art thou, / In weighty varied solid frightful form. . . ." Yet at the same time Weber's reverence for the mask's hieratic repose expresses itself in the same old-fashioned diction and inverted syntax that characterizes his poem to Chac Mool. In short, an inconsistent attitude toward the art emerges as an aesthetic inconsistency in the poetry: insofar as the art is "frightful," full of "virility brutality and blackness," it inspires syntactical and rhythmic structures that exceed the ordinary bounds of English verse; insofar as this same art seems full of the peace of the eternal it brings out an old-fashioned, pseudobiblical language of reverence.[62]

Almost ten years later, William Carlos Williams also measured his own art against an African artifact. Looking back at the poems published in the last issue of *Contact*, but also by implication at the poems published during the entire brief existence of the magazine, Williams measures them against a "native paddle" brought back from Africa by a cousin: "[S]lightly curved in haft, six feet long, heavy, tapering to the tridentate spear's edge—wild nigger's work. What is poetry? What shall I say? What is their worth, these six poems in this issue judged absolutely—what? beside the cut of a West Coast nigger's surf paddle. . . ." The paddle becomes a physical measure of aesthetic success, the fineness of its proportions a model of practical engagement with the concrete world of fact. It is, in other words, what Williams called "the thing itself."[63]

By implication, the African paddle stands for everything that Williams had tried to achieve in *Contact,* a magazine dedicated, as its name implies, to an art as much a part of local conditions as that paddle. But *Contact* had another editor as well, one who featured "wild nigger's work" of a different sort. Robert McAlmon's *"Jazz Opera* Americano" uses the black model to rebel vociferously against repression: "[T]om tom, a hunter's horn, with a high yodel and the rattle of a string of missionary teeth . . . and I feinting but never fainted in a swirling vortex of colored rhythms, uneven dissonant and tragic—wild, wild, wildman, why are you shouting wild man? Dance jazzo, swirl me. . . ."[64] This is a far cry from Williams's reverence for the workmanship and care of the African paddle. Both editors romanticize "wild nigger's work," but McAlmon puts all the emphasis on the adjective, Williams on the noun, and the derogatory possessive hovers in the middle as a kind of ambiguous cipher, looking both ways at once.

It was in this ambiguous way that blackness entered and affected the language of the avant-garde. The works produced by that influence range from the conventional dialect of Alice Corbin's "Mandy's Religion" and "The Old Negro Alone" to things like *"Jazz Opera* Americano" or Charles Galway's "La Rumba Cubano," which finally dithered into pure noise:

> I am colossal elephant buttocks
> That have learned to sway stupidly
> And writhe the old Bowery plantation negroes Voodoo
> Bum— bum— bum— bum
> Madness . . .

Galway is apparently trying to construct a challenging poetic out of the very metaphors that Cortissoz and Johnson had applied to modernism: "Out of desert and jungle I become infection / Slippery sinister green of tropic heat that lures / To vileness . . . Pestilence loud trumpeted accurate and frantic."[65] But even in this absurd performance, with its juvenile desire to shock, there is equivocation. Galway wants his loud trumpetings to be "accurate" as well as frantic. It is hard to see any way in which this frenzy might be accurate, especially since Galway gives up on description altogether and resorts to pure noise: "bum— bum— bum." The word *accurate* seems to suggest that, despite its frenzy, there is something about the rumba that is incisive and sure, something that might even meet Williams's desire for solid workmanship or Weber's for eternal form.

In one sense such differences simply represent the use of quite different if equally familiar stereotypes: the racial other as natural and basic versus the racial other as perverse and mysterious. In another sense these aesthetic differences are perfectly natural variations within the movement. As Josephson said, "Revolt against traditional style takes many shapes; one writer employs violent thought-dissociations; another ripe colloquialisms, and the terminology of our popular magazines, newspapers, advertisements; others, again, employ the most shocking opposition in word-relationships, distort syntax, and punctuation and typography."[66] But the peculiarity of many of these works is that they try to deploy both stereotypes and to revolt against tradition in all these ways at once.

In "The Widow's Jazz," published in 1931, Mina Loy sums up a whole decade of such confused white attempts to understand, absorb, emulate, or dismiss black language and culture. The poem begins with a line that captures the whole genre to which "Hope" and "Southern Woman" belong: "The white flesh quakes to the negro soul." Beyond mere description, the poem also linguistically enacts the effect of this earthquake by slipping into dialect: "White man quit his actin' wise / colored folk hab de moon in dere eyes." Though this is the only line of actual dialect in the poem, it clearly functions as a linguistic model for the style of the whole, the modernist tangle of interjected phrases, contradictory syntax, mixed metaphors, and choppy rhythmic refrains that is apparently supposed to represent what happens when wisdom catches the moon in its eyes. The "impish musics" of black performers, the "dissonance" of black music and language, what Loy finally calls "this cajoling jazz . . . with its tropic breath," inspire the writer with a modernist style.[67]

Jazz is for Loy "a synthesis / of racial caress," an aural version of the black–white congress that occurs in stories like "Hope." From this congress, in Loy's version, is born a language, the very language, in fact, that the Americanist avant-garde had been talking about. Yet this language is presented in two quite different ways. Toward the end of the poem the language becomes almost biblical in its reverence for itself:

> The seraph and the ass
> in this unerring esperanto
> of the earth
> converse
>
> of everlit delight. . . .[68]

A universal language of the earth, joining opposites and contraries in unerring communication: this sounds like the loftiest ambitions of the avant-garde for the American language. The notion of Esperanto neatly combines an international character with a notion of universality and simplicity: this language is to be both various and basic. But elsewhere in the poem the same language is an "uninterpretable wail."[69] How could Esperanto be uninterpretable? How could the universal language break down in incomprehension? The fact is that Loy seems to favor *this* situation just as much as she favors the other, for this kind of language provides the poem its most arresting lines: "An electric clown / crashes the furtive cargoes of the floor." This is hardly the language of conversation, not even the conversation of seraph and ass.

Instead of providing an "unerring esperanto," the meeting of black and white produces a contradiction that works at several levels at once. Loy's own attitude toward jazz is inconsistent, for she celebrates both its availability and its mystery. The style she evolves from jazz has the same attributes: her poem is a curious composite of direct appeal and cryptic word painting:

> Husband
> how secretly you cuckold me with death
>
> while this cajoling jazz
> blows with its tropic breath[70]

Her attitude toward the poem is similarly divided, for she clearly wants on one level to communicate and to further communication, while on another level romanticizing the aloofly incomprehensible.

In one poem Loy nearly touches the two extremes reached by white modernists under the influence of the "racial caress." These extremes were not, finally, just the two distant ends of a continuum but radically incompatible alternatives, since one of these was to confirm the sanctity of language as the ultimate guarantor of American cultural unity, while the other undermined and attacked all language, even if it was solidly American. The ultimate threat of the "uninterpretable wail," of McAlmon's juvenile hooting, of Galway's "bum— bum— bum," was that they exceeded language altogether and in so doing imperiled the whole cultural project of the avant-garde. That project depended just as much as the American Academy did on the notion that language is the surest representation of a people to itself. The avant-garde wanted that language to be more flexible and inclusive, but it did not dispute the essential notion, derived from Romance philology, that identified a culture with its language. Stretching narrow notions of the English language, Galway, McAlmon, and Loy stretch language itself until it snaps. Without any unity or harmony of its own, without any meaning, this language could hardly perform its traditional function as symbol of cultural or political unity.

One of the contributors to the January 1923 issue of *Broom* that promised so much was the Baroness Else von Freytag-Loringhoven, who produced what may have been meant as a Mayan poem written in a kind of "Me Tarzan, You Jane" dialect: "Where youth? / No find her."[71] The baroness also caused a long-running controversy in the *Little Review* with works that ended like this:

> Vé—O—voorrr—!
> Vrmbbbjjj—sh—
> Sh—sh— —
> Ooh! ! !
> Vrmbbbjjj—sh—sh—
> *Sh—sh—*
> *Vrmm.*[72]

Maxwell Bodenheim defended this poem as the work of "a conscious savage," and the paradox of his term says a good deal about the mixed motives of the avant-garde and the ultimate contradiction inherent in the language of the baroness's two contributions.[73] On one hand, savagery was to be a refuge from consciousness, and its language the language of earth itself; on the other hand, savagery was the avant-garde's conscious disruption of the natural order, especially the natural order of language. Though this contradiction worked itself out in many works by the Americanist avant-garde, Bodenheim himself offered the best illustration of the direction the contradiction would take when forced to resolve itself.

Bodenheim had published two poems on racial themes in the first days of *Others,* and by the mid-1920s he constituted one of the few real links between the white modernist avant-garde and Harlem. His poem "Lynched Negro," from the *Little Review,* was reprinted in *Opportunity,* and he served as judge for one of the annual literary contests that magazine sponsored.[74] Though he wrote a number of jazz poems, Bodenheim tended to make greater use in fiction of the Harlem slang he had learned: *Naked on Roller Skates* includes a glossary for the uninitiated.[75] But his most interesting use of these materials occurs in *Ninth Avenue,* a novel that Countee Cullen called "well worth reading," despite the fact that he appears in it himself in a rather unflattering light.[76]

Ninth Avenue is in part a roman à clef, a takeoff on the Harlem fad, an elaborate send-up of the way white aesthetes like "Paul Vanderin" fawned over young black poets like "Christopher Culbert." Into this structure Bodenheim inserts another, somewhat more serious if equally symbolic, about the growing love between Blanche Palmer and another young writer, Eric Starling. Blanche, as we can tell merely from her name, is white and also quite unlettered, Eric an accomplished writer who only seems white. There is a recognition scene that does not seem to be a takeoff, though it duplicates almost to the letter the scene in *Autobiography of an Ex-Colored Man* when the protagonist is forced to confess his race. Despite her rather limited background, Blanche decides to marry Eric, throwing off every prejudice except one. With a vision of Eric in her mind urging her on, Blanche settles down "with a little grammar she had purchased" to rid her speech of the crudities of Ninth Avenue and become a writer.[77]

One of the reasons the scene rings so hollow is that Blanche already speaks perfect American: "'Oh, for Gawd's sake, what a dump,' she said. 'How'm I going to sit down with gue and coffee all over the chairs?'"[78] Why she should have to abandon this language to join a literary circle made up of thinly disguised members of the Greenwich Village avant-garde—"Max Oppendorf" is in part James Oppenheim—is very hard to say. In fact, it seems an exact reversal of the situation in Loy's poem in that the result of communion between the races is nothing other than standard English. Yet this is precisely why Bodenheim's novel is so revealing, because the meeting between the races depends on a mutual reverence for language, a reverence too strong to allow for any trifling. When they first meet Blanche says, "You've got to help me with my grammar—that's the big, weak sister with me," to which Eric replies, "You can bet I will."[79] A romance begun over grammar lessons may not sound very promising, but it proves strong enough to defy every convention—except the one with which it begins.

In one sense the marriage of Blanche and Eric is a fulfillment, albeit a fictional one, of the multiracial program of the avant-garde. But somehow the American language gets lost in the process. The irony is perfectly revealing, however, because Eric and Blanche can meet only in a language utterly stripped of particular characteristics, a language that allows them to live together because it robs them of their own cultures and backgrounds. In other words, the only way that Bodenheim could imagine a multiracial unity was in terms of a language so conventional it was indistinguishable from the standard. Thus his own language in *Ninth Avenue* is utterly inoffensive and unimaginative. Though the novel is as enlightened in its social attitudes as any of the period, its linguistic conservatism reveals quite well what would happen to the Americanist avant-garde whenever it was finally forced to rconcile its competing desires for diversity and unity: it would cease to be an avant-garde at all.

V

The same issue of *Opportunity* that included Cullen's notice of *Ninth Avenue* also included the second part of a story that must have seemed a virtual mirror image of Bodenheim's novel. Claude McKay's "High Ball" is also about grammar, racial impersonation, and mixed marriage, but it turns out far less happily than its counterpart. In fact, it may well be a fictional rendition of McKay's own difficulties with "Color Scheme," his first attempted novel, which he burned after Knopf rejected it. "Color Scheme" was unsuccessful with white publishers and the black sponsors to whom McKay entrusted it because of its language, because in it McKay tried to move back into dialect, or at least into "the everyday language of the streets."[80] "High Ball" seems to be about the pitfalls that await a black artist who attempts to use this language.

"High Ball" tells the story of Nation Roe, a blues singer who is taken up and lionized by the white press. The black press welcomes his fame but also criticizes him, embarrassed by the "bad grammar and false rhymes" of his songs: "The Negro journals said that Nation was among the few living men of the race who served as an example and incentive to all Afro-Americans. But those very journals also said that Nation's bad grammar and false rhymes were not interpretative of the modern spirit of the Negro." Here McKay wickedly captures the tone of critics like Locke and Johnson, who said in *The Book of American Negro Poetry* that dialect is no longer "capable of giving the fullest interpretation of Negro character and psychology."[81] Whether McKay is mocking his old friend and long-suffering supporter is uncertain, but when Nation reforms his grammar he also loses his audience: "At last Nation's manager put his foot down on all academic improvements."[82]

In the process Nation almost loses his distinctive style, but he finds it again, oddly enough, in the company of George Lieberman, "a successful black-face actor." With Lieberman and his colleagues, Nation finds "the finest accents of his voice," a voice that now acquires "a wider range and greater power." McKay goes out of his way to purge this situation of its ironies, which would have been all the more obvious when the story was originally published, the very month Al Jolson, to much publicity, signed the contract to make *The Jazz Singer*.[83] George, his wife, and his blackface cronies are made out to be touchstones of honesty and goodwill. In fact, they might have saved Nation from his worst mistake, which is to marry Myra Peck simply because he wants "a brilliant-talking wife like one of the white actresses."[84]

Thus McKay describes from the point of view of the black artist a situation that seems the very dream of the Americanist avant-garde: black and white artists in league together on behalf of ordinary American language, facing down standardization and convention on all sides. In fact, McKay's story, in which black and white make a compact over bad grammar, seems much truer to the avant-garde vision than Bodenheim's story, in which the compact requires that both sides acquire good grammar. But George finally cannot save Nation from the "brilliant-talking Myra" because he cannot find a way honestly to express his reasons for disliking her. George and Nation share a language only onstage; offstage they are tongue-tied and clumsy: "Yet sometimes in a burning wave of resentment he felt that his white friends made cruel blunders that bit into his flesh like this, because they had never suffered so deeply."[85] When Myra finally reveals the crude racism beneath her brilliant talk it seems a judgment on them all: on Nation's own linguistic snobbism, on George's linguistic slumming, on "brilliant talk" itself, which is just a shell over the most insidious form of discrimination.

McKay's story describes a situation in which the black artist finds himself surrounded on all sides by falsehood: on one side the pretensions of those who would have him become a brilliant talker himself; on the other, the facile enthusiasm of George and his friends, which is finally nothing more than a mask, a role that despite themselves they leave behind in the theater. The real Nation is alone in what seems a hall of mirrors. Just a few months before Locke described with high hopes the way a common interest in "folk music and poetry" would bring the white avant-garde and the Harlem writers together, McKay showed the complex dynamic that kept them apart.

"High Ball" is, in fact, an uncannily accurate allegory of the conflicts facing the Harlem Renaissance. Black artists did in fact seek out alliances with those McKay later castigated as "impersonators," alliances against the restrictions of the African-American and Anglo-American genteel traditions. As Locke said in *The New Negro*, African-American writers "have too long been the victims of the academy tradition. . . ."[86] Thus he welcomed the new "revolt against Puritanism" even though he realized it would often involve a shallow primitivism.[87] White dialect writers like DuBose Heyward, Julia Peterkin, T. S. Stribling, and Clement Wood became important allies of the Harlem movement and were welcomed as significant modern writers.[88]

Opportunity also formally welcomed the new work in "our modern journals" because it promised to break the hold of old stereotypes that had dominated establishment journals like *Harper's* and the *Atlantic*.[89] The alliance of black and white writers against academic authority thus comes to resemble the one in "High Ball" between Nation and the blackface actors, and in the end it falls subject to the same dangers. It may have been simply insensitive of Knopf to advertise Johnson's *Autobiography of an Ex-Colored Man* and Van Vechten's *Nigger Heaven* together in *Opportunity* as if they were of equal and similar interest to a black audience, as if "THE NEGRO as author and as subject" were pretty much the same thing.[90] But the Bonis went a good deal farther when they advertised *The New Negro* and R. Emmett Kennedy's folk song collection *Mellows* together in the *Crisis*. The idea that there might be something appealing to the audience of "new Negroes" in Kennedy's bayou romanticism was insulting by itself; there was no need to add injury to insult by offering *Mellows* "bound in a special bandanna cloth."[91]

The younger Harlem writers were willing to accept the white modernists even if they often played a blackface role because any encouragement of African-American folklore and language helped to break down stifling academic traditions of the past.[92] As in "High Ball," the point of contact was a mutual interest in "bad grammar," in language, that is to say, that refused to conform to standard English. But in reality, as in "High Ball," white use of "bad grammar" was often nothing more than a stage convention like blackface or bandanna cloth. There always seemed to come a moment that exposed the basic asymmetry of the situation, the unbalancing fact that George Lieberman and friends were black only onstage and thus could take off the burnt cork and eat in whatever restaurant they chose, while Nation was the same, on stage and off, and had to be careful not to go where he would be refused service.

McKay's story thus exposes the reality behind Locke's blithe hope that "deep and unbiased interest [in] Negro materials as themes and Negro idioms of speech" would make for common cause between white modernists and the Harlem writers. For it is hard to say that that interest was always "deep and unbiassed," and even when it was, as in the fictional case of George Lieberman, personal sincerity counted for very little in the face of social and political inequality. Without any changes in that underlying reality, the avant-garde combination of patronization and masquerade simply created a temporary space of racial cooperation, which Nation Roe always had to leave for a real America in which his position had changed, if at all, for the worse.

7

Two Strangers in the American Language: William Carlos Williams and Jean Toomer

I

The December 1922 issue of *Broom* included a brief sketch that already seemed to justify its high hopes for a new art as American as skyscrapers and jazz. Aesthetically Jean Toomer's "Seventh Street" was as original as anything *Broom* would publish, and its subject matter was immediate, timely, and American: "Seventh Street is a bastard of Prohibition and the War. A crude-boned, soft-skinned wedge of nigger life breathing its loafer air, jazz songs and love, thrusting unconscious rhythms, black reddish blood into the white and whitewashed wood of Washington."[1] The same month this appeared, Waldo Frank took a whole book of such sketches to Horace Liveright, who had just published *The Waste Land*.[2] A year and a day after he had agreed to publish that poem, Liveright accepted Toomer's manuscript, which was entitled *Cane*.[3]

When Toomer returned his signed contract to Liveright, he expressed his gratification at entering "the fold" along with Eliot.[4] However, Toomer's manuscript had a good deal more in common with a work that was written as a direct challenge to *The Waste Land*, a work that, if it had had any readers, would have seemed the very epitome of *Broom*'s campaign of modern writing in "plain American." Like *Cane*, Williams's *Spring and All* was a curious mixture of prose and poetry, of pastoralism and urbanism, of political fears and cultural hopes. The two works depended for their hopes on the same organic metaphor: Williams's spring shoots come struggling out of the muddy waste of weeds in the same miraculous way that Toomer's November cotton flower blooms out of season. The very titles of the two works suggest spontaneous growth from the American soil, and yet nothing could be less organic than the organization of *Cane* and *Spring and All*. The two works proved even more difficult to read and resolve than *The Waste Land* itself, so much so that they both languished in obscurity, unread and virtually unknown, for decades.

Originally, these two works, along with the others Williams and Toomer were writing at the time, were intertwined in the ambitions of the Americanist avant-garde. Even before *Broom* had linked their names in its manifesto/advertisement, Toomer and Williams had appeared together in the *Little Review* for autumn 1922. Williams contributed a letter/essay praising the *Little Review* "because it maintains contact with common sense in America. It is the only important reaction to the American environment. . . ." But the only reactions to the American environment in the autumn 1922 issue were a story by Kenneth Burke and Toomer's "Fern."[5] The January 1923 issue of *Broom* that had been promised with a jazz fanfare included "Karintha," the opening section of *Cane*, and Williams's "Destruction of Tenochtitlan," later included in *In the American Grain*. Both contributions were decorated with the Mayan motifs that were supposed to provide a unifying point of comparison for the whole issue.[6] *Broom* published part of "Kabnis," the concluding section of *Cane*, in its August issue, and a second part in September, along with Williams's "Fountain of Eternal Youth," also from *In the American Grain*. In November it published two sections of *Spring and All*, including what became the title poem.[7]

Both writers were to continue publishing in the *Little Review*, a journal that listed Toomer as a collaborator on its cover, but they did not appear together again until 1932.[8] In fact, what was to be one of Toomer's last literary publications of any kind appeared in that year in *Pagany*, which took its title from a novel by Williams and its aesthetic principles from his criticism. *Pagany*, which was subtitled "A Native Quarterly," began its life with a critical manifesto from Williams and included a contribution from him in nearly every issue of its brief life.[9] Richard Johns, the editor, also knew Margery Latimer, Toomer's first wife, which is perhaps how *Pagany* came to print in its winter 1932 issue Toomer's "Brown River, Smile," the first published version of a lifelong project that eventually became "The Blue Meridian." Williams was no longer reviewing contributions for Johns by this time, but the winter 1932 issue did include a chapter of his novel *White Mule*.[10]

Williams and Toomer appeared together for the last and perhaps the most significant time in *America and Alfred Stieglitz*, a collective portrait organized by Waldo Frank and several of his colleagues from *Seven Arts*. Their joint appearance is so significant because Stieglitz was such a powerful symbol for the Americanist avant-garde. The conjunction in the title of the collection was meant to suggest a virtual identity, to present Stieglitz as an "incarnation," in the words of the editors, of the modern effort "in American terms and on American soil." Both Williams and Toomer took him as such and, though Williams was always wary of Stieglitz, as an ego ideal as well. Williams produced one of his finest essays, "The American Background," for this volume, an essay that restated much that he had been saying about the American idiom and "the local effort." Toomer used his essay to reconstruct Stieglitz as a type of the new American, an individual who fit into no race and no place except what Stieglitz had called "An American Place," a term Williams always felt Stieglitz had taken from him.[11]

Clearly, it was natural for someone like Frank to think of Williams and Toomer as collaborators in the effort to define "an American place." Matthew Josephson did so when he reviewed *Cane* and Williams's *Great American Novel* together in *Broom* in October 1923, as did Gorham Munson when he included

Toomer and Williams in *Destinations*, one of the many collective portraits that the American avant-garde produced of itself at this time. Paul Rosenfeld produced two, one including Toomer, the other including Williams.[12] If anything, Toomer was more solidly ensconced within this group than was Williams. When Harold Loeb listed the new writers who were going to help *Broom* establish modernism in America, he included Toomer but not Williams.[13] When Munson listed the new writers on whose work he intended to found the new journal *Secession*, he did the same.[14]

For Munson it was Toomer who was the "major" writer, Williams who had not quite managed to rise above "the category of minor." Munson arranged *Destinations* so that it culminated in a chapter on Toomer, who thus became, much like Stieglitz, "a dynamic symbol of what all artists of our time should be doing." According to Munson, Toomer had virtually solved the problem of modernity by pulling his own authentic speech from the "folk ways" of his ancestors.[15] Toomer played much the same role of salvific example in Frank's *Re-Discovery of America*.

Despite this extravagant praise, these claims that Toomer represented something of significance for America as a whole, it was hard for these writers to speak of him without a certain old-fashioned condescension. Rosenfeld assured his readers that *Cane* was "prophetic not only for men of negro blood," but he also thought that Toomer's contribution to American letters was primarily musical: "He tunes his fiddle like a tavern minstrel. . . ."[16] Josephson also felt Toomer was primarily a sensuous and emotional writer who would do better to skirt large ideas and modern forms.[17] Even Munson advised Toomer to stick to what he called "negroid lyricism."[18] This line of reasoning reached its nadir in Alfred Kreymborg's massive survey *Our Singing Strength: An Outline of American Poetry*, in which he praised Toomer as "one of the finest artists among the dark people, if not the finest," but then remarked the "frankly lyrical strain native to the darky everywhere."[19]

Perhaps such language is only too predictable, the condescension only the inevitable reverse of the excessive praise, which was itself often couched in terms that would make any writer uncomfortable. But it is less predictable that such language would also have been applied to Williams. In *Destinations* Munson dwelt relatively little on the issue of Toomer's race, but he found Williams "minor" because he remained "alien" to the great American background, a "primitive" lost in a great uncharted country.[20] Rosenfeld found the source of Williams's peculiar charm "in his crassness, in his dissonant mixed blood," an opinion that was also held by Kreymborg.[21] As late as 1961, Van Wyck Brooks traced Williams's character to the mixed racial influence of the Caribbean: "Dr. Williams's father and mother had grown up with the colored people in their West Indian islands, and he himself had, ingrained in his very bones, a love of the Negroes, 'furnaces of emotional power.'"[22] Though it was not at all unfriendly, this habit of finding Williams's crassness, his dissonance, his "wild swiftness of temper," his bluntness, his primitiveness ingrained in his very bones and blood was, nonetheless, thoroughly racist.

Thus Williams and Toomer share a peculiar and ironic place within the Americanist avant-garde. Both writers saw themselves and their works as expressions of a new world, what Williams called the "Nuevo Mundo" as if to restore for his American readers some of the linguistic freshness of its discovery. As he put it in 1939, "Of mixed ancestry, I felt from the earliest childhood that America was the only home I could ever possibly call my own. I felt that it was expressly founded for me, personally, and that it must be my first business in life to possess it . . ." (*SL*, p. 185). Toomer also felt that he and his work were "the result of racial blending here in America which has produced a new race or stock," and he struggled all his life with the poem he began as "The First American," a poem that was to define and express that race.[23] Williams and Toomer were perhaps the most appropriate symbols of the program announced over and over by the Americanist avant-garde—by *Seven Arts* in 1916, by *Broom* in 1922, in the very title of *Others*—and yet they finally proved as unreadable as their works. Despite its enthusiasm for Africa and Meso-America, despite its promises of a transnational America and a multiethnic American modernism, the avant-garde proved ill prepared to include within its conception of the new American writing any examples that actually stretched the old categories of race and ethnicity.

In fact, such are the ironies of the American racial situation that it finally proved easier for Williams than for Toomer to identify himself with African America. In the early 1930s, when Nancy Cunard proposed her *Negro* anthology, Williams was thrilled, and he contributed an overheated and utterly inappropriate piece on his fascination with black women, "The Colored Girls of Passenack—Old and New."[24] Toomer refused to contribute for the simple reason that, as he put it, "I am not a Negro."[25] This avant-garde collaborative effort in which the two did not appear together thus proves more revealing than all of those in which they did so appear. For Williams became more and more interested in black language and culture, to the point of beginning a novel with a black protagonist, as Toomer more adamantly refused to affiliate himself with African America.[26] Toomer's stance can be interpreted quite negatively as a loss of faith and courage, but it does demonstrate nonetheless the fundamental asymmetry of the American racial situation, in which Williams was free to define himself, even if it meant defining himself vicariously as black, while Toomer was not. Thus two writers who might have established a new racial understanding in American literature ended instead by acting out the old illogic of the American racial masquerade.[27]

II

For Williams the New World and its new language shared a relationship so close it threatened to become circular: "We are still struggling to express, as we could not do it with the old language, that which must require a new coinage, the economic, social-esthetic liberation of which we still believe America capable, the Nuevo Mundo! of the discoverers."[28] The crabbed syntax of this sentence, with its free-floating relative clauses and its question-begging hyphen between the social and the aesthetic, betrays some of the difficulty against which Williams himself was still struggling. How could a new language will itself into being if the agency of all change is language itself? How can aspirations for a new language even be expressed, if they require for their expression the utter transformation of the language now in use? In content and in form, Williams's tortured sentence reveals the answer, for the new language really exists in and as the struggle against the old, in the very deformity and strangeness forced on a speaker who has something new to say.

It was this crabbed and twisted quality in Williams's writing that his colleagues called his dissonance, his slantwise relationship to the linguistic world around him. They were suggesting that Williams wrote in dialect, in an idiolect motivated against the standard language by the user's ethnic or racial difference. Williams quite agreed, but he felt that his dialect was nothing more or less than the American language put into service by modernism. That language was every bit as dissonant as he was himself; it was, in fact, defined by its dissonance, "as if the whole of the words in the world had broken loose from books and come deluging upon us to realize themselves in a new condition, under new circumstances, to form a new language" (*SE*, p. 173). Because the standard was defined by its fixity, "a restricted and disciplined tongue," a dialect would have to be defined by its freedom, its indiscipline, even its ugliness: "I am an American. A United State-ser. Yes it's ugly, there is no word to say it better" (*I*, p. 175).

Any attempt to define or catalogue what Williams loved to call "the American idiom" would therefore violate its very nature, for it was not to be thought of as a particular kind of language but as a particular use of language. Like the avant-garde around him, Williams defined his language in terms of its resistance to the English standard. It was a language he had first to "un-English," as he said of Joyce (*I*, p. 334). Williams's metaphors for this process are necessarily negative—smashing, breaking, even maiming: "[E]very time anyone today tries to use a word it's like trying to get a few nails out of an old box to fix something with. You have to smash and pull and straighten—and then what have you got?" (*SE*, p. 163). At times Williams wanted his readers to hear the nails squeal as he pulled them loose: "Break the words. . . . One cannot break them— Awu tsst granj splith gra pragh og bm— Yes, one can break them. One can make them" (*I*, p. 160).

Yet Williams also showed real indecision between breaking and making, which often seemed to him mutually exclusive alternatives to taking. There was finally a world of difference between breaking a word "off from the European mass" (*I*, p. 175) and making a new word: "If I make a word I make myself into a word. Such is progress. I shall make myself into a word. One big word. One big union" (*I*, p. 160). Breaking shivers words and people to bits; making makes one big union. In its ideal state, as Williams said in an essay on Pound, modern American poetry would make by breaking: "It is not by a huge cracking up of language that you will build new work . . . nor by use of an embalmed language, on the other hand. But by poetry—that will strike through words whipping them into a shape—clarity and motion . . ." (*SE*, p. 110). Poetry is language that makes by breaking, that makes a shape by transfixing some old shape through the heart, that achieves both clarity and motion, Heisenberg be damned. Thus it is also language that achieves the "social-esthetic liberation" of which America is both the cause and the effect. The stranger, the racially dissonant, is the agent of the new country, which exists in a continuous matrix of making and breaking.

It is in this sense that *Spring and All* is a piece of American dialect poetry. Shirley Brice Heath has called it a masterwork of "oral or unplanned discourse" rendered in written form. Its characteristic devices are those, she says, of oral debate rebelling against the official forms and subjects of academic discourse: "incomplete sentences, mixed genres, numerous openings of subgenres without closure of these, repetitious false starts, switches across topics within the midst of paragraphs, incomplete or unclear pronoun reference, incomplete references to other actual texts upon which this text depends, and direct dialogue cited without indication of speaker."[29] The generic indeterminacy of *Spring and All*, its formal jaggedness, the breathless incompletion of its style, even the sophomoric dadaism of its inconsistent numbering and oddly printed "chapter" heads, mimic the constant violation that speech visits on the categories of standard written discourse, even though very little in the work actually sounds like speech itself.

Williams's own metaphors for this poetic project are frequently those of cutting or breaking, as in "The Rose":

> Sharper, neater, more cutting
> figured in majolica—
> the broken plate
> glazed with a rose

The new modernist rose makes itself by cutting away the old poetic rose, sometimes so violently and spontaneously the edges show:

> The place between the petal's
> edge and the[30]

Williams is so fascinated by edges in this poem, so intent on cutting, that he describes by not writing, simply letting the empty space name itself.

Yet the line that cuts also grows: "But if it ends / the start is begun . . ." (*CP*, p. 195). And this is true as well for all the violent metaphors of *Spring and All*, even the holocaust that sweeps the world clean at the beginning of the sequence: "This final and self inflicted holocaust has been all for love, for sweetest love, that together the human race, yellow, black, brown, red and white, agglutinated into one enormous soul may be gratified with the sight and retire to the heaven of heavens content to rest on its laurels" (*CP*, pp. 179–80). Despite the sarcasm that tinges this as it tinges nearly everything in the prose of *Spring and All* no matter how deeply felt, Williams truly believed that the negative freedom of the avant-garde gesture would become the positive freedom of an egalitarian society:

> American verse of today must have a certain quality of freedom, must be "free verse" in a sense. It must be new verse, in a new conscious form. But even more than that it must be free in that it is free to include all temperaments, all phases of our environment, physical as well as spiritual, mental and moral. It must be truly democratic, truly free for all—and yet it must be governed.[31]

Here, too, making and breaking would coalesce as one American alternative to passive taking.

Where *Spring and All* approaches real dialect most overtly, however, is just where this dialectic breaks down. Poem XVII, later titled "Shoot it Jimmy!," includes some of the most extremely demotic lines in the whole sequence. In fact, Williams had to tone down one piece of slang that was apparently too crude for the *Dial:* "Our orchestra / is the cat's nuts" (*CP*, pp. 216, 504). What remained was, however, quite crude enough:

> Man
> gimme the key
>
> and lemme loose—
> I make 'em crazy
> (*CP*, p. 216)

The elisions render the rhythm and drive of the American language, its impatience with ordinary boundaries, even those between words. That same drive can take a word around the corner on two wheels:

> That sheet stuff
> 's a lot a cheese.

Or perhaps it would be better to accept the poem's own metaphor for itself: jazz improvisation. Staves and stanzas receive the same impatient scorn, one from the speaker, the other from his alter ego the poet. The two share a fierce emphasis on an originality that can only come from improvisation, an art form whose products are unique because they respect no predetermined rules:

> Nobody
> Nobody else
>
> but me—
> They can't copy it

This last line brings into the poem, however, an odd note of challenge. The democratic freedom of the jazz artist has a weirdly dual effect: on one hand he takes the language and art of the mass and uses it to set them free—"I make 'em *crazy*"; on the other hand, improvisation sets him up above and apart from the mass, antagonistic to it—"I *make* 'em crazy." The poem begins with a collective first person pronoun—"Our orchestra"—but ends with a stark division between them and me.

Of course, a lot depends on who "they" are. Nowadays, in the *Collected Poems*, the pronoun can seem to have as broad and vague a reference as any reader wants, but in the *Dial* for August 1923, when the poem appeared along with Gilbert Seldes's essay "Toujours Jazz," it probably seemed to most readers to mean something fairly specific. Like Williams, Seldes celebrated jazz for its American independence, carelessness, frankness, and gaiety, all of which, he said, were found more commonly among black Americans than white ones. But Seldes also says quite frankly that before jazz can amount to much as an art form it must be appropriated by white musicians with conventional training, and to make his point he tries to float a leaden joke about the surname of Paul Whiteman.[32] In short, Seldes takes a very distinct position on a raging controversy of the time, whether jazz could or could not, should or should not, be copied by white musicians.[33] Williams seems to take the opposite point of view, especially if one assumes that the speaker of the poem is black.

There is one very strong reason to do so. Williams was quite fond of Bert Williams's signature song, "Nobody," which he mentioned in the "Advent of the Slaves" chapter of *In the American Grain*, still in manuscript when "Shoot it Jimmy!" was published (*IAG*, p. 209).[34] Bert Williams had died suddenly and under rather dramatic circumstances in the spring of 1922, when Williams was placing the poems he had written up to that point for *Spring and All*.[35] It is not at all unlikely that William Carlos Williams would have quoted the title and refrain of Bert Williams's song in his poem on jazz as he did in his chapter on the slaves.

If this is true, however, then the whole poem simply consumes itself. If the white Williams is putting himself in the role of the black Williams, making a play on surnames quite the reverse of Seldes's, then the proud boast "They can't copy it" becomes ironic nonsense. Even the single word *nobody* curls up on itself. In Bert Williams's song, the word is a complaint against all those who have refused him help.[36] William Carlos Williams unfairly inverts this situation in *In the American Grain* to convict the entire black race of being "nobody": "When they try to make their race an issue—it is nothing. In a chorus singing *Trovatore*, they are nothing. But saying *nothing*, dancing *nothing*, 'NOBODY,' it is a quality" (*IAG*, p. 209). In fact, Williams puts African Americans in a seamless trap: they are nothing whenever they try to say anything but that they are nothing. As quoted in *Spring and All*, however, the term is turned outward at the audience, at "them," who become a collective nobody because the speaker is so full of himself and his own originality. How is it that a term that makes a black man invisible and impotent can, when used in blackface, as it were, make for a white poet's assertion of difference and originality? The difference that made jazz appealing in the first place has been replaced here by a perfect simulacrum of itself.

Williams produces his own oddly melancholy exposition of these inconsistencies in the very next poem in *Spring and All,* usually called "To Elsie." He turns the jazz musician's bold boast, "I make 'em crazy," inside out to make the first line of the new poem: "The pure products of America go crazy" (*CP,* p. 217). In the colloquial confines of "Shoot it Jimmy!" "crazy" has positive connotations, produced when slang "rags" or "jazzes" or "signifies" on the standard language by reversing its value judgments. In this sense craziness is both the central value and the chosen method of the poem, if not of the whole sequence. Somewhere in the gap between these two poems, however, craziness loses this unconventional meaning: the craziness in "To Elsie" is a state of "numbed terror," not a state of hedonistic exaltation. This mood swing from the manic to the depressive continues on its downward course throughout the poem, revaluing much that "Shoot it Jimmy!" had celebrated. The music that was "the cat's nuts" to one protagonist now appears in quite a different light as the "young slatterns" trick themselves out for a Saturday night of empty pleasure and numb, emotionless sex. As the sequence shifts its gaze to the audience, the jazz musician's boast, "I make 'em crazy," begins to seem the sheerest cruelty.

Thus Williams concentrates the pressure on the variant possibilities of a single word and especially on the tension between its colloquial and its standard meaning. It is the common tactic of dialect, and yet Williams does not merely undermine the authority of the standard. The rebellious quality of the colloquial, it seems, must be paid for. The process of linguistic jazzing, prizing as it does a craziness that refuses all ties of commonality along with the claims of convention, turns the people against itself. Breaking, that is to say, does not become making, and the dissonance of art does not conduce to a new unity but merely becomes another symptom of cultural disunity. Williams's final metaphor for this disunity returns to Bert Williams:

> No one
> to witness
> and adjust, no one to drive the car
> (*CP,* p. 219)

Here the tune returns to its original key of lonely desolation, almost as if Williams intended to play it back against the ending of the previous poem. The defiant self-assertion of "Nobody / Nobody else // but me" becomes the melancholy searching of "No one / to witness / and adjust, no one to drive the car."

The inconsistency within "Shoot it Jimmy!" thus becomes an inconsistency between it and another poem and in so doing reveals itself as an inconsistency in this whole sequence. In *Spring and All* Williams violently breaks his language away from the standard, but he also wants that language to serve as the basis for a new American unity. The fear that lurks in the white space between "Shoot it Jimmy!" and "To Elsie" is that these are incompatible aims. And if this is true, then Williams's whole project of a new America founded on the dissonance of the American idiom might be in danger of coming apart.

III

With the lines "The pure products of America / go crazy" Williams also entered the raging debate in the early 1920s about who the pure products of America were. *In the American Grain*, the book he wrote and published in the little magazines along with *Spring and All*, took up position in a field already delimited on one side by Stuart Sherman's *Americans* and on the other by Waldo Frank's *Our America*.[37] Like Frank, Williams disputed the notion that the only pure Americans were Anglo-Saxon Americans, and so he tilted away from the blunt unity of Sherman's title toward the broader inclusiveness of Frank's. But Williams also agreed, at least some of the time, with Frank's feeling that the pure products of America go crazy because they lack "peasant traditions to give them / character" (*CP*, p. 219).[38] How to manage the conflicting imperatives of variety and unity was a problem Williams was so little able to solve that he finally ended up sounding more like Sherman after all.

The purest products of America that appear in *In the American Grain* are those who brush their fellow citizens against the grain. As he was to say some years later in the Stieglitz essay, "the pure American addition to world culture" was produced by men who were "themselves foreigners—in their own country" (*SE*, pp. 141–42). Before there was a country to be foreign to, the truest Americans were those who had no country at all: Red Eric, who begins the whole book by complaining of his fellow Norsemen, "Because I am not like them, I am evil" (*IAG*, p. 1); Columbus accused of treason; Cortez attacked from the rear by his own countrymen; Champlain, who brought his own would-be murderer with him from France. For Williams, even Washington is transformed from the revered father of his country into a great voluptuary gnawed on and hated by the "crawling mass" (*IAG*, p. 143). It is no wonder, then, that the sequence culminates with Aaron Burr, an accused traitor, and Edgar Allan Poe, best known still as a dipsomaniac.

Williams does not merely accept but insists on this paradox. Burr is great precisely because he is universally despised: "[I]f a verdict be unanimous, it is sure to be a wrong one, a crude rush of the herd . . ." (*IAG*, p. 190). Poe is a great American poet *because* he abhorred everyone and everything around him. Thus there creeps into this book on the American grain an increasingly shrill denunciation of the masses, the herd, to which Williams applies the traditional metaphors of the Right: the masses are low, dirty, fecal, insectlike, rodentlike. And there is an almost palpable inconsistency in the central metaphor of the whole volume, namely, that of touch. The pivotal chapter of *In the American*

Grain insists on a dichotomy between the Catholic and the Protestant coloniza-tions of the new continent, only the first of which had the "apt sensual touch" that allowed for a true approach to the new (*IAG*, pp. 128–29). Touch comes to sym-bolize everything Williams values: it is a concrete approach to the local, without preconceptions. And yet there is also a physical flinching from the mass that appears overtly in Williams's hatred for Franklin, who "only wanted to touch" (*IAG*, p. 155). In this case "there is a kind of nastiness in his TOUCHING" be-cause it is "sly, covert, almost cringing." It is the touching of the mass man, in other words, who cannot stand it that some things remain "clean, aloof" (*IAG*, p. 157).

Thus the final dichotomy of the book utterly undoes its central dichotomy, as Williams closes by comparing Hawthorne's "closeness to the life of his locality" unfavorably to Poe's "flying to the ends of the earth" (*IAG*, p. 228). Hawthorne remains conventional and timid because he lacks Poe's saving "repugnance," because he handles what Poe avoids. As Williams finally announces with some-thing of a flourish, "By such a simple, logical twist does Poe succeed in being the more American . . . by standing off to SEE instead of forcing himself too close" (*IAG*, pp. 228–29).

There is certainly a measure of wishful self-justification here.[39] Williams had been preaching the virtues of the low and the local to a tiny audience for years. The very titles of books like *Al Que Quiere* and *Sour Grapes* breathe the resent-ment he felt at his lack of success, especially when measured against contempo-raries like Eliot, who he felt had taken a smoother road. As the 1920s dragged on into the 1930s, he suffered the further perverse indignity of having his socially conscious poetry appear only in limited-edition printings that very few readers could afford. The notion that a poet becomes more truly American by standing off from the embrace of his fellow Americans was no doubt personally tempting to him.

In a way this notion is simply a development of an idea that Williams had been advancing for some time. Poe, he says, was unrecognized because Americans can never recognize themselves "until someone invent the ORIGINAL terms. As long as we are content to be called by somebody else's terms, we are incapable of being anything but our own dupes" (*IAG*, p. 226). In other words, Poe serves as the dissonant voice that, in the absence of a true American language, reminds us of the need for one. As Williams says in *Spring and All*, "the first American poet had to be a man of great separation . . ." (*CP*, p. 198). Thus the true American poet is defined in the same way that the true American language is defined, by its ability to cut itself off from the English standard: Poe himself said, according to Williams, "that we should cut ourselves loose from the lead strings of our British grandmama" (*SE*, p. 144). This desire to cut himself loose became "a mono-maniacal driving to destroy, to annihilate the copied, the slavish, the FALSE literature about him" (*IAG*, p. 223).

All the truest Americans, it turns out, "cut themselves off from the old at once and set to work with a will" (*SE*, p. 143). Thus the language of cutting, breaking, and tearing free returns in a new situation adapted, as it were, from a linguistic to a political context. In this analysis the pure products of America might always be crazy, because their very purity would be based on their eccentricity. But with this language there returns the problem of basing a new unity on an ethic of separation. How could Poe's desire to cut himself loose, to destroy, to annihilate, ever become the basis for a democratic union? How could this language of cutting loose be reconciled with the equally insistent metaphors of touch and contact? Certainly Williams means in general that Americans should stay in contact with the low and democratic and cut themselves off only from foreign influences, but he finally pushes the emphasis on separation and the disdain for the herd so far as to turn democracy inside out, transforming it into aristocracy, "since an aristocracy is the flower of a locality and so the *full* expression of a democracy" (*IAG*, p. 231). Being in the American grain requires such sharp cutting against the American grain that what seems the most democratic of all modernist masterworks ends with the aloofness of the aristocrat.

Thus *In the American Grain* requires its reader to conceive of America as a democracy best represented by its aristocrats, especially if those aristocrats were also outcasts like Aaron Burr. But it also offers another model that resolves the basic paradox of Williams's work in a different way, by presenting a race composed entirely of outcasts. Over and over, Williams describes the true Americans as a lost race, not a race still to come into its own but one forever in arrears. As early as the prologue to *Kora in Hell*, he insisted that "The New World is Montezuma or, since he was stoned to death in a parley, Guatemozin who had the city of Mexico leveled over him before he was taken" (*I*, p. 24). He returned to the same image many years later, in "The American Background," where he says that "the pure American addition to world culture" is a secret that lies buried in Tenochtitlán (*SE*, p. 143). He makes this definition plainest in *In the American Grain:* "I do believe the average American to be an Indian, but an Indian robbed of his world . . ." (*IAG*, p. 128).

Thus the elemental American scene of creation is also one of racial murder, Cortez slaughtering the Aztecs, or Ponce de León exterminating the Caribs. In fact, it is by being defeated that Aztecs or Caribs come to be representative of America: "These are the inhabitants of our souls, our murdered souls that lie . . . agh. . . . In the heart there are living Indians once slaughtered and defrauded . . ." (*IAG*, p. 39, 42). Here the cutting and slashing that Williams so often associates with the truly American are turned on America's first inhabitants—"cut them down if they fainted, slashed off breasts, arms—women, children. Gut souls" (*IAG*, p. 42)—but the more they are cut down and cut off the more the Indians rise and become the soul of America. The more thoroughly exterminated the tribe, the more effffectively does it resolve Williams's paradox because then it becomes a collective of outcasts, a democracy somehow made up of those rejected by the mass.

This logic describes its tightest circle around the African slaves whom Williams brings so casually into *In the American Grain*. At first he seems uncertain of how to account for the charm that African Americans exert over him: "[I]t is a sunken quality, or it is a living quality—it is no matter which" (*IAG*, p. 209). But it soon develops that where the slaves are concerned sunken and living are the same thing, for they have "a solidity, a racial irreducible minimum, which gives them poise in a world where they have no authority." If they try to assert that solidity, insisting on the distinctness and value of their race, "it is nothing." But singing "Nobody," "that's SOMETHIN'." Only by being nothing, by admitting their nothingness, can African Americans exert that substantial solidity, that elemental vitality that makes them so real to Williams he tries to emulate their language: "waggin', wavin', weavin', shakin'; or alone, in a cabin, at night, in the stillness, in the moonlight—bein' nothin'— . . ." (*IAG*, p. 209).

"Bein' nothin'" is a paradoxical activity, but it is also for Williams the quintessentially American activity, deriving self-assertion from defeat, originality from abnegation. African Americans are such a powerful symbol for him because they seem to share as a race the obliqueness of the American outcast and thus to turn it into a vital culture. Moreover, it is a race that speaks a language cut loose from the standard, symbolized for Williams by the eliding apostrophe, and yet solid and concrete. It is a minor detail but perhaps not entirely an unimportant accident that the black man whose speech seems to Williams a spring "never ending, never failing" comes to him with an injured larynx: "'Doc, I got a hemorrhage of the FLUTE,' he said. 'Cocaine for horses, cocaine for mules, IN THE TRENCHES!' he yelled as I removed the bandage" (*IAG*, p. 210). Williams seems unaware of the irony in the fact that the man whose eloquence he admires so much he wants to write a book either with him or about him demonstrates that eloquence most in expostulations about his injured voice.[40] On the other hand, who could better demonstrate the peculiar charms of "saying *nothing*" (*IAG*, p. 209)?

Actually, there is one other, one whom Williams is even more taken with, one who does all her talking with a knife. "I remember with thrilling pleasure and deep satisfaction," he says, "E. K. Means' tale, *Diada Daughter of Discord*, an outstanding story of a wild nigger wench. . . . Read *Diada* . . ." (*IAG*, p. 210). "Diada, Daughter of Discord" is in many ways one of the crudest stories of one of the crudest of the dialect writers who flourished at this time, but it is not hard to see why it fascinated Williams. Though Diada is herself Polynesian, brought to a Mississippi plantation only for a visit, her story contains all the elements of the American drama that gripped Williams. Huge, deformed, animalistic, and powerful, Diada terrifies everyone on the plantation, and she soon collects all the sharp objects in sight and takes off for the swamp. The scene that Williams remembers most vividly, "cutting cane stalks, sharpening them with lightning speed and driving them through the attacking hounds" (*IAG*, p. 210), occurs when Diada is cornered, a moment of extremity in which she utters the only sound she makes in the entire story: "Whoosh! Whoo-ash!" This "long, plaintive, howling scream" seems a mere animalistic cry to her pursuers, but it turns out in the end that it means, quite simply and logically, *"Help! I am in trouble!"*[41]

The lurid drama of the "wild nigger wench" slashing her way through the swamp with a knife thus turns out to have a moral. It is for lack of a common language that Diada is driven into the swamp, because her Polynesian syllables seem to European-tuned ears mere noise. Though what she has to say is as eloquent as anything in the story, she seems to be "saying *nothing,*" and thus she has to talk with a knife. And though this is a miniature version of the whole American tragedy, a people cut off and isolated because there are no words for their condition, Williams is clearly thrilled by the drama of Diada's last stand. Black, female, enslaved, and inarticulate, Diada provides nonetheless a romantic drama of resistance in which "saying nothing" is more potent than any words could ever be.

Dialect literature thus provides Williams with one of his most persistent symbols of America, a symbol he would repeat and elaborate throughout the rest of his work. A young woman, preferably black or American Indian, bathed in filth, was the shape in which he preferred to see his country. This is Elsie, "bathed in filth" in *Spring and All* (*CP*, p. 217); and the foreign woman who seems to him "America personified in the filth of its own imagination" in *Contact;* and Kathleen, who is called "an exquisite chunk of mud" in "K. McB." (*CP*, p. 106); and Georgie Anderson, the black maid who may have started the whole series by allowing the young Williams to watch through a keyhole while she bathed. All of these women converge in certain abstract figures who anchor some of Williams's most important work: the "black eyed susan" in the last poem of *Spring and All;* the "beautiful thing" of *Paterson.*

When Columbus first walks on the soil of the New World, a scene Williams cleverly saves for the end of his chapter in *In the American Grain,* he says it is "the most beautiful thing which I had ever seen . . ." (*IAG*, p. 26). Williams cherishes this phrase until it becomes a keynote of his longest work, where it acquires a complex irony. For the woman called "Beautiful Thing" in *Paterson* is beautiful only in the same way that Diada is, as a defiled and inarticulate outcast. Like Diada, this woman is an elemental and destructive force, "a dark flame, / a wind, a flood" (*P*, p. 100) and yet, also like Diada, she is driven into a corner, beaten, and, in this version, raped: "they maled / and femaled you jealously / Beautiful Thing" (*P*, p. 128). Yet her broken nose is her beauty: "I must believe that all / desired women have had each / in the end / a busted nose / and lived afterward marked up" (*P*, p. 128). And the very fact that she is defiled and even expelled is the source of her importance: "[T]hat which should be / rare, is trash; because it contains / nothing of you. They spit on you, / literally, but without you, nothing" (*P*, p. 123). Thus Williams plays with a familiar pun as nothing is converted back into the thing itself, the expelled and the defiled become the very definition of beauty.

It is so difficult to measure the ratio of willful to unwillful self-revelation in

Williams's work that it is impossible to say whether he is aware of the violently sexual wish-fulfillment that runs through his many descriptions of black female victims. Or whether he consciously plays both roles in the drama. For the black female victim is certainly the last version of a role that Williams had played for some time, as Montezuma, as a Carib, as an American Indian, "the brutal thing itself," as he called himself in the chapter of *In the American Grain* in which he confronts Europe in the form of Valery Larbaud (*IAG*, p. 107). Perhaps more extensively than any of his colleagues, Williams played the role of the modern artist as racial outcast, "madmen at Paris, . . . the Caribs leaping out," as he put it in *In the American Grain* (p. 40). Thus there is an element of sentimental self-pity in the descriptions of the rape and beating in *Paterson*, in the examination of the scarred legs of the black maid who fascinates Williams in the same section of the poem: "I can't be half gentle enough, / half tender enough / toward you, toward you, / inarticulate, not loving half enough . . ." (*P*, p. 128). And yet at other times, Williams quite consciously plays the role of bully and defiler:

> (Then, my anger rising) TAKE OFF YOUR
> CLOTHES! I didn't ask you
> to take off your skin . I said your
> clothes, your clothes. You smell
> like a whore. I ask you to bathe in my
> opinions, the astonishing virtue of your
> lost body (I said) .
>
> (*P*, p. 106)

The way that Williams stands on both sides of this racial drama of power and submission reveals a good deal about the instability of his basic metaphor for America. In one sense the black female victim is the ultimate metaphorical version of his concept of American literature and art: cut off, abused, misunderstood, and all the more truthful and beautiful for it. She expresses as well the way that different racial stereotypes conveniently fit this paradigm, for someone like Diada is at once so elemental and real as to be a virtual animal and at the same time so different as to be sheer mystery. She is nothing and at the same time the most beautiful thing. This is what, at many stages of his career, Williams wanted to accomplish himself, and he certainly wanted to see himself as belonging to a tribe of outcasts. And yet, when the violence and distaste that always lurk within the sentimental version of the black victim finally come into the open, they reveal how little able Williams was to join this tribe.

Despite his own situation on the margins of the Americanist avant-garde, Williams reproduces in his own work its contradiction of racial cross-identification and racial hatred. More obviously than some of his less "dissonant" colleagues, he shows how easily praise of wholeness can dissolve into a critique of nothingness, how variously African Americans served as symbols of some all-encompassing psychic health and simultaneously as ciphers of total lack. And Williams also demonstrated more obviously than most how these inconsistencies derailed the cultural project of the Americanist avant-garde, which attempted to phrase its language as a dialect of rebellion but also as a national language of unity. Speaking a dialect, "saying *nothing,*" the black alter ego stands at the very intersection of these contradictions.

IV

The contributions Williams and Toomer made to the September 1923 issue of *Broom* show a surprising commonality of concern. When Ponce de León slaughters the Caribs in Williams's "Fountain of Eternal Youth," he also slaughters "a language," but slaughter seems simply to give that language a secret life: "Do these things die? Men who do not know what lives, are themselves dead. In the heart there are living Indians once slaughtered and defrauded . . ." (*IAG*, p. 42). Perhaps Williams is referring to the actual language of the Caribs, lost but for secret survivals like "hurricane," but it is more likely that he means the American language that was lost when the first settlers submitted themselves to English words and forms instead of inventing their own. The problem of all of Williams's work in one sense is to find the surviving remnants of this slaughtered language and restore them to life.

This is also the problem of Toomer's contribution, a section of "Kabnis" in which the title character struggles with "misshapen, split-gut, tortured, twisted words" (*C*, p. 111). The language he might have spoken, the language of poetry, has "gone down t hell in a holy avalanche of words" (*C*, p. 111), an avalanche started by racial hatred. Thus both writers seek a language submerged in slaughter, a language apprehensible only in the deformations of contemporary speech. The broken forms of the works they produced at this time testify to the difficulty of approaching this language, especially if that meant reconciling the racial history that had killed it.

Like his protagonist, Toomer felt that history as an internal pressure. In the most candid of several statements he made about his background Toomer said, "Racially, I seem to have (who knows for sure) seven blood mixtures: French, Dutch, Welsh, Negro, German, Jewish, and Indian. Because of these, my position in America has been a curious one."[42] One of the most curious things about this experience was the number of different racial and ethnic groups into which Toomer could superficially fit: "According to their own subjective experiences, various people have taken me for American, English, Spanish, French, Italian, Russian, Hindu, Japanese, Romanian, Indian, and Dutch."[43] In Toomer's view this very variability made him the more quintessentially American: "And, I alone, as far as I know, have striven for a spiritual fusion analagous [*sic*] to the fact of racial intermingling. . . . What am I? From my own point of view, naturally and inevitably an American."[44] Taking very seriously rhetoric like Bourne's about a transnational America, Toomer argued that America had brought forth a distinct type, "the American type,"[45] from its mixture of races and stocks: "[A]nd in this America I saw the divisions mended, the differences reconciled—saw that (1) we would in truth be a united people existing in the *United* States, saw that (2) we would in truth be once again members of a united human race."[46] Toomer's first and most fully considered literary work was "The First American," later retitled "The Blue Meridian," an attempt to give poetic account of this type.[47]

Unfortunately for this project, Toomer matured at a time when American racial classifications, both official and unofficial, were becoming more, not less, rigid. As George Hutchinson has recently pointed out, the term *mulatto* was removed from U. S. census forms in 1920.[48] On the one hand, this may simply have retired an outmoded concept, one as surrounded by myth and misinformation as any, but, on the other hand, it also made the choice of racial allegiance for someone like Toomer a good deal starker. This insistence on racial boundaries emerged with almost hysterical shrillness when *Time* magazine learned of Toomer's marriage to Margery Latimer. It quoted his ideas about the new American race with scorn and affected alarm under the ironic title of "Just Americans." The article suggested that some states, like Wisconsin, where Toomer and Latimer were married, were insufficiently vigilant against marriages between the races.[49]

"The First American" was Toomer's attempt to counter such rigid ideas about race, and it was simultaneously a technical attempt to put into practice theories Toomer had gleaned from "the poems and programs of the Imagists. Their insistence on fresh vision and on the perfect clean economical line was just what I had been looking for."[50] Moving to New York, Toomer also "stepped into the literary world" he had been reading about: "Frank, Gorham Munson, Kenneth Burke, Hart Crane, Matthew Josephson, Malcolm Cowley, Paul Rosenfeld, Van Wyck Brooks, Robert Littell—*Broom*, the *Dial*, the *New Republic* and many more."[51] He met with especial enthusiasm from Lola Ridge, who was helping to edit *Broom*, and she invited him to her parties, where he met a number of writers, possibly including Williams.[52] But if he was hoping to find there a truly "fresh vision" about race, he was ultimately to be disappointed.

The most important acquaintance Toomer made at Ridge's was Waldo Frank, to whom he quite hopefully sent "The First American."[53] It is not hard to see why these two should have greeted one another with enthusiasm: for Toomer, Frank was a theorist whose works had virtually predicted "The First American"; to Frank, Toomer seemed the embodiment of his predictions. Soon Toomer was writing to Frank that "the Experiment here in America has an almost complete hold upon my interests and imagination," and that "I cannot think of myself as being separated from you in the dual task of creating an American literature, and of developing a public. . . ."[54] They corresponded copiously, traveled together, and even arranged to have their two books, *Cane* and *Holiday*, published on the same day.

Even at the very beginning, however, there were omens of the eventual breakup of this happy relationship. Toomer was distressed that the all-inclusive vision of *Our America* did not include African Americans: "In your Our America, I missed your not including the Negro. . . . Of the Negro, what facts are known have too often been perverted for the purpose of propaganda, one way or the other."[55] Any hopes he might have had that Frank would avoid such propaganda when he *did* include "the Negro" were to be disappointed. Toomer's very tactful review of *Holiday* in the *Dial* shows how he had to haul that work around to his own way of thinking. "Frank is too subtle," he says, "for an abitrary portioning of repression, in a block, to the whites of the South; for a rigid symbolizing of the blacks as expression." But this is exactly what Frank did when he characterized blacks: "[T]he nigger world is a music filling the world from the trees right down to the earth."[56] And Toomer was well aware of this, as he grudgingly admits: "In contrast with each other, however, it may be said that in this novel the blacks generally represent a full life; while the whites stand for a denial of it."[57] In a very short time, Toomer had come to realize that the all-inclusive vision of *Our America* was riven by some very old-fashioned dichotomies.

Toomer's discomfort was even greater when he realized that these dichotomies were to be applied to him. His first exposure to "modern American writing" had been a lecture by Williams's friend Alfred Kreymborg, the founding editor of *Others*. Four years after this first glimpse, Frank arranged to have Toomer join Kreymborg for a reading, but only on certain rather restrictive terms: "I told K. I was sure you could do your Negro stuff. It will of course be necessary, in case you are used, to feature something special like that, as by yourself you are not a drawing card,—AS YET."[58] Despite his later protestations, Toomer had realized from the beginning, "As I become known, I shall no doubt be classed as a Negro."[59] He had prepared himself for this eventuality, but he was still struck by the crudity and bluntness with which his "Negro stuff" was to be commercialized. Horace Liveright also proposed "that right at the very start there should be a definite note struck about your colored blood," and this the ad department of Boni & Liveright did with a vengeance: in ads for *Cane* it offered "negro life whose rhythmic beat, like the primitive tom-tom of the African jungle, you can feel because it is written by a man who has felt it historically, poetically, and with deepest understanding."[60] Toomer's racial status had to be simplified in this way so that his books could be sold. Even worse, Toomer never lost the suspicion that his racial status had been simplified so that Waldo Frank's books could be sold.[61]

Toomer was aghast at Liveright's campaign not simply because he was reluctant to see his complex background presented so crudely but also because he resented the idea that others were to have the power of defining him at all. "My racial composition and my position in the world," he wrote to Liveright, "are realities which I alone may determine. . . . I do not expect to be told what I should consider myself to be."[62] It seemed an especially cruel irony that literary success should have robbed him of this essential right of self-definition and more ironic still that he should have suffered thus at the hands of a literary movement that was at that very moment advertising the sparkling newness of its approach to race.

The praise that Toomer received from the avant-garde seemed uncomfortably close to the stereotypes it supposedly reversed. Toomer was so pleased to receive a note of encouragement from Sherwood Anderson, for example, that he composed a long letter of tribute in return. But it soon became clear that Anderson appreciated Toomer only in an especially restricted sense. Anderson confessed that he had long envied the sure touch of the African Americans he had seen doing manual labor: "What they touch with their great black fingers is something definite. I am envious of them. . . . What would I not give to accomplish something definite— related to trees, the earth, the sky, the seas." This sure touch also extended to language, which Anderson felt was dying under the pressure of "standardization, big editions, money rolling in. . . ."[63] Anderson seized on Toomer as an antidote to that death, a literate and articulate man who was nonetheless in touch with raw reality: "A man like yourself can escape. You have a direct and glowing genius[?] that is, I am sure, a part of your body, a part of the way you walk, look at things, make love, sleep and eat. Such a man goes rather directly from feeling to expression."[64]

Toomer shrewdly observed in a letter to Frank: "Sherwood Anderson has doubtless had a very deep and beautiful emotion by way of the Negro. Here and there he has succeeded in expressing this. But he is not satisfied. He wants more. He is hungry for it. I come along. I express it. It is natural for him to see me in terms of this expression. I see myself that way. But also I see myself expressing *myself,* expressing *Life.* " Anderson, he felt, "limits me to Negro. As an approach, as a constant element (part of a larger whole) of interest, Negro is good. But to try to tie me to one of my parts is surely to loose me."[65] What Toomer had been proposing since "The First American" was something quite new; what Anderson was looking for was quite old, though it was tricked out in an up-to-date costume.

One of the things that made Toomer uncomfortable about such praise was its closeness to the old stereotypes it seemed superficially to reverse. The enthusiasm of Anderson and Frank could easily edge off into the condescension shown by the *Dial*'s brisk, dismissive review of *Cane*, which stressed the accuracy of the author's "negro ear."[66] Toomer was also praised in the *New York Tribune* for having rendered "the hopes and fears of the genuine darky," an entity whose passions, according to the *Boston Evening Transcript*, are "untutored and entirely unconnected with the brain." Perhaps the most demeaning of all these reviews, however, was the one that suggested that "Jean Toomer" was merely a nom de plume for Waldo Frank.[67] To this reviewer, apparently, a black writer was incapable even of rendering his own unbridled authenticity.

Yet Toomer faced the same sort of distorting incomprehension from his closest associates in the Americanist avant-garde, an incomprehension all the more insidious because it was rooted in the very language they were supposed to share. When Gorham Munson first read "Theater," he compared it unfavorably to Frank's "Hope," assuming, on the basis of a very flawed reading of the story, that it was about interracial attraction. Toomer pointed out in response that "Theater" was not another in the seemingly endless string of stories and poems about white longing for the release of black sensuality: the barrier between the two characters, he told Munson, is "not of race, but of respectability." Munson, embarrassed by his misreading, explained, "Much depends on the word 'dictie,' whose meaning I did not know."[68] This puts a vast problem in a nutshell: because he did not speak the American language that Toomer was using, Munson could not read his story, could only read it, in fact, by turning it into a story by Waldo Frank. Like Nation Roe, Toomer was faced by a white associate who really did not speak his language at all, who could only read him in light of the clichés of white impersonators.

By the time he was hailed in *The New Negro* as "a bright morning star of a new day of the race in literature," Toomer refused to be considered black at all.[69] And the writer who could most successfully have embodied Locke's hopes for a dual renaissance, a confluence of Harlem and the moderns, had also abandoned all but a few of his friends in the avant-garde. In 1930 Toomer told a correspondent, "I have been associated in New York and Paris with some of the men who have been trying to bring about a renaissance in American art and life."[70] In one way, the lack of specificity is intriguing: does he mean the Harlem Renaissance or what was often called the New York Little Renaissance, associated with Frank? In another way, the ambiguity simply illustrates how loosely connected Toomer was with both movements, and how the possibility of a link between them had in his case turned into an estranging distance from both.

V

Toomer made it clear to several of his friends and correspondents that he had discovered an important part of his identity during the two months he spent in Sparta, Georgia. As he wrote to the staff at the *Liberator:*

> A visit to Georgia last fall was the starting point of almost everything of worth that I have done. I heard folk-songs come from the lips of Negro peasants. I saw the rich dusk beauty that I had heard many false accounts about, and of which, till then, I was somewhat skeptical. And a deep part of my nature, a part that I had repressed, sprang suddenly to life and responded to them.

But discovering anew this particular aspect of his heritage did not make Toomer any the less insistent on its other aspects or on the importance of the mixture to which they belonged. As he said in the same letter, "Without denying a single element in me, with no desire to subdue one to the other, I have sought to let them function as complements. I have tried to let them live in harmony. Within the last two or three years, however, my growing need for artistic expression has pulled me deeper and deeper into the Negro group."[71]

For Toomer, apparently, it was not impossible to be pulled into one particular part of his background and yet still remain faithful to the various whole. This is so because Toomer saw the African-American part of his heritage quite differently from Frank and Anderson. For him there was no romantic temptation to return to a simpler past and, therefore, no temptation to make one race a metaphor for the lost innocence of another. As he wrote in "On Being an American":

> Back to nature, even if desirable, was no longer possible, because industry had taken nature unto itself. Even if he wanted to, a city person could not become a soil person by changing his locale and living on a farm or in the woods. . . . Those who sought to cure themselves by a return to more primitive conditions were either romantics or escapists.[72]

This is one reason why Toomer was baffled and annoyed at people who wanted him to continue to write *Cane* over and over, because he saw that way of life as vanished and untouchable.

If, on one hand, this seems sad and even defeatist, it did, on the other, open up a "new life" as well. In a letter to Frank, Toomer lamented the fact that "the Negro of the folk-song has all but passed away," but he also said, "When I come up to Seventh Street and Theatre, a wholly new life confronts me. A life, I am afraid, that Sherwood Anderson would not get his beauty from. For it is jazzed, strident, modern. Seventh Street is the song of crude new life. Of a new people. Negro? Only in the *boldness* of its expression. In its healthy freedom. American."[73] The new, modern life of Seventh Street resists any attempt to primitivize it, to exploit it. Toomer's acidly ironic comment about Anderson reveals that he also had a personal stake in this new life, because it helped him resist the push Anderson was giving him into a primitive, rural past. Toomer is asserting, in other words, that he is far more of a modernist than Anderson. This also means that he has a far less static notion of race, one that allows him to assert a particular black identity and a various American one at the same time. In fact, it might seem that on Seventh Street Toomer discovered that in some ways at least black identity *was* the American identity he had been seeking, as long as it was not defined as a static thing lodged in some mythical primitive past but as a position of "healthy freedom" and "boldness" of expression.

Thus it was possible for Toomer to say almost in the same breath that *Cane* was a "lyric essence" of the rural South and a "spiritual form analogous to the fact of racial intermingling."[74] Toomer tended to express this relationship in the form of a circle: "Aesthetically, from simple forms to complex ones, and back to simple forms. Regionally, from the South up into the North, and back into the South again."[75] But it would be more accurate to say that there is a constant shuttling back and forth between literary forms such as lyric in a simple state and complex variations on them or mixtures of them. It is in this freedom from fixed forms, in this boldness of expression, that Toomer is faithful at once to the African-American experience he discovered in the South and to his vision of the new American. According to James Kraft, "[T]he blackness of *Cane* is in its noncategorical and freely creative capacity to transform the forms of the 'white' novel and create its own black existence."[76] Yet it would be far too simplistic to see the book in terms of a black–white tension between freedom and form, for there are obviously black forms, such as the spiritual, that Toomer stretches just as he stretches the lyric, and there are black forms, such as call and response, that incorporate tension and interplay into their very structure. What Toomer was trying to accomplish was too complex for any mere dichotomy.

The same might be said of Toomer's conception of the American language. Even before his trip to Georgia, he had been interested in the literary possibilities of dialect: there are two or three dialect poems in an early notebook probably kept during 1920.[77] While in Georgia he seems to have kept a list of dialect expressions, possibly for later use in *Cane*.[78] But readers who looked in *Cane* for fidelity to a particular kind of speech were disappointed.[79] *Cane* bore little resemblance to contemporaneous works like *Birthright, Nigger,* or the collections of Bradford and Gonzales because its aim was not to preserve a particular language but to use the disjunctive strategies of that language to invent new forms.

As Alain Locke put it in *The New Negro*, writers like Toomer were "thoroughly modern, some of them ultra-modern," even as they dug "deep into the racy peasant undersoil of the race life." The key characteristic of the new generation was, according to Locke, "the increasing tendency to evolve from the racial substance something technically distinctive. . . ." This technical distinction came from the way these writers managed to "transpose the dialect motive and carry it through the idioms of imagery rather than the broken phonetics of speech. . . ."[80] Such transposition is possible, Locke leaves his readers to assume, because the "dialect motive" is not to be associated with any particular patterns of speech, much less with those traditionally represented by the white dialect writers, but with the habit of bringing "technical distinction" to speech itself. When the dialect motive of disarranging and rearranging standard speech patterns is brought to literature, the result is not primitivism but modernism.

The dust jacket of the first edition of *Cane* identified it as "a vaudeville out of the South."[81] This is a metaphor easily subject to misunderstanding: it was picked up and used in unsympathetic reviews to suggest that the book was an incomprehensible mélange.[82] But Toomer may have had something both distinct and complex in mind. For vaudeville is "out of the South" in that its sources are largely rural and black, but it is also "out of the South" in that these forms have been transplanted into an urban setting and subjected to violent stretching and scrambling. Vaudeville is also highly formulaic, dependent on an almost ritualistic repetition of acts and situations, but it is also improvisatory, as the performers interact differently with different audiences on different nights. Vaudeville is also, most obviously, an oral form, but it is not for that reason a simple one. It most closely approximates the oral forms that Heath compares to *Spring and All:* "mixed genres, numerous openings of subgenres without closure of these, repetitious false starts, switches across topics within the midst of paragraphs, . . . incomplete references to other actual texts upon which this text depends. . . ."[83] Vaudeville is, in other words, an art in which the simple reveals its infinite complexity, in which popular culture lives by absorbing and rearranging high culture, in which oral communication is not subgeneric to literature but supergeneric. It is an apt metaphor for what Toomer was trying to accomplish, which was quite similar to what Williams was trying to accomplish in *Spring and All.* Unfortunately, the similarities extend to the difficulties the two writers ultimately faced.

VI

The multiplicity of Toomer's ambition, and the difficulties he encountered, can be illustrated by a comparison of two of the shortest sections of *Cane,* "Her Lips Are Copper Wire" and "Reapers." The first is one of two or three poems in the book that represent Toomer's earlier imagist period. It is prosodically irregular, syntactically discontinuous, and devoid of punctuation. The pronoun references shift from second to third person abruptly and without explanation, and there is a queasy inconsistency of mood: "telephone the power-house" is almost certainly in the imperative, but "whisper of yellow globes," the first line of the poem, could be indicative or imperative. As in many modernist poems, these formal discontinuities are meant to mimic the jaggedness of modern urban life, in this case the on/off patterns of the lights on the city signs: "(her words play softly up and down / dewy corridors of billboards)" (*C*, p. 57). Here Toomer is apparently describing the same Seventh Street scene that appears in "Gum":[84]

STAR
J E S U S
The Light of the World

· · ·

WRIGLEYS

eat it
after
every meal
It Does You Good

Intermittently, their lights flash
Down upon the streets of Washington . . .

(*CPJT*, p. 18)

In "Her Lips Are Copper Wire," Toomer's words play up and down in the same way, flashing on and off with the electrical current that is the gathering metaphor for the whole poem.

The reconnection of a circuit, the jump of electricity across a gap, is, in fact, a gathering metaphor for most of this, the second, section of *Cane*. For much of this section the sexual tension between the characters crackles across a physical or social gap. In "Theater" John silently watches Dorris dance while Dorris watches him watch, until a "shaft of light goes out the window high above him" and somehow sweeps both of them up into the same dream (*C*, p. 55). In "Box Seat" Dan and Muriel yearn for one another, but they remain separated by the intrusive Mrs. Pribby, so that "Muriel's lips become the flesh-notes of a futile, plaintive longing" (*C*, p. 62). In "Her Lips Are Copper Wire" the restrictions are stripped off and the electricity fairly hums:

> then with your tongue remove the tape
> and press your lips to mine
> till they are incandescent

Until this moment of release, "the main wires are insulate," but once that insulation is stripped off, lips touch, lights light up the city street, and words flow.

The incandescence is not simply sexual because its glow is the glow of words released from inhibition and restriction. In "Box Seat" Dan is wooed not just by Muriel's physical lips but also by "Lips, flesh-notes of a forgotten song. . . ." This song emerges from the black urban culture of street and theater: "Dark swaying forms of Negroes are street songs that woo virginal houses" (*C*, p. 59). In "Her Lips" these songs break free and "play softly up and down / dewy corridors of billboards." The energy is released when it jumps a gap, like a spark, or overcomes resistance, like an incandescent filament. It almost seems as if the songs require a prior moment of forgetting or the obstacle of repression so as to release all their energy. And this does seem to be the way Toomer looks at the relationship between the "forgotten" songs and their urban re-realizations, as if the discontinuity of modern life were not the death of an old organic existence but the release of it in a new form.

Thus Toomer defines the form he himself uses in most of the second, urban section of *Cane*, where even the prose is choppy and asyntactic: "Stale soggy wood of Washington. Wedges rust in soggy wood . . . Split it! In two! Again! Shred it! . . the sun" (*C*, p. 41). Like Williams, Toomer uses ellipses to suspend ordinary syntax and to mimic the action of splitting or breaking indispensable to creation. Out of these breaks in the ordinary, leaping across them, comes a speech and a poetic, both associated with jazz. It is not really an accident that the idiom used for jazz improvisation is "tore it down," that when the piano player does this in "Bona and Paul," "the picture of Our Poets hung perilously" (*C*, p. 75). Like *Cane* itself, jazz has an old, rural basis, but it mobilizes that influence against standard European forms in a way that makes it seem both simple and complex at once.

If jazz provides a general formal model for this section of *Cane*, imagism provides the specific metaphor of electricity. "Her Lips" was written around 1920, before most of the poems in *Cane;* in fact, it was composed when Toomer was preparing a response to Richard Aldington's essay on imagism entitled "The Art of Poetry."[85] In that essay, which used examples from Pound and H.D., Aldington declared that a successful imagist poem included "phrases which give me a sudden shock of illumination. . . ."[86] This is Aldington's metaphor—not a particularly lively one—for Pound's doctrine of the image as "that which presents an intellectual and emotional complex in an instant of time. . . . It is the presentation of such a 'complex' instantaneously which gives that sudden sense of liberation . . . which we experience in the presence of the greatest works of art."[87] Toomer copied Aldington's electrical metaphor into his notebook and literalized it in "Her Lips Are Copper Wire," and in so doing he puts the doctrine of the image to work in an urban American setting.

Toomer wrote a number of poems under this influence, including "Evening Song" and "Face," which appear in *Cane*. His closeness to the imagist movement at this time can be demonstrated by the uncanny similarity between the fifth of his "Five Vignettes" and a poem by Williams on a similar subject:

> In Y. Don's laundry
> A Chinese baby fell
> And cried as any other.
> (*CPJT*, p. 3)

> Long before dawn your light
> Shone in the window, Sam Wu;
> You were at your trade.
> (*CP*, p. 59)

Toomer also followed the modernist movement in the other direction, away from this extreme simplicity to the sort of sound poems the dadaists were doing:

> Mon sa me el kirimoor,
> Ve dice kor, korrand ve deer . . .
> (*CPJT*, p. 15)

At either extreme, however, it was difficult for modern poetry to satisfy Toomer's desire for ethical and political engagement. As he wrote to Munson in 1922, "I still demand an extra-artistic consciousness in works of art."[88] Thus he quarrels at length with Aldington's assumption that "the old cant of a poet's message is now completely discredited." He disagrees with imagism's shift of emphasis from explanation to presentation: "Overnight, our voice and our hearing have not shrunk to an eye." And when he accuses Aldington of turning his back on "the mighty voices of the past," Toomer links at least four different issues: imagism's repudiation of tradition; its deprecation of poetry with a message; its emphasis on visual imagery over verbal music; and its refusal of the old prosodic forms.[89]

The task that faced him in *Cane*, then, was somehow to produce a modern literature that was in all four ways more faithful to "the mighty voices of the past." Like Williams, he wanted to make a cohesive and unified culture out of an aesthetic of breaks and discontinuities. However, the formal structure of most of the poems in the collection—and certainly of those in the first section of the book—suggests that Toomer could not imagine how to make the imagist aesthetic of breaks and discontinuities serve this function. "Reapers," to take a significant example, is written in rhymed quatrains, rhymed so insistently, in fact, that it is possible to read the poem as having only two rhyming sounds for its eight lines. It is also rendered in complete, conventional sentences, and it has a fairly consistent iambic rhythm. The appropriateness of these conventions appears where they are most consistent:

> Black reapers with the sound of steel on stones
> Are sharpening scythes. I see them place the hones
> In their hip-pockets as a thing that's done,
> And start their silent swinging, one by one.
>
> (*C*, p. 5)

The rhymthic repetitions of the form stand for the repetitive nature of the work, which appears most obviously in the nearly perfect iambic line that represents the resumed swinging of the scythes. This sort of work is repetitive in a physical sense, relying as it does on a few movements reiterated again and again, and in a temporal sense, since it must be done every day, every season, season after season. It is "a thing that's done," a habit.

Toomer does not print the break between stanzas as a physical break, but everything changes there nevertheless:

> Black horses drive a mower through the weeds,
> And there, a field rat, startled, squealing bleeds,
> His belly close to ground. I see the blade,
> Blood-stained, continue cutting weeds and shade.
>
> (*C*, p. 5)

The break represents a major change in the life of this rural area, the change from manpower to machines, which changes everything else as well. As Toomer put it in a letter to Frank, "The supreme fact of mechanical civilization is that you become part of it, or get sloughed off (under)."[90] The line describing the death of the field rat embodies this change in meaning and in sound. Instead of working slowly and rhythmically, the mower moves on ineluctably, even killing the living things before it, which make a sound that is the very antithesis of the soft silent swinging of the scythes. The dying squeal of the rat affects the poetry itself, which is least iambic and most interrupted just here, as if the line itself were cut mindlessly and inorganically.

Interruption thus has quite a different meaning in this poem, even in this whole section of *Cane*. Though the break is still associated with modernity, it is not creative but destructive. When the narrator calls Karintha "a wild flash," a thorough reader of *Cane* may suspect some connection with the electrical imagery of "Her Lips Are Copper Wire," but in this story the brief flash, no matter how passionate, is sad, the flash of "a growing thing ripened too soon" (*C*, pp. 3–4). The whole balance between the organic and the mechanical has shifted. Whereas in "Seventh Street" the iron wedge is cheered as it slices the soggy life of Washington, in "Reapers" and "Karintha" the machine seems a cruel violation of the organic.

Perhaps the ultimate realization of this violation in language is the taut, wordless hum of the lynch mob in "Blood Burning Moon." Like the mechanical mower in "Reapers," the lynch mob rolls forward, breaking both sound and body: "The moving body of their silence preceded them over the crest of the hill into factory town. It flattened the Negroes beneath it" (*C*, p. 36). Years later, when Toomer prepared a statement of support for the Scottsboro Boys, he used the machine as a metaphor for this kind of mob violence and racist repression: "Those who have been caught in a machine will sympathize with the plight of the Scottsboro boys. . . . Most of us at one time or another have been caught in a machine."[91] The unmistakably personal reference seems to give both "Reapers" and "Blood Burning Moon" a new, almost intimate, resonance, and to pose another challenge to any modernism that would cut off the venerable repetitions of work, culture, or voice. The formal antithesis of such interruptions is the refrain, as in "Song of the Son," which transforms lynching into "an everlasting song, a singing tree" (*C*, p. 14), by the simple faithfulness of repetition.

And yet, at the very moment that Waldo Frank was carrying this and the other poems of *Cane* to Liveright, Toomer wrote to Munson, "I rejected 'The Poetry of the People' for such things as motorcycle motors, dynamos, and generators," and he praised the position recently taken in *Secession* of "acceptance of the machine" as "the attitude (the only healthy, the only *art* attitude) which uses modern forms. . . ."[92] In the context of the time, this is not a trivial inconsistency, because Toomer's friends Frank and Munson were in the process of mounting a major aesthetic battle on precisely this issue: Frank against and Munson for the machine. Toomer's inconsistency represents, perhaps, a painfully dual allegiance in this battle, but it also betrays his own inability to choose when "modern forms" and "ancient voices" come into conflict.

In their opposition, the first two parts of *Cane* lay out in formal and thematic terms the conundrum that faced Toomer as a writer and an individual. The formal task that Toomer set for himself was to use the tools of modernism in such a way as to draw from them something more socially responsible than he found in the imagists. At the same time, he needed to use traditional forms in a way that would not conduce to the sort of primitivism he loathed in Anderson and Frank. His hope, in other words, was to meet the expectations of Locke, to create a modernist race literature that would find in the African-American past not some placebo against progress but a self-conscious tradition ultimately fit for an urban American future.

The difficulty of doing this, of drawing out of conflict a living language, is what tortures Kabnis in the third section of *Cane*. Kabnis is both tormented and tempted by the southern life around him. On one hand he sees the folk life around him as a healthy model of a new language. Halsey tells him, speaking of moonshine: "Th boys what made this stuff—are y listenin t me, Kabnis? th boys what made this stuff have got th art down like I heard you say youd like t be with words" (*C*, p. 95). But no matter how much he may admire the artists of moonshine, Kabnis cannot reconcile himself to a life of rural repetition: "Great God Almighty, a soul like mine cant pin itself onto a wagon wheel an satisfy itself in spinnin round" (*C*, p. 115). But there does not seem to be any alternative, any other way of shaping words.

The personal drama of "Kabnis" has to do with allegiance, with the contradictory pull of North and South and of black and white. For Kabnis, concerned as he is with self-expression as a means of self-definition, this conflict occurs most acutely as a choice of languages: "Th form thats bound int my soul is some twisted awful thing that crept in from a dream, a godam nightmare, an wont stay still when I feed it. An it lives in words" (*C*, p. 111). But the only words it can have are crossed by violence and conflict. In a sense Kabnis *is* this conflict: he insists on a sense of difference. But he also longs for some sort of community, some unity and wholeness. This is his dilemma, as it is the dilemma of *Cane*.

For Kabnis's unpleasant choice between words that go round and round like a wheel and the broken words of his own soul is the choice presented in *Cane* itself, most notably in the contrast between "Reapers" and "Her Lips Are Copper Wire." And Kabnis's distress betrays Toomer's fear that he had not managed to reconcile these two forms with their competing motives, that the broken modern forms remained aloof and socially unresponsive, idiosyncratic, while the repetitive forms were outmoded, repressive, or primitivistic. This is one of the reasons *Cane* remains such an important work for an understanding of the 1920s, because it distills a dilemma that faced the Americanist avant-garde and the Harlem writers at the same time. Whether it was the avant-garde, trying to make modernism into a dialect so as to challenge the cultural supremacy of the English, or the Harlem writers, trying to make dialect into a modern literature so as to avoid the primitivizing pressures of the past, the central problem of reconciling competing linguistic motives remained. In the end, perhaps it was simply this dilemma that the two groups shared and nothing else.

8

"Characteristics of Negro Expression": Zora Neale Hurston and the *Negro* Anthology

I

Zora Neale Hurston's first significant publication, the short story "Drenched in Light," which appeared in *Opportunity* in December 1924, was autobiographical in more ways than one. Hurston had written into the story her past as a girl in Eatonville, Florida, and she had given to her protagonist, Isie Watts, a set of habits and aspirations she would later describe as her own.[1] But she could not have known when she wrote the story how much the conclusion would come to seem autobiographical as well. The way that Isie is picked up and cosseted by a patronizing white traveler oddly predicts the way that Hurston herself, arriving in New York hard on the heels of "Drenched in Light," was virtually adopted, first by Fannie Hurst and then by the grimly philanthropic Mrs. Charlotte Osgood Mason.[2]

Though Hurston could not have foreseen this turn of events, she must have known that white exploitation of African-American folkways was the subject of lively complaint in the press that published her story. In the review of *Cane* that *Opportunity* published in December 1923, Montgomery Gregory complained that black middle-class abhorrence of "mass life" had "enabled the white artist to exploit the Negro race for personal recognition or commercial gain."[3] A few months after "Drenched in Light" was published, Charles Johnson noted in an *Opportunity* editorial, "The first significant exploitation of the materials of Negro life has come not from Negro but from white writers."[4] Surrounded by such editorial comment, "Drenched in Light" could easily have been read as a fictional account of the way that all the best of black life was picked off by white romantics on the prowl. It would have appeared, that is to say, as the other side of the story told in Waldo Frank's "Hope," the story of interracial transfusion told over and over again in the white avant-garde press of the early 1920s.

"Drenched in Light" was therefore the perfect calling card, to use Robert Hemenway's term, for a young writer unintimidated by the possibility of white patronization and black middle-class disapproval, determined to use the positive aspects of her past whether they had been romanticized or not.[5] And yet the story became cruelly autobiographical over the years, as the reception and later reputation of Hurston's work were dominated by questions about Mrs. Mason. Until the "stunning reversal" largely brought about by Alice Walker, discussions of Hurston's work dwelt almost obsessively on her willingness to be patronized.[6] Richard Wright's famous review of *Their Eyes Were Watching God* set the tone by charging that Hurston used a "minstrel technique" to appeal to "a white audience whose chauvinistic tastes she knows how to satisfy."[7]

In her own eyes Hurston was addressing the very issue raised by Gregory and Johnson, reviving black folklore that had been widely misused, "debunking," as she put it, "the current mammy-song-Jolson conception of the Southern Negro." Her own folklore research was meant to correct the distorted image created by dialect writers like Octavus Roy Cohen and Roark Bradford.[8] It was to take back a language obscured by travesty and stereotype, so negatively charged that educated blacks were afraid to use it. Thus when students at Howard University objected to the grammar of the spirituals they were asked to sing, Hurston weighed in on the other side.[9] This proved the beginning of an argument Hurston carried on throughout her life, as a novelist and ethnographer, on behalf of "Negro expression" against the forces of standardization.

"Color Struck," the play Hurston submitted to the first *Opportunity* literary contest, seems to open this argument. The title describes a young woman who is so obsessed with the possibility of colorism in others that she loses her lover. "Color struck" is a term for her obsession but also for the retreat it causes: in military terms, she strikes the colors and leaves the field. The term has become most famous, however, as part of an anecdote about Hurston herself, who is said to have arrived at a party after the 1925 *Opportunity* awards dinner with the triumphant cry, "Calaaaah struuuuck."[10] Thus what had denoted retreat and shame becomes a cry of triumph. This must have been what Hurston intended to accomplish within the play itself, which has for its dramatic center the far from innocuous subject of the cakewalk.

From the earliest days of the minstrel show, the cakewalk had been an irresistible inspiration to white audiences, spawning dance crazes, vaudeville routines, and even entire dramatic productions such as *Clorindy, the Origin of the Cakewalk*, by Will Marion Cook and Paul Laurence Dunbar. At the turn of the century, when "Color Struck" is set, the cakewalk was an international fad, made famous by Bert Williams and George Walker, who had taken over *Clorindy* and toured the world in it.[11] The show installed the cakewalk forever as a cliché of black life, a position exemplifed by the sheet music for a 1905 hit called "The Coon's Paradise," which shows a cakewalking couple between a chicken stealer and a card game.[12]

Perhaps the most significant thing about "Color Struck" is the fact that it makes no reference to this notoriety at all; there is no hint in the play that the dance performed by the various Florida contingents was simultaneously being performed onstage by Williams and Walker and in New York society by William Vanderbilt. In Hurston's play the cakewalk is a black rural ritual that has no reference to anything outside itself, certainly not to the possibility that its routines and usages might provide ammunition for white stereotyping. The play simply removes the white frame that had been placed around the cakewalk, as it had been placed around the dialect stories told by Uncle Remus.[13] Thus what seems a piece of pure folk art is in fact a self-conscious and even polemical act, for Hurston constructs the drama so that the one defensively race-obsessed character in the play finds herself shut out of the cakewalk, cut off from her fellows and her culture because of her obsession with color. Thus the play recommends its own sublime indifference to white opinion as a way of redeeming black folk culture from its popularized and vulgarized white versions.

In this sense "Color Struck" is Hurston's actual calling card vis-à-vis New York literary society, the work whose title she used to announce her unintimidated arrival on the scene. And it also focuses many of the issues raised so far in this study: the status of dialect, the preemptive power of white patronage and emulation, and the relation of literature and ethnography. In many ways Hurston seems the best exemplification of Locke's prediction that renewed acceptance of "folk music and poetry as an artistic heritage" would bring Harlem into an alliance with white American modernists.[14] Hurston became the only professionally trained ethnographer/folklorist among the Harlem Renaissance writers, and she used the materials she collected in a series of interpenetrating works: "The Eatonville Anthology," *Mules and Men,* and *Their Eyes Were Watching God.* She also belonged to that group of young writers that Locke called "modernists among the moderns."[15] "Color Struck" was first published in *Fire!!,* the anthology "devoted to younger Negro artists" that Wallace Thurman, Langston Hughes, Richard Bruce, Gwendolyn Bennett, Hurston, and others brought out in the fond hope that it would offend someone.[16] The one contribution that *was* found offensive, Bruce's "Smoke, Lilies and Jade," associates Hurston, Hughes, Cullen, and Toomer with Mencken, Cabell, Van Vechten, Wilde, Schnitzler, and Freud.[17]

It may have seemed the fulfillment of Locke's prediction, therefore, that Hurston's ethnographic theories were first published in another anthology, a quintessentially modernist production entitled *Negro.* This massive work was the last publishing project of Nancy Cunard, who had bought her press from William Bird, publisher of Pound, Williams, McAlmon, and Hemingway. She had herself published Pound and Beckett, and she enlisted both, with varying degrees of success, in her last project, which finally proved too large to publish herself. There is an intriguing similarity between the anthological nature of Hurston's own works and this miscellaneous, collective, disorganized, supergeneric sprawl of a book, which was in some ways the perfectly appropriate place for her to appear. And yet Cunard herself struck certain potential contributors, including Louise Thompson, as uncomfortably like the woman who had been both Thompson's and Hurston's patron: Mrs. Charlotte Osgood Mason.[18] And she seriously alienated one friend and potential contributor, Claude McKay, by her lofty assumption that he would be willing to write for her collection without pay.[19]

Such conflicts may suggest that it was somewhat more difficult to escape the distorting enthusiasms of white patronage than Hurston may have thought. They may also suggest that Hurston's appearance in *Negro* marks not the fruition but the final failure of Locke's high hopes.

II

The white traveler of "Drenched in Light" picks up Isie Watts because, as she says, "I want a little of her sunshine to soak into my soul. I need it."[20] Mrs. Mason apparently said something like this to the adult Zora Neale Hurston, as she revealed in her autobiography: "I must tell the tales, sing the songs, do the dances, and repeat the raucous sayings and doings of the Negro farthest down. She is altogether in sympathy with them, because she says truthfully they are utterly sincere in living" (*DT*, p. 177). Such passages naturally provoke questions about Hurston's own sincerity, which was apparently less than perfect. Indeed, Louise Thompson recalled for Robert Hemenway how Hurston would surreptitiously mock the primitive role she was encouraged by her patron to play.[21]

Anyone who believes she can buy sincerity obviously deserves exactly what she gets, but the duplicity of Hurston's position has more significant implications as well. Franz Boas, under whom Hurston studied at Columbia, apparently felt that the peculiar merit of her ethnographic work also lay in its sincerity: "[S]he entered into the homely life of the southern Negro as one of them and was fully accepted as such by the companions of her childhood. Thus she has been able to penetrate through that affected demeanor by which the Negro excludes the White observer effectively from participating in his true inner life."[22] Hurston herself told Alan Lomax that she collected folk songs by singing along and gradually memorizing what she was singing. It was this participation, Lomax felt, that made her work so "genuine."[23]

If, however, she appeared to others as a genuine participant in the folk life she observed, Hurston appeared to herself in a more complicated role. In her own introduction to *Mules and Men*, she says she had known the folklore virtually from birth. "But it was fitting me like a tight chemise. I couldn't see it for wearing it. It was only when I was off in college, away from my native surroundings, that I could see myself like somebody else and stand off and look at my garment. Then I had to have the spy-glass of Anthropology to look through at that" (*MM*, p. 1). There is an intriguing gap between the image that Boas and Lomax have of Hurston as a full participant in the folklore she studied and her own conception, which, as Hemenway says, requires a certain "dissociation of sensibility."[24] Even the "chemise" that Hurston uses to symbolize her heritage is turned inside out, as it were, in the course of *Mules and Men*. When she shows up in Polk County wearing a $12.74 dress from Macy's, Hurston must tell a hurried lie about a bootlegging boyfriend in order to defuse the suspicion (*MM*, pp. 63–64). It was *this* dress, a fancy one from the city, that she was actually wearing without noticing it; the plain, cheap dress she resolved to wear the next day was thus something of a disguise.

At times Hurston seems almost to relish the tension between revelation and disguise, sincerity and masquerade. In one of her most famous statements of self-definition, "How It Feels to Be Colored Me," she throws herself into a stereotype that made at least a few of her Harlem contemporaries cringe: the jazz-crazy savage.

> This orchestra grows rambunctious, rears on its hind legs and attacks the tonal veil with primitive fury, rending it, clawing it until it breaks through to the jungle beyond. I follow those heathen—follow them exultingly. I dance wildly inside myself; I yell within, I whoop; I shake my assegai above my head, I hurl it true to the mark *yeeeeooww!* I am in the jungle and living in the jungle way. (*ILM*, p. 154)

Here Hurston is both naive and affectedly naive at the same time, affected in the purposely overblown role of spear-shaking savage, genuinely naive in the assumption that she can simply ignore the misunderstanding the role will cause. It can hardly matter, though, because within the space of a page she goes on to dismantle the whole pose of primitive authenticity:

> But in the main, I feel like a brown bag of miscellany propped against a wall. Against a wall in company with other bags, white, red and yellow. Pour out the contents, and there is discovered a jumble of small things priceless and worthless. A first-water diamond, an empty spool, bits of broken glass, lengths of string, a key to a door long since crumbled away, a rusty knife-blade, old shoes saved for a road that never was and never will be, a nail bent under the weight of things too heavy for any nail, a dried flower or two still a little fragrant. (*ILM*, p. 155)

So much for the true inner life.

The shift from spear-shaking savage to miscellaneous brown bag is a shift from primitivism to modern, ironic, cultural relativism, to the role that James Clifford describes so well as that of the contemporary anthropologist.[25] It seems to enclose the savage and defuse it by suggesting that it is no more authentic than anything else in the brown bag. And yet there is certainly something lost in this process, some vigor and enthusiasm at the very least. And it is hard to invest much cultural pride in a jumble of items randomly thrown into a shapeless bag. Hurston's dilemma, which was the same as that faced by McKay and Toomer, was not so much to resolve the contradiction between these two choices as to figure out why they were so often the only choices available. As a black Floridian, as an anthropologist, as a writer of fiction and drama, she faced this question over and over.

III

In Henry Louis Gates, Jr.'s influential analysis of *Their Eyes Were Watching God*, it is free indirect discourse that exists as the third term between speech and narrative commentary, dialect and standard English, participation and observation. Yet there is an intriguing and significant inconsistency in the way this third term is deployed. At times Gates speaks of it as a strategy that "resolves that implicit tension between standard English and black dialect," a strategy that on another level allows *Their Eyes Were Watching God* to "resolve that implicit tension between the literal and the figurative, between the semantic and the rhetorical" and thus to become what he calls a signifying text.[26] At other times, however, Gates speaks of a "rhetoric of division" in the text, and free indirect discourse becomes not a resolution but "a dramatic way of expressing a divided self."[27] In his afterword to *Their Eyes Were Watching God*, Gates speaks of free indirect discourse as "a *divided* voice, a double voice unreconciled."[28] Thus the same technique seems to figure as resolution and lack of resolution at the same time.

This inconsistency seems to arise from a more basic conflict of critical motives. On one hand Gates sees free indirect discourse as a magnificent creative triumph over the division between oral and literary texts and over the associated division between individual and collective voices. Free indirect discourse of this kind represents "not only an individual character's speech and thought, but also the *collective* black community's speech and thoughts. . . ." Thus "the ultimate sign of the dignity and strength of the black voice" is the way it makes these distinctions disappear, so that individual and community, narrator and characters, standard English and dialect, simply become one. The speakerly text, in this analysis, exposes the opposition between these various terms "as a false opposition."[29]

On the other hand, Gates joins Barbara Johnson in seeing free indirect discourse as a celebration of division. Of *Dust Tracks in the Road* he says, "Hurston's unresolved tension between her double voices signifies her full understanding of modernism. Hurston uses the two voices in her text to celebrate the psychological fragmentation both of modernity and of the black American."[30] In this analysis Hurston's self-conscious play with voices and points of view makes her a triumphant example of modern, or perhaps more properly postmodern, irony, triumphant because it demolishes essentialist definitions of self and of race. Used as it is in these two quite inconsistent ways, the theory of free indirect discourse neither resolves nor celebrates division but restages on another level the whole intriguing problem of Hurston's life and work, as she had already stated it in "How It Feels to Be Colored Me." Moreover, it restages the very dichotomy Locke hoped to overcome, the dichotomy between African-American folk culture and modernism, as long as the first is seen in terms of reconciliation and the second in terms of division.

Hurston's own theories about dialect and standard English, oral and literary discourse, speech and narration are, if anything, even less consistent, but they deserve a good deal more attention than they have received because of the way they investigate the very process by which these pairs are originally produced. In "Characteristics of Negro Expression," first published in the *Negro* anthology, Hurston begins by laying out a number of parallel dichotomies that are quite similar to those deployed by Gates and Johnson. "It is easier to illustrate than it is to explain," she says, "because action came before speech."[31] Just as action comes before speech, a language of action comes before a language of abstraction. Playing with her terms a bit, Hurston compares action words to "actual goods," which come before coins and checks. Thus the difference between *mimesis* and *diegesis*, between illustration and explanation, becomes the associated difference between motivated and conventional signs, between actual goods and conventional signifiers like coins, or to use Hurston's own linguistic terms, between "close-fitting" and "detached" expressions (*SC*, p. 49).

"Negro expression" is associated with the first in all these pairs: it is actual, full of action, illustrative, and close-fitting. Nevertheless, it is also highly dramatic and, what is somewhat harder to see given the fact that it is supposed to be "close-fitting," highly metaphorical. Playing with her terms again, Hurston turns "action" and "actual" inside out to reveal their opposite: "Every phase of Negro life is highly dramatized. . . . Everything is acted out" (*SC*, p. 49). To "act" is obviously to do something effectual in the real world, but it is also to feign to do so, to pretend. When Hurston says that in order to make "detached words" as "close-fitting" as he wants, "the Negro . . . must add action to it to make it do," she turns the idiom on a dime. To make something do is simply to make it suffice, to make it cover the situation, to pull and haul something until it comes as close to fitting as possible, but here it also means to make the language work, perform, accomplish something actual. Thus the difference between the kind of acting that simply makes do and the kind of acting that actually does something is balanced on a razor's edge.

Despite her insistence on the actuality of black speech, Hurston can also insist that all characteristic "Negro expression" is "acted out," a process she illustrates with a few anecdotes about the "little plays by strolling players [that] are acted out daily in a dozen streets in a thousand cities" (*SC*, p. 50). These "players" are constantly "posing," and they illustrate a propensity for "adornment," a delight in "decorating the decoration" that Hurston also finds characteristic of her race (*SC*, p. 53). She seems not at all concerned that her reader may see a resemblance between the "decorated" and the "detached," so that the actual, active language of black speakers may come round to merge with its opposite, the feigned, conventional, artificial language of the other race.

Hurston is not concerned because she is working with definitions of originality and mimicry radically different from those in conventional use. She notes with scorn the widespread prejudice that "the Negro is lacking in originality" not because it is false in itself but because it rests on a false notion of originality: "It is obvious that to get back to original sources is much too difficult for any group to claim very much of a certainty. What we really mean by originality is the modification of ideas" (*SC*, p. 58). Given the unapproachability of the truly original, whatever that might mean, Hurston feels that the most original is the one who most thoroughly modifies: "So if we look at it squarely, the Negro is a very original being. While he lives and moves in the midst of a white civilization, everything that he touches is re-interpreted for his own use" (*SC*, p. 58).

What may seem in this like special pleading or mere playing with paradox is actually rooted in a very shrewd observation of American society. For Hurston notices that white writers and performers are desperate to mimic black ways: "Everyone seems to think that the Negro is easily imitated when nothing is further from the truth" (*SC*, p. 66). Thus she mocks Paul Whiteman, Mae West, and George Gershwin for trying to imitate the race that is itself criticized as imitative. But she is not merely turning the tables, trying to claim that black art and language are too original to be imitated. On the contrary, it is precisely because it is already imitative that it cannot be further imitated. It is precisely the self-conscious awareness, the ironic indirection, of black art and language that makes it original and impossible to mimic. White performers, because they are unself-conscious, naive, and obsessed with a false concept of originality, are helpless to rival the race they long to emulate.

An originality founded on mimicry may sound a bit too good to be true, and yet it is an old and well-established product of the American racial drama. An 1845 playbill advertised the performance of Juba, the first black minstrel performer, in these terms: "The entertainment to conclude with the Imitation Dance, by Mast. Juba, in which he will give correct Imitation Dances of all the principal Ethiopian Dancers in the United States. After which he will give an imitation of himself— and then you will see the vast difference between those that have heretofore attempted dancing and this WONDERFUL YOUNG MAN."[32] One difference between Juba and all the other "Ethiopian Dancers" is that only Juba was black, but he does not found his claim to superiority on this simple fact, that he was in a sense the original of what the white blackface performers were imitating. Instead, he rises supreme because of his ability to imitate himself best of all. In a sense Hurston is making the same claim in "Characteristics of Negro Expression," that black performers are original because they can produce the best imitation of what Whiteman, West, and Gershwin are all trying to imitate: themselves. Black performers *are* original not because they possess originality as a quality but because they produce originality as a commodity.

Thus Hurston applies in theoretical terms the insight of "Drenched in Light." When originality, sincerity, the actual become commodities that are bought and sold, then the difference between the real world of action and the symbolic world of coins and checks has disappeared. In the most cynical terms, one might say that she is original who can generate originality for sale or use, for

Mrs. Mason to enjoy or Franz Boas to publish. But "Characteristics of Negro Expression" is not merely, or even primarily, cynical, for it presents the ability to produce originality out of the materials of an alien and repressive society as the great triumph of African-American culture. The example she gives in the essay is jazz, in which African-American musicians so thoroughly recreated European music and instrumentation that white music became "an imitation of a Negro orchestra making use of white-invented musical instruments in a Negro way" (*SC*, p. 59). But she might just as easily have had reference to her own earlier work and used the cakewalk as an example, for it was originally a slave imitation of the master's ballroom dancing, but made so new that William Vanderbilt ended up imitating black slaves imitating white aristocrats.

Posing, acting out, playing thus become highly original actions. They also become *actual*, to use the terminology of the essay itself. Gates finds a distinction in *Their Eyes* between verbal work and verbal play, between the figurative wordplay of the folk and Jodie Stark's instrumental desire to become a "big voice." The example of figurative play he uses is the mock courtship that takes place on the porch of Stark's store, which the novel describes in this way: "They know it's not courtship. It's acting out courtship and everybody is in the play."[33] Here the porch echoes accepted linguistic theory, which teaches that certain utterances—"I do," for example—constitute action in themselves but not when they occur onstage or in a book. Someone who says "I do" in a play, Austin reminds us, is not therefore married.[34] Thus there seems to be a strict line between performance and the performative, but this is precisely the line that Hurston toys with when she balances "action" and the "actual" against "acting out."

Hurston frequently applies to verbal play various metaphors of work: "poets of the swinging blade," she calls the lumberjacks of Polk County, who can sing and swing the axe equally well (*DT*, p. 179). "Hurry up," says one of her Polk County informants, "so somebody else kin plough up some literary and lay-by some alphabets" (*MM*, p. 86). "Playing the dozens" may be figurative but it is not therefore frivolous: Hurston frequently compares it to some immediate physical action, such as "'putting your foot up' on a person" (*DT*, p. 187). Of all Hurston's works, *Their Eyes Were Watching God* turns most notoriously on a statement that is also an act, Janie's low-rating of her husband Jodie, which seems actually to kill him. Mary Helen Washington says of the men on the porch, "Their talking is either a game or a method of exerting power," but Janie's own most independent act shows that talking on the porch is a game that is simultaneously a method of exerting, and perhaps of resisting, power.[35] In other words, talk is both work and play, a game and a deadly reality.

Perhaps this sort of language is best thought of as *behavior*, which Hemenway helpfully defines as "performed interpretations of the world which influence action."[36] Several of the genres in which Hurston was most interested fall usefully within this definition. Conjure is the most obvious example, but other, more conventionally Christian, ceremonies qualify as well. The sacrament of communion is taken seriously enough that in at least two stories estranged wives go to great lengths to avoid partaking with their abusive husbands.[37] The other side of this story appears in "The Gilded Six-Bits," which almost seems an illustrative case study of the linguistic practices discussed in "Characteristics of Negro Expression."

In this story Missie May and her husband, Joe, represent and reinforce their happy marriage with a set of playful rituals: every Saturday afternoon, Joe throws his pay, nine silver dollars, through the front door and then hides while his wife picks it up. After she affects alarm he enters with pockets full of treats, which she must extract. The routine is, on one level, mere childish play; on another level it is adult play, since the struggling with pockets arouses an appetite that the author decorously redirects toward food. On yet another level the routine is an example of sacramental play, since it revivifies the marriage: the exchange of treats for the meal that Missie May has prepared makes this an informal communion. And the silver dollars represent the whole: as symbols they are no more or less conventional than anything else that happens during the ritual, including the speeches of mock threat, concern, and reconciliation, and yet they solidify nonetheless the marriage they represent.

Into this happy relationship steps the interloper, Mr. Otis D. Slemmons, with gold pieces for jewelry and a mouth full of gold teeth and "Chicago talk." The one example of such talk given in the story is rather cleverly built out of a commonly misunderstood word:

> He asted me, "Who is dat broad wid de forte shake?" Dat's a new word. Us always thought forty was a set of figgers but he showed us where it means a whole heap of things. Sometimes he don't say forty, he jes' say thirty-eight and two and dat mean de same thing. . . . He say, "Ah have to hand it to you, Joe. Dat wife of yours is jes' thirty-eight and two. Yessuh, she's forte!" Ain't he killin'? (*ILM*, p. 212)

While Joe is fascinated with the man's talk, May succumbs to his gold, which, she discovers too late, is merely gilded.

The difference between Otis Slemmons's fake gold and Joe's real silver suggests a relatively easy way of aligning behavior, speech, and money so as to interpret this story. But the speeches that Joe makes to preserve the marriage are not really any more genuine than the speeches Slemmons makes to break it up: both rely on pretense. But Joe's is a ceremonial pretense that Missie May shares, while Slemmons's pretense is his alone. His money is no good not because it lacks some intrinsic characteristic of value—all money is conventional and, therefore, to some extent misleading—but because it is not shared in a reciprocal system of exchange. All behavior, all speech, like all money, is conventional, imitative, and yet this does not undermine the distinction between truth and falsehood. The truth is any variety of language that works in a ceremony that affects people's daily lives. Joe's word is his bond, to take one of Austin's favorite locutions, because it is given as part of a performative exchange with another person; Slemmons's word, like his money, is only valuable to himself.[38]

In practice, then, Hurston links performance and the performative, acting out and action. From the same set of terms she draws an associated theory of genre. Two of the main characteristics of African-American performance listed in "Characteristics of Negro Expression" are "angularity" and asymmetry. As Hurston admits, these clash with a third important characteristic: rhythm. "The presence of rhythm and lack of symmetry are paradoxical, but there they are" (*SC*, p. 55). Yet there can be asymmetrical rhythms, syncopated ones, as Hurston notes in using blues and tap dancing as examples. Here the rhythm "is a rhythm of segments. Each unit has a rhythm of its own, but when the whole is assembled it is lacking in symmetry. But easily workable to a Negro who is accustomed to the break in going from one part to another . . ." (*SC*, p. 55). In another contribution to *Negro* Hurston speaks of the "jagged harmony" of the spirituals, the dissonances that break in "at any old time" (*SC*, p. 80).

Here Hurston is giving a shape to the performance she calls "Negro expression," a shape typified by the spirituals, the blues, jazz, tap, dialect, and, in the case of literature, the anthology. In fact, the prototype in literature of the form Hurston is describing might be Du Bois's *The Souls of Black Folk*, which is both an anthology of essays and an anthology of spirituals, a collection of miscellaneous pieces that aspires to be a collective portrait of a people. *Cane* is another obvious precursor. Hurston's own works were often, in Hemenway's comment on *Jonah's Gourd Vine*, "less a narrative than a series of linguistic moments."[39] This has caused some difficulty in reading and interpreting Hurston's works, which have many "breaks" between one part and another, between one voice and another. But it simply stands to reason that, having defined "Negro expression" as she does, Hurston would also redefine the fictional structures as well.

Hurston does not reconcile or celebrate the divisions within her texts or within the African-American folk texts she found in her travels. Instead, she utterly redefines the dichotomies that seem to produce these divisions. She dismisses the conventional distinction between the language of work and the language of play, denotative language and its figurative shadow, through a conception of performative language in which even the most playful utterances accomplish serious social work. With this distinction goes the associated distinction between the original and the imitation. Thus it is possible for her to avoid in her social linguistics the idea that dialect is an inept imitation of the standard language, and she avoids in the same way the notion that other African-American arts and folkways are inept imitations of European forms. Since these folk expressions are performative and more self-consciously imitative than standard literary productions, it presents no difficulty for a self-conscious literature to use them; the problem is rather for the literary to keep up to the signifying speed set by oral performance. In fact, Hurston, like later linguists such as Shirley Brice Heath, sees the oral not as derivative from but as supergeneric on the written.[40] It is inherently anthological, receptive in form to individual utterances of any kind, so long as they respect the basic performative ethic on which the social linguistic system depends.

This is quite possibly what Toomer was trying to get at when he called *Cane* a vaudeville, an oral, popular form that absorbed the various forms around it in an anthology of performance. It may even have been what Eliot was trying to get at in *Sweeney Agonistes*, another work that is anthological and vaudevillian. It is almost certainly what Locke was talking about when he noted in the younger generation of Harlem writers "an increasing tendency to evolve from the racial substance something technically distinctive. . . ."[41] By this evolution the younger Harlem writers were to bring African-American writing into the forefront of literary experimentation and thus to make of it their own kind of modernism.

IV

Hurston published "Characteristics of Negro Expression," appropriately enough, in a modernist anthology in 1934, but she had formulated most of the ideas that were to go into the essay as early as 1928 and had already embodied them in her own anthology by 1926. Though "The Eatonville Anthology" is a minor work, it is in a sense the prototype for everything Hurston would do in literature and anthropology. As she put it in a letter to Langston Hughes about a particularly rewarding field trip: "I can *really* do a Village Anthology now. . . ."[42] Yet the material she was collecting on this trip and the rules of dialect expression that she formulated from it appeared not in her own enlarged "Village Anthology" but in an international modernist one. A detailed comparison of the two anthologies can show both the possibilities of the anthology form as Hurston defined it and the distortions that form suffered as it passed from her own work into the realm of Anglo-American modernism.

"The Eatonville Anthology" that was published in the *Messenger* in 1926 is so scrappy in form that the end of one segment was simply left out, apparently unnoticed.[43] It is utterly miscellaneous as to form and genre, including sketches, parables, animal tales, dramatizations, and short stories. These also mix fact, fiction, and folklore in varying degrees. One tale included as if it had actually happened in Eatonville is in fact a variation on a folktale so common it has been classified by folklorists as Type 660.[44] The missing end of the incomplete segment is to be found in Hurston's autobiography, where it is reported as fact.[45] And a number of segments would reappear in Hurston's later fiction, sometimes as kernels of much larger works.

In fact, "The Eatonville Anthology" is something of an autoanthology, if in a somewhat prospective sense. A rather lame pun is lifted from "Color Struck" to reappear in the segment entitled "Double Shuffle." Portions of the concluding animal tale and one of the folktales will reappear in *Mules and Men,* and three of the segments will give rise to entire novels, two of them becoming parts of *Their Eyes Were Watching God* and a third transformed into *Seraph on the Suwanee.*[46] Such reuse poses an intriguing problem that goes beyond genre, because it shows how easily Hurston transposed materials back and forth between fictional forms and forms that were at least ostensibly factual. A certain amount of the material reported in *Mules and Men* as the result of collecting trips conducted after 1927 actually appears in Hurston's fictional work before that date. But it is difficult to say whether she fictionalized her ethnographic reports or whether her fiction had always been in part the product of ethnographic collecting. "The Eatonville Anthology" itself is utterly ambiguous in this respect, since it is presented in such a vague way that it might be considered ethnographic reportage or storytelling.

According to Hemenway, "'The Eatonville Anthology' is, finally, hardly fiction at all. It is pure Zora Neale Hurston: part fiction, part folklore, part biography, all told with great economy, an eye for authentic detail, and a perfect ear for dialect."[47] As Hemenway says, it is the best recorded version of the performances that so entranced Hurston's friends and associates in Harlem, and this is clearly the only genre to which it comfortably belongs, the genre of performance. "The Eatonville Anthology" is an anthology of performances in the sense defined in "Characteristics of Negro Expression," each segment with its own rhythm, the whole with a kind of jagged harmony. Distinctions between fact and fiction, reportage and storytelling, part and whole, all are blurred within the genre of performance.

Hurston's definition of performance also explains how the various voices of the anthology achieve their jagged harmony. The segments are generally introduced and narrated in the third person, with a few lapses, as, for example, when "The Way of a Man with a Train" suddenly seems to be the narrative of "we children" (*ILM,* p. 179). This third-person narrative voice also sticks fairly closely to standard English, again with a few lapses. The narrator tells the story of Coon Taylor in perfectly conventional English, except for saying that Joe Clarke "set up in the melon patch one night" (*ILM,* p. 180). The dialogue, on the other hand, is entirely in dialect, and there is a small amount of free indirect discourse, such as Mitchell Potts's summary judgment, "'Nough was 'nough" (*ILM,* p. 186). But the narrator apparently feels it necessary to break into this kind of discourse with explanatory glosses for the urban and northern reader: "His African soup-bone (arm) was too strong to let a woman run over him" (*ILM,* p. 186).

This sort of gloss seems to establish the standard English third-person narrator as an authoritative, nonparticipating frame within which the dialect speech of the fictional characters can be securely lodged. But this frame is completely open at one end as the narrator gives way entirely to a dialect speaker who tells the concluding animal tale: "Once 'way back yonder before the stars fell all the animals used to talk just like people" (*ILM,* p. 187). And it is this folk voice that finishes the whole anthology by shrugging off the issues of symmetry and formal unity: "Stepped on a tin, mah story ends" (*ILM*, p. 188). The suggestion is that this voice has enclosed the whole anthology, standard English narrator and all, from the very beginning, that it is only within this voice, with its insouciance toward such matters as consistency and conclusiveness, that the anthology can leap from seemingly factual accounts of real people, to parabolic folktales to stories in which animals talk, and then simply saunter off without concluding. Unlike the free indirect discourse, which, in this work at least, still falls subject to the narrator's parenthetical power to frame and explain, the dialect voice sails along without interruption, brushing off any hint that the reader may speak a different language: "'Oh, Miss Nancy,' he says, 'Ma'am, also Ma'am, if you'd see me settin' straddle of a mud-cat leadin' a minnow, what would you think? Ma'am also Ma'am?' Which is a out and out proposal as everybody knows" (*ILM*, p. 187). This linguistic confidence, this conviction that it is the dialect that encloses the standard, is the source of Hurston's power as a writer.

"The Eatonville Anthology" makes it clear how she derives that power from the original folk genre of verbal performance. The segment called "Village Fiction" might easily lend its title to the whole anthology, especially if it is read without subordinating one of the two terms. As in *Their Eyes Were Watching God*, the Eatonville of "The Eatonville Anthology" is its fictions, or, to use the terms Hurston uses, the town is the collective voice assembled to tell stories on the porch of the general store: "The *town* was collected at the store-postoffice as is customary on Saturday nights. The *town* has had its bath and with its week's pay in pocket fares forth to be merry. The men tell stories and treat the ladies to soda-water and peppermint candy" (*ILM*, p. 184).

This setting explains the one consistent formal element of the anthology, the formulaic beginning of the segments, all but two of which start with the name of one of the townspeople. There is, in other words, a formal identity between an individual citizen and the story told about him or her. In fact, each person becomes that story, so much so that he or she is often reduced to a single dramatic attribute such as "The Pleading Woman." Jim Merchant is always in good humor; Becky Moore has lots of children; the entire Jones family shoots craps. Bit by bit the porch renders the town into anecdote until the anthology and the town are coextensive and synonymous.

Elsewhere, especially in *Their Eyes Were Watching God*, Hurston faces up to the repressive potentialities of this sort of anecdotal reduction. Of her own case she says in *Dust Tracks*, "If the village was singing a chorus, I must have missed the tune" (*DT*, p. 46). But in "The Eatonville Anthology" there always seems to be a way to modify the tune so as to include a few new singers. The process of fictional rendering is, in fact, reciprocal, and the respect of the porch can be won and its narrative drive deflected by a clever performer. Even a silenced woman might accomplish this, as the downtrodden Mrs. Joe Clarke does when she "shakes the hand of fellowship with everybody in the Church with her eyes closed, but somehow always misses her husband" (*ILM*, p. 181). This might seem a desperately minimal reaction to a wife-beating husband, but it is a powerfully subtle gesture in a town founded on sacramental performance, and it is thus the true ancestor of the far more vocal gesture by which Janie Stark will repudiate her husband in the novel that grew from this brief anecdote.

By performances of this kind, individuals in the town of Eatonville make their reality and take their place in the anthology constantly evolving on the porch. The porch provides the performative context within which even a silent woman like Sister Ca'line Potts can take action: "Did all of her laughing down inside, but did the thing that kept the town in an uproar of laughter. It was the general opinion of the village that Ca'line would do anything she had a mind to. And she had a mind to do several things" (*ILM*, p. 186). It is no accident that Sister Ca'line stages her revenge on her unfaithful husband in such a way that it entertains the porch. The humiliation she inflicts is her punishment and her revenge.

It can certainly be said that what transpires on the porch and in front of it is only a play, a game, and Gates is surely correct to remind us that courtship in such a context is not a serious thing. But the animals of the final segment of "The Eatonville Anthology" have a different notion. When Mr. Dog wants to commit himself to a serious proposal of marriage, he says, "Miss Coon . . . Ma'am, also Ma'am which would you ruther be—a lark flyin' or a dove settin'?" (*ILM*, p. 187). This, like Mr. Rabbit's even more indirect question, "is a out and out proposal as everybody knows." It is not just that the animals have an expanded notion of the limits of implication; they also have a far more important expanded notion of the performative. To play with words really is to commit oneself under certain circumstances, under the circumstances, that is, set up by the porch, which witnesses and actualizes verbal performance by rendering it into the town's collective notion of reality. Acting out becomes action, and the individual rhythm joins the overall jagged harmony in these linguistic moments, out of which the anthology is made.

V

On the surface Nancy Cunard's *Negro* anthology is vastly more capacious and miscellaneous than Hurston's brief collection of sketches. Over eight hundred pages long and too heavy to lift comfortably, the anthology is global in reach, miscellaneous as to contributors, and generically indiscriminate in the extreme. It includes poems, music, pictures, maps, tables, arguments, essays, letters, and bibliographies. In a very practical sense it is a direct heir of such other omnivorous and generically indiscriminate works as *The Waste Land* and *The Cantos*. In 1928 Cunard bought her press from William Bird, who had published under the imprint of Three Mountains Press Pound, Williams, Hemingway, and others. Under the name of the Hours Press Cunard published Pound's *XXX Cantos* and Beckett's *Whoroscope*. *Negro* was to have been the last and greatest product of

Hours Press, but it proved so difficult and costly that it outgrew the press, which accordingly folded.[48]

In its final form *Negro* brought together virtually every kind of writing discussed in this study: the French surrealists, like Aragon, from whom Cunard had originally derived her enthusiasm about Africa; collectors of African art such as Paul Guillaume; transatlantic modernists like Pound; members of the Americanist avant-garde such as Williams and Kreymborg; Harlem Renaissance writers and older African-American authorities like Du Bois; Afro-Caribbean and African scholars and revolutionaries like George Padmore, who actually collaborated on the volume, and Jomo Kenyatta, who was studying with Malinowski at the time. Indeed, the final volume did include a fair amount of serious scholarship and journalism from black writers, from Padmore, Du Bois, Locke, and Matheus, as well as Hurston. And it might have served as solid evidence of the rapprochement between African-American writing and Anglo-American modernism if the contributions from the modernists had not been either diffident or condescending.

Pound makes a kind of conspicuous absence, with his own brief, cranky letter about Frobenius and another from an unnamed correspondent pleading with him to get involved in "Negro education," a rather grim possibility considering the drift of his political and racial views at this time.[49] Williams, on the other hand, contributed his testimony that "I have had my breath taken away by sights of colored women that no white woman has equalled for me." These sightings have been so profoundly striking because of the "simplicity of mind" and the "muscular . . . contours" of the black women he has seen.[50] It is more than a little incongruous to have this analysis followed by Arthur Schomburg's pleas for a university chair in Negro history.

Another incongruity exists between Hurston's essays on "Negro Expression," Sterling Brown's contributions from *Southern Road,* and the dialect poems provided by some of the white contributors. Carl Rakosi's "Black Crow" actually features a Sambo, while Alfred Kreymborg's "Miss Sal's Monologue," ostensibly a tribute to Bert Williams, reads more like a tribute to William Carlos Williams as mouthpiece for Bert Williams:

> "nobody
> no-day
> no-how—"
> (*N*, p. 431)

There was very little in such works to show that white emulation of African-American language and culture had advanced beyond the stage of exaggerating a few verbal clichés.

As a whole, however, the anthology was riven by a more consequential dichotomy. Cunard made sure that it was constantly informed by her own fierce insistence on political protest against injustice. The defense of the Scottsboro Boys provides a background for article after article, as does outrage against lynching. The first page of "Characteristics of Negro Expression," for example, faces a huge, clumsily retouched photograph of a lynch mob (*N*, p. 39). This makes the anthology a good deal more serious than previous modernist efforts. While advising Eliot on *The Waste Land* and *Sweeney Agonistes,* Pound, to take a contrasting example, had made heavy fun of the Dyer antilynching bill then before Congress.[51]

This difference might be taken as an index of changing times, the turn toward radical politics in the 1930s, which had touched Pound as well as Cunard, though not in exactly the same way. On the other hand, *Negro* preserves a good deal of the more frivolous interests of the 1920s, which it represents in the form of a lengthy section on black performers. This includes large photographs of figures like Louis Armstrong, Duke Ellington, and Josephine Baker, some of which seem to stretch farther back in time than the 1920s. Bill "Bojangles" Robinson, for example, is presented staring at a rabbit's foot (*N*, p. 303), while Tim Moore, whose career took him from the Gold Dust Twins to "Amos 'n' Andy," is shown in "blackface."[52]

Any responsible anthology would have had to show all of this, the repression as well as the art and music, which in the 1930s would inevitably have included examples now considered outrageous. There certainly were valid ways of discussing the relationship between white repression and black art, as Cunard herself suggested in her foreword, where she spoke of the "Negro folk-imagination, the poetic and rhythmic intensity of their religious expression, the sole emotional outlet that was permitted in slavery days" (*N*, p. iii). But what is most remarkable about *Negro* is how little connection there is between the outrage about the Scottsboro Boys and the relish expressed for black popular art. The episodic nature of the anthology form has a weirdly dissociative effect that is nonetheless quite distinct. For in this way the anthology reinstates and reinforces the old dichotomy that James Weldon Johnson had complained against back in 1922, the dichotomy confining dialect to "two full stops, humor and pathos."[53] For all the space it gave to responsible black commentary, the anthology still tended to present African Americans as objects of pity or comedy. And in so doing it divided what Hurston's contribution did so much to connect, political action and performance.

Part of this effect is attributable to the micropolitics of the period. Because the National Association for the Advancement of Colored People (NAACP) and the American Communist party were at loggerheads about the defense of the Scottsboro Boys, Cunard, who was a fierce Communist party supporter, allowed what could have been the common cause of the whole volume to become a source of division. She cannot resist making a preemptive strike against Du Bois's contribution, which she virtually urges her readers to ignore because the NAACP is "a reactionary Negro organization" (*N*, p. 142). She sneers at the *Crisis* for its habit of publishing photogenic baby pictures and graduation portraits, and she even stoops to this sort of noxious innuendo: "That Dr. Du Bois has only a little Negro blood has nothing to do with it, he is known as and professes to be a Negro" (*N*, p. 147).

Yet this is just the most heinous example of Cunard's heavy editorial hand, which blots the volume over and over with reminders, exhortations, challenges, and corrections, all aimed at convincing the reader that "the Communists *alone* are really helping the Negro" (*N*, p. 146). In retrospect, with current knowledge of what was happening in the Soviet Union in 1934, it is infuriating to be told that "To-day in Russia alone is the Negro a free man, a 100 per cent. equal" (*N*, p. iv). That Stalin's Soviet Union could have been held up in 1934 as a model for the treatment of minorities is simply beyond irony.

The more subtle result of this hectoring is that it succeeds in defining political action in an exceedingly narrow way, a way that most definitely excludes the performers who receive such interest elsewhere in the anthology. But this does not mean that the performers are criticized in the same terms Cunard uses for Du Bois. Far from it. In fact, the stern and uncompromising voice that finds every sort of action short of Communist revolution to be mere frivolity meets its symmetrical counterpart in an emotional adulation of black performers precisely because they resist all seriousness. Cunard herself complained, "A number of the younger writers are race-conscious in the wrong way, they make of this a sort of forced, *self*-conscious thing . . ." (*N*, p. 73). According to Cunard, "the Negro is very real; he is *there*" (*N*, p. 69), but this is true only if he remains unconscious of being there. Thus she laments the success of Josephine Baker, who is no longer *"free, perfect and exact"* now that she has become so refined and self-conscious (*N*, p. 329).

The same tone runs through the various jazz articles translated by Samuel Beckett: "Oh you musicians of my life, prophets of my youth, splendid Negroes informed with fire, how shall I ever express my love for your saxophones writhing like orchids . . . your rhythms as inexorable as tom-toms beating in an African nostalgia!" (*N*, p. 291). Perhaps the apotheosis of this mood occurs in the contribution of George Antheil, the composer, friend of Pound, and the one who had apparently arranged for Hurston to contribute to the anthology. Antheil traced the source of black musical creativity to "the groins, the hips, and the sexual organs." He praised the infusion of African forms into European music and art in the same sexual terms: "Europe has been impregnated, and impregnated deeply. We need no longer be surprised by our black children" (*N*, p. 349). One can only imagine what it must have felt like for Clarence Cameron White to see his very decorous article on "The Musical Genius of the American Negro" grouped with this fevered effusion, or for Edward G. Perry to read his "Negro Creative Musicians," which concentrated heavily on Samuel Coleridge-Taylor, after Antheil's benediction: "Therefore we welcomed this sunburnt and primitive feeling, we laid our blankets in the sun and it killed all of our civilised microbes" (*N*, p. 351).

Hurston's own "Spirituals and Neo-Spirituals" was placed in the same section, cheek by jowl with "John Henry," by Guy Johnson, whom she despised.

The double bind this imposes on the African-American contributors to *Negro* is exposed by Michael Gold's supererogatory "A Word as to Uncle Tom," which implicitly divides the whole race into two categories, those going Red in increasing numbers and those named in the title. This is the same Michael Gold who forced Claude McKay to resign from the *Liberator* in 1919 because he insisted on greater coverage of racial issues. It is also the same Michael Gold whose political revue, *Hoboken Blues*, was performed in 1928 by a white cast in burnt cork.[54] The contradiction might be comic if it were not so binding for the black writers involved. For African Americans were told on one hand that they were Uncle Toms unless they signed on with the Communist party; all other forms of political action were virtual race treason. Like Gold, Cunard rolled out the term "white man's nigger" (*N*, p. 147). Yet if they became self-conscious and left their primitive and sunburnt arts behind, African Americans also became unreal. Though the anthology did provide a tremendous amount of space for commentary by African-American scholars and writers, many of the white contributors seemed to take the definitive tone of the title as sanction to lay down a definition that no individual could meet.

This situation is especially ironic where Hurston is concerned. Cunard's anthology provided an outlet for her ethnographic theories, but at the same time it helped to promulgate the literary theory that would effectively silence her best work. For it was the same narrow definition of political effectiveness that Richard Wright applied to *Their Eyes Were Watching God* and that set the tone for those who disapproved of Hurston's work for the next forty years. So thoroughly riven was the discursive context of the time by the dichotomy between acting and action, performance and the performative, that no one could see how Hurston had attempted to rethink it.

This, then, is the source of all the difference between the two anthologies. Cunard's narrative voice is both intrusive and ineffective just as her method of organization is simultaneously heavy-handed and hopelessly lax. For Cunard believes that there are two different kinds of language, even two kinds of human activity, instrumental and decorative. Where the first is concerned she is ruthless; for the second she has a simpering fondness that leads her into the worst kind of editorial solecism. Out of this basic opposition come all the discontinuities and contradictions of the anthology, which despite its miscellaneous and even messy appearance really has only two rather simple and incompatible points to make.

For Hurston, on the other hand, there is no such stark distinction between performance and political action because she does not recognize, at least where African-American art and language are concerned, the more basic distinction between kinds of language. In her anthology the editorial voice disappears, but there is a successful community nonetheless because the performative ethic provides a collective forum. The most important irony posed by the *Negro* anthology, then, is that it encloses its most significant African-American contribution within a context that effectively negates its central message.

The *Negro* anthology is a very elaborate, if temporally somewhat belated, act of modernist racial rebellion. It was certainly meant, on one level at least, to be a massive elucidation of *Black Man, White Ladyship,* Cunard's defiant display of her black lover, Henry Crowder. McKay had called that work "a Negro stick to beat the Cunard mother," and the later far more massive work sometimes performed the same function, as in the case of the uncaptioned photograph of Lady Cunard with an Indian rajah, which was supposed to illustrate her hypocrisy where race was concerned.[55] But the anthology is also a detailed demonstration of how easily that rebelliousness could coexist with an attitude capable of finding W. E. B. Du Bois frivolous. It is intriguing to watch the contradiction develop as Cunard simultaneously praises African Americans for their free and open spontaneity, and enlists that spontaneity on her own side in the generational conflict, while castigating the leaders of African America for insufficient political seriousness. Potentially, this puts Hurston in the same bind that traps a fictional character like McKay's Bita Plant, who is caught between Squire Gensir's romanticized primitivism and the rigid moral demands of the Craigs. It was her genius, as it was McKay's and even Toomer's, to work past this false dichotomy in which both sides lead to the same conclusion.

VI

In a different part of the *Negro* anthology, John Frederick Matheus had used *The Nigger of the "Narcissus"* as a metaphor for the white fascination that finally issued in the anthology itself. Matheus's choice may have been appropriate in more ways than one, for the awful contradiction represented by Wait's "veiled" face, the uncanny mixture of the crude and the mysterious, informs the anthology as it seemed to inform virtually every literary product touched by the racial fascination of the time. But Conrad had put himself squarely in the midst of this conundrum, straddling the apparent gap between the concrete and the uncanny, the familiar and the foreign, and this is where Hurston puts herself as well. As unlike in virtually every practical way as these two writers were, they both used the participant–observer position to conceptualize a performative theory of language that made it communal without making it metaphysical or politically exclusive.

This unexpected confluence suggests that the racial commonality that the Americanist avant-garde had hoped for was not to be found in any nationalistic theory of language, no matter how democratic. Instead, it was to be found in the remapping of language across national boundaries and also across boundaries between the practical and the decorative, the concrete and the ephemeral, motivated and conventional, dialect and standard. The struggle of these modern writers was not to choose but to refuse to make a choice between these false alternatives. Everything was against them, because white prejudice and white romanticism colluded in making the line between nature and culture as rigid as possible. But a few writers, enlightened by their own disabling linguistic displacement, did manage to turn the racial masquerade of modernism into a displacement of the dichotomies themselves.

The fact remains, of course, that in a practical sense even the success of the white avant-garde made life more difficult for African-American and Afro-Caribbean writers like McKay, Toomer, and Hurston. Stein's example was an irritation to McKay, Frank's a real roadblock for Toomer, and Cunard's a smothering embrace for Hurston. The theoretical renovation of language taking place in the white avant-garde was of little practical consequence where these writers were concerned; indeed, it seems that the avant-garde had a good deal to do with the fact that none of the three black writers considered here managed to make a lifetime career of literature. It is certainly the case that all three felt it necessary to struggle just as diligently against the standards of the avant-garde as against the standards of its opponents.

And yet the power of this renovation was not entirely squandered. At least, it seems to have survived to take effect in another day, in a time when African, African-American, and Caribbean writers look past the overt racism of writers like Conrad, Stein, Eliot, and Williams to find there powerful linguistic examples. Ngugi's continuing interest in Conrad and Brathwaite's testimony to Eliot are just the most surprising examples in a category that also includes Gayl Jones's attention to Stein and Anthony Appiah's tribute to Williams. Salman Rushdie has suggested that such writers are the forebears of the international English literature of which he himself is perhaps the most prominent example. If it is now unthinkable to describe literature in English in the tones of Stuart Sherman or Robert Bridges, much of the credit must go to those modernists who were most peripatetic, linguistically and geographically.

However, much of the credit must also go to the culture that inspired and led them. The dialect that James Weldon Johnson ceremonially buried in 1922 died a well-deserved death, but the dialect that Johnson himself used, the characteristic "Negro expression" that Hurston defined and that both Toomer and McKay struggled to put into their works, has exerted a profound influence, determining the course of literature written in English. It now does so directly, as African-American writers of the early part of the century come into ever greater prominence, but for many years it had done so indirectly, serving as the linguistic model for some of the most prominent writers of the century. Literary modernism in English, whether it be dated from *The Nigger of the "Narcissus,"* from Stein's *Three Lives,* from *The Waste Land,* or even from *Spring and All,* could not have arisen without the example of dialect. Thus a stigmatized and despised language transformed the literature of one century and prepared the way for the literature of another.

Notes

Preface

1. Michael S. Harper, *Images of Kin: New and Selected Poems* (Urbana: University of Illinois Press, 1980), p. 10. John Berryman, *The Dream Songs* (New York: Farrar, Straus & Giroux, 1969), p. v.

2. Harper, p. 10. For an example of the kind of language Harper has in mind, see Dream Song 60, Berryman, p. 67.

Chapter 1

1. Bernard Shaw, "Preface: A Professor of Phonetics," *Collected Plays with Their Prefaces,* 7 vols. (New York: Dodd, Mead, 1975), 4:664, 734. In a fragment included in this edition, Shaw claims that he wrote the play purely to publicize phonetics as a way of achieving a standard English pronunciation (p. 800). See also Shaw's "Plea for Speech Nationalisation," in *The English Language: Essays by Linguists and Men of Letters, 1858–1964,* 2 vols., ed. W. F. Bolton and D. Crystal (Cambridge: Cambridge University Press, 1966–1969), 2:80–85.

2. Compare this scene to a famous episode in American advertising. To counter protests about the grammatical error in its slogan claiming that its brand "tastes good like a cigarette should," the company ran another ad defiantly asking, "What do you want, good grammar or good taste?" Dennis Baron calls this "the glorious defeat of artificial grammatical prescriptions by the democratic representatives of realistic language." See his *Grammar and Good Taste: Reforming the American Language* (New Haven, Conn.: Yale University Press, 1982), p. 169.

3. Robert L. Carringer, *The Jazz Singer* (Madison: University of Wisconsin Press, 1979), p. 140; Ronald Haver, audio essay, *Singin' in the Rain* (Criterion, 1988, laserdisc).

4. All the details in this paragraph are included in Havers's audio essay, included on one track of the 1988 Criterion laserdisc reissue of *Singin' in the Rain.*

5. In fact, this scene is itself frequently omitted from televised versions of *Singin' in the Rain.*

6. *The Jazz Singer* (Warner Bros./Vitaphone, 1927). The title cards refer to him as "Ragtime Jakie." Carringer, p. 143.

7. *The Jazz Singer,* title cards. The corresponding scene in the screenplay is much milder and lacks the generational rebelliousness. Carringer, pp. 98–99.

8. The movie retains a useful ambiguity about this "tear." Is it a function of Jack's Jewishness or sorrow at separation from his heritage and family? Yudelson says, "[T]hat's Jakie—with the cry in the voice, just like in the temple." Carringer, p. 122.

9. Carringer, p. 120. In the film itself this becomes, "He talks like Jakie—but he looks like his shadow."

10. For a penetrating discussion of these questions, to which I am greatly indebted, see Michael Rogin, "Blackface, White Noise: The Jewish Jazz Singer Finds His Voice," *Critical Inquiry* 18 (Spring 1992): 417–53, esp. pp. 429, 430–431.

The Jazz Singer was hardly unique in bringing these old routines to the screen. In fact, what is remarkable about this period is the prevalence of blackface routines in film, onstage, and even on radio. Within a year of the premiere of *The Jazz Singer*, the following productions appeared, each with significant blackface roles (all page citations are to William Torbert Leonard, *Masquerade in Black* [Metuchen, N.J.: Scarecrow Press, 1986]): Carl Laemmle's lavish film version of *Uncle Tom's Cabin* (pp. 186–89); D. W. Griffith's comic version of the same story, *Topsy and Eva* (p. 192); Eddie Cantor's feature film debut in *Kid Boots* (p. 241); Moran and Mack (a.k.a. "Two Black Crows") in *Two Flaming Youths*, with W. C. Fields (p. 278); First National's *An Octoroon* (p. 372); and MGM's *Heart of Maryland* with a large white cast in blackface (pp. 370–71). Onstage there were premieres as different as Oscar Hammerstein's extravaganza *Golden Dawn* (pp. 203, 206–7); Jay C. Flippen in *Padlocks of 1927* (p. 250); David Belasco's *Lulu Belle* (p. 322); Maxwell Anderson and Laurence Stallings's *Deep River* (pp. 331–32); and the return of McIntyre and Heath to vaudeville after their "retirement" (p. 275). At the same time, Amos 'n' Andy, then known as Sam 'n' Henry, made their radio debut (pp. 234–37).

11. Carringer, p. 148.

12. Ibid., p. 145. Jolson ad-libbed most of the extended sound sequences in the film. These are transcribed and printed in Carringer.

13. Al Jolson, "Maaaaam-my! Maaaaam-my! The Famous Mammy-Singer Explores His Native(?) Sunny Southland," *Vanity Fair* 24 (April 1925): 42, 98. This kind of interchange of material did actually take place, however. Shelton Brooks, a black composer, wrote at least two songs for Jolson, and Garland Anderson, a black bellhop who had written a play, took it to Jolson, who arranged to have it performed. The result, *Appearances*, was the first full-length Broadway production of the work of a black playwright. As a kind of ultimate reversal, John Mason, a black performer, was made up to look like Jolson in blackface for the 1929 *Deep Harlem*. Bruce Kellner, *The Harlem Renaissance: An Historical Dictionary for the Era* (1984; rpt. New York/London: Methuen/Routledge & Kegan Paul, 1987), pp. 54, 14, 111.

14. Another way of putting this would use the terminology advanced by Werner Sollors, who focuses on "the conflict between contractual and hereditary, self-made and ancestral, definitions of American identity—between *consent* and *descent.*" See his *Beyond Ethnicity: Consent and Descent in American Culture* (New York: Oxford University Press, 1986), pp. 5–6. In *The Jazz Singer* Jakie Rabinowitz seems to move from an ethnicity defined by descent to a citizenship defined by consent. And yet the use of another ethnicity, another form of descent, to manage this transition shows how complexly the two modes are intertwined, at least in the modern period.

15. Raphaelson's story is reprinted in Carringer, pp. 147–67. *Pygmalion* made its first American appearance in the same magazine in 1914.

16. Rudolf Fisher, "The Caucasian Storms Harlem," *The American Mercury* 11 (August 1927): 398.

17. José M. Salaverria, "The Negro of the Jazz Band," trans. Dorothy R. Peterson, in *Ebony and Topaz: A Collectanea*, ed. Charles S. Johnson (1927; rpt. Freeport, N.Y.: Books for Libraries Press, 1971), pp. 65–66.

18. Carl Van Vechten, *"Keep A-Inchin' Along": Selected Writings of Carl Van Vechten About Black Art and Letters*, ed. Bruce Kellner (Westport, Conn.: Greenwood Press, 1979), pp. 4–5, 69; John R. Cooley, *Savages and Naturals: Black Portraits by White Writers in Modern American Literature* (Newark: University of Delaware Press/London and Toronto: Associated University Presses, 1982), p. 73. There is a letter preserved in the Jean Toomer papers that records Frank's decision to travel as black, if Toomer were going to do the same. Waldo Frank to Jean Toomer, nd (1922?), Jean Toomer papers, box 2, folder 83,

James Weldon Johnson Collection of Negro Literature and Art, Beinecke Rare Book and Manuscript Library, Yale University.

19. Holly Stevens, *Souvenirs and Prophecies: The Young Wallace Stevens* (New York: Knopf, 1977), p. 199; Ezra Pound, *The Selected Letters of Ezra Pound, 1907–1941*, ed. D. D. Paige (1950; rpt. New York: New Directions, 1971), p. 294.

20. *The Letters of T. S. Eliot*, ed. Valerie Eliot (New York: Harcourt, Brace, 1988), p. 350; James R. Mellow, *Charmed Circle: Gertrude Stein and Company* (New York: Praeger, 1974), pp. 64, 69, 77.

21. John Berryman, *The Dream Songs* (New York: Farrar, Straus & Giroux, 1969), p. v. For a discussion of Berryman and a number of the other writers mentioned here see Aldon L. Nielsen, *Reading Race: White American Poets and the Racial Discourse in the Twentieth Century* (Athens: University of Georgia Press, 1988).

22. Nathan Irvin Huggins, *Harlem Renaissance* (New York: Oxford University Press, 1971), p. 93.

23. Sherwood Anderson to Jean Toomer, January 3, 1924, Jean Toomer papers, box 1, folder 8, James Weldon Johnson Collection of Negro Literature and Art, Beinecke Rare Book and Manuscript Library, Yale University. The whole correspondence is of the greatest interest. See Darwin T. Turner, "An Intersection of Paths: Correspondence Between Jean Toomer and Sherwood Anderson," in *Jean Toomer: A Critical Evaluation*, ed. Therman B. O'Daniel (Washington, D.C.: Howard University Press, 1988), pp. 99–110; and Mark Helbling, "Sherwood Anderson and Jean Toomer," in O'Daniel, ed., pp. 111–20.

24. H.D., *HERmione* (New York: New Directions, 1981), p. 26. For a discussion of this passage and the whole issue of racial crossidentification in H.D., see Susan Stanford Friedman, "Modernism of the 'Scattered Remnant': Race and Politics in the Development of H.D.'s Modernist Vision," in *H.D.: Woman and Poet*, ed. Michael King (Orono: University of Maine Press/National Poetry Foundation, 1986), pp. 99–116.

25. Alice Corbin, "Mandy's Religion," *Seven Arts* 2 (September 1917): 600; Carl Sandburg, "Jazz Fantasia," *Dial* 68 (March 1920): 294; Malcolm Cowley, "Farewell Blues," in *The American Caravan*, ed. Van Wyck Brooks et al. (New York: Literary Guild, 1927), pp. 57–58; Mina Loy, "The Widow's Jazz," *Pagany* 2 (Spring 1931): 68–70. Lindsay's most famous contribution to this genre is, of course, "The Congo." See as well "Booker Washington Trilogy," *Poetry* 8 (June 1916): 109–21; and "Notes on the Booker Washington Trilogy," *Poetry* 8 (June 1916): 146–48.

26. Peter Ackroyd, *T. S. Eliot: A Life* (New York: Simon & Schuster, 1984), pp. 65, 91. Just before his father's death, Eliot wrote to John Quinn about the importance of having a book published soon: "You see I settled over here in the face of strong family opposition, on the claim that I found the environment more favourable to the production of literature. This book is all I have to show for my claim—it would go toward making my parents contented with conditions—and towards satisfying them that I have not made a mess of my life, as they are inclined to believe." *Letters*, p. 266.

27. Eliot, *Letters*, pp. 42–43, 125. Aiken called these poems "a cynical counterpoint to the study of Sanskrit and the treatise on epistemology." Conrad Aiken, "King Bolo and Others," in *T. S. Eliot: A Symposium*, ed. Richard March and Tambimuttu (1949; rpt. Freeport, N.Y.: Books for Libraries Press, 1968), p. 21.

28. Eliot, *Letters*, p. 77. For discussions of other early literary treatments of racial subjects see Robert Crawford, *The Savage and the City in the Work of T. S. Eliot* (Oxford: Clarendon Press, 1987), pp. 83–85.

29. Clive Bell, *Since Cézanne* (New York: Harcourt, Brace, 1922), p. 222. "Plus de Jazz," the essay from which this comment is quoted, is dated 1921.

30. For a full discussion of the role of minstrel songs in the *Waste Land* drafts, see chapter 4 in the present study.

31. Michael J. Sidnell, *Dances of Death: The Group Theatre of London in the Thirties* (London: Faber, 1984), pp. 263–65; Arnold Bennett, *The Journals of Arnold Bennett*, ed. Newman Flower (London: Cassell, 1933), 3:52.

32. At the same time, racial masquerade was becoming an accepted part of ordinary white middle-class American life. Books such as Herbert Preston Powell's *World's Best Book of Minstrelsy* (Philadelphia: Penn Publishing, 1926) were published to guide churches, charitable organizations, schools, and fraternal organizations in producing their own authentic minstrel shows.

33. James Weldon Johnson, *God's Trombones: Seven Negro Sermons in Verse* (1927; rpt. New York: Penguin, 1990), p. 8.

34. James Weldon Johnson, ed., *The Book of American Negro Poetry*, 2nd ed. (1931; rpt. New York: Harcourt, Brace & World, 1969), pp. 4, 41. Johnson quoted from this preface in the preface to *God's Trombones*.

35. Alain Locke, "Negro Youth Speaks," in *The New Negro*, ed. Alain Locke (1925; rpt. New York: Atheneum, 1968), p. 51.

36. Van Vechten, p. 59. For other comments about "the chain of dialect" see: Locke, pp. 5, 48; Walter M. Brasch, *Black English and the Mass Media* (Amherst: University of Massachusetts Press, 1981), p. 149; and Henry Louis Gates, Jr., *The Signifying Monkey: A Theory of African-American Literary Criticism* (New York: Oxford University Press, 1988), pp. 176–78.

37. Racial masquerade, that is to say, is allowable only for whites. As James Weldon Johnson said, it is deemed "quite seemly for a white person to represent a Negro on the stage, but a violation of some inner code for a Negro to represent a white person." *Black Manhattan* (1930; rpt. New York: Atheneum, 1969), p. 191.

38. By 1931 Johnson had modified his opinion of dialect somewhat under the influence of Langston Hughes and Sterling Brown. See his "Preface to the Revised Edition," *Book of American Negro Poetry*, p. 4. For a more complete discussion, see chapter 6 in the present study. It is interesting that Johnson and Locke both felt a resemblance between their linguistic situation and that of Irish writers like Synge: "What the colored poet in the United States needs to do is something like what Synge did for the Irish . . ." (*Book of American Negro Poetry*, p. 41). It is also ironic that Synge should have seemed a successful model, when, in fact, he was attacked in Ireland for perpetuating the clichés of the stage Irishman, in many ways a British equivalent of the black minstrel. For a fuller discussion of such correspondences, see C. L. Innes, *The Devil's Own Mirror: The Irishman and the African in Modern Literature* (Washington, D.C.: Three Continents Press, 1990).

39. For the details of this anticipated alliance, see chapter 6 in the present study.

40. Houston A. Baker, Jr., *Modernism and the Harlem Renaissance* (Chicago: University of Chicago Press, 1987), pp. 1–8. For another opinion, one that that stresses the similarity between the linguistic tactics of Anglo-American modernism and African-American writers, see Clyde Taylor, "Salt Peanuts," *Callaloo* 5 (1982): 1–11.

41. Hugh Kenner, *The Pound Era* (Berkeley: University of California Press, 1971), pp. 94–103.

42. "Proposal for the Publication of a New English Dictionary by the Philological Society," in *Proper English? Readings in Language, History and Cultural Identity*, ed. Tony Crowley (London: Routledge, 1981), p. 154. Crowley has since discovered a usage of the term dating back to 1844. See Roy Harris, "Murray, Moore and the Myth," in *Linguistic Thought in England, 1914–1945*, ed. Roy Harris (London: Duckworth, 1988), p. 20. It still remains significant that the OED dated the term to its own first circulars.

43. Shaw, *Collected Plays*, 4:800. For the increasing popularity of the phrase "standard language," see John Earl Joseph, *Eloquence and Power: The Rise of Language Standards and Standard Languages* (London: Frances Pinter, 1987), pp. 3–5.

44. Shaw, "A Plea for Speech Nationalisation," p. 84. Linda Dowling finds irony in the fact that Clara Hill mistakes Eliza's "bloody" as the newest fashionable slang. See her *Language and Decadence in the Victorian Fin de Siècle* (Princeton, N.J.: Princeton University Press, 1986), p. 95.

45. James Milroy and Leslie Milroy, *Authority in Language: Investigating Language Prescription and Standardisation*, 2nd ed., (London: Routledge, 1991), p. 36; Edward Finegan, *Attitudes Toward English Usage: The History of a War of Words* (New York: Teacher's College of Columbia University Press, 1980), p. 20. As Richard Bailey shows, such demands were often countered by another line of reasoning, that English was especially strong and vital because it was various. See his *Images of English: A Cultural History of the Language* (Ann Arbor: University of Michigan Press, 1991), pp. 32–59.

46. Kenneth Cmiel, *Democratic Eloquence: The Fight Over Popular Speech in Nineteenth-Century America* (New York: William Morrow, 1990), pp. 123, 263–65.

47. Elsa Nettels, *Language, Race, and Social Class in Howells's America* (Lexington: University Press of Kentucky, 1988), pp. 8–9.

48. Baron, p. 82; Bailey, p. 210.

49. Joseph, pp. 14, 109.

50. Tony Crowley, *Standard English and the Politics of Language* (Urbana: University of Illinois Press, 1989), pp. 107–24.

51. Society for Pure English, Tract No. 1 (1919), p. 6; Tract No. 2 (1919), pp. 37–39; Tract No. 4 (1921), pp. 14–19; Tract No. 9 (1922), pp. 24–26. See Bailey, pp. 206–8.

52. Robert Graves, *Impenetrability, or The Proper Habit of English* (London: Hogarth, 1926), pp. 30–31. In 1921 Graves had written to the society to protest its doctrine of "one word, one meaning." See Tract No. 4 (1921), pp. 22–26.

53. Shaw, *Collected Plays*, 4:663; John Honey, *Does Accent Matter? The Pygmalion Factor* (London: Faber & Faber, 1989), p. 31.

54. *The Teaching of English in England* (London: His Majesty's Stationery Office, 1921), p. 19. See Crowley, *Standard English*, pp. 236–49.

55. Paul Elmer More et al., *Academy Papers: Addresses on Language Problems by Members of the American Academy of Arts and Letters* (New York: Scribner's, 1925), p. v.

56. Charles A. Fenton, "The American Academy of Arts vs. All Comers: Literary Rags and Riches in the 1920's," *South Atlantic Quarterly* 58 (1959): 575. This campaign will be discussed in greater detail in chapter 6 of the present study.

57. George Sampson, *English for the English: A Chapter in National Education* (1921; rpt. Cambridge: Cambridge University Press, 1952), p. 47; Adams Sherman Hill, *Our English* (New York: American Book Co., 1888), p. 113. Hill was Boylston Professor of Rhetoric and Oratory at Harvard and was instrumental in introducing the first English composition courses there.

58. H. Rider Haggard, *The Annotated She*, ed. Norman Etherington (Bloomington: Indiana University Press, 1991), p. 99.

59. "The Linguistic Conscience," *Cambridge Magazine* 10 (Summer 1920): 31. The broadside is unsigned, but W. Terence Gordon reports that it was written by C. K. Ogden, who edited the magazine. See his *C. K. Ogden: A Bio-Bibliographic Study* (Metuchen, N.J.: Scarecrow Press, 1990), pp. 9–10.

60. Richard Grant White, *Words and Their Uses, Past and Present* (Boston: Houghton Mifflin, 1889), p. 423.

61. Leonard Forster, *The Poet's Tongues: Multilingualism in Literature* (Cambridge:

Cambridge University Press, 1970), pp. 54–55; Joseph, p. x. Forster uses the phrase "language loyalty" on p. 19. For a rather different account of the growth of linguistic nationalism, see Benedict Anderson, *Imagined Communities: Reflections on the Origin and Spread of Nationalism,* rev. ed. (London: Verso, 1991). Of particular interest here is Anderson's account of the way that linguistic nationalism passes to the Third World (pp. 113–40).

62. Linda Dowling, "Victorian Oxford and the Science of Language," *PMLA* 97 (March 1982): 163.

63. George Steiner, *After Babel: Aspects of Language and Translation* (London: Oxford University Press, 1975), pp. 75, 78–81; Dowling, *Language and Decadence,* p. 35.

64. Edward Steiner, quoted in Shirley Brice Heath, "Standard English: Biography of a Symbol," in *Standards and Dialects of English,* ed. Timothy Shopen and Joseph M. Williams (Cambridge, Mass.: Winthrop, 1980), p. 29.

65. Etienne Balibar, "Paradoxes of Universality," in *Anatomy of Racism,* ed. David Theo Goldberg (Minneapolis: University of Minnesota Press, 1990), pp. 285–86.

66. R. W. Chapman, quoted in Bailey, p. 8. See the entire introduction, pp. 1–16.

67. Paul Elmer More, *Academy Papers,* p. 23. For a progressive demolition of all possible standards for theorizing the standard, see Crowley, *Standard English,* chaps. 3, 4, and 5.

68. Sampson, pp. 47–48.

69. Henry Alford, *A Plea for the Queen's English,* 2nd ed. (London: A. Strahan, 1869), p. 279.

70. Milroy and Milroy, p. 21.

71. Bailey, p. 11.

72. Crowley, *Standard English,* p. 156; E. J. Hobsbawm, *The Age of Empire, 1875–1914* (New York: Pantheon, 1987), pp. 36–37, 56–73.

73. Otto Jespersen, *Mankind, Nation and Individual from a Linguistic Point of View* (1925; rpt. London: George Allen & Unwin, 1946), pp. 44–45. See also Cmiel, pp. 142–46.

74. Bailey, pp. 114–15; Crowley, *Standard English,* pp. 207–57.

75. Robert Bridges, "The Society's Work," Society for Pure English, Tract No. 21 (1925), p. 4.

76. Bailey, p. 123; Alford, p. 6. This attack, occasioned by the slaughter of the Civil War, was removed from later editions.

77. Bridges, p. 5. Bailey reports that Bridges scuttled plans for cooperation with an American version of the SPE (p. 207).

78. Quoted in Bailey, p. 157.

79. T. L. Kington-Oliphant, *The New English,* 2 vols. (London: Macmillan, 1886), 2:230.

80. A. Lloyd James, "Broadcast English," in Bolton and Crystal, eds., p. 100.

81. Henry Reeve, quoted in Bailey, p. 242; Dowling, "Victorian Oxford," pp. 171–72. See also Sampson, p. 51, and Dowling, *Language and Decadence,* p. 87.

82. White, p. 44; Williams Roscoe Thayer, quoted in Allen Walker Read, "Amphi-Atlantic English," *English Studies* 17 (1935): 174. Read's article is a rich compendium of statements about the tension between English and American English. See also Bailey, pp. 124–25.

83. William Fowler, *English Grammar* (1887), quoted in Heath, pp. 28–29.

84. More, *Academy Papers,* p. 10. See the dissent by another American Academy member, Brander Matthews, *Academy Papers,* pp. 63–93, and *Essays on English* (New York: Scribner's, 1922), pp. 4–6.

85. Quoted in Thomas F. Gossett, *Race: The History of an Idea in America* (1963; rpt.

New York: Schocken, 1965), p. 306. For a discussion of the antiimmigration agitation of the time, and especially the role played in it by writers and intellectuals, see pp. 134–43, 287–309.

86. William Mathews, *Words; their use and abuse* (Chicago: Griggs, 1892), pp. 47–48.

87. Quoted in Nettels, p. 19.

88. Henry James, *The Question of Our Speech* (Boston: Houghton Mifflin, 1905), pp. 44–45, 41.

89. Paul Shorey, "The American Language," in *Academy Papers*, p. 161. Shorey praises James's address on page 129.

90. See Michael Taussig, *Shamanism, Colonialism, and the Wild Man: A Study in Terror and Healing* (Chicago: University of Chicago Press, 1987), for the "deformation of good speech" that is a necessary component of the defense of colonialism (p. 70).

91. For a discussion of this process in an American context, see Cmiel, p. 38.

92. Milroy and Milroy, pp. 98–103.

93. Quoted in Heath, pp. 23–24. See also Crowley, *Standard English*, p. 67.

94. More, *Academy Papers*, p. 9. See also Crowley, *Standard English*, p. 126.

95. Shorey, *Academy Papers*, p. 135.

96. Bridges, Society for Pure English, Tract No. 9 (1922), p. 21; C. Alphonso Smith, "Dialect Writers," in *The Cambridge History of American Literature*, 4 vols., ed. W. P. Trent et al. (New York: Putnam, 1918), 2:361; Logan Pearsall Smith, "Robert Bridges: Recollections," Society for Pure English, Tract No. 35 (1931): 487. In *The Dialect of the Tribe*, Margery Sabin uses Smith's *Words and Idioms* as an example of English taste for the concrete and idiomatic, apparently unaware that much of this material originally appeared as Tract No. 12 of the SPE. Its appearance there illustrates the point to be made, that the SPE accommodated those like Smith who defended "the idiomatic loopholes in rational language" and those like Fowler who spent long hours attempting to close them. See Logan Pearsall Smith, "English Idioms," Society for Pure English, Tract No. 12 (1923); and Margery Sabin, *The Dialect of the Tribe: Speech and Community in Modern Fiction* (New York: Oxford University Press, 1987), p. 18.

97. *Teaching of English in England*, p. 275.

98. Ibid., p. 65. There was some controversy on this point within the commission, with some sentiment for the idea that dialect speakers should simply become bilingual (p. 67).

99. Dowling, "Victorian Oxford," p. 169. See also Dowling, *Language and Decadence*, p. 83.

100. N. F. Blake, *Non-Standard Language in English Literature* (London: Deutsch, 1981), p. 166; Dowling, *Language and Decadence*, pp. 182, 214, 226–30; Crowley, *Standard English*, pp. 160–61.

101. Norman Page, *Speech in the English Novel*, 2nd ed. (London: Macmillan, 1988), pp. 75–76; Sabin, p. 17.

102. George Philip Krapp, *The English Language in America* (1925; rpt. New York: Frederick Ungar, 1960), p. 225.

103. Crowley, *Standard English*, p. 140.

104. Alford, p. 245; James, pp. 40–41. See also Blake, p. 160.

105. Graves, p. 42.

106. Patrick Brantlinger, *Rule of Darkness: British Literature and Imperialism, 1830–1914* (Ithaca, N.Y.: Cornell University Press, 1988), pp. 231–32.

107. Taussig, p. 87.

108. James, p. 40.

109. Shorey, *Academy Papers*, pp. 152–53.

110. Society for Pure English, Tract No. 4 (1921), p. 42; and Tract No. 6 (1921), p. 28.

111. Baron, pp. 21–24; Read, pp. 161, 167.

112. James Adams (1799), quoted in Read, p. 161.

113. Joel Chandler Harris, quoted in Brasch, p. 86. Krapp, p. 251. See also Annie Weston Whitney, "Negro American Dialects," *The Independent* 53 (August 22, 1901, and August 29, 1901): 1981, 2039. For discussions in the black press see "Negro Dialect," *Opportunity* 2 (September 1924): 260; and Edwin D. Johnson, "The Speech of the American Negro Folk," *Opportunity* 5 (July 1927): 196. J. L. Dillard has attacked Krapp's theory with such vehemence it seems necessary to observe that it may have had a certain strategic usefulness at the time it was offered.

114. R. Emmett Kennedy, *Black Cameos* (New York: Albert & Charles Boni, 1924), pp. x, xii; Ambrose E. Gonzales, *The Black Border* (Columbia, S.C.: State Printing Co., 1922), p. 12. The same sort of thing had been said in England about the rural peasantry since at least the beginning of the nineteenth century. See Page, *Speech in the English Novel*, p. 60.

115. "Daddy Jake the Runaway," in *Critical Essays on Joel Chandler Harris*, ed. R. Bruce Bickley (Boston: G. K. Hall, 1981), p. 17.

116. Bailey, p. 130; Brasch, p. 4.

117. Quoted in Baron, p. 26.

118. Smith dates the dialect boom to Russell's poem (*Cambridge History*, p. 353), as do Page and A. C. Gordon in their collection *Befo' de War: Echoes in Negro Dialect* (1888; rpt. New York: Scribner's, 1906), which was dedicated to "Irwin Russell Who Awoke the First Echo." Harris's *Uncle Remus: His Songs and Sayings* was first published in 1880. Page says that the idea for "Marse Chan," his first dialect story, came to him in the same year. *The Novels, Stories, Sketches and Poems of Thomas Nelson Page*, 12 vols. (New York: Scribner's, 1906), 1:ix–x.

119. T. C. De Leon, "The Day of Dialect," *Lippincott's Magazine* 60 (November 1897): 680; Thomas Nelson Page, "The Immortal Uncle Remus," *Book Buyer* 12 (December 1895): 642–45, reprinted in Bickley, p. 56; Joseph Boskin, *Sambo: The Rise and Demise of an American Jester* (New York: Oxford University Press, 1986), p. 108; Rayford W. Logan, *The Negro in American Life and Thought: The Nadir, 1877–1901* (New York: Dial Press, 1954), pp. 239–74; Bruce Jackson, ed., *The Negro and His Folklore in Nineteenth-Century Periodicals* (Austin: University of Texas Press, 1967), p. 211. See also Brasch, pp. 114–17; and Nettels, pp. 65–66.

120. Smith, *Cambridge History*, p. 351. Smith is hardly alone in this. The extensive article by J. A. Harrison on "Negro English," *Anglia* (1884), is indebted to the writings of white writers like Harris, Macon, and Sherwood Bonner. See *Perspectives on Black English*, ed. J. L. Dillard (The Hague: Mouton, 1975), pp. 143–95.

121. Boskin, pp. 101–2; Bernard Wolfe, "Uncle Remus and the Malevolent Rabbit," *Commentary* 8 (July 1949): 31–41, reprinted in Bickley, pp. 82–83.

122. Gossett, pp. 264–65. See the long and finely nuanced discussion of Harris in Eric J. Sundquist, *To Wake the Nations: Race in the Making of American Literature* (Cambridge, Mass.: Harvard University Press/Belknap Press, 1993), pp. 323–59.

123. Gossett, pp. 274–75, 280–81.

124. Smith, *Cambridge History*, p. 354; Page, "The Immortal Uncle Remus," p. 56. The former slave pining for the old plantation had been a staple of the minstrel show since the 1850s. See Hans Nathan, *Dan Emmett and the Rise of Negro Minstrelsy* (Norman: University of Oklahoma Press, 1962), p. 243.

125. E. K. Means, *E. K. Means: Is this a title? It is the name of a writer of negro stories, who has made himself so completely* the *writer of negro stories that his book needs no title.* (New

York: Putnam's, 1918), pp. vi–vii. This book was of particular importance to William Carlos Williams. See chapter 7 of the present study.

126. See Page, "The Immortal Uncle Remus," p. 56; Jackson, p. xxiii; and George M. Fredrickson, *The Black Image in the White Mind: The Debate on Afro–American Character and Destiny, 1817–1914* (New York: Harper & Row, 1971), pp. 208, 211.

127. Quoted in Edgar P. Billups, "Some Principles for the Representation of Negro Dialect in Fiction," *Texas Review* 8 (January 1923): 100.

128. Quoted in Alain Locke, "Our Little Renaissance," in Johnson, ed., *Ebony and Topaz*, p. 117.

129. Smith, *Cambridge History*, p. 361.

130. Charles W. Chesnutt, *The Marrow of Tradition* (Boston: Houghton Mifflin, 1901), pp. 95, 96. See Sundquist's massive contextualization of this novel in *To Wake the Nations*, pp. 271–454.

131. "The Poet," in *The Complete Poems of Paul Laurence Dunbar* (New York: Dodd, Mead, 1913), p. 191. See the discussion in Brasch, pp. 126–35.

132. Gossett, pp. 390, 371.

133. Billups, p. 101; Brasch, p. 171. See also "Negro Dialect," *Opportunity* 2 (September 1924): 259.

134. As distorted and demeaning as most of this work now seems, it actually established a threshold for the Harlem Renaissance. In 1927, when Alain Locke looked for evidence that "Our Little Renaissance" had made a difference, he actually began by citing Peterkin and Du Bose Heyward. Charles Johnson's introduction to *Ebony and Topaz* mentions Peterkin, Heyward, Paul Green, and Guy Johnson, all of whom except Heyward contributed to the volume themselves. Locke, "Our Little Renaissance," in Johnson, ed., *Ebony and Topaz*, p. 117; Johnson, "Introduction," in Johnson, ed., *Ebony and Topaz*, p. 12. Dorothy Scarborough, author of *In the Land of Cotton*, was invited to the banquet for Jessie Fauset from which the Harlem Renaissance is sometimes dated, and she also served, along with Clement Wood, author of *Nigger*, as judge for the *Opportunity* literary awards. *Opportunity* 2 (May 1924): 144; and 2 (September 1924): 277.

135. Huggins, p. 63. Huggins specifically includes the modernist generation in this description.

136. For the impact of Uncle Remus on Pound, see Humphrey Carpenter, *A Serious Character: The Life of Ezra Pound* (London: Faber, 1988), pp. 22, 414. Vachel Lindsay was also strongly affected by early reading from Uncle Remus (Cooley, p. 51). The first poetry read aloud to William Carlos Williams was that of Paul Laurence Dunbar, which was also very popular at the time. See *The Autobiography of William Carlos Williams* (New York: New Directions, 1951), p. 15. Nor was the dialect fad limited to America. In 1926 Henry Newbolt reported, with some satisfaction, that the popularity of O. Henry, Mark Twain, and Bret Harte, which had swept through English schools like "a prairie fire," was now as dead as "Uncle Remus." "The Future of the English Language," in *Studies in Green and Gray* (London: Thomas Nelson, 1926), p. 232.

137. James Weldon Johnson, *Fifty Years and Other Poems* (Boston: Cornhill, 1917), pp. xi–xiv. For a discussion of Johnson's long association with Matthews, see Lawrence J. Oliver, *Brander Matthews, Theodore Roosevelt, and the Politics of American Literature, 1880–1920* (Knoxville: University of Tennessee Press, 1992), pp. 47–62.

138. *Cambridge Magazine* 10 (Summer 1920): 55–59. The headnote, presumably by Ogden, claims that McKay's almost severely conventional poems display "some of those peculiar qualities which rendered the visit of the Southern Syncopated Orchestra so memorable last Autumn. . . ."

139. Carl Van Vechten, *Nigger Heaven* (1926; rpt. New York: Octagon, 1980), p. 57. In Johnson's correspondence there is a brief letter from Stein that, in a trivial sense, completes this circle. She thanks him for sending her a copy of *God's Trombones*, which, she says, she is reading with great interest. James Weldon Johnson correspondence, series I, folder 459, James Weldon Johnson Collection of Negro Literature and Art, Beinecke Rare Book and Manuscript Library, Yale University.

140. *The Complete Prose of Marianne Moore*, ed. Patricia C. Willis (New York: Viking, 1986), p. 167. Moore was also responsible for publishing two or three of the last published writings of Jean Toomer in the *Dial*.

141. Robert Underwood Johnson, "The Glory of Words," in More et al., pp. 276–77.

142. Moore, p. 167.

143. T. S. Eliot, "Marianne Moore," *Dial* 75 (1923): 596. A few lines in "Black Earth," a poem originally published in the *Egoist* in 1918 and in *Others for 1919*, apparently convinced Pound that Moore might herself be black: "And are you a jet black Ethiopian Othello–hued, or was that line in one of your *Egoist* poems but part of your general elaboration and allegory and designed to differentiate your colour from that of the surrounding menagerie?" *Selected Letters*, p. 143.

144. Johnson, "The Glory of Words," pp. 265–66. See Nathan, pp. 147, 154, for the role of the triangle in early minstrel shows.

145. Richard S. Kennedy, *Dreams in the Mirror: A Biography of E. E. Cummings* (New York: Liveright, 1980), p. 294. *Sweeney Agonistes* will be discussed in greater detail in chapter 4 of the present study.

146. E. E. Cummings, *Three Plays and a Ballet*, ed. George J. Firmage (London: Peter Owen, 1968), pp. 45–46, 52, 58, 43–44.

147. Cummings, p. 44.

148. Carringer, p. 63.

149. Sherwood Anderson, *Sherwood Anderson's Notebooks* (New York: Boni & Liveright, 1926), p. 135. Quoted in Helbling, "Sherwood Anderson and Jean Toomer," pp. 119–20.

150. Stuart P. Sherman, *Americans* (New York: Charles Scribner's Sons, 1922), pp. 20, 316–17.

151. Dowling, "Victorian Oxford," p. 162; idem, *Language and Decadence*, p. 14.

152. Shaw, *Collected Plays*, 4:735–36.

153. Dowling, "Victorian Oxford," p. 165.

154. Ibid., p. 169; idem, *Language and Decadence*, pp. 101–2.

155. Cmiel, pp. 150–66.

156. Franz Boas, "On Alternating Sounds," *American Anthropologist* 2 (January 1889): 47–53; reprinted in *The Shaping of American Anthropology, 1883–1911: A Franz Boas Reader*, ed. George W. Stocking, Jr. (New York: Basic Books, 1974), pp. 72–77. The implications of this idea for the different varieties of the American language are worked out in Sundquist.

157. Bronislaw Malinowski, "The Problem of Meaning in Primitive Languages," supplement to *The Meaning of Meaning*, by C. K. Ogden and I. A. Richards, 10th ed. (London: Routledge & Kegan Paul, 1949), pp. 299, 309, 328.

158. For other discussions of the way that ethnography and linguistic and cultural relativism have grown up together, see Steiner, p. 87; Dowling, "Victorian Oxford," p. 169; and, most especially, James Clifford, *The Predicament of Culture: Twentieth-Century Ethnography, Literature, and Art* (Cambridge, Mass.: Harvard University Press, 1988).

159. Gail Levin, "American Art," in *"Primitivism" in 20th Century Art: Affinities of*

the Tribal and the Modern, ed. William Rubin, 2 vols. (New York: Museum of Modern Art, 1984), 2:454–55.

160. Steiner, pp. 176–87. For the influence of Worringer on the primitivism of English avant–garde art, see Richard Cork, *Vorticism and Abstract Art in the First Machine Age* (Berkeley: University of California Press, 1976), pp. 115, 175. For his influence on the primitivism of English writers of the period, see Michael North, *The Final Sculpture: Public Monuments and Modern Poets* (Ithaca, N.Y.: Cornell University Press, 1985), pp. 111–21. For the influence of Lévy-Bruhl on Eliot, see Crawford, pp. 87–92; for his influence on the French avant–garde, see Evan Maurer, "Dada and Surrealism," in Rubin, *"Primitivism" in 20th Century Art*, 2:542.

161. Richard Huelsenbeck, *Memoirs of a Dada Drummer*, ed. Hans J. Kleinschmidt, trans. Joachim Neugroschel (New York: Viking, 1974), p. xxxi.

162. Ezra Pound, *Ezra Pound and the Visual Arts*, ed. Harriet Zinnes (New York: New Directions, 1980), p. 181.

163. Huelsenbeck, p. 9.

164. Maurer, 2:536–41.

165. Richard Huelsenbeck, "Chorus Sanctus," *Little Review* 10 (Spring 1924): 20.

166. Nathan, p. 217.

167. Maurer, 2:538–39. The collages date to 1926.

168. Blaise Cendrars, *The African Saga*, trans. Margery Bianco (New York: Payson & Clarke, 1927). The importance of this work in American racial politics is signified by the introduction of Arthur Spingarn. See also Alain Locke, "A Note on African Art," *Opportunity* 2 (May 1924): 137. Cendrars's actual qualifications in the 591 languages supposedly represented in the anthology have been pretty thoroughly debunked. See Jean-Claude Blachère, *Le Modèle nègre: Aspects littéraires du mythe primitiviste au XXe siècle chez Apollinaire–Cendrars–Tzara* (Dakar: Nouvelles Editions Africaines, 1981), pp. 76–77; and Jay Bochner, *Blaise Cendrars: Discovery and Re–creation* (Toronto: University of Toronto Press, 1978), pp. 66–67.

169. Jean–Louis Paudrat, "From Paris," in Rubin, *"Primitivism" in 20th Century Art*, 1:158. Though Cendrars was not a dadaist, a number of his early poems, including "Mee Too Buggi," to be discussed later, were published in dada journals such as Hugo Ball's *Cabaret Voltaire*. See Bochner, pp. 61, 124.

170. Blachère, p. 112.

171. Ibid., p. 19. See also the excellent discussion of Cendrars in Marjorie Perloff, *The Futurist Moment: Avant–Garde, Avant Guerre, and the Language of Rupture* (Chicago: University of Chicago Press, 1986), pp. 2–43.

172. Jean–Pierre Goldenstein, *Dix–neuf poèmes élastiques de Blaise Cendrars: édition critique et commenté* (Paris: Méridiens Klincksieck, 1986), pp. 98–100, 146. Goldenstein reprints the French translation—*Histoire des Naturels des îles Tonga ou des Mais, situées dans l'Ocean Pacifique depuis leur découverte par le capitaine Cook* (1817)—of the English book from which virtually every word of the poem has been taken.

173. Goldenstein, p. 146.

174. Ibid., pp. 99, 148.

175. "Mee Too Buggi" (1914) is also reprinted and discussed in Blachère, pp. 75–76, 210–11. Its sources are discussed in Monique Chefdor, *Blaise Cendrars* (Boston: Twayne, 1980), p. 51. On its nature as collage see Bochner, pp. 126–27, 137.

176. James Joyce to Frank Budgen, *Letters*, ed. Stuart Gilbert and Richard Ellmann, 3 vols. (New York: Vintage, 1966) 1:139–40.

177. Seamus Heaney, *The Government of the Tongue* (New York: Noonday/Farrar, Straus & Giroux, 1988), p. 40.

178. Edward Said makes this point in "Reflections on Exile," *Granta* 13 (Autumn 1984): 159–72.

179. Raymond Williams, *The Politics of Modernism* (London: Verso, 1989), pp. 78–79.

180. Marianna Torgovnick, *Gone Primitive: Savage Intellects, Modern Lives* (Chicago: University of Chicago Press, 1990), pp. 188, 193.

181. Johnson, ed., *Ebony and Topaz*, pp. 65–66.

182. Stephen J. Greenblatt, *Learning to Curse: Essays in Early Modern Culture* (New York: Routledge, 1990), p. 32; Sara Suleri, *The Rhetoric of English India* (Chicago: University of Chicago Press, 1992).

183. In fact, even this version of the romance of the foreign has its roots in modernism, as is shown by an outburst in the *Anti-Oedipus:* "Strange Anglo-American literature: from Thomas Hardy, from D. H. Lawrence to Malcolm Lowry, from Henry Miller to Allen Ginsberg and Jack Kerouac, men who knew how to leave, to scramble the codes. . . . They overcome a limit, they shatter a wall, the capitalist barrier. And of course they fail to complete the process, they never cease failing to do so." This is postmodernism looking back at modernism, and making of its restless cultural peregrinations a new aesthetic. Gilles Deleuze and Félix Guattari, *A Thousand Plateaus*, trans. Brian Massumi (Minneapolis: University of Minnesota Press, 1987), pp. 379, 98; idem, *Anti-Oedipus*, trans. Robert Hurley, Mark Seem, and Helen R. Lane (Minneapolis: University of Minnesota Press, 1983), pp. 132–33.

184. From "Frammento alla morte" (1960), quoted in Chris Bongie, *Exotic Memories: Literature, Colonialism, and the Fin de Siècle* (Stanford, Calif.: Stanford University Press, 1991), p. 201.

185. Salman Rushdie, *The Satanic Verses* (New York: Viking, 1989), p. 60.

186. Salman Rushdie, *Imaginary Homelands, Essays and Criticism, 1981–1991* (New York: Viking, 1991), p. 64. Rushdie's optimism might be contrasted here with the far sterner conclusion of Ngugi wa Thiong'o, who has maintained in a number of publications over the last twenty years that African writers can never write honestly in English.

187. Rushdie, *Imaginary Homelands*, p. 394.

Chapter 2

Where modern critical editions of Conrad's novels exist, I have used them for all references. These are identified in the text by the following abbreviations:

HD *Heart of Darkness*, ed. Robert Kimbrough (New York: Norton, 1988)

LJ *Lord Jim*, ed. Thomas C. Moser (New York: Norton, 1968)

NN *The Nigger of the "Narcissus,"* ed. Robert Kimbrough (New York: Norton, 1979)

For the other fiction referred to here, I have used the Concord Edition (Garden City, N.Y.: Doubleday, Page, 1923), with individual volumes identified in the text by the following abbreviations:

AF *Almayer's Folly*

OI *An Outcast of the Islands*

R *The Rescue*

SA *The Secret Agent*

T *Typhoon and Other Stories*

TU *Tales of Unrest*

V   *Victory*

Y   *Youth and Two Other Stories.*

1. Michael H. Levenson, *A Genealogy of Modernism: A Study of English Literary Doctrine, 1908–1922* (Cambridge: Cambridge University Press, 1984), pp. 2–3. Levenson's statement later in this paragraph appears on the same pages.

2. In "To My Readers in America" Conrad says, "After writing the last words of that book, in the revulsion of feeling before the accomplished task, I understood that I had done with the sea, and that henceforth I had to be a writer. And almost without laying down the pen I wrote a preface, trying to express the spirit in which I was entering on the task of my new life" (*NN*, p. 168). For a discussion of the preface, with a comparison to the preface to *Lyrical Ballads*, see Ian Watt, *Conrad in the Nineteenth Century* (Berkeley: University of California Press, 1979), pp. 76–88.

3. In *Joseph Conrad: Narrative Technique and Ideological Commitment* (London: Edward Arnold, 1990), Jeremy Hawthorn complains that previous writers have refused to take this issue seriously (p. 101). Even critical discussions such as Eugene B. Redmond's "Racism or Realism? Literary Apartheid, or Poetic License? Conrad's Burden in *The Nigger of the 'Narcissus'*" (*NN*, pp. 358–68) tend to be mere inversions of the metaphysical analysis of blackness first laid out by Albert Guerard in *Conrad the Novelist* (Cambridge: Harvard University Press, 1958), pp. 100–125. Among the exceptions I would include Michael J. C. Echeruo, *The Conditioned Imagination from Shakespeare to Conrad* (London: Macmillan, 1978), pp. 93–112. See also Marianne DeKoven's *Rich and Strange: Gender, History, Modernism* (Princeton, N.J.: Princeton University Press, 1991).

4. John Frederick Matheus, "Some Aspects of the Negro Interpreted in Contemporary American and European Literature," in *Negro: An Anthology*, ed. Nancy Cunard (London: Wishart, 1934), p. 111. It is worth noting that Matheus specifically exempts Cendrars from his criticisms in this essay.

5. Watt, p. 80.

6. D. C. R. A. Goonetilleke, *Joseph Conrad: Beyond Culture and Background* (London: Macmillan, 1990), p. 185. This work substantially restates arguments already made in *Developing Countries in British Fiction* (Totowa, N.J.: Rowman & Littlefield, 1977).

7. This, and a good deal of other very valuable information, is derived from the textual notes in Kimbrough's edition of *NN*. See p. 115.

8. *The Collected Letters of Joseph Conrad*, ed. Frederick Karl and Laurence Davies, 4 vols. (Cambridge: Cambridge University Press, 1986), 2:21.

9. For a discussion of other similar European reactions to racially different faces, see Sara Suleri, *The Rhetoric of English India* (Chicago: University of Chicago Press, 1992), pp. 19–20. The word used by one of Suleri's sources is the same as that used by Conrad: *repulsive.*

10. Guerard, *Conrad the Novelist*, p. 109; quoted in *NN*, p. 226.

11. Conrad, *Collected Letters*, 4:101.

12. Levenson, *Genealogy of Modernism*, p. 32. It is worth noting that the revolutionary language of the anarchist pamphlets in *The Secret Agent* is called *charabia*, or gibberish, and these are written by Comrade Ossipon, whose face is repeatedly described as having at least some features "of the negro type" (*SA*, pp. 26, 44, 50).

13. Conrad, *Collected Letters*, 2:16. The very form of the letter, with its pronoun capitalized in the Polish fashion, illustrates Conrad's problem.

14. Goonetilleke, p. 185; Levenson, *Genealogy of Modernism*, p. 10. It is also worth noting that in his most recent work Levenson finds exile a necessary condition for both

James and Conrad: "In *The Ambassadors* and *Heart of Darkness* it requires two cultures to construct an individual" (Michael Levenson, *Modernism and the Fate of Individuality: Character and Novelistic Form from Conrad to Woolf* [Cambridge: Cambridge University Press, 1991], p. 77). If this is so, then there is always going to be some tension, some dissonance, between the constitution of the individual writer and that of the culture to which he appeals.

15. Zdzislaw Najder, *Joseph Conrad: A Chronicle*, trans. Halina Carroll-Najder (New Brunswick, N.J.: Rutgers University Press, 1983), p. 100.

16. Alfred Russel Wallace, *The Malay Archipelago* (1869; rpt. London: Macmillan, 1984), pp. 468–69; Sherard Osborn, *The Blockade of Kedah in 1838: A Midshipman's Exploits in Malayan Waters* (1857; rpt. Oxford: Oxford University Press, 1987), p. 11. Osborn's book was also a favorite of Conrad's. For an account of Conrad's reading in such sources, see Norman Sherry, *Conrad's Eastern World* (London: Cambridge University Press, 1966), pp. 139–70. For a detailed discussion of linguistic variety in present-day Indonesia, see the following by Benedict R. O'G. Anderson: *Language and Power: Exploring Political Culture in Indonesia* (Ithaca, N.Y.: Cornell University Press, 1990); and *Imagined Communities: Reflections on the Origin and Spread of Nationalism*, rev. ed. (London: Verso, 1991), pp. 132–33.

17. Goonetilleke, p. 49.

18. Clifford, a longtime civil official in various parts of the empire and the compiler of a Malay dictionary, criticized Conrad's knowledge of Malay details in the *Singapore Free Press*, September 1, 1898. After Conrad admitted his relative ignorance, the two became correspondents and friends. See Conrad, *Collected Letters*, 2:129–30; 179–81; Najder, p. 100; and Goonetilleke, p. 43.

19. See Wallace, pp. 134–35; and Osborn, pp. 73, 125.

20. Christopher L. Miller, *Blank Darkness: Africanist Discourse in French* (Chicago: University of Chicago Press, 1985), pp. 26–27; Stephen J. Greenblatt, *Learning to Curse: Essays in Early Modern Culture* (New York: Routledge, 1990), p. 27. Todorov reminds us that this denial of speech is not restricted to European imperialists: Mayans and Aztecs both referred to other peoples as "mutes." Tzvetan Todorov, *The Conquest of America: The Question of the Other*, trans. Richard Howard (New York: Harper & Row, 1984), p. 76. One of the earliest representations of the speech of the New World used Conrad's favorite word: "[W]e began to hear in the men's house . . . a very low murmur." Stephen J. Greenblatt, *Marvelous Possessions: The Wonder of the New World* (Chicago: University of Chicago Press, 1991), p. 14.

21. Wallace, pp. 351, 325, 349. See John E. Saveson, *Joseph Conrad: The Making of a Moralist* (Amsterdam: Rodopi, 1972), p. 17.

22. Osborn, pp. 332, 55–56; Linda Dowling, *Language and Decadence in the Victorian Fin de Siècle* (Princeton, N.J.: Princeton University Press, 1986), p. 102.

23. Conrad describes this trip in "Geography and Some Explorers," *Last Essays* (London: Dent, 1926), pp. 26–31. See also Najder, p. 107.

24. George W. Stocking, Jr., "The Ethnographic Magic: Fieldwork in British Anthropology from Tylor to Malinowski," in *Observers Observed: Essays in Ethnographic Fieldwork*, ed. George W. Stocking, Jr. (Madison: University of Wisconsin Press, 1988), pp. 77, 80, 82. See also the discussion of Haddon in Adam Kuper, *The Invention of Primitive Society: Transformations of an Illusion* (London: Routledge, 1988), pp. 152–58.

25. Bronislaw Malinowski, *A Diary in the Strict Sense of the Term*, trans. Norbert Guterman (New York: Harcourt, Brace & World, 1967), pp. 16, 27, 41, 54, and passim; James Clifford, *The Predicament of Culture: Twentieth-Century Ethnography, Literature, and Art* (Cambridge, Mass.: Harvard University Press, 1988), p. 96; Stocking, p. 82.

26. Frederick Karl reports that at least one known letter from Conrad to Malinowski remains untraced. Conrad, *Collected Letters*, 1:xliv. See also Najder, p. 483; and David W. Tutein, *Joseph Conrad's Reading: An Annotated Bibliography* (West Cornwall, Conn.: Locust Hill Press, 1990), p. 65.

27. Clifford, pp. 101–2; Conrad, *Collected Letters*, 2:xxvi, 5, 89, 125. Clifford compares Malinowski's diary to "Heart of Darkness." It seems much more logical, in generic terms, to compare the diary to Conrad's letters, and, in terms of subject matter, to the Malay novels and stories.

28. Stocking, p. 78; Wallace, p. 326; Conrad, *The Rescue*, p. 160.

29. It is somewhat unclear as to whether the word itself gave offense or merely the subject. See *NN*, p. 113, and Hamlin Garland's commentary, reprinted in Martin Ray, ed., *Joseph Conrad: Interviews and Recollections* (London: Macmillan, 1990), p. 41.

30. Stocking, p. 102, n. 2.

31. Malinowski, *A Diary*, pp. 69, 279. The italicized passages are in English in the original.

32. Malinowski, *A Diary*, p. 197. Not having been able to consult the manuscript of the diary, I do not know whether this word actually appears in English, as the italics suggest, or whether it is the Polish–English hybrid that appears in the entry for April 22, 1918.

33. Malinowski, *A Diary*, pp. 63, 163, 119.

34. "From the start of my own field-work, it has been my deepest and strongest conviction that we must finish by studying ourselves through the same methods and with the same mental attitude with which we approach the exotic tribes." Bronislaw Malinowski, "A Nation–Wide Intelligence Service," in *First Year's Work (1937–1938) by Mass Observation*, ed. Charles Madge and Tom Harrisson (London: Lindsay Drummond, 1938), p. 103.

35. Bronislaw Malinowski, "The Problem of Meaning in Primitive Languages," supplement to *The Meaning of Meaning*, by C. K. Ogden and I. A. Richards, 10th ed. (London: Routledge & Kegan Paul, 1949), pp. 309, 312, 315. See also Bronislaw Malinowski, *Coral Gardens and their Magic*, 2 vols. (New York: American Book Co., 1935), 2:7–9.

36. Malinowski, "Problem of Meaning," p. 315. For a discussion of Malinowski's linguistic ideas and their effect on later British philosophers such as J. L. Austin, see Jerzy Szymura, "Bronislaw Malinowski's 'Ethnographic Theory of Language,'" in *Linguistic Thought in England 1914–1945*, ed. Roy Harris (London: Duckworth, 1988), pp. 106–31. For the influence of Malinowski's contextual self-consciousness on later anthropologists, some called "Malinowski's children" by Clifford Geertz, see Clifford, p. 113.

37. Edward W. Said, *Joseph Conrad and the Fiction of Autobiography* (Cambridge: Harvard University Press, 1966), p. 21; Joseph Conrad, *Notes on Life and Letters* (Garden City, N.Y.: Doubleday, Page, 1921), p. 13. Conrad could make statements, in a somewhat more skeptical mode, that sounded exactly like those of Malinowski on "word-magic": "Words alone strung upon a convention have fascinated us as worthless glass beads strung on a thread have charmed at all times our brothers the unsophisticated savages of the islands" (*Notes*, pp. 27–28).

38. Malinowski, *Coral Gardens*, 2:57.

39. "I want to make it quite clear that I am not speaking here only of the Trobriand language, still less only of native speech in agriculture. I am trying to indicate the character of human speech in general . . ." (*Coral Gardens*, 2:8).

40. Joseph Conrad, *A Personal Record* (1912; rpt. Garden City, N.Y.: Doubleday, Page, 1925), pp. xiii–xiv.

41. See Edward Said's argument that, like Nietzsche, Conrad displaces the linguistic focus from *logos* to *melos*. "Conrad and Nietzsche," in *Joseph Conrad: A Commemoration*,

ed. Norman Sherry (London: Macmillan, 1976), p. 71. See also Jeremy Hawthorn, *Joseph Conrad: Language and Fictional Self–Consciousness* (Lincoln: University of Nebraska Press, 1979), chap. 6.

42. See Clifford: "But once culture becomes visible as an object and ground, a system of meaning among others, the ethnographic self can no longer take root in unmediated identity" (p. 106). Recent commentaries on Conrad and Malinowski, including Clifford's, have neglected the linguistic theories of both. Careful attention to these would show that Marianna Torgovnick's view of Malinowski as withdrawing behind a screen of "pure, untainted theory" is simply wrong. Marianna Torgovnick, *Gone Primitive: Savage Intellects, Modern Lives* (Chicago: University of Chicago Press, 1990), pp. 229–32. Even a reasonably complete investigation of Malinowski's most basic anthropological ideas would give a different result. For two essays that emphasize the practical political engagement of Malinowski, while differing as to its character and effect, see Wendy James, "The Anthropologist as Reluctant Imperialist," and Stephen Feuchtwang, "The Discipline and Its Sponsors," in *Anthropology and the Colonial Encounter*, ed. Talal Asad (London: Ithaca Press, 1973).

43. Conrad, *Collected Letters*, 3:488, n. 5. It is this status as outsider in England and in English that makes Conrad of continuing interest to African writers like Peter Nazareth and Ngugi wa Thiong'o. Peter Nazareth, "Out of Darkness: Conrad and Other Third World Writers," *Conradiana* 14 (1982): 173–87; Ngugi wa Thiong'o, *Writers in Politics* (London: Heinemann, 1981).

44. Robert Graves, *Impenetrability: or The Proper Habit of English* (London: Hogarth, 1926), pp. 31–33; Ford Madox Ford, *Joseph Conrad: A Personal Remembrance* (London: Duckworth, 1924), p. 214. See also Martin Ray, "The Gift of Tongues: The Languages of Joseph Conrad," *Conradiana* 15 (1983): 93.

45. *NN*, p. 118; Conrad, *Collected Letters*, 1:199, 2:20. See also Watt, p. 58; and Ray, ed., *Joseph Conrad*, pp. 208–10.

46. Many of the major developments of the period, from the pronunciation guides and dictionaries of Jones and Wyld to Basic English, were aimed first at foreign speakers of English. See Richard W. Bailey, *Images of English: A Cultural History of the Language* (Ann Arbor: University of Michigan Press, 1991), p. 5.

47. Roy Harris, "Murray, Moore and the Myth," in *Linguistic Thought in England 1914–1945*, ed. Roy Harris (London: Duckworth, 1988), p. 18.

48. Gunnar Landtman, *The Kiwai Papuans of British New Guinea* (London: Macmillan, 1927), p. 453.

49. Malinowski, *Coral Gardens*, p. 12. Fear of this situation has not exactly died out. As late as 1962 Dwight MacDonald complained that without prescriptive linguistic authority "the result will be a jargon as cut off from the race's culture and traditions as the Pidgin English of the South Seas." Edward Finegan, *Attitudes Toward English Usage: The History of a War of Words* (New York: Teacher's College of Columbia University Press, 1980), p. 15.

50. Conrad, *Notes on Life and Letters*, p. 155.

51. G. Jean-Aubry, *Joseph Conrad: Life and Letters*, 2 vols. (Garden City, N.Y.: Doubleday, Page, 1927), 2:94–95.

52. Anderson, *Language and Power*, pp. 195–96; Bailey, pp. 64, 79, 127; J. L. Dillard, *All–American English* (New York: Random House/Vintage, 1976), pp. 4–6, 30–39.

53. As early as Puttenham, the language of the coastal English towns fell under suspicion because of the influence on it of maritime English. Bailey, pp. 126–28.

54. Dillard, pp. 6–7. See also Dillard's *Black English: Its History and Usage in the United States* (New York: Random House, 1972), p. 83; idem, *Toward a Social History of*

American English (Berlin: Mouton, 1985), pp. 7–12; and Walter M. Brasch, *Black English and the Mass Media* (Amherst: University of Massachusetts Press, 1981), p. xxvi. Suzanne Romaine surveys the evidence for the theory that maritime pidgins influenced *all* global pidgins and creoles in *Pidgin & Creole Languages* (London: Longmans, 1988), pp. 84–86.

55. See also *The Rescue*, p. 136.

56. Bailey, pp. 64–66, 76; Greenblatt, *Marvelous Possessions*, p. 139; Todorov, pp. 98–101; Peter Hulme, *Colonial Encounters: Europe and the Native Caribbean, 1492–1797* (London: Methuen, 1986), p. 142. As Greenblatt says, the "primal crime in the New World" was Columbus's kidnapping of Arawaks to serve as interpreters (*Learning to Curse*, p. 17). This is true in the Old World as well. The first Africans brought to England as slaves were meant to return to Africa and serve as interpreters. Folarin Shyllon, *Black People in Britain 1555–1833* (Oxford: Oxford University Press, 1977), p. 6. Romaine reports that captured Africans were taught a simplified Portuguese as early as 1435 so as to serve as interpreters for Prince Henry's expeditions (p. 82).

57. Conrad, *Collected Letters*, 1:170.

58. See Frederick Karl, *Joseph Conrad: The Three Lives* (New York: Farrar, Straus & Giroux, 1979), pp. 331–33.

59. Ray, ed., *Joseph Conrad*, pp. 40, 74, 138. Saveson, p. 11. For other comments on Conrad's accent see Ray, ed., *Joseph Conrad*, pp. 59, 82, 109, 215; and Najder, p. 357. For testimony on Conrad's difficulty with written English see Ray, ed., *Joseph Conrad*, p. 98, and Najder, pp. 222–23, 373. For Conrad's own frustrations with his command of the language, see *Collected Letters*, 2:16, 460, and 3:401; and Najder, pp. 332–33, 408.

60. Ray, ed., *Joseph Conrad*, p. 67; Najder, p. 373.

61. Ray, ed., *Joseph Conrad*, pp. 109, 104, 115. For other comments on Conrad's appearance see pp. 22, 28, 67. It was Newbolt to whom Conrad appealed for official patronage in 1905. The vast difference between himself and Newbolt in worldly success, despite their similar interests, demonstrates how far Conrad really was from the standardization movement. See *Collected Letters*, 3:248. Newbolt did not care for *The Nigger of the "Narcissus"* (Ray, ed., *Joseph Conrad*, p. 115).

62. Ray, ed., *Joseph Conrad*, p. 96; Conrad, *Collected Letters*, 3:482.

63. Conrad, *A Personal Record*, p. xiii.

64. Conrad, *Collected Letters*, 1:397, 399. See Ray, "The Gift," p. 86.

65. Zygmunt Frajzyngier, "James Wait's Polish Idiom," *Conradiana* 17 (1985): 143.

66. Conrad, *Notes on Life and Letters*, pp. 131, 138, 147. Wincenty Lutoslawski claimed in 1930 that the "oriental passion between persons of different race and education . . . have been peculiar to Poles more than to any other nation of Europe. . . . Poles are as passionate and reckless as the Outcast" (Ray, ed., *Joseph Conrad*, p. 90). Lutoslawski is not, however, the most reliable or representative informant. Conrad's uncle Tadeuz Bobrowski did perhaps establish a metaphor for Conrad by calling the Poles "pariahs" (Karl, p. 211).

67. *Selected Writings of Cunninghame Graham*, ed. Cedric Watts (East Brunswick, N.J.: Associated University Press, 1981), p. 66.

68. Sherry, p. 37.

69. Conrad, *Collected Letters*, 2:323. For discussions of the biographical ramifications of Conrad's names, see Najder, p. 272; and Karl, pp. 20–21, 130, 188–89.

70. Conrad, *Last Essays*, pp. 25–26. See also *Collected Letters*, 3:89, where Conrad says that the English "never made me feel a foreigner."

71. Watt, p. 19.

72. Najder, p. 85. See also pp. 163 and 182 for discussions of Conrad's loneliness at sea.

73. Karl, p. 115.

74. Patrick Brantlinger, *Rule of Darkness: British Literature and Imperialism, 1830–1914* (Ithaca, N.Y.: Cornell University Press, 1988), pp. 162, 244. For Burton, see also Miller, p. 15.

75. Conrad, *Collected Letters*, 2:60. Conrad often assumed a mock Arabic role in addressing Cunninghame Graham.

76. Najder, p. 205; *NN*, pp. 112–13.

77. For a good discussion of this issue and a review of critical responses to it, see Watt, *NN*, pp. 239–43.

78. See Hawthorn's discussion of free indirect discourse and editorial comment in *The Nigger of the "Narcissus"* (pp. 18–19).

79. See, for example, Martin Ray, "Language and Silence in the Novels of Joseph Conrad," *Conradiana* 16 (1984): 29. It is hard to see how technical language can enjoy "a direct correspondence with the things" it designates if that language is the creation of a polyglot crew.

80. Conrad, *Collected Letters*, 1:423. In this phase Conrad did sound like some of the spokesmen for the standardization movement. Richard Grant White, for example, thought it a danger that speakers were becoming self–conscious instead of speaking their language intuitively. *Words and Their Uses, Past and Present* (Boston: Houghton Mifflin, 1889), p. 27.

81. Najder's translation (p. 338) differs slightly from that in *Collected Letters*, 4:288.

82. Najder, pp. 77–78. See also Conrad's discussion of the English nature of the crews he served with in *Notes on Life and Letters*, pp. 180–81.

83. As N. F. Blake says in his discussion of nonstandard speech in Conrad's novels, there is no attempt to make Wait speak in dialect. *Non–Standard Language in English Literature* (London: Deutsch, 1981), p. 179.

84. See Hawthorn, *Narrative Technique*, pp. 111–115.

85. Suleri, p. 6.

86. See Hawthorn's discussion in *Narrative Technique*, p. 52.

Chapter 3

1. "The modern movement in art gets its inspiration undoubtedly from African art, and it could not be otherwise." Paul Guillaume, "African Art at the Barnes Foundation," *Opportunity* 2 (May 1924): 140–41. Quoted in Chidi Ikonné, *From Du Bois to Van Vechten: The Early New Negro Literature, 1903–1926* (Westport, Conn.: Greenwood Press, 1981), pp. 3–4. Though current scholarly opinion is a good deal cooler on the subject, it still acknowledges the force of European fascination with African masks and statues. See the catalogue of the Museum of Modern Art exhibition *"Primitivism" in 20th Century Art: Affinity of the Tribal and the Modern*, ed. William Rubin (New York: Museum of Modern Art, 1984), in which Rubin takes issue with previous opinions like Guillaume's but also argues at length for an important but rather vaguely defined "affinity" between "tribal" art and the modern. The controversy surrounding this exhibition gives a good indication of current opinion about this "affinity." See, for example, James Clifford, "Histories of the Tribal and the Modern," *Art in America* 73 (April 1985): 164–77, 215; reprinted in *The Predicament of Culture* (Cambridge, Mass.: Harvard University Press, 1988); Hal Foster, "The 'Primitive' Consciousness of Modern Art," *October* 34 (Fall 1985): 45–70; and Rosalind Krauss, "Preying on 'Primitivism,'" *Art & Text* 17 (April 1985): 58–62.

2. "Dr. Barnes," *Opportunity* 2 (May 1924): 133; Alain Locke, "A Note on African Art," *Opportunity* 2 (May 1924): 134–38.

3. There is a good deal of dispute about the timing and significance of this discovery. For Stein's account, in which Matisse surprises Picasso with an African statue, see *The Autobiography of Alice B. Toklas* (1933; rpt. New York: Random House/Vintage, 1960), p. 63. For the most minute investigation see William Rubin, "Picasso," in Rubin, ed., esp. pp. 337, n. 86 and 339, n. 138.

4. Stein, *Autobiography of Alice B. Toklas*, p. 64. See the critical commentary on this and other passages in Stein's work in Aldon Lynn Nielsen, *Reading Race: White American Poets and the Racial Discourse in the Twentieth Century* (Athens: University of Georgia Press, 1988), pp. 22–24. Picasso's later dismissals of African art as an influence are considered strategic by William Rubin. See his "From Narrative to 'Iconic' in Picasso: The Buried Allegory in *Bread and Fruitdish on a Table* and the Role of *Les Demoiselles D'Avignon*," Art Bulletin 65 (December 1983): 645; and "Picasso," p. 335, n. 52. See also Gertrude Stein, *Picasso: The Complete Writings*, ed. Edward Burns (1970; rpt. Boston: Beacon, 1985), p. 47.

5. Rubin, "Picasso," pp. 297–98. In the surviving correspondence Picasso asks Stein to look for "les statues negres" for him and then refers to the objects Stein subsequently purchased as "les negres." Pablo Picasso to Gertrude Stein, December 1917 (letter 101), and April 26, 1918 (letter 104), Stein correspondence, American Literature Collection, Beinecke Rare Book and Manuscript Library, Yale University.

6. Rubin, "Picasso," pp. 247–48. For Stein's account of her sittings for the portrait see *Autobiography of Alice B. Toklas*, pp. 46–47, 49, 53.

7. Stein, *Autobiography of Alice B. Toklas*, p. 54.

8. Among many accounts of the similarities between these two works, the most interesting is still Richard Bridgman's "Melanctha," *American Literature* 33 (November 1961): 350–59. See also Bridgman's *Gertrude Stein in Pieces* (New York: Oxford University Press, 1970); and Jayne L. Walker, *Gertrude Stein: The Making of a Modernist* (Amherst: University of Massachusetts Press, 1984), pp. 27–38.

9. James R. Mellow, *Charmed Circle: Gertrude Stein & Company* (New York: Praeger, 1974), p. 44.

10. Cary D. Wintz, *Black Culture and the Harlem Renaissance* (Houston: Rice University Press, 1988), pp. 45–47.

11. Ikonné, pp. 27–28. It should be noted that the exact relationship between African art and African–American art and literature was discussed from a number of different points of view in *The New Negro*. Alain Locke himself was at least ambivalent on the subject, as shown by his own essay "The Legacy of the Ancestral Arts," which he significantly bracketed with Countee Cullen's poem "Heritage," which begins, "What is Africa to me?" *The New Negro*, ed. Alain Locke (1925; rpt. New York: Atheneum, 1968), pp. 250–67.

12. Carl Van Vechten, *Nigger Heaven* (1926; rpt. New York: Octagon, 1980), pp. 55, 57. Van Vechten's curious preface to *Three Lives* is worth noting here, because in it he praises Stein as "so distinguished, so instinct with *race* and force and character . . . [original emphasis]" *Three Lives* (Norfolk: New Directions, 1933), p. viii.

13. I. A. Richards, "Preface," *Spring in New Hampshire*, by Claude McKay (London: Richards, 1920), p. 1; Zora Neale Hurston, *The Sanctified Church* (Berkeley: Turtle Island, 1981), p. 54.

14. Rubin, "Picasso," p. 254. Rubin is particularly fond of this comparison. See "Iconic," pp. 632, 634.

15. Leo Steinberg, "The Philosophical Brothel, Part 2," *Art News* 71 (October 1972): 41. For Steinberg's latest thoughts on this painting see the updated version of this essay in *October* 44 (Spring 1988): 7–74.

16. Thus Walter von Ruckterschell, who did a number of the drawings for *The New Negro*, exactly reverses Conrad's prejudice about the mask of the African face: "You should see the natives bathing," he said once. "The ugly white mask, it is we who wear it." Louise Herrick Wall, "Walter von Ruckterschell," *Opportunity* 2 (May 1924): 148.

17. Quoted in Steinberg, p. 20.

18. D. H. Kahnweiler, "Negro Art and Cubism," *Horizon* 18 (1948): 415.

19. Kahnweiler, p. 414; Stein, *Picasso*, p. 73. See Picasso's own discussion of signs in André Malraux, *Picasso's Mask*, trans. June Guicharnaud (New York: Holt, Rinehart & Winston, 1976), p. 120.

20. For a brief discussion of British colonial language policy as it related to schooling, see Carol Sicherman, *Ngugi wa Thiong'o: The Making of a Rebel* (London: Hans Zell, 1990), pp. 27–28. Sicherman's notes list a number of more detailed studies.

21. Patricia Leighten, "The White Peril and *L'Art nègre:* Picasso, Primitivism, and Anticolonialism," *Art Bulletin* 72 (1990): 627.

22. Yve-Alain Bois, "Kahnweiler's Lesson," *Representations* 18 (Spring 1987): 33–68.

23. Quoted in Walker, p. 1.

24. Gertrude Stein, *Three Lives* (1909; rpt. New York: Random/Vintage, 1936), pp. 94, 92. All subsequent parenthetical page references will be to this edition.

25. Walker, for example, fails to follow up on the reference to Caliban in her discussion of "Melanctha," though she says at the beginning of her book that Stein's motive is "to give speech to Caliban, to a 'reality' that lies this far outside *vraisemblance*" (pp. 1–2). An example of the more recent trend is Marianne DeKoven's *Rich and Strange: Gender, History, Modernism* (Princeton, N.J.: Princeton University Press, 1991), pp. 67–85.

26. Tzvetan Todorov, *The Conquest of America*, trans. Richard Howard (New York: Harper & Row, 1984), p. 36.

27. Alfred Simson, quoted in Michael Taussig, *Shamanism, Colonialism, and the Wild Man: A Study in Terror and Healing* (Chicago: University of Chicago Press, 1987), p. 91.

28. Sara Suleri, *The Rhetoric of English India* (Chicago: University of Chicago Press, 1992), p. 163. See also p. 31.

29. See also Etienne Balibar, "Paradoxes of Universality," in *Anatomy of Racism*, ed. David Theo Goldberg (Minneapolis: University of Minnesota Press, 1990), pp. 283–94.

30. Rubin, "Picasso," pp. 241–42.

31. Carl Van Vechten, *"Keep A-Inchin' Along": Selected Writings of Carl Van Vechten About Black Art and Letters*, ed. Bruce Kellner (Westport, Conn.: Greenwood Press, 1974), pp. 4–5.

32. The Radcliffe themes are reprinted in Rosalind S. Miller, *Gertrude Stein: Form and Intelligibility* (New York: Exposition Press, 1949). See esp. pp. 139–44.

33. Trial dust wrapper for *Three Lives*, reproduced in Robert A. Wilson, *Gertrude Stein: A Bibliography* (New York: Phoenix, 1974), p. 4.

34. Rubin, "Picasso," pp. 241–42.

35. Mellow, pp. 113–14.

36. Whether Stein's Jewish heritage played a role here is a question too large to be answered at this time. See Michael Rogin's deft analysis of the way black roles eased assimilation for American Jews, who, unlike Stein, stayed in America. "Blackface, White Noise: The Jewish Jazz Singer Finds His Voice," *Critical Inquiry* 18 (Spring 1992): 449.

37. Malraux, pp. 10–11.

38. Gelett Burgess, "The Wild Men of Paris," *Architectural Record* 5 (May 1910): 407–14; Ezra Pound, "The New Sculpture," *Egoist*, February 16, 1914, pp. 67–68, rpt. in

Ezra Pound and the Visual Arts, ed. Harriet Zinnes (New York: New Directions, 1980), p. 182.

39. Nathan I. Huggins, *Harlem Renaissance* (New York: Oxford University Press, 1971), p. 93.

40. The term *transcendental homelessness* is from Georg Lukács, *The Theory of the Novel,* trans. Anna Bostock (Cambridge, Mass.: MIT Press, 1971); its application to modernist primitivism Marianna Torgovnick's. See her *Gone Primitive: Savage Intellects, Modern Lives* (Chicago: University of Chicago Press, 1990), p. 188.

41. *Collected Early Poems of Ezra Pound,* ed. Michael John King (New York: New Directions, 1976), p. 34; *The Variorum Edition of the Poems of W. B. Yeats,* ed. Peter Allt and Russell K. Alspach (New York: Macmillan, 1940), p. 263. A year later, Gordon Craig signified the importance of masks in modern drama by beginning to publish the *Mask* (1908–1929). Walter Sorell, *The Other Face: The Mask in the Arts* (Indianapolis: Bobbs–Merrill, 1973), p. 71.

42. A similar point has been made about costume by Kaja Silverman, "White Skin, Brown Mask: The Double Mimesis, or With Lawrence in Arabia," *differences* 1 (1989): 48.

43. A. David Napier, *Masks, Transformation, and Paradox* (Berkeley: University of California Press, 1986), p. 4. See also Sorell, p. 11.

44. Paul Laurence Dunbar's "We Wear the Mask" was written about the same time as *The Nigger of the "Narcissus"* but from the other side, from behind the barrier of enforced unreadability. *The Complete Poems of Paul Laurence Dunbar* (New York: Dodd, Mead, 1913), p. 71. When W. E. B. Du Bois picked up the metaphor a few years later, it was to dramatize the immense social and psychological costs of the "veil" that had been drawn over the lives of African Americans. W. E. B. Du Bois, *The Souls of Black Folks* (1903; rpt. New York: Library of America, 1986), pp. 3–4, 12, 16. The power of the mask as a distorting stereotype is further exemplified by the fact that many African-American performers of the period, most notably Bert Williams, had to wear blackface makeup because their real faces did not conform to the caricature made popular by white minstrels.

45. Rubin, "Picasso," pp. 263–64. Rubin believes that the left–hand figure was "unquestionably reworked after Picasso had completed the painting in its original, Iberian form" (p. 264). But he hypothesizes that there were *"two* periods of repainting," with the left–hand figure being reworked before the visit to the Trocadéro and the two right–hand figures repainted after the visit.

46. This is an interpretation of the evolution of the painting supported by Rubin ("Narrative to 'Iconic,'" pp. 630–32); and Steinberg (pp. 39–40, and 59, n. 32), though Steinberg does propose other models, including Max Jacob, and Rubin discusses a drawing of André Salmon that is in some ways similar to the original figure on the left ("Picasso," p. 285). In fact, the "thanatophobic" interpretation of the painting that Rubin and Steinberg have made current rests on the assumption that Picasso is himself implicated in the scene it portrays. Many of the studies for *Les Demoiselles d'Avignon* are reproduced and discussed in Steinberg. See especially page 25 for the transition discussed here. All the materials relating to this painting have been collected and discussed in *Les Demoiselles d'Avignon 3* (Paris: Musée Picasso, 1988), 2 vols. The sketchbook Picasso kept in March 1907, while planning *Les Demoiselles,* has been published with a text by Brigitte Leal as *Picasso: "Les Demoiselles d'Avignon": A Sketchbook* (London: Thames & Hudson, 1988).

47. Steinberg, pp. 40, 26. Rubin has quite successfully demonstrated that the masks in *Les Demoiselles* could not have been based on any particular African masks available to Picasso in Paris at the time of the painting ("Picasso," pp. 262–66). However, it is clear that Picasso did handle and purchase African masks, as well as African sculpture, at this

time. Inez Haynes Irwin, who visited Picasso at his studio in April 1908, reports seeing *Les Demoiselles* and simultaneously being shown "a mask of the Congo and some totem-pole like hideosities that he [Picasso] made himself." *Les Demoiselles d'Avignon 3*, 2:560.

48. John Richardson, *A Life of Picasso*, 2 vols. (New York: Random House, 1991–), 1:408.

49. Leal, unpaged introduction.

50. Silverman, p. 11. See also Suleri, p. 142.

51. See Patrick Brantlinger on India as "a realm of imaginative license . . . a place where the fantastic becomes possible in ways that are carefully circumscribed at home." *Rule of Darkness: British Literature and Imperialism, 1830–1914* (Ithaca, N.Y.: Cornell University Press, 1988), p. 13. But this is not entirely a European mode of thought. See Taussig's discussion of the fact that "wherever you go, the great *brujos* [magicians or sorcerers] are elsewhere" (p. 179).

52. Henry Louis Gates, Jr., *Figures in Black: Words, Signs, and the "Racial" Self* (New York: Oxford University Press, 1987), p. 168. See also Dennis Duerden, *The Invisible Present: African Art & Literature* (New York: Harper & Row, 1975), esp. p. 117.

53. Rubin, "Picasso," pp. 255; 335, n. 53.

54. Stein, *Picasso*, p. 52.

55. Ibid., p. 34. Note also Picasso's famous comment, quoted in Mellow (p. 93) among other places, that, though Stein does not now resemble her portrait, "She will."

56. Kahnweiler, p. 418.

57. For one use of the idea of the dialectical image see Walter Benjamin, *Charles Baudelaire: A Lyric Poet in the Era of High Capitalism*, trans. Harry Zohn (London: NLB, 1973), p. 171. See also Adorno's attack in Bloch et al., *Aesthetics and Politics*, ed. Ronald Taylor (London: Verso, 1977), pp. 111–15; and W. J. T. Mitchell's application in *Iconology: Image, Text, Ideology* (Chicago: University of Chicago Press, 1986), pp. 93, 158. Most important for my discussion is Taussig's application of the idea to the popular art of South America. See Taussig, pp. 200–201.

58. Adam Gopnik, "'High and Low': Caricature, Primitivism, and the Cubist Portrait," *Art Journal* 43 (Winter 1983): 374.

59. Gates, *Figures in Black*, pp. 169, 171. See also the discussion of dialect and mask in Benedict R. O'G. Anderson, *Language and Power: Exploring Political Cultures in Indonesia* (Ithaca, N.Y.: Cornell University Press, 1990), pp. 129–31, 144, 149–51.

60. Gilles Deleuze and Félix Guattari, *A Thousand Plateaus: Capitalism and Schizophrenia*, trans. Brian Massumi (Minneapolis: University of Minnesota Press, 1987), p. 104. See also Deleuze and Guattari's *Kafka: Toward a Minor Literature*, trans. Dana Polan (Minneapolis: University of Minnesota Press, 1986).

61. Shirley Brice Heath, *Ways with Words: Language, Life, and Work in Communities and Classrooms* (Cambridge: Cambridge University Press, 1983).

62. George F. Whicher, quoted in Bridgman, "Melanctha," p. 356. This has been said in more recent criticism as well: "The syntactical devices Stein uses to probe the psyches of her characters, recorded in black English, are authentic." Bettina L. Knapp, *Gertrude Stein* (New York: Continuum, 1990), p. 86. And see the lengthy, quite favorable, discussion in Sylvia Wallace Holton, *Down Home and Uptown: The Representation of Black Speech in American Fiction* (London and Toronto: Associated University Presses, 1984), pp. 96–98.

63. Mellow, p. 87; Stein, *Autobiography of Alice B. Toklas*, p. 68. There is an intriguing resemblance between this episode and Edward Garnett's expectation that because he wrote of the East Conrad might be Asian himself.

64. Mellow, pp. 69, 64. See also p. 77.

65. A few exceptions might be found, such as the invariant *be* in Melanctha's promise to Jeff: "I be home Jeff to-night to see you" (p. 196). Yet even here the usage is incorrect, because the invariant *be* usually expresses an ongoing condition.

66. R. Emmett Kennedy, *Black Cameos* (New York: Albert & Charles Boni, 1924), p. xiv. This was a claim made over and over at the time. For a summary statement see C. Alphonso Smith, "Dialect Writers," in *The Cambridge History of American Literature*, ed. W. P. Trent et al. (New York: Putnam, 1918), p. 356.

67. Richard Bridgman, *The Colloquial Style in America* (New York: Oxford University Press, 1966), p. 92.

68. Kenneth Burke, *A Grammar of Motives* (1945; rpt. Berkeley: University of California Press, 1969), p. 52.

69. Gertrude Stein, *Selected Writings*, ed. Carl Van Vechten (1962; rpt. New York: Random/Vintage, 1972), p. 519.

70. Gertrude Stein, *Lectures in America* (1935; rpt. Boston: Beacon Press, 1985), p. 210.

71. Heath, *Ways with Words*, p. 141.

72. Stein, *Lectures in America*, p. 214.

73. Thus Heath herself has cited Stein as an inspiring literary example of oral or unplanned discourse rebelling against the standard language. Shirley Brice Heath, "Literacy and Language Change," *Georgetown University Round Table on Language and Linguistics 1985*: 282–93. Her primary example here is William Carlos Williams's *Spring and All*. See chapter 7 of the present volume.

74. Henry Alford, *A Plea for the Queen's English* (London: A. Strahan, 1864), p. 244.

75. Quoted in Edward Finegan, *Attitudes Toward English Usage: The History of a War of Words* (New York: Teacher's College of Columbia University Press, 1980), p. 67.

76. Dennis E. Baron, *Grammar and Good Taste: Reforming the American Language* (New Haven, Conn.: Yale University Press, 1982), p. 26.

77. Hurston, *The Sanctified Church*, pp. 49–55.

78. Gates, p. 171. For a more complete discussion of Gates's interpretation of Hurston, see chapter 8 of the present volume.

79. For a very useful discussion of this strategy, see Marjorie Perloff, *The Poetics of Indeterminacy: From Rimbaud to Cage* (1981; rpt. Evanston, Ill.: Northwestern University Press, 1983), pp. 67–108. Other useful discussions of such representational strategies in Stein include Randa Dubnick, *The Structure of Obscurity: Gertrude Stein, Language, and Cubism* (Urbana: University of Illinois Press, 1984); and Wendy Steiner, *Exact Resemblance to Exact Resemblance: The Literary Portraiture of Gertrude Stein* (New Haven, Conn.: Yale University Press, 1978). For a brief analysis linking Stein to African–American antiphonal oral literature, see Gayl Jones, *Liberating Voices: Oral Tradition in African American Literature* (Cambridge, Mass.: Harvard University Press, 1991), pp. 74–75.

80. Richard Wright, "Gertrude Stein's Story Is Drenched in Hitler's Horrors" (rev. of *Wars I Have Seen*), *P.M.*, March 11, 1945, p. 15. For a discussion of this and other statements by Wright in praise of *Three Lives*, see Eugene E. Miller, "Richard Wright and Gertrude Stein," *Black American Literature Forum* 16 (Fall 1982): 107–12. For the reactions of other African-American writers, favorable and unfavorable, to *Three Lives*, see John Malcolm Brinnin, *The Third Rose* (Boston: Little, Brown, 1959), p. 121.

81. Rosalind Krauss, *The Originality of the Avant-Garde and Other Modernist Myths* (Cambridge, Mass.: MIT Press, 1986), pp. 23–40. See also Rubin's association of the mask with Picasso's creation of collage. *"Primitivism,"* p. 64.

Chapter 4

1. Alain Locke, Advertising flyer–program, "Announcing Great Day," Jan. 10, 1932; quoted in Robert E. Hemenway, *Zora Neale Hurston: A Literary Biography* (Urbana: University of Illinois Press, 1977), p. 179.

2. Humphrey Carpenter, *A Serious Character: The Life of Ezra Pound* (London: Faber & Faber, 1988), pp. 22, 414.

3. For a pertinent critique of the uses white Americans have made of the "trickster" figure, see Ralph Ellison, *Shadow and Act* (1964; rpt. New York: Random House/Vintage, 1972), pp. 45–59. Ellison's analysis is also pertinent to what is said later in this chapter about the minstrel tradition. But he also says, "I use folklore in my work not because I am Negro, but because writers like Eliot and Joyce made me conscious of the literary value of my folk inheritance" (p. 58).

4. *The Letters of T. S. Eliot*, ed. Valerie Eliot (New York: Harcourt Brace Jovanovich, 1988), p. 350; Carpenter, p. 414. Hereafter, Eliot's letters will be cited parenthetically as *EL*.

5. *The Selected Letters of Ezra Pound, 1907–1941*, ed. D. D. Paige (1950; rpt. New York: New Directions, 1971), p. 304. Hereafter, Pound's letters will be cited parenthetically as *PL*.

6. From a 1935 letter in the Pound archive, Beinecke Rare Book and Manuscript Library, Yale University; quoted in Wendy Stallard Flory, *The American Ezra Pound* (New Haven, Conn.: Yale University Press, 1989), p. 76.

7. Herbert Read, "T. S. E.—A Memoir," in *T. S. Eliot: The Man and His Work*, ed. Allen Tate (New York: Delacorte, 1966), p. 15. Half a century earlier, Noah Webster had suffered the same sort of anxiety when New Englanders mocked his strange Middle American pronunciation. See Dennis E. Baron, *Grammar and Good Taste: Reforming the American Language* (New Haven, Conn.: Yale University Press, 1982), p. 57.

8. Ezra Pound, "The Revolt of Intelligence," *New Age*, January 8, 1920, p. 153, January 15, 1920, p. 176.

9. Ezra Pound, "The Revolt of Intelligence," *New Age*, December 18, 1919, p. 106.

10. For a very critical study of the role of race in the work of these two poets, see Aldon Lynn Nielsen, *Reading Race: White American Poets and the Racial Discourse in the Twentieth Century* (Athens: University of Georgia Press, 1988), pp. 58–60, 65–72.

11. James Weldon Johnson, "Preface to the First Edition," *The Book of American Negro Poetry*, 2nd ed. (1931; rpt. New York: Harcourt, Brace & World, 1969), pp. 40–42. Such objections had been made to the conventional representations of black dialect since the 1890s. See Henry Louis Gates, Jr., *The Signifying Monkey: A Theory of African–American Literary Criticism* (New York: Oxford University Press, 1988), pp. 176–77; idem, *Figures in Black: Words, Signs, and the "Racial" Self* (New York: Oxford University Press, 1987), pp. 167–95. Among these could be included the objections in *The New Negro*, ed. Alain Locke (1925; rpt. New York: Atheneum, 1968), by Arthur Huff Fauset (p. 239) and Alain Locke (pp. xii, 48), which fall at about the same time as Johnson's first preface. However, in the preface and elsewhere in his work, Johnson spoke of *Uncle Remus* as "the greatest body of folk lore that America has produced" (p. 10). See also *The Autobiography of an Ex–Colored Man* (1912; rpt. New York: Penguin, 1990), p. 63. In the preface to later editions of *The Book of American Negro Poetry*, Johnson acknowledged that writers such as Sterling Brown had freed dialect from its questionable past and made it a possible language for poetry again.

12. See Joseph Boskin, *Sambo: The Rise and Demise of an American Jester* (New York: Oxford University Press, 1986); and Rayford W. Logan, *The Negro in American Life and*

Thought: The Nadir, 1877–1901 (New York: Dial Press, 1954). The black press of the 1920s was remarkably tolerant of the white dialect writers, but Cohen seems to have exhausted even this tolerance. See "That Obnoxious White Character," *Opportunity* 2 (October 1924): 309–10. On the other hand, J. L. Dillard defends Cohen, even against what he calls near-universal contempt from blacks. *Black English: Its History and Usage in the United States* (New York: Random House, 1972), p. 250.

13. Malcolm Cowley, *Exile's Return: A Literary Odyssey of the 1920's* (New York: Viking, 1951), p. 5. Nathan Huggins relates this sense of linguistic dispossession to the even more serious one suffered by African Americans. Nathan Irvin Huggins, *Harlem Renaissance* (New York: Oxford University Press, 1971), pp. 60–62. For a different opinion see Cary D. Wintz, *Black Culture and the Harlem Renaissance* (Houston, Tex.: Rice University Press, 1988), p. 4.

14. Bernard Shaw, *Collected Plays with Their Prefaces*, 7 vols. (New York: Dodd, Mead, 1975), 4:664.

15. Lewis is quoted in Peter Ackroyd, *T. S. Eliot* (London: Hamish Hamilton, 1984), p. 56. For the mockery of Pound see Read, p. 14. A "nasal twang" may seem a minor linguistic deviation, but it was the term traditionally used by the English to demean American dialect. See Baron, p. 27.

16. Quoted in Donald Davie, *Ezra Pound* (New York: Viking, 1975), pp. 46–47. Davie's suggestion that in *Homage* Pound is dramatizing the colonial relationship of his own American English to English English and of that English to Latin is a most useful one (pp. 43–61).

17. "English for the English," quoted in Henry Alford, *A Plea for the Queen's English*, 2nd ed. (London: A. Strahan, 1869), pp. 266–71.

18. H. W. Fowler and F. G. Fowler, *The King's English*, 2nd ed. (Oxford: Clarendon Press, 1922), p. 24.

19. Society for Pure English, Tract No. 10 (1922), p. 7. (In the same issue the *New York Evening Post* was quoted as welcoming the SPE in the hopes that it might end "the tiresome wrangle over English English versus American English" [p. 27].) Society for Pure English, Tract No. 21 (1925), p. 5. See also Richard W. Bailey, *Images of English: A Cultural History of the Language* (Ann Arbor: University of Michigan Press, 1991), p. 206–7; and Tony Crowley, *Standard English and the Politics of Language* (Urbana: University of Illinois Press, 1989), pp. 236–50.

20. Robert Bridges, "The Society's Work," Society for Pure English, Tract No. 21 (1925), p. 5.

21. Henry Newbolt, "The Future of the English Language," in *Studies in Green and Gray* (London: Thomas Nelson, 1926), p. 228.

22. Christopher Ricks, *T. S. Eliot and Prejudice* (Berkeley: University of California Press, 1988), p. 198. For a discussion of this whole issue as it concerns Eliot, see Ricks's chapter "An English Accent" (pp. 154–203).

23. *EL*, p. 318. See Lyndall Gordon, *Eliot's New Life* (New York: Farrar, Straus & Giroux, 1988), p. 208. For a contemporary's account of the social and linguistic antipathy between Pound and Edwardian England, see Wyndham Lewis, "Ezra Pound," in *Ezra Pound: A Collection of Essays*, ed. Peter Russell (London: Peter Nevill, 1950), pp. 257–66. For more recent discussions see the following by Donald Davie: "Ezra Among the Edwardians," "Ezra Pound Abandons the English," and "Ezra Pound and the English," in *Studies in Ezra Pound* (Manchester: Carcanet, 1991), pp. 218–42, 259–69.

24. Gilles Deleuze and Félix Guattari, *Kafka: Toward a Minor Literature*, trans. Dana Polan (Minneapolis: University of Minnesota Press), p. 19.

25. Deleuze and Guattari, *Kafka*, p. 27. For practical applications and theoretical

discussions of this work, see Louis A. Renza, *"A White Heron" and the Question of Minor Literature* (Madison: University of Wisconsin Press, 1984), pp. 29–38; and David Lloyd, *Nationalism and Minor Literature: James Clarence Mangan and the Emergence of Irish Cultural Nationalism* (Berkeley: University of California Press, 1987), pp. 23–25. Lloyd states that the theory of a minor literature applies only to "the negative critical aspect of modernism," from which he excludes Eliot, Pound, and Yeats because of "the claims to transcending division and difference that constantly inform their works." For a discussion of "minor literature" and the literature of "minorities," see David Lloyd, "Genet's Genealogy: European Minorities and the Ends of the Canon," *Cultural Critique* 6 (Spring 1987): 161–85.

26. T. S. Eliot, review of *Tarr*, *The Egoist*, September 1918, p. 106.

27. Ezra Pound, *Ezra Pound and the Visual Arts*, ed. Harriet Zinnes (New York: New Directions, 1980), pp. 181–82.

28. Robert C. Toll, *Blacking Up: The Minstrel Show in Nineteenth–Century America* (New York: Oxford University Press, 1974), pp. 270–72. See also Constance Rourke's discussion of the simultaneous growth of the "Yankee" role and the black minstrel stereotype (*American Humor: A Study of the National Character* [1931; rpt. New York: Doubleday Anchor, 1955], pp. 70–90); Huggins, pp. 244–301; and Berndt Ostendorf, *Black Literature in White America* (Sussex: Harvester Press, 1982), p. 80.

29. Robert Bone, "The Oral Tradition," in *Critical Essays on Joel Chandler Harris*, ed. R. Bruce Bickley, Jr. (Boston: G. K. Hall, 1981), pp. 137, 139. Eric J. Sundquist, *To Wake the Nations: Race in the Making of American Literature* (Cambridge, Mass.: Harvard University Press/Belknap Press, 1993), pp. 345–47.

30. Robert O'Meally, "Introduction," *Tales of the Congaree*, by E. C. L. Adams (Chapel Hill: University of North Carolina Press, 1987), pp. xix, xxxv.

31. The prevalence of blackface at this time is indicated by the careers of other white actors who seemed to specialize in such roles: besides the very active Tom Wilson, Nick Cogley, Pauline Dempsey, and Lucretius C. Harris each had eight such roles in roughly the same time period. Between 1926 and 1932, burnt cork transformed Myrna Loy, who became famous as the ultrasophisticated Nora Charles in the *Thin Man* movies, into the following: Roma, a half-caste; a mulatto; a Chinese girl; a slave girl; Yasmani, a Hindu; Azuri, an Arab of the desert; a "native girl"; the Gypsy Nubi; Manuella, a half-breed; Moira, another "native girl"; and Fu Manchu's daughter. See Appendix B, "Whites in Blackface—Films," in William Torbert Leonard, *Masquerade in Black* (Metuchen, N.J.: Scarecrow Press, 1986), pp. 370–78.

32. Conrad Aiken, *Ushant* (New York: Duell, Sloan and Pearce, 1952), pp. 143, 135, 137. Evidence that Eliot would have concurred in Aiken's account of their feelings is provided in "Eeldrop and Appleplex," *Little Review* 4 (May 1917): 7–11, which is generally held to be about the collaboration of Eliot and Pound but which also bears a number of close similarities to the relationship of Eliot and Aiken. For example, Eeldrop and Appleplex rush out whenever there is a disturbance in the street so that Eeldrop can listen to the lower orders and register "in his mind their oaths, their redundance of phrase, their various manners of spitting."

33. Aiken, *Ushant*, p. 137. See also Aiken's later account in "King Bolo and Others," in *T. S. Eliot: A Symposium*, comp. Richard March and Tambimuttu (1949; rpt. Freeport, N.Y.: Books for Libraries Press, 1968), p. 21. As Aiken's title suggests, the infamous King Bolo poems were supposed to be part of this modernist affront to literary and scholarly respectability and, of course, they too depended heavily on racist slurs and stereotypes. For a discussion see chapter 1 of the present volume.

34. Aiken, *Ushant*, p. 137.

35. Aiken, "King Bolo," p. 21.

36. Gilles Deleuze and Félix Guattari, *Anti–Oedipus: Capitalism and Schizophrenia*, trans. Robert Hurley, Mark Seem, and Helen R. Lane (Minneapolis: University of Minnesota Press, 1983), pp. 77, 105. For brief discussions of "Mélange Adultère de Tout," a poem not much noticed in the criticism on Eliot, see Grover Smith, *T. S. Eliot's Poetry and Plays: A Study in Sources and Meaning*, 2nd ed. (Chicago: University of Chicago Press, 1974), p. 35; and A. D. Moody, *Thomas Stearns Eliot Poet* (Cambridge: Cambridge University Press, 1979), p. 57.

37. T. S. Eliot, *The Complete Poems and Plays, 1909–1950* (New York: Harcourt, Brace & World, 1971), p. 28. Subsequent citations will be from this edition, identified in the text as *CPP*.

38. Deleuze and Guattari, *Kafka*, p. 26.

39. Note the revealing use of the word *adulterate* in *After Strange Gods* (New York: Harcourt, Brace, 1933): "The population should be homogeneous; where two or more cultures exist in the same place they are likely either to be fiercely self-conscious or both to become adulterate" (p. 20).

40. T. S. Eliot, *The Waste Land: A Fascimile and Transcript of the Original Drafts Including the Annotations of Ezra Pound*, ed. Valerie Eliot (New York: Harcourt Brace Jovanovich, 1971), p. 5, n. 125. "By the Watermelon Vine" is listed as "Negro Song" in Minnie Earl Sears's *Song Index* (1934; rpt. Shoe String Press, 1966), p. 41, and under "Minstrel" in Anthony and Anne Stecheson, *The Stecheson Classified Song Directory* (Hollywood, Calif.: Music Industry Press, 1961), p. 237. Valerie Eliot gives its date of first performance as 1904, but both Roger Lax, *The Great Song Thesaurus* (New York: Oxford University Press, 1984), and Julius Mattfeld, *Variety Music Cavalcade, 1620–1969* (Englewood Cliffs, N.J.: Prentice-Hall, 1971), give the date as 1914, suggesting that Eliot might have heard it close to the time when the earliest shards of *The Waste Land* were assembled. For information on the original performance of "My Evaline" in 1901, see Ken Bloom, *American Song: The Complete Musical Theatre Companion* (New York: Facts on File, 1985), p. 1529.

41. Charles Sanders has suggested that in draft form *The Waste Land* resembled the traditional minstrel-show form, with the last four sections corresponding to the olio and Tiresias as Mr. Interlocuter. "*The Waste Land*: The Last Minstrel Show?" *Journal of Modern Literature* 8 (1980): 23–38.

42. For a discussion of the source of the Shakespeherian Rag, see Brude McElderry, "Eliot's Shakespeherian Rag," *American Quarterly* 9 (Summer 1957): 185–86. For opera burlesque see Julian Mates, *America's Musical Stage: Two Hundred Years of Musical Theatre* (Westport, Conn.: Greenwood Press, 1985), p. 86; and Hans Nathan, *Dan Emmett and the Rise of Early Negro Minstrelsy* (Norman: University of Oklahoma Press, 1962), pp. 65, 67. For mock oratory see Toll, pp. 55–56; and Nathan, p. 133. In both cases the parody worked in two directions, against the ignorant "darky" and against the threatening cultural product his fumbling brought down to earth. See also Gates's discussion of "Follit's Black Lectures," a popular English phenomenon of the mid-nineteenth century (*Signifying Monkey*, pp. 92–94).

43. Eliot, *Facsimile*, p. 95, n. 129.

44. Clive Bell, *Since Cézanne* (New York: Harcourt, Brace, 1922), p. 222.

45. Ricks, pp. 209–15.

46. In the draft Eliot has substituted "an alien" for "the sullen" and removed the *s* from "campfires" without correcting the grammar. *Facsimile*, p. 99.

47. Eliot, *Facsimile*, p. 125.

48. Moody, p. 120.

49. Ezra Pound, *Guide to Kulchur* (1938; rpt. New York: New Directions, 1970), p. 93.

50. *EL,* p. 505. This line has been excised from the severely bowdlerized version of this letter printed in Pound's *Selected Letters,* pp. 171–72. There is no room here to investigate the intricate relationship between Pound's racial masking and the convoluted cross-sexual role he casts himself in in these letters. The latter has been investigated by Wayne Koestenbaum, *Double Talk: The Erotics of Male Literary Collaboration* (New York: Routledge, 1989).

51. See the discussion of this typescript, on deposit with the Hayward bequest in the library of King's College, Cambridge, in Michael J. Sidnell, *Dances of Death: The Group Theatre of London in the Thirties* (London: Faber & Faber, 1984), pp. 263–65. I am indebted to Ronald Bush for this reference. For a useful discussion of *Sweeney* in light of Eliot's interest in the primitive, see Robert Crawford, *The Savage and the City in the Work of T. S. Eliot* (Oxford: Clarendon Press, 1987).

52. *Sweeney* was in draft by April 1923, a few months before Eliot called for a new kind of contemporary drama that would be "something like a performance of the *Agamemnon* by the Guitrys" (*Selected Essays, 1917–1932* [New York: Harcourt, Brace, 1932], p. 94). See Moody, p. 114, for the date. Late in 1924, Eliot told Arnold Bennett he "wanted to write a drama of modern life . . . 'perhaps with certain things in it accentuated by drum beats.'" *Sweeney* was apparently the "jazz play" they discussed (*The Journals of Arnold Bennett,* 3 vols., ed. Newman Flower [London: Cassell, 1933], 3:52). See also the reference in *The Use of Poetry and the Use of Criticism* (London: Faber & Faber, 1933) in which Eliot describes an attempt to write a verse play with different "levels" appealing to different segments of his audience (p. 153). This is often taken to be a reference to *Sweeney.* As Crawford shows, Eliot wrote his play virtually by filling in the blanks of F. M. Cornford's synopses of Aristophanes (pp. 160–90). Eliot mentions Cornford's *Origins of Attic Comedy* in a letter to Hallie Flanagan about her production of the play (*Dynamo* [New York: Duell, Sloan & Pearce, 1943], pp. 82–83). The account also includes an additional fragment, obviously derived from Auden.

53. Barbara Everett, "The New Style of *Sweeney Agonistes,*" *The Yearbook of English Studies* 14 (1984): 251.

54. Ibid., p. 246.

55. "'[R]ing up' is English, 'call up' the American; 'trunk line,' if applied to the telephone service, is English, the American is, if I remember, 'long distance'" (*EL,* p. 455).

56. Gates, *Figures in Black,* p. 289.

57. Brander Matthews, "The Englishing of French Words," Society for Pure English, Tract No. 4 (1921), p. 6.

58. Eugene Levy, *James Weldon Johnson: Black Leader, Black Voice* (Chicago: University of Chicago Press, 1973), p. 86. "Under the Bamboo Tree" was one of the most popular American songs of the period, selling four hundred thousand copies in less than a year. Yale undergraduates turned it into a football fight song (Levy, p. 89), and it became so prevalent among black audiences that children in Washington, D.C., used an adaptation of it as a mildly obscene street chant. Jean Toomer, *The Wayward and the Seeking,* ed. Darwin T. Turner (Washington, D.C.: Howard University Press, 1982), p. 51. It is possible that the song was recalled to Eliot's memory by the death of Bert Williams, who had become world famous in the Ziegfeld Follies. Early in 1922 Williams collapsed on the stage of a production that had been retitled *Under the Bamboo Tree.* See Leonard, pp. 203, 237.

59. Levy, pp. 88–90.

60. Mates, p. 85; Toll, p. 54.

61. Gates, *Signifying Monkey,* p. 100.

62. Deleuze and Guattari, *Kafka,* p. 21.

63. Houston A. Baker, Jr., *Modernism and the Harlem Renaissance* (Chicago: University of Chicago Press, 1987), p. 52.

64. Eliot, "Eeldrop," p. 9.

65. T. S. Eliot, *For Lancelot Andrewes: Essays on Style and Order* (Garden City, N.Y.: Doubleday, Doran, 1929), p. vii.

66. Eliot himself said at about this time, "I lost my southern accent without ever acquiring the accent of the native Bostonian . . ." ("Preface," *This American World*, by Edgar Mowrer [London: Faber & Gwyer, 1928], pp. xiii–xiv). Many listeners would agree that Eliot's voice remained peculiarly without character (Ricks, pp. 182–85).

67. Edward Kamau Brathwaite, *History of the Voice: The Development of Nation Language in Anglophone Caribbean Poetry* (London: New Beacon Books, 1984), pp. 30–31.

68. Ezra Pound, "How to Read," quoted in Davie, *Studies in Ezra Pound*, pp. 239–40.

69. Ezra Pound, *The Cantos* (New York: New Directions, 1972). Quotations from *The Cantos* will be identified in the text by canto and page number in this edition.

70. Logan Pearsall Smith, "A Few Practical Suggestions," Society for Pure English, Tract No. 3 (1920), pp. 7–9.

71. For later repetitions of this list, which also included Yeats, Hardy, and Ford, see *Pound/Ford: The Story of a Literary Friendship*, ed. Brita Lindberg–Seyersted (New York: New Directions, 1982), p. 172; and Donald Hall, *Remembering Poets: Reminiscences and Opinions* (New York: Harper & Row, 1978), p. 227.

72. Robert Bridges, "On English Homophones," Society for Pure English, Tract No. 2 (1919); Smith, pp. 13–16; Robert Graves, *Impenetrability: or, The Proper Habit of English* (London: Hogarth, 1926), pp. 30–33.

73. Carpenter, pp. 140, 115; 1914 SPE member list, Society for Pure English, Tract No. 1 (1919), n.p.

74. *Ezra Pound and Dorothy Shakespear: Their Letters, 1909–1914*, ed. Omar Pound and A. Walton Litz (New York: New Directions, 1983), p. 316.

75. *Pound/Ford*, p. 172; Carpenter, p. 249. Herbert N. Schneidau says that "Sir Henry Newbolt, Frederic Manning, and G. W. Prothero (editor of the *Quarterly Review*) were treated with great deference in Pound's early letters and writings." *Ezra Pound: The Image and the Real* (Baton Rouge: Louisiana State University Press, 1964), p. 15. For a very useful account of these relationships, see Davie, *Studies in Ezra Pound*, pp. 222–27.

76. Henry Newbolt, *New Paths on Helicon* (London: Thomas Nelson, [1928?]). Newbolt was in fact quite receptive to the new movements, and in his note on Pound in *New Paths* calls himself "one of his oldest admirers" (p. 386). Ironically, he is much harsher toward Eliot, whom he criticizes quite extensively (pp. 401–3, 426). See also *Selected Poems of Henry Newbolt*, ed. Patric Dickinson (London: Hodder & Stoughton, 1981), p. 25. Davie reports that Newbolt referred approvingly to Pound, at least as a critic, as early as 1912 (*Studies in Ezra Pound*, p. 226).

77. Newbolt, *Selected Poems*, p. 35; Ezra Pound, *Personae: Collected Shorter Poems* (New York: New Directions, 1971), p. 33. See Carpenter, p. 118.

78. Ezra Pound, "Leo Frobenius," in *Negro: An Anthology*, ed. Nancy Cunard (London: Wishart Press, 1934), p. 623. According to Pound, Blaise Cendrars was the only person he had met who was interested in discussing Frobenius.

79. To be fair to Pound, he could not have known of McKay's discussion, since it appeared in Russian and was not translated back into English until 1979. See Claude McKay, *The Negroes in America*, trans. Robert J. Winter (Port Washington, N.Y.: Kennikat Press, 1979), p. 57. For Senghor and Césaire see A. James Arnold, *Modernism and Negritude: The Poetry and Poetics of Aimé Césaire* (Cambridge, Mass.: Harvard University

Press, 1981), pp. 35–37, and Senghor's foreword to *Leo Frobenius, 1873–1973: An Anthology*, ed. Eike Haberland (Wiesbaden: Franz Steiner Verlag, 1973), p. vii.

80. *"Ezra Pound Speaking": Radio Speeches of World War II*, ed. Leonard W. Doob (Westport, Conn.: Greenwood Press, 1978), p. 99.

81. J. J. Wilhelm, *The American Roots of Ezra Pound* (New York: Garland, 1985), pp. 30–32, 34.

82. See George Steiner, *After Babel: Aspects of Language and Translation* (London: Oxford University Press, 1975), pp. 191–97.

83. Ezra Pound, *The Classic Anthology Defined by Confucius* (Cambridge, Mass.:Harvard University Press, 1954), p. 100.

84. Davie, *Studies in Ezra Pound*, pp. 11–22; L. S. Dembo, *The Confucian Odes of Ezra Pound* (London: Faber & Faber, 1963), p. 3.

85. Pound, *Classic Anthology*, p. 8.

86. Ibid., p. 35.

Chapter 5

Works by Claude McKay will be identified in the text by the following abbreviations:

ALWH   *A Long Way from Home* (New York: Lee Furman, 1937)

  B   *Banjo* (New York: Harper & Brothers, 1929)

  BB   *Banana Bottom* (New York: Harper & Brothers, 1933)

  CB   *Constab Ballads* in *The Dialect Poetry of Claude McKay* (Salem, N.H.: Ayer, 1987) (separate pagination)

  GHJ   *My Green Hills of Jamaica*, ed. Mervyn Morris (Kingston: Heinemann, 1979)

  HH   *Home to Harlem* (New York: Harper & Brothers, 1928)

  HS   *Harlem Shadows* (New York: Harcourt, Brace, 1922)

  PCM   *The Passion of Claude McKay: Selected Poetry and Prose, 1912–1948*, ed. Wayne F. Cooper (New York: Schocken, 1973)

  SJ   *Songs of Jamaica* in *The Dialect Poetry of Claude McKay*

1. Wayne F. Cooper, *Claude McKay: Rebel Sojourner in the Harlem Renaissance* (1987; rpt. New York: Schocken, 1990), p. 184.

2. Quoted in Tyrone Tillery, *Claude McKay: A Black Poet's Struggle for Identity* (Amherst: University of Massachusetts Press, 1992), p. 18.

3. In *Banana Bottom*, Hopping Dick is turned away from the Craig's door for "murdering his h's" (p. 210), though it is not at all clear where he could have picked up this Cockneyism.

4. As McKay put it in *My Green Hills of Jamaica:* "He felt that . . . modernism and industrialism were ruining the world. He was especially critical of the rapid modernization of the American system" (p. 82).

5. Cooper, p. 381, nn. 81, 82.

6. Logan Pearsall Smith, *Reperusals and Recollections* (New York: Harcourt, Brace, 1937), pp. 49–65.

7. Cooper, p. 381, n. 82.

8. Alice Werner, "Introduction," *Jamaican Song and Story: Annancy Stories, Digging Sings, Ring Tunes, and Dancing Tunes*, coll. and ed. Walter Jekyll (London: David Nutt, 1907), p. xii.

9. Cooper, pp. 35–47. For another version of McKay's meeting with Jekyll see *ALWH*, p. 13, and for discussions of the relationship see Cooper, p. 27, and Tillery, pp. 10–12.

10. *Banana Bottom* is dedicated to "Pâcjo," which was McKay's name for Jekyll (see *GHJ*, p. 78). An author's note says that "all the characters, as in my previous novels, are imaginary, excepting perhaps Squire Gensir."

11. Surprised that Jekyll would prefer his company to that of Jamaica's British governor, McKay was told, "English gentlemen have always liked their peasants, it's the ambitious middle class that we cannot tolerate" (*GHJ*, p. 71). This condescension actually gratified what McKay called a certain snobbishness in himself. This episode shows how much Jekyll's folklore collecting resembled Yeats's in Ireland as well as Harris's in America.

12. See, for example, Tillery, pp. 13, 40.

13. Cooper, pp. 81, 118, 126.

14. "He was a full-blooded African, of middle height and dark chestnut color." Max Eastman, "Biographical Note," *Selected Poems of Claude McKay* (1953; rpt. New York: Harcourt Brace Jovanovich, n.d.), p. 7. Over the years, it seems, Eastman's vision of his friend had become more benighted rather than less so: "His laughter at the frailties of his friends and enemies, no matter which—that high, half-wailing falsetto laugh of the recklessly delighted Darky—was the center of my joy in him throughout our friendship of more than thirty years" (p. 7). Thirty years before this, McKay had written sourly to Eastman, "You have been entirely deceived about me, Max. I suppose it is due to this everlastingly infectious smile of mine" (*PCM*, p. 89).

15. I. A. Richards, "Preface," *Spring in New Hampshire*, by Claude McKay (London: Grant Richards, 1920), p. 5.

16. Again, Richards did the same, though he was a bit cagier: "[T]his is the first instance of success in poetry with which we in Europe at any rate have been brought into contact." *Spring in New Hampshire*, p. 5.

17. Jean-Paul Sartre, "Black Orpheus," in *The Black American Writer: Poetry and Drama*, ed. C. W. E. Bigsby (Deland, Fla.: Everett/Edwards, 1969), pp. 14–16. See also the classic discussion of Frantz Fanon, "The Negro and Language," in *Black Skin, White Masks*, trans. Charles Lam Markmann (New York: Grove, 1967), pp. 17–40.

18. See, for example, the discussion of the creole continuum in *The Empire Writes Back: Theory and Practice in Post-Colonial Literatures*, ed. Bill Ashcroft, Gareth Griffiths, and Helen Tiffin (London: Routledge, 1989), p. 47.

19. Sartre, p. 24.

20. Gilles Deleuze and Félix Guattari, *Anti–Oedipus: Capitalism and Schizophrenia*, trans. Robert Hurley, Mark Seem, and Helen R. Lane (Minneapolis: University of Minnesota Press, 1983), pp. 77, 105.

21. C. K. Ogden, "The Linguistic Conscience," *Cambridge Magazine* 10 (Summer 1920): 31. In the same issue Ogden published two dozen of McKay's poems. For biographical testimony and details about Basic English, see W. Terrence Gordon, *C. K. Ogden: A Bio-Bibliographic Study* (Metuchen, N.J.: Scarecrow, 1990); and P. Sargant Florence and J. R. L. Anderson, eds., *C. K. Ogden: A Collective Memoir* (London: Pemberton, 1977).

22. George Wolf, "C. K. Ogden," in *Linguistic Thought in England, 1914–1945*, ed. Roy Harris (London: Duckworth, 1988), pp. 85–105.

23. Ibid., pp. 103–5.

24. C. K. Ogden, headnote to "Poems: Claude McKay," *Cambridge Magazine* 10 (Summer 1920): 55.

25. James Weldon Johnson, ed., *The Book of American Negro Poetry*, 2nd ed. (1931; rpt. New York: Harcourt, Brace & World, 1969), p. 165. McKay's dialect poetry continues to receive significant praise, along with serious criticism. See Lloyd W. Brown, *West Indian Poetry*, 2nd ed. (London: Heinemann, 1984), pp. 39–62; and Edward Kamau Brathwaite, *History of the Voice: The Development of Nation Language in Anglophone Caribbean Poetry* (London: New Beacon Books, 1984), pp. 19–22. Note also how Cooper distinguishes McKay's dialect from "the Dunbar school" (*DP*, p. ii).

26. Jekyll, ed., pp. xxxix, 6, 157.

27. Patrick Taylor, *The Narrative of Liberation: Perspectives on Afro-Caribbean Literature, Popular Culture, and Politics* (Ithaca, N.Y.: Cornell University Press, 1989), p. 140. In some parts of the West Indies, according to Roger Abrahams, Anancy speaks so brokenly that the name Nansi becomes synonymous with nonsense. *The Man-of-Words in the West Indies: Performance and the Emergence of Creole Culture* (Baltimore, Md.: Johns Hopkins University Press, 1983), pp. 164–65.

28. Brown, p. 49.

29. Ralph Ellison, *Shadow and Act*, pp. 46–47. For a nuanced discussion of the trickster tradition in African-American folklore, see Lawrence W. Levine, *Black Culture and Black Consciousness* (New York: Oxford University Press, 1977), pp. 102–33. The most influential contemporary analysis is Henry Louis Gates, Jr., *The Signifying Monkey: A Theory of African-American Literary Criticism* (New York: Oxford University Press, 1988).

30. According to Abrahams, Anancy is a liminal figure, in between and isolated (pp. 170–71). See also Barbara Johnson's discussion of the liminal position Zora Neale Hurston takes up at the beginning of *Mules and Men*. "Thresholds of Difference: Structures of Address in Zora Neale Hurston," in *"Race," Writing and Difference*, ed. Henry Louis Gates, Jr. (Chicago: University of Chicago Press, 1986), pp. 324–27.

31. Jekyll, ed., pp. 238, 53.

32. As such, it would be an early example of what Louise Bennett calls, in the title of a well-known Jamaican dialect poem, "Colonisation in Reverse." *Jamaica Labrish* (Kingston: Sangster's Book Stores, 1966), p. 179. Another strategy one might sense in McKay's work is the one assumed by John Agard in "Palm Tree King":

> Because I come from the West Indies
> certain people in England seem to think
> I is a expert on palm trees
>
> So not wanting to sever dis link
> with me native roots (know what ah mean?)
> or to disappoint dese culture vulture
> I does smile cool as seabreeze
>
> an say to dem
> which specimen
> you interested in
> *Mangoes and Bullets* (London: Serpent's Tail, 1990), p. 36.

33. Note the way "Old England" is referred to when McKay recounts his actual trip to England (*ALWH*, pp. 59, 66). On the other hand, there is an unpublished sonnet from the mid-1920s entitled "London" that is a good deal more negative about British culture. "London," in "Cities" manuscript, Claude McKay papers, James Weldon Johnson Collection of Negro Literature and Art, Beinecke Rare Book and Manuscript Library, Yale University.

34. Brathwaite, p. 20; Edouard Glissant, *Caribbean Discourse: Selected Essays*, trans. J. Michael Dash (Charlottesville: University Press of Virginia, 1989), p. 124.

35. Jekyll, ed., p. 6.

36. *The Autobiography of William Butler Yeats* (New York: Collier, 1965), p. 47.

37. Note the very similar episode in Michelle Cliff's *No Telephone to Heaven* (New York: Vintage, 1987), when the protagonist's mother, a Jamaican immigrant to New York, discovers a few small markets carrying Jamaican produce: "She came home with these things laden in her arms, as if to say, Family, this is for you. In these shops she broke her silence, here she felt most the loss of home, of voice, even as she brushed the dirt off the yam-skin . . ." (p. 65).

38. Hans Nathan, *Dan Emmett and the Rise of Early Negro Minstrelsy* (Norman: University of Oklahoma Press, 1962), pp. 5, 243. The latter genre was, of course, the basis of "Dixie."

39. Quoted in C. K. Ogden, "Recent Verse," *Cambridge Magazine* 10 (January–March 1921): 117.

40. See the analysis of Jean-Claude Bajeux, *Antilia retrouvée: Claude McKay, Luis Palés Matos, Aimé Césaire, poètes noirs antillais* (Paris: Editions Caribéennes, 1983), which is one of the few to give serious attention to the form of McKay's poetry and the linguistic issues it raises (pp. 52–53).

41. Cary D. Wintz, *Black Culture and the Harlem Renaissance* (Houston, Tex.: Rice University Press, 1988), p. 88. For detailed discussions of McKay's dealings with these journals, see Cooper, p. 81; Tillery, pp. 29–32, 39.

42. Tillery, p. 30.

43. Cooper, p. 166.

44. C. K. Ogden, "Poems: Claude McKay," *Cambridge Magazine* 10 (Summer 1920): 55; and "Recent Verse," *Cambridge Magazine* 10 (January–March 1921): 113, 116–17.

45. Tillery, p. 32.

46. Claude McKay, *The Negroes in America*, trans. Robert J. Winter, ed. Alan L. McLeod (Port Washington, N.Y.: Kennikat Press, 1979), pp. 63–64. This edition is a translation back into English of a work McKay published in Russian translation while visiting the Soviet Union in 1922–23. Cooper reads this passage as optimistic and positive, missing, I think, the clear note of personal resentment and ignoring the obvious animus against figures such as Roger Fry and Clive Bell (Cooper, p. 187).

47. For a general discussion of the difficulties modernism presents for Caribbean writers, see Gikandi. McKay's formalism is briefly discussed in Houston Baker's analysis of the conflict between modernist standards and the Harlem Renaissance, *Modernism and the Harlem Renaissance* (Chicago: University of Chicago Press, 1987), pp. 85–86.

48. Claude McKay, "Black Belt Slummers," in "Cities" manuscript, Claude McKay papers, James Weldon Johnson Collection of Negro Literature and Art, Beinecke Rare Book and Manuscript Library, Yale University.

49. See Bajeux, pp. 73–79. For a different and more positive reading of the poem, see Brown, p. 60.

50. Cooper, p. 38.

51. Johnson, *Book of American Negro Poetry*, p. 167. Johnson does maintain, however, that the "passion found in his poems of rebellion, transmuted, is felt in his love lyrics."

52. Tillery, p. 79.

53. Claude McKay, letter to W. A. Bradley (1928), quoted in Michel Fabre, "Aesthetics and Ideology in *Banjo*," in *Myth and Ideology in American Culture*, ed. Régis

Durand (Lille: Publications de L'Université de Lille, 1976), p. 203. According to Fabre, McKay aims to achieve in his fiction "a mosaic of outlooks."

54. For useful accounts of this controversy, see Cooper, pp. 240–48; Tillery, pp. 87–106. See also the annotated list of reviews in John E. Bassett, *Harlem in Review: Critical Reactions to Black American Writers, 1917–1939* (Selinsgrove, Pa.: Susquehanna University Press, 1992), pp. 90–95.

55. Herschel Brickell, review of *Home to Harlem, Opportunity* 6 (May 1928): 151–52.

56. T. S. Matthews, "What Gods! What Gongs!" *New Republic* 55 (May 30, 1928): 50–51.

57. Allison Davis, "Our Negro 'Intellectuals,'" *Crisis* (August 1928): 268–69, 284–86. The aesthetic conservatism of the established African-American intelligentsia meant that it was generally antimodernist. See Chidi Ikonné, *From Du Bois to Van Vechten: The Early New Negro Literature, 1903–1926* (Westport, Conn.: Greenwood Press, 1981), p. 96; and the unsigned editorial "The New Generation," *Opportunity* 2 (March 1924): 69. The younger generation, as the last item implies, was more receptive both to modernism and to McKay. See David Levering Lewis, *When Harlem Was in Vogue* (New York: Oxford University Press, 1981), pp. 228–29; and Arnold Rampersad, "Langston Hughes and Approaches to Modernism in the Harlem Renaissance," in *The Harlem Renaissance: Revaluations,* ed. Amrijit Singh, William S. Shriver, and Stanley Brodwin (New York: Garland, 1989), pp. 49–71.

58. In a letter to James Weldon Johnson, McKay expressed more sympathy with the position of the "nice Negroes": "[B]etween the devil of Cracker prejudice and the deep sea of respectable white condescension I can certainly sympathise, though I cannot agree, with their dislike of the artistic exploitation of low-class Negro life." Claude McKay to James Weldon Johnson, April 30, 1928, James Weldon Johnson correspondence, series I, folder 308, James Weldon Johnson Collection of Negro Literature and Art, Beinecke Rare Book and Manuscript Library, Yale University.

59. In general it is true, as so many critics have said, that the reason–insight, culture–nature split dominates McKay's first two novels. But to put all the emphasis here is to miss the clearly satirical edge that McKay often gives to what was elsewhere a deadly serious controversy. See Michael B. Stoff, "Claude McKay and the Cult of Primitivism," in *The Harlem Renaissance Remembered,* ed. Arna Bontemps (New York: Dodd, Mead, 1972), pp. 130–32; and Edward Margolies, *Native Sons: A Critical Study of Twentieth-Century Black American Authors* (Philadelphia: Lippincott, 1968), pp. 31–32, 41–42.

60. Margolies, pp. 41–42. Perhaps the most positive view of the use of stereotypes in the Harlem Renaissance is given by Robert Bone, *The Negro Novel in America,* rev. ed. (New Haven, Conn.: Yale University Press, 1965), p. 66, but even he observes that it is a short step from "Melanctha" or Jean le Nègre to Banjo (p. 74).

61. Both Stoff (p. 142) and Bone (p. 72) consider *Banana Bottom* to be intellectually superior to McKay's other fiction. On the other hand, Saunders Redding calls it "utterly inexcusable filth" without offering any further explanation. "The Negro Writer and American Literature," in *Anger, and Beyond: The Negro Writer in the United States,* ed. Herbert Hill (New York: Harper & Row, 1966), p. 15.

62. Alain Locke, "Spiritual Truancy," *New Challenge* 2 (Fall 1937): 81–85, reprinted in *The Spiritual Temper of Alain Locke,* ed. Jeffrey C. Stewart (New York: Garland, 1983), pp. 63–66.

63. Tillery, pp. 145–46.

64. Claude McKay, "Cycle" manuscript, Claude McKay papers, James Weldon Johnson Collection of Negro Literature and Art, Beinecke Rare Book and Manuscript Library, Yale University.

Chapter 6

1. For McKay's return to the United States in 1934 and his stay in the work camp, see Wayne F. Cooper, *Claude McKay: Rebel Sojourner in the Harlem Renaissance* (1987; rpt. New York: Schocken, 1990), pp. 291, 301. Eliot's return in 1932 was the occasion for the lectures later printed as *After Strange Gods* (New York: Harcourt Brace, 1933).

2. *Broom* 4 (December 1922): inside back cover.

3. *Broom* 4 (January 1923): back cover. For a full text of the poem, which first appeared in the *Dial* in 1920, see *The Complete Poems of Marianne Moore* (New York: Macmillan/Viking, 1967), pp. 46–47.

4. William Carlos Williams, *Paterson*, ed. Christopher MacGowan (New York: New Directions, 1992), p. 2.

5. T. S. Eliot, "American Literature and the American Language," *To Criticize the Critic* (New York: Farrar, Straus & Giroux, 1965) (originally given as a lecture in 1956). Quoted in David Simpson, *The Politics of American English, 1776–1850* (New York: Oxford University Press, 1986), p. 12. Pound's reaction to the same sort of thing was a bit more unpredictable and rambunctious. The *Little Review* for spring 1922 contained a spoof entitled "The Western School of Poesy, Synthese," by Pound's alter ego Abel Sanders: "Say, bo! I heard about that fourty-niner./Say, Bo! I've heard erbout that Perarie Schooner!/Say, Bo!!" (p. 34).

6. For a survey of American literary nationalism in this century, see Charles C. Alexander, *Here the Country Lies: Nationalism and the Arts in Twentieth–Century America* (Bloomington: Indiana University Press, 1980).

7. Alain Locke, "Beauty Instead of Ashes," *Nation* 126 (April 18, 1928): 433; reprinted in *The Critical Temper of Alain Locke*, ed. Jeffrey C. Stewart (New York: Garland, 1983), p. 24. Locke was consistent in referring to the younger Harlem writers as modernists. See also Stewart, ed., pp. 45, 47; and "Negro Youth Speaks," in *The New Negro*, ed. Alain Locke (1925; rpt. New York: Atheneum, 1968), pp. 50–51.

8. Alain Locke, "The Negro Poets of the United States," in *Anthology of Magazine Verse 1926 and Yearbook of American Poetry*, ed. William S. Brathwaite (Boston: Brimmer, 1926), p. 150; reprinted in Stewart, ed., p. 45. For a more recent expression of the same idea, that the white modernist search for new expressions coincides with "Negro idioms of speech," see Clyde Taylor, "Salt Peanuts," *Callaloo* 5 (1982): 1–11.

9. There is an undated letter with the Jean Toomer papers at Yale from Toomer to Lola Ridge, who was doing most of the American editorial work for *Broom* at this time, inquiring about the "Negro number," rumors of which had reached him from as far away as California. Jean Toomer to Lola Ridge, [1922?], Jean Toomer papers, box 1, folder 18. Toomer mentioned the same rumor in an undated letter to Waldo Frank. Jean Toomer to Waldo Frank, [1923?], Jean Toomer papers, box 3, folder 84. Ridge referred to the January 1923 number of *Broom* as the "All-American number" in a letter to Toomer. Lola Ridge to Jean Toomer, November 19, 1922, Jean Toomer papers, box 1, folder 18. James Weldon Johnson Collection of Negro Literature and Art, Beinecke Rare Book and Manuscript Library, Yale University.

10. Herbert S. Gorman, "Tradition and Experiment in Modern Poetry," *New York Times Book Review*, March 27, 1927, p. 2.

11. Frederick J. Hoffman, *The Twenties: American Writing in the Postwar Decade* (1955; rev. ed., 1962; rpt. New York: Free Press, 1965). The closest Hoffman comes to discussing the Harlem Renaissance is a two-page discussion of jazz and white primitivism (pp. 306–8).

12. Houston A. Baker, Jr., *Modernism and the Harlem Renaissance* (Chicago: Univer-

sity of Chicago Press, 1987). See also Arnold Rampersad, "Langston Hughes and Approaches to Modernism in the Harlem Renaissance," in *The Harlem Renaissance: Revaluations*, ed. Amrijit Singh, William S. Shriver, and Stanley Brodwin (New York: Garland, 1989), pp. 49–71.

13. James Oppenheim, "Poetry—Our First National Art," *Dial* 68 (February 1920): 240. See also Editorial, *Seven Arts* 1 (December 1916): 156. This plea in support of the vernacular has a long history in America. See Elsa Nettels, *Language, Race, and Social Class in Howells's America* (Lexington: University Press of Kentucky, 1988), p. 62, for similar pronouncements from Emerson and Howells; Kenneth Cmiel, *Democratic Eloquence: The Fight over Popular Speech in Nineteenth-Century America* (New York: William Morrow, 1990), pp. 107–11, for Lowell; and Whitman's "Slang in America," *North American Review* 141 (1885), reprinted in *The English Language: Essays by Linguists and Men of Letters, 1858–1964*, ed. W. F. Bolton and D. Crystal (Cambridge: Cambridge University Press, 1969), pp. 54–55. For a survey bringing such nineteenth-century ideas into the twentieth century, see Richard Bridgman, *The Colloquial Style in America* (New York: Oxford University Press, 1966).

14. Matthew Josephson, *Life Among the Surrealists* (New York: Holt, Rinehart & Winston, 1962), pp. 62–63.

15. Skipwith Cannell, "On a London Tennis Court," *Others* 3 (July 1916): 9. See also Skipwith Cannell, "To England," *Others* 1 (August 1915): 27.

16. Richard Aldington, "English and American," *Poetry* 16 (May 1920): 94–98. Mencken quoted a generous portion of this article in the third edition of *The American Language*. H. L. Mencken, *The American Language*, 3rd ed. (New York: Knopf, 1923), pp. 19–20. See also Alice Corbin Henderson, "American Verse and English Critics," *Poetry* 11 (January 1918): 207–12.

17. Malcolm Cowley, *Exile's Return: A Literary Odyssey of the 20's* (New York: Viking, 1951), p. 28.

18. Baker Brownell, "Irrational Verse," *Others* 5 (December 1918): 25.

19. See Emmy Veronica Sanders, "America Invades Europe," *Broom* 1 (November 1921): 93, for such an adaptation of the *Others* motto.

20. Lawrence J. Oliver, *Brander Matthews, Theodore Roosevelt, and the Politics of American Literature, 1880–1920* (Knoxville: University of Tennessee Press, 1992), p. 55.

21. Quoted, from an 1892 article in *Harper's*, in Nettels, p. 43. Matthews may have had in mind such categorical pronouncements as this from Ruskin's *Fors Clavigera*: "England taught the Americans all they have of speech, or thought, hitherto. What thoughts they have not learned from England are foolish thoughts; what words they have not learned from England, unseemly words; the vile among them not being able even to be humourous parrots, but only obscene mocking-birds" (XLII). Quoted in Allen Walker Read, "Amphi-Atlantic English," *English Studies* 17 (1935): 167.

22. For a discussion of this article and the ensuing controversy, see Edmund Wilson, *The Shores of Light: A Literary Chronicle of the Twenties and Thirties* (New York: Farrar, Straus & Young, 1952), pp. 421–28.

23. Benjamin T. Spencer, paraphrasing Richard Grant White, in *The Quest for Nationality: An American Literary Campaign* (Syracuse, N.Y.: Syracuse University Press, 1957), p. 301. For the antiimmigration opinions of two generations of New England literary authorities, see Nettels, pp. 101–2; and Arthur Frank Wertheim, *The New York Little Renaissance: Iconoclasm, Modernism, and Nationalism in American Culture, 1908–1917* (New York: New York University Press, 1976), pp. 3–4.

24. Malcolm Cowley, "The Revolt Against Gentility," in *After the Genteel Tradition: American Writers, 1910–1930*, ed. Malcolm Cowley (Carbondale: Southern Illinois Uni-

versity Press, 1964), p. 13. It is worth noting that the magazines of the genteel tradition had consistently printed the most offensive dialect humor. See Nettels, pp. 69–70; and Rayford W. Logan, *The Negro in American Life and Thought: The Nadir, 1877–1901* (New York: Dial Press, 1954), pp. 239–74. See Du Bois's complaint against *Harper's, Scribner's,* the *Atlantic,* and the *Century:* "The Browsing Reader," *The Crisis* 30 (May 1925): 24–26.

25. Harold E. Stearns, "Preface," *Civilization in the United States,* ed. Harold E. Stearns (1922; rpt. Westport, Conn.: Greenwood Press, 1971), p. vii.

26. Mencken, p. viii; Stearns, ed., p. 150.

27. Charles A. Fenton, "The American Academy of Arts vs. All Comers: Literary Rags and Riches in the 1920's," *South Atlantic Quarterly* 58 (1959): 575–76.

28. Royal Cortissoz, *American Artists* (New York: Scribner's, 1923), pp. 18, 324. See also Dickran Tashjian, *William Carlos Williams and the American Scene, 1920–1940* (New York: Whitney Museum of American Art, 1978), p. 102.

29. Robert Underwood Johnson, "The Glory of Words," in *Academy Papers: Addresses on Language Problems by Members of the American Academy of Arts and Letters,* ed. Paul Elmer More et al. (New York: Scribner's, 1925), pp. 276–77.

30. Quoted in Hoffman, p. 169.

31. Stuart P. Sherman, *Americans* (New York: Scribner's, 1922), pp. 2–4. For Sherman's role in the American Academy campaign see Fenton, pp. 578–79; Oliver, pp. 171–73.

32. Sherman, *Americans,* pp. 25, 22.

33. Stuart Sherman, *Points of View* (New York: Scribner's, 1924), pp. 255–56. It was in this book that Sherman preserved his attack on Gertrude Stein, in which he produced a synthetic Stein work by cutting up pieces of paper with words written on them (pp. 261–68).

34. A further irony lies in the fact that Brander Matthews, whom Sherman cast as the enemy of the Mohawks, had been and was continuing to serve as literary advisor and mentor to James Weldon Johnson. See Oliver, pp. 54–55. This is an irony that cuts both ways: at the very moment the younger generation was attacking Matthews as hopelessly hidebound, he was attempting to secure favorable reviews for *The Book of American Negro Poetry.*

35. Waldo Frank, *Our America* (New York: Boni & Liveright, 1919), pp. 9, 77, 126–46, 177–80, 163–64. For similar sentiments from another seminal figure of the avant–garde, see Harriet Monroe, rev. of *Chicago Poems* by Carl Sandburg, *Poetry* 8 (May 1916): 90–93; and idem, "At Noon," *Others* 3 (September 1916): 55–56.

36. Romain Rolland, "America and the Arts," trans. Waldo Frank, *Seven Arts* 1 (November 1916): 50; Barry Benefield, "Simply Sugar-Pie," *Seven Arts* 1 (November 1916): 3–14. The precursor to all such efforts was Robert J. Coady's magazine *The Soil,* an eclectic mixture of Jack Johnson, Bert Williams, ragtime, machine art, and localism, which Robert Alden Sanborn celebrated in *Broom* as "first cousin to the free verse movement in America." "A Champion in the Wilderness," *Broom* 3 (November 1922): 175. See also Tashjian, pp. 71–74.

37. Claude McKay, "Two Sonnets," *Seven Arts* 2 (October 1917): 741–42.

38. Randolph Bourne, *The History of a Literary Radical* (New York: S. A. Russell, 1956), pp. 262–84.

39. Bourne, pp. 269, 271. The concept of transnational America applied most directly to the European immigrants of the time, but Bourne intended that it should apply as well to African Americans. Like Zora Neale Hurston about fifteen years later, Bourne studied with Franz Boas at Columbia, and his views on race are set out in a review of Boas's *Mind of Primitive Man.* See Edward Abrahams, *The Lyrical Left: Randolph Bourne, Alfred Stieg-*

litz and the Origin of Cultural Radicalism in America (Charlottesville: University Press of Virginia, 1986), p. 68.

40. Gorham Munson, *The Awakening Twenties: A Memoir–History of a Literary Period* (Baton Rouge: Louisiana State University Press, 1985), p. 28.

41. Waldo Frank, *In the American Jungle [1925–1936]* (New York: Farrar & Rinehart, 1937), pp. 129–30.

42. Waldo Frank, "For a Declaration of War," *Secession* 7 (Winter 1924): 5–14.

43. Gorham B. Munson, "Syrinx," *Secession* 5 (July 1923): 9–10; Malcolm Cowley, "Love and Death," *Secession* 5 (July 1923): 19. The two sides in this controversy, which uncannily replicates the slightly earlier controversy between Frank's group and the American Academy, were represented in a fictional dialogue between Josephson and Paul Rosenfeld: Edmund Wilson, "Imaginary Dialogues: The Poet's Return," in *The Shores of Light*, pp. 125–40 (originally published April 9, 1924).

44. Wilson, p. 246.

45. Emmy Veronica Sanders, "Fourth of July Crackers," *Broom* 2 (July 1922): 288.

46. William Carlos Williams, *I Wanted to Write a Poem: The Autobiography of the Works of a Poet*, ed. Edith Heal (Boston: Beacon Press, 1958), pp. 28–29. Quoted (and the cover illustrated) in Tashjian, p. 61.

47. V. F. Calverton, "Introduction," *Anthology of American Negro Literature* (New York: Modern Library, 1929), pp. 3–4. This is a commonplace that was current at least by 1856. See Bruce Jackson, ed., *The Negro and His Folklore in Nineteenth-Century Periodicals* (Austin: University of Texas Press, 1967), pp. 24–25, 72–79, 51–54. A number of the dialect writers made the same point. See R. Emmett Kennedy, *Black Cameos* (New York: Albert & Charles Boni, 1924), p. xii; and Ambrose E. Gonzales, *The Black Border: Gullah Stories of the Carolina Coast* (Columbia, S.C.: State Printing Co., 1922), p. 12.

48. Quoted in Bruce Kellner, ed., *The Harlem Renaissance: A Historical Dictionary for the Era* (1984; rpt. New York: Methuen, 1987), p. 111.

49. John Rodker, "W. H. Hudson," *Little Review* 7 (May–June 1920): 20.

50. Alice Corbin Henderson, "The Folk Poetry of These States," *Poetry* 16 (August 1920): 266.

51. Alice Corbin, "Echoes of a Childhood: A Folk–Medley," *Seven Arts* 2 (September 1917): 598–601; idem, "Poetry of the American Negro," *Poetry* 10 (June 1917): 158–59.

52. Quoted, from Munson's book on Frank, in Tashjian, p. 131. For general discussions of the psychology of white primitivism as it relates to the Harlem Renaissance, see Chidi Ikonné, *From Du Bois to Van Vechten: The Early New Negro Literature, 1903–1926* (Westport, Conn.: Greenwood Press, 1981), p. 29; Daniel Levering Lewis, *When Harlem Was in Vogue* (1981; rpt. Oxford: Oxford University Press, 1989), pp. 91–92; Nathan Irvin Huggins, *Harlem Renaissance* (Oxford: Oxford University Press, 1971), pp. 244–301; and Cowley, *Exile's Return*, pp. 236–37.

53. Mark Turbyfill, "Sloth," *Others* 4 (June 1917): 28.

54. Stephen Hudson, "Southern Woman," *Little Review* 7 (September–December, 1920): 44–46. "Stephen Hudson" was the nom de plume of Sidney Schiff, an English writer and patron who knew Eliot quite well at this time. In fact, it is possible that the *Little Review* received and published his work because of Eliot's recommendation. Eliot did give Schiff advice about American publications in 1919. A later Hudson piece was referred to the *Dial* by him. See *The Letters of T. S. Eliot*, ed. Valerie Eliot (New York: Harcourt Brace Jovanovich, 1988), pp. 375, 509.

55. Waldo Frank, "Laughter and Light," *Dial* 79 (December 1925): 513. This is a review of Sherwood Anderson's *Dark Laughter*.

56. Waldo Frank, *City Block* (New York: Scribner's, 1922), pp. 149, 173–74. "Hope"

originally appeared in *Secession* 3 (August 1922): 1–4. The editors noted somewhat proudly that *City Block* might have to be printed privately because "Hope" was so outré.

57. *Memoirs of Waldo Frank*, ed. Alan Trachtenberg (Amherst: University of Massachusetts Press, 1973), pp. 105–6.

58. Aldous Huxley, "Happy Families," *Little Review* 6 (September 1919): 18–30.

59. Ben Hecht, "Rouge," *Little Review* 6 (September 1919): 12–18.

60. Huxley, of course, was not an American at all, and Hecht not exactly a consistent member of the avant–garde, and so in one sense their works can merely serve to illustrate the abiding presence of the negative stereotype on which Frank and others built their romantic constructions. Hecht was, however, a close friend of Bodenheim's and a regular associate of the *Little Review* crowd in its Chicago period. See Doug Fetherling, *The Five Lives of Ben Hecht* (Toronto: Lester & Orpen, 1977). The same trope, with an individual divided into black and white selves, appears in the work of a writer who was more of an American than Huxley and more of a modernist than Hecht. See Mina Loy's "To You," *Others* 3 (July 1916): 27–28.

61. Max Weber, *Cubist Poems* (London: Elkin Mathews, 1914), p. 24 Some of Weber's woodcuts of African and Mesoamerican subjects later appeared in *Broom* 3 (August 1922).

62. Weber, *Cubist Poems*, p. 14.

63. "Critical Note," *Contact* 5 (June 1923): 12. This note is attributed to Williams in Emily Mitchell Wallace's *Bibliography of Williams Carlos Williams* (Middletown, Conn.: Wesleyan University Press, 1968), p. 178. For a discussion of "the thing itself" that associates it with solid American workmanship, see "Yours, O Youth," *Contact* 3 (n.d.): 14–16.

64. Robert McAlmon, "*Jazz Opera* Americano," *Contact* 3 (n.d.): 17.

65. Alice Corbin, "Mandy's Religion" and "The Old Negro Alone," *Seven Arts* 2 (September 1917): 600, 601; Charles Galway, "La Rumba Cubano," *Broom* 4 (March 1923): 235–36.

66. Matthew Josephson, "Toward a Professional Prose," *Broom* 5 (August 1923): 59.

67. Mina Loy, "The Widow's Jazz," *Pagany* 2 (Spring 1931): 68–70. "The Widow's Jazz" is about Loy's longing for the vanished Arthur Cravan. Loy was born in England and lived part of her life in Paris, and though she did not write as a self-consciously American poet until the Second World War, she has always been considered part of the American avant–garde. See Virginia M. Kouidis, *Mina Loy: American Modernist Poet* (Baton Rouge: Louisiana State University Press, 1980), p. 24.

68. Loy, "The Widow's Jazz," pp. 69–70.

69. Ibid., p. 68.

70. Ibid.

71. Else von Freytag-Loringhoven, "Circle," *Broom* 4 (January 1923): 128. The title of this poem was printed in a circle and the whole was paralleled by a Mayan design. One of the few analyses of modern American poetry to take von Freytag-Loringhoven's work at all seriously is Cary Nelson's *Repression and Recovery: Modern American Poetry and the Politics of Cultural Memory 1910–1945* (Madison: University of Wisconsin Press, 1989), pp. 71–72.

72. Else von Freytag-Loringhoven, "Poems," *Little Review* 6 (March 1920): 10–12.

73. Maxwell Bodenheim, "Reader Critic," *Little Review* 6 (April 1920): 61.

74. Maxwell Bodenheim, "The Cotton Picker," *Others* 1 (September 1915): 50; idem, "An Old Negro Asleep," *Others* 2 (April 1916): 207; idem, "Lynched Negro," *Little Review* 11 (Spring 1925): 9, and *Opportunity* 3 (September 1925): 271. See also *Opportunity* 5 (March 1927).

75. Maxwell Bodenheim, *Selected Poems, 1914–1944* (New York: Beechwood Press, 1946), pp. 152–62.

76. Countee Cullen, "The Dark Tower," *Opportunity* 5 (June 1927): 180–81.

77. Maxwell Bodenheim, *Ninth Avenue* (New York: Boni & Liveright, 1926), p. 242.

78. Ibid., p. 11.

79. Ibid., p. 216.

80. For the demise of "Color Scheme," the manuscript of which was destroyed, see Cooper, pp. 193–222. Cooper does not mention "High Ball," nor does Tyrone Tillery in his study of McKay.

81. James Weldon Johnson, "Preface to the First Edition," *The Book of American Negro Poetry*, 2nd ed. (1931; rpt. New York: Harcourt Brace & World, 1969), p. 42.

82. Claude McKay, "High Ball," *Opportunity* 5 (May 1927): 142. All quotations from "High Ball" in this paragraph are taken from the same page.

83. Robert L. Carringer, "Introduction: History of a Popular Culture Classic," *The Jazz Singer*, ed. Robert L. Carringer (Madison: University of Wisconsin Press, 1979), p. 18. The hero of *The Autobiography of an Ex-Colored Man* also finds himself patronized by blackface performers who come looking for authentic material. James Weldon Johnson, *The Autobiography of an Ex-Colored Man* (1912; rpt. New York: Penguin, 1990), p. 78.

84. McKay, "High Ball," p. 142.

85. Claude McKay, "High Ball [Part 2]," *Opportunity* 5 (June 1927): 170.

86. Locke, ed., *The New Negro*, p. 264. See also Edward Margolies, *Native Sons: A Critical Study of Twentieth-Century Black American Authors* (Philadelphia: Lippincott, 1968), pp. 30–32.

87. Alain Locke, "American Literary Tradition and the Negro," *Modern Quarterly* 3 (May–July 1926): 221.

88. "The New Generation," *Opportunity* 2 (March 1924): 69; "Out of the Shadow," *Opportunity* 3 (May 1925): 131.

89. Editorial, "New Patterns in the Literature About the Negro," *Opportunity* 3 (June 1925): 162–63. This editorial singles out Williams for praise.

90. *Opportunity* 5 (September 1927).

91. *The Crisis* 31 (January 1926): 151; *The Crisis* 31 (February 1926): 203.

92. Even the more conservative critics distinguished between what the Harlem Renaissance was doing and the scurrilous dialect tradition of the "genteel" magazines. See Du Bois, p. 26.

Chapter 7

The following abbreviations will be used for works by Williams:

CP   *The Collected Poems of William Carlos Williams*, vol. 1 (1909–1939), ed. A. Walton Litz and Christopher MacGowan (New York: New Directions, 1986)

I   *Imaginations*, ed. Webster Schott (New York: New Directions, 1970)

IAG   *In the American Grain* (1925; rpt. New York: New Directions, 1956)

P   *Paterson*, ed. Christopher MacGowan (New York: New Directions, 1992)

SE   *Selected Essays* (New York: New Directions, 1954)

The following abbreviations will be used for works by Toomer:

C   *Cane*, ed. Darwin T. Turner (New York: Norton, 1988)

CPJT   *The Collected Poems of Jean Toomer*, ed. Robert B. Jones and Margery Toomer Latimer (Chapel Hill: University of North Carolina Press, 1988)

WS   *The Wayward and the Seeking: A Collection of Writings by Jean Toomer*, ed. Darwin T. Turner (Washington, D.C.: Howard University Press, 1980)

1. Jean Toomer, "Seventh Street," *Broom* 4 (December 1922): 3.

2. For Liveright's negotiations concerning *The Waste Land* see Lawrence Rainey, "The Price of Modernism: Publishing *The Waste Land*," in *T. S. Eliot: The Modernist in History*, ed. Ronald Bush (Cambridge: Cambridge University Press, 1991), pp. 91–133.

3. Cary D. Wintz, *Black Culture and the Harlem Renaissance* (Houston, Tex.: Rice University Press, 1988), p. 158.

4. Jean Toomer to Horace Liveright, August 11, 1923, Jean Toomer papers, box 1, folder 16, James Weldon Johnson Collection of Negro Literature and Art, Beinecke Rare Book and Manuscript Library, Yale University. Subsequent references to this collection will be abbreviated JTP, with box and folder number following: JTP 1:16. It should be noted that the papers have been recatalogued since being moved from Fisk University to Yale, so that these numbers will not necessarily agree with box and folder numbers given in earlier studies.

5. William Carlos Williams, "Reader Critic," *Little Review* 9 (Autumn 1922): 59–60; Jean Toomer, "Fern," *Little Review* 9 (Autumn 1922): 25–29.

6. Jean Toomer, "Karintha," *Broom* 4 (January 1923): 83–85; William Carlos Williams, "The Destruction of Tenochtitlan," *Broom* 4 (January 1923): 112–20.

7. Jean Toomer, "Kabnis," *Broom* 5 (August 1923): 12–16, and *Broom* 5 (September 1923): 83–94; William Carlos Williams, "The Fountain of Eternal Youth," *Broom* 5 (September 1923): 73–77; idem, "Spring and All," *Broom* 5 (November 1923): 209. Given this publishing history, it is certain that the two writers knew one another's work. Despite this fact, and despite the number of close friends and literary associates they shared, including Gorham Munson and Kenneth Burke, there is no solid evidence to suggest that the two were acquainted or that they were much interested in one another's writing. I have been able to find no references to Toomer in Williams's published works or in accounts of his life. Toomer mentions Williams in a letter to Munson about *Secession* 4, but all he says is "Williams—good" (Jean Toomer to Gorham Munson, n.d. [ca. May 1923]; JTP 6:184). There is also a reference to Williams's "tart acceptance" of American life in an unpublished review of Paul Rosenfeld's *Port of New York* (undated typescript, p. 6; JTP 57:1332).

8. Jean Toomer, "Oxen Cart and Warfare," *Little Review* 10 (Autumn–Winter 1924–25): 44–48; idem, "Easter," *Little Review* 11 (Spring 1925): 3–7; William Carlos Williams, "A Tentative Statement," *Little Review* 12 (May 1929): 95–98.

9. William Carlos Williams, "Manifesto," *Pagany* 1 (January–March 1930): 1. See Emily Mitchell Wallace, *A Bibliography of William Carlos Williams* (Middletown, Conn.: Wesleyan University Press, 1968), pp. 185–90, for other contributions.

10. Jean Toomer, "Brown River, Smile," *Pagany* 3 (Winter 1932): 29–33. For a brief account of other publications of versions of this poem, see *CP*, p. 108. For correspondence between Margery Latimer and Richard Johns, see Daniel P. McCarthy, "'Just Americans': A Note on Jean Toomer's Marriage to Margery Latimer," in *Jean Toomer: A Critical Evaluation*, ed. Therman B. O'Daniel (Washington, D.C.: Howard University Press, 1988), pp. 60–61. Latimer had contributed to the first issue of *Pagany* along with Williams. See also Williams's *Selected Letters* (New York: New Directions, 1984), p. 118.

11. The Editors, "America and Alfred Stieglitz: A Collective Portrait," p. 5; William Carlos Williams, "The American Background," p. 32; and Jean Toomer, "The Hill," p. 302, all in *America and Alfred Stieglitz: A Collective Portrait*, ed. Waldo Frank et al. (New

York: Literary Guild, 1934). For Williams's more negative feelings about Stieglitz see Bram Dijkstra, pp. 83–84. For the assertion about "An American Place" see *A*, p. 236.

12. M[atthew] J[osephson], "Great American Novels," *Broom* 5 (October 1923): 177–79; Gorham B. Munson, *Destinations: A Canvass of American Literature Since 1900* (New York: J. H. Sears, 1928); Paul Rosenfeld, *Port of New York* (1924; rpt. Urbana: University of Illinois Press, 1961); idem, *Men Seen: Twenty-Four Modern Authors* (New York: The Dial Press, 1925).

13. Harold A. Loeb, "Comment: Broom: 1921–1923," *Broom* 5 (August 1923): 58.

14. See Munson's letter to Stieglitz, reprinted in Gorham Munson, *The Awakening Twenties: A Memoir–History of a Literary Period* (Baton Rouge: Louisiana University Press, 1985), pp. 175–76.

15. Munson, *Destinations*, pp. 135, 184–86.

16. Rosenfeld, *Men Seen*, pp. 227, 231.

17. Josephson, pp. 178–79.

18. Gorham Munson to Jean Toomer, October 29, 1922, JTP 6:183.

19. Alfred Kreymborg, *Our Singing Strength: An Outline of American Poetry* (New York: Coward-McCann, 1929), pp. 575–76.

20. Munson, *Destinations*, pp. 121–22.

21. Rosenfeld, *Port of New York*, p. 109; Kreymborg, quoted in Mike Weaver, *William Carlos Williams: The American Background* (Cambridge: Cambridge University Press, 1971), p. 160.

22. Van Wyck Brooks, "Introduction," *The Farmer's Daughters: The Collected Stories of William Carlos Williams* (New York: New Directions, 1961), p. xii.

23. Quoted, but with the footnote information omitted, in S. P. Fullinwider, "Jean Toomer: Lost Generation, or Negro Renaissance?" in O'Daniel, ed., p. 24.

24. For Williams's fascination with Cunard see Bryce Conrad, *Refiguring America: A Study of William Carlos Williams' In the American Grain* (Urbana: University of Illinois Press, 1990), p. 154, n. 48. For his enthusiasm about the anthology see Dickran Tashjian, *William Carlos Williams and the American Scene, 1920–1940* (New York: Whitney Museum of American Art, 1978), p. 113.

25. Jean Toomer to Nancy Cunard, February 8, 1932. Quoted and discussed in Wintz, p. 186, and Nellie Y. McKay, *Jean Toomer, Artist* (Chapel Hill, N.C.: University of North Carolina Press, 1984), p. 200.

26. For discussions of *Man Orchid*, the novel in question, see Paul Mariani, *William Carlos Williams: A New World Naked* (New York: McGraw-Hill, 1981), pp. 514–16; Aldon Lynn Nielsen, *Reading Race: White American Poets and the Racial Discourse in the Twentieth Century* (Athens: University of Georgia Press, 1988), pp. 80–84; and Nathaniel Mackey, "Sound and Sentiment, Sound and Symbol," *Callaloo* 10 (Winter 1987): 42–48.

27. Williams has been cited more and more frequently of late as an example for writers and scholars struggling toward multicultural conceptions of American language and literature. Books like John F. Callahan's *In the African-American Grain: Call-and-Response in Twentieth-Century Black Fiction*, 2nd ed. (Middletown, Conn.: Wesleyan University Press, 1990), and Vera M. Kutzinski's *Against the American Grain: Myth and History in William Carlos Williams, Jay Wright, and Nicolas Guillen* (Baltimore, Md.: Johns Hopkins University Press, 1987) make their tribute in their titles. See also Kwame Anthony Appiah, *In My Father's House: Africa in the Philosophy of Culture* (London: Methuen, 1992), p. 95. On the other hand, a very determined attack on Williams's racial attitudes has been mounted by Aldon Lynn Nielsen in *Reading Race*, pp. 72–89.

28. William Carlos Williams, "The American Language," *New English Weekly*, October 19, 1933, p. 10.

29. Shirley Brice Heath, "Literacy and Language Change," *Georgetown University Roundtable on Language and Linguistics* 1985: 287–88.

30. *The Collected Poems of William Carlos Williams*, ed. A. Walton Litz and Christopher MacGowan, 2 vols. (New York: New Directions, 1986), 1:195. For a discussion of these metaphors see James E. B. Breslin, *William Carlos Williams: An American Artist* (1970; rpt. Chicago: University of Chicago Press, 1985), p. 80.

31. William Carlos Williams, "America, Whitman, and the Art of Poetry," *Poetry Journal* 8 (November 1917): 29. Quoted in Frail, p. 78.

32. Gilbert Seldes, "Toujours Jazz," *Dial* 75 (August 1923): 170–72.

33. For an early skirmish see Hiram Kelly Moderwell, "A Modest Proposal," *Seven Arts* 2 (July 1917): 368–73; and Charles L. Buchanan, "Ragtime and American Music," *Seven Arts* 2 (July 1917): 376–82. The subject also received a good deal of attention in *Vanity Fair* during the 1920s. See Gilbert Seldes, "American Noises: How to Make Them, and Why," *Vanity Fair* 22 (June 1924): 59, 85; John Peale Bishop, "The Formal Translation of Jazz," *Vanity Fair* 23 (October 1924): 57, 90, 100; and Virgil Thomson, "The Cult of Jazz," *Vanity Fair* 24 (June 1925): 54. The subject was naturally of great interest to the Harlem writers as well. For an example see J. A. Rogers, "Jazz at Home," in Locke, ed., *The New Negro*, pp. 216–24. For a survey of these controversies see Kathy J. Ogren, *The Jazz Revolution: Twenties America & the Meaning of Jazz* (New York: Oxford University Press, 1989).

34. For a comment on this passage see Nielsen, p. 75.

35. Mariani, p. 201. For Bert Williams's death see Ann Charters, *Nobody: The Story of Bert Williams* (New York: Macmillan, 1970), pp. 146–47; and Eric Ledell Smith, *Bert Williams: A Biography of the Pioneer Black Comedian* (Jefferson, N.C.: McFarland, 1992), pp. 221–28.

36. For a text of the song see Charters, pp. 135–37.

37. See Breslin, p. 88.

38. For a discussion of the resemblances between Williams and the rest of the avantgarde on this issue, see Bram Dijkstra, *The Hieroglyphics of a New Speech: Cubism, Stieglitz, and the Early Poetry of William Carlos Williams* (Princeton, N.J.: Princeton University Press, 1969), pp. 176–78. For an interesting discussion of the tensions inherent in "To Elsie," see James Clifford, *The Predicament of Culture: Twentieth–Century Ethnography, Literature, and Art* (Cambridge, Mass.: Harvard University Press, 1988), pp. 3–7.

39. See Breslin, p. 105.

40. See Weaver, pp. 74–75.

41. E. K. Means, *More E. K. Means* (New York: Putnam's, 1919), pp. 66–69 (emphasis in original). For a discussion of this story, which Williams also mentions in *The Great American Novel*, see Bryce Conrad, p. 138.

42. Jean Toomer to the *Liberator*, August 19, 1922, JTP 4:150. Though this letter is sometimes described as being addressed to Claude McKay, it is in fact a reply to a note from the staff of the *Liberator* and bears the salutation "Dear Friends." The account given here of Toomer's racial background is repeated almost verbatim from a letter of June 30, 1922, to John McClure, editor of the *Double Dealer*, which published some of Toomer's early work (JTP 2:46). For a survey of the various comments Toomer made about his racial background, see Cynthia Earl Kerman and Richard Eldridge, *The Lives of Jean Toomer* (Baton Rouge: Louisiana State University Press, 1987), pp. 95–99; *WS*, p. 18.

43. From "Reflections of an Earth–Being," one of several unpublished autobiographical accounts included in the Jean Toomer papers in the James Weldon Johnson Collection at Yale. As excerpted in *WS*, p. 18.

44. Jean Toomer to John McClure, June 30, 1922, JTP 2:46. See also excerpts from "On Being an American," *WS*, p. 93.

45. Jean Toomer, "Race Problems and Modern Society," in *Problems of Civilization*, ed. Ellsworth Huntington et al. (New York: D. Van Nostrand, 1929), p. 96.

46. Jean Toomer, "On Being an American," typescript p. 36, JTP 20:513.

47. For Toomer's explanation of this project see "On Being an American," typescript, pp. 36–37, JTP 20:513; quoted in *WS*, pp. 121–22.

48. George B. Hutchinson, Jean Toomer and the 'New Negroes' of Washington," *American Literature* 63 (December 1991): 687.

49. McCarthy, pp. 59–60.

50. "Outline of an Autobiography," as excerpted in *WS*, p. 120.

51. Ibid., p. 126.

52. See "Outline of an Autobiography," quoted in *WS*, p. 113. Letters to and from Ridge in the Jean Toomer papers show that she gave Toomer rather detailed advice about his early work (JTP 1:18). According to Kerman and Eldridge, Toomer was first invited to Ridge's in August 1920 (p. 72). Williams attended these parties regularly and was definitely there in July 1920, when he first met Robert McAlmon. See Mariani, p. 173, and Williams's *Autobiography* (New York: New Directions, 1967), pp. 163, 171–72.

53. "Outline of an Autobiography," quoted in *WS*, p. 114; Kerman and Eldridge, p. 86.

54. Jean Toomer to Waldo Frank, July 23, 1922, JTP 3:83; and Jean Toomer to Waldo Frank, August 21, 1922, as quoted in Kerman and Eldridge, p. 89.

55. Jean Toomer to Waldo Frank, March 24, 1922, quoted in Kerman and Eldridge, p. 87. See Jean Toomer to Waldo Frank, July 25, 1922, JTP 3:83, for Toomer's pleasure at Frank's plans to include "The Negro" in a revised *Our America*.

56. Waldo Frank, *Holiday* (New York: Boni & Liveright, 1923), p. 146.

57. Jean Toomer, "Waldo Frank's Holiday," *Dial* 75 (October 1923): 383.

58. Jean Toomer, "On Being an American," typescript p. 32, JTP 20:513; Waldo Frank to Jean Toomer, n.d. [1923?], JTP 3:84.

59. Jean Toomer to John McClure, June 30, 1922, JTP 2:46.

60. Horace Liveright to Jean Toomer, August 29, 1923, JTP 1:16; publicity clipping for *Cane*, JTP 26:612.

61. Frank candidly wrote to Toomer that Liveright planned to use him to get "a possible Negro public for *Holiday.*" Waldo Frank to Jean Toomer, n.d. [1923?], JTP 3:84. Years later, Toomer speculated to himself as to why Frank had "deliberately misrepresented me." "Some motive was at work. I have my guesses." "On Being an American," typescript verso p. 41, JTP 20:513.

62. Jean Toomer to Horace Liveright, September 5, 1923, JTP 1:16.

63. Sherwood Anderson, quoted in Helbling, "Sherwood Anderson and Jean Toomer," in O'Daniel, ed., pp. 119–20.

64. Sherwood Anderson to Jean Toomer, January [?] 1924, JTP 1:8.

65. Two undated letters, Jean Toomer to Waldo Frank, JTP 3:83.

66. "Briefer Mention: *Cane*," *Dial* 76 (January 1924): 92.

67. John E. Bassett, *Harlem in Review: Critical Reactions to Black American Writers, 1917–1939* (Selinsgrove, Pa.: Susquehanna University Press, 1992), pp. 42–44.

68. Jean Toomer to Gorham Munson, October 31, 1922; Gorham Munson to Jean Toomer, November 11, 1922, JTP 6:183.

69. William Stanley Brathwaite, "The Negro in American Literature," in *The New Negro*, ed. Alain Locke (1925; rpt. New York: Atheneum, 1968), p. 44.

70. Jean Toomer to Mrs. Beardsley, November 1, 1930, JTP 1:1; quoted in McKay, p. 199.

71. Jean Toomer to the *Liberator*, August 19, 1922, JTP 4:150. See also McKay, p. 32; Kerman and Eldridge, pp. 82–85; and Helbling, "Jean Toomer and Waldo Frank," in O'Daniel, ed., p. 91.

72. Jean Toomer, "On Being an American," typescript p. 45, JTP 20:513. See also Helbling, "Jean Toomer and Waldo Frank," in O'Daniel, ed., pp. 95–96.

73. Jean Toomer to Waldo Frank, undated, JTP 3:83; slightly misquoted in Kerman and Eldridge, eds., p. 98.

74. Notes quoted in Kerman and Eldridge, eds., p. 100; Jean Toomer to the *Liberator*, August 19, 1922, JTP 4:150.

75. Jean Toomer to Waldo Frank, December 12, 1922, JTP 3:83; quoted in Kerman and Eldridge, eds., p. 99.

76. James Kraft, "Jean Toomer's *Cane*," in O'Daniel, ed., p. 150. See also Barbara E. Bowen, "Untroubled Voice: Call and Response in *Cane*," in *Black Literature and Literary Theory*, ed. Henry Louis Gates, Jr. (New York: Methuen, 1984), pp. 187–203.

77. JTP 60:1411.

78. There is a small notebook in the Jean Toomer papers that includes an early draft of "Reapers" and a list of expressions: "too heavy to tote; A Way Out of No Way; get shed of; done et; little biddie; Theyre not as high as they has bee[n]; Yassum, theyre off quite sharp," etc. JTP 60:1410.

79. See, for example, McClure's complaint, in a letter to Anderson that Anderson forwarded to Toomer, that "his dialect is weak." John McClure to Sherwood Anderson, January 29, 1924, JTP 1:8.

80. Locke, ed., *The New Negro*, p. 51.

81. McKay, p. 83.

82. Bassett, p. 42.

83. Heath, "Literacy and Language Change," pp. 287–88.

84. It is no wonder that Alfred Kreymborg enthusiastically accepted "Gum" for an American number of the *Chapbook* that he was compiling (Alfred Kreymborg to Jean Toomer, n.d. [ca. 1922–23], JTP 4:125). Its play with urban signage was a technique particularly popular with American and European modernists of the time. See Williams's version of this technique in "The Attic Which Is Desire" (*CP*, 1:325).

85. Robert B. Jones, "Introduction," *The Collected Poems of Jean Toomer*, ed. Robert B. Jones and Margery Toomer Latimer (Chapel Hill: University of North Carolina Press, 1988), pp. x–xii, xxx. This response is contained in an unpaged and undated notebook included in the Jean Toomer papers, JTP 60:1411.

86. Richard Aldington, "The Art of Poetry," *Dial* 69 (1920): 170.

87. Ezra Pound, "A Retrospect," in *Literary Essays*, ed. T. S. Eliot (New York: New Directions, 1968), p. 4.

88. Jean Toomer to Gorham Munson, October 8, 1922, JTP 6:183.

89. Notebook, unpag., JTP 60:1411.

90. Jean Toomer to Waldo Frank, n.d., JTP 3:83.

91. Statement included with reply to Langston Hughes letter of November 17, 1933, JTP 4:111.

92. Jean Toomer to Gorham Munson, December 20, 1922, JTP 6:183. This lettter was also printed as part of the ongoing controversy about machine forms in art in *S4N* 25 (March–April 1923), unpag.

Chapter 8

Works by Zora Neale Hurston will be identified in the text by the following abbreviations:

DT   *Dust Tracks on a Road: An Autobiography*, ed. Robert Hemenway (Urbana: University of Illinois Press, 1984)

ILM   *I Love Myself When I Am Laughing . . .: A Zora Neale Hurston Reader*, ed. Alice Walker (New York: Feminist Press, 1979)

MM   *Mules and Men* (1935; rpt. New York: Harper & Row, 1990)

SC   *The Sanctified Church: The Folklore Writings of Zora Neale Hurston* (Berkeley: Turtle Island, 1981)

1. Zora Neale Hurston, "Drenched in Light," *Opportunity* 2 (December 1924): 371–74; Robert E. Hemenway, *Zora Neale Hurston: A Literary Biography* (Urbana: University of Illinois Press, 1977), pp. 9–11.

2. Robert Hemenway has recently described the exact nature and extent of these relationships to support his argument that they were not nearly as intense or extensive as is usually supposed. Nonetheless, the adoption metaphor may be allowable, considering that Hurston routinely referred to Mason as Godmother. Robert Hemenway, "The Personal Dimension in *Their Eyes Were Watching God*," in *New Essays on Their Eyes Were Watching God*, ed. Michael Awkward (Cambridge: Cambridge University Press, 1990), pp. 29–50.

3. Montgomery Gregory, review of *Cane, Opportunity* 1 (December 1923): 374–75.

4. Charles S. Johnson, editorial, "Out of the Shadow," *Opportunity* 3 (May 1925): 131.

5. Hemenway, *Hurston*, p. 10.

6. Mary Helen Washington, "Introduction: Zora Neale Hurston: A Woman Half in Shadow," *ILM*, pp. 10–11, 17–18, and "Foreword," *Their Eyes Were Watching God* (New York: Harper & Row, 1990), p. vii.

7. Richard Wright, "Between Laughter and Tears," *New Masses* 5 (October 1937): 22, 25.

8. Quoted in Hemenway, *Hurston*, pp. 205, 163.

9. Zora Neale Hurston, "The Hue and Cry About Howard University," *Messenger* 7 (September 1925): 315–19, 338; Hemenway, *Hurston*, p. 52.

10. Hemenway, *Hurston*, p. 60. This episode provides the opening of Alice Walker's essay "On Refusing to Be Humbled by Second Place in a Contest You Did Not Design: A Tradition by Now," *ILM*, pp. 1–5.

11. For an excellent discussion of the cakewalk and its implications for turn–of–the–century black writing, see Eric J. Sundquist, *To Wake the Nations: Race in the Making of American Literature* (Cambridge, Mass.: Harvard University Press/Belknap Press, 1993), pp. 276–94. See also Nathan I. Huggins, *Harlem Renaissance* (New York: Oxford University Press, 1971), pp. 273–301; and Ann Charters, *Nobody: The Story of Bert Williams* (New York: Macmillan, 1970), pp. 34–40.

12. Sam Dennison, *Scandalize My Name: Black Imagery in American Popular Music* (New York: Garland, 1982), p. 384.

13. See Gayl Jones's discussion of the way that Hurston's early stories break out of the frame of the dialect tale. Gayl Jones, *Liberating Voices: Oral Tradition in African American Literature* (Cambridge, Mass.: Harvard University Press, 1991), p. 68.

14. Alain Locke, "Beauty Instead of Ashes," *The Nation* 126 (April 18, 1928): 433; reprinted in *The Critical Temper of Alain Locke*, ed. Jeffrey C. Stewart (New York: Garland, 1983), p. 24.

15. Locke, in Stewart, ed., p. 47.

16. Hemenway, *Hurston*, pp. 43–50.

17. Richard Bruce, "Smoke, Lilies and Jade," *Fire!!* 1 (1926): 34.

18. Anne Chisholm, *Nancy Cunard* (London: Sidgwick & Jackson, 1979), pp. 202–3.

19. Cary D. Wintz, *Black Culture and the Harlem Renaissance* (Houston, Tex.: Rice University Press, 1988), pp. 185–86. Cunard's side of the correspondence and part of McKay's is preserved in the Claude McKay papers, James Weldon Johnson Collection of Negro Literature and Art, Beinecke Rare Book and Manuscript Library, Yale University.

20. Hurston, "Drenched in Light," p. 374.

21. Hemenway, *Hurston*, p. 139.

22. Franz Boas, "Preface," *MM*, p. xiii.

23. Hemenway, *Hurston*, p. 168; Arnold Rampersad, "Foreword," *MM*, p. xvi.

24. Hemenway, *Hurston*, p. 62.

25. James Clifford, *The Predicament of Culture: Twentieth-Century Ethnography, Literature, and Art* (Cambridge, Mass.: Harvard University Press, 1988), pp. 79–80, 120–21.

26. Henry Louis Gates, Jr., *The Signifying Monkey: A Theory of African–American Literary Criticism* (New York: Oxford University Press, 1988), pp. 191–93. See also p. 215.

27. Gates, *Signifying Monkey*, pp. 203, 207.

28. Henry Louis Gates, Jr., "Afterword: Zora Neale Hurston: 'A Negro Way of Saying,'" *Their Eyes Were Watching God*, p. 193.

29. Barbara Johnson and Henry Louis Gates, Jr., "A Black and Idiomatic Free Indirect Discourse," in *Zora Neale Hurston's Their Eyes Were Watching God: Modern Critical Interpretations*, ed. Harold Bloom (New York: Chelsea House, 1987), pp. 83–85.

30. Gates, "Afterword," p. 194. See also Barbara Johnson, "Metaphor and Metonymy in *Their Eyes Were Watching God*," in *Black Literature and Literary Theory*, ed. Henry Louis Gates, Jr. (London: Methuen, 1984), p. 218; and idem, "Thresholds of Difference: Structures of Address in Zora Neale Hurston," in *"Race," Writing, and Difference*, ed. Henry Louis Gates, Jr. (Chicago: University of Chicago Press, 1986), p. 327.

31. Hurston's essays from *Negro* are most readily available today in *SC*, which reprints the original texts with a few minor errors of transcription.

32. Quoted in Eric Lott, "'The Seeming Counterfeit': Racial Politics and Early Blackface Minstrelsy," *American Quarterly* 43 (June 1991): 229.

33. Gates, *Signifying Monkey*, p. 195.

34. J. L. Austin, *How to Do Things with Words*, 2nd ed., ed. J. O. Urmson and Marina Sbisà (Cambridge, Mass.: Harvard University Press, 1975), pp. 5, 22.

35. Washington, "Foreword," p. xiii.

36. Hemenway, *Hurston*, p. 80. Hemenway's example is jazz.

37. See "Sweat," *ILM*, p. 204; "The Eatonville Anthology," *ILM*, p. 181.

38. Austin, p. 10.

39. Hemenway, *Hurston*, p. 192.

40. Shirley Brice Heath, "Literacy and Language Change," *Georgetown University Round Table on Language and Linguistics* 1985: 287–88.

41. Alain Locke, "Negro Youth Speaks," in *The New Negro*, ed. Alain Locke (1925; rpt. New York: Atheneum, 1968), p. 51.

42. Zora Neale Hurston to Langston Hughes, April 12, 1928, Langston Hughes correspondence, James Weldon Johnson Collection of Negro Literature and Art, Beinecke Rare Book and Manuscript Library, Yale University. It is in this letter that she first sets down the rules of "Negro expression" that she would develop into "Characteristics of Negro Expression." See Hemenway, *Hurston*, pp. 114–15.

43. Zora Neale Hurston, "The Eatonville Anthology," *The Messenger* (September,

October, November 1926): 261–62, 297, 319, 332. The anthology is most readily available today in *ILM*, which is the text referred to here. For an account of the printing mistake see Hemenway, *Hurston*, p. 69.

44. Hemenway, *Hurston*, p. 69.

45. See "The Eatonville Anthology," *ILM*, pp. 186–87; *DT*, p. 35.

46. For a summary discussion of these relationships, see Hemenway, *Hurston*, pp. 69–70.

47. Ibid., p. 70.

48. For a book-by-book account of the Hours Press see Nancy Cunard, *These Were the Hours*, ed. Hugh Ford (Carbondale: Southern Illinois University Press, 1969). See also Chisholm, pp. 137–55.

49. *Negro: An Anthology*, ed. Nancy Cunard (London: Wishart Press, 1934), p. 212. Subsequent citations in the text are identified with the abbreviation *N*.

50. "The Colored Girls of Passenack—Old and New" is now most readily available in *The Farmer's Daughters: The Collected Stories of William Carlos Williams* (New York: New Directions, 1961), pp. 50–57.

51. Ezra Pound to T. S. Eliot, January 27[?], 1922, in *The Letters of T. S. Eliot*, ed. Valerie Eliot (New York: Harcourt Brace Jovanovich, 1988), p. 505.

52. *N*, p. 304. Moore had a long and complicated relationship with blackface makeup. In 1908 he did a one-man version of *Uncle Tom's Cabin*, in which half his face was made up to look white and the other half to look black. Bruce Kellner, ed., *The Harlem Renaissance: A Historical Dictionary for the Era* (New York: Methuen, 1984), pp. 248–49.

53. James Weldon Johnson, "Preface to the First Edition," *The Book of American Negro Poetry*, 2nd ed. (1931; rpt. New York: Harcourt Brace & World, 1969), p. 41.

54. Kellner, p. 170. Significantly, it was McKay who objected most strongly to Cunard's unqualified support for the Communist party. See her letter to McKay of September 20, 1932, and his very strong anti-Communist comments in the poems of the "Cycle" manuscript. Claude McKay papers, James Weldon Johnson Collection of Negro Literature and Art, Beinecke Rare Book and Manuscript Library, Yale University.

55. Claude McKay, *A Long Way from Home* (New York: Lee Furman, 1937), p. 344. *N*, p. 552.

Index